INTERNATIONAL ORGANIZATIONS

INTERNATIONAL ORGANIZATIONS

John McCormick

BLOOMSBURY ACADEMIC
LONDON • NEW YORK • OXFORD • NEW DELHI • SYDNEY

BLOOMSBURY ACADEMIC
Bloomsbury Publishing Plc
50 Bedford Square, London, WC1B 3DP, UK
1385 Broadway, New York, NY 10018, USA
29 Earlsfort Terrace, Dublin 2, Ireland

BLOOMSBURY, BLOOMSBURY ACADEMIC and the Diana logo are trademarks of
Bloomsbury Publishing Plc

First published in Great Britain 2024

Cover design: Eleanor Rose
Cover images © FG Trade / Getty; © Anadolu Agency / Getty Images; © Saul Loeb / Pool / AFP / Getty Images;
© Waseem Andrabi / Hindustan Times / Getty Images; © honglouwawa / Getty Images; © Getty Images.

A catalogue record for this book is available from the British Library.

Library of Congress Cataloging-in-Publication Data
Names: McCormick, John, 1954- author.
Title: International organizations / John McCormick.
Description: New York : Bloomsbury Publishing, 2024. | Includes bibliographical references and index. |
Summary: "International organizations such as the World Health Organization and the United Nations have never been so
important in addressing global challenges. This new textbook from bestselling author John McCormick introduces readers to
nature, structure and purpose of international organizations. It considers both their historical development and their place in
the contemporary world, along with the problems they face and solutions they offer"– Provided by publisher.
Identifiers: LCCN 2023028327 (print) | LCCN 2023028328 (ebook) | ISBN 9781350337336 (paperback) |
ISBN 9781350337343 (hardback) | ISBN 9781350337350 (pdf) | ISBN 9781350337367 (ebook)
Subjects: LCSH: International agencies. | International cooperation.
Classification: LCC JZ4850 .M378 2024 (print) | LCC JZ4850 (ebook) | DDC 327.1/7–dc23/eng/20230826
LC record available at https://lccn.loc.gov/2023028327
LC ebook record available at https://lccn.loc.gov/2023028328

ISBN:	HB:	978-1-3503-3734-3
	PB:	978-1-3503-3733-6
	ePDF:	978-1-3503-3735-0
	eBook:	978-1-3503-3736-7

Typeset by Integra Software Services Pvt. Ltd.
Printed and bound in Great Britain by Bell and Bain Ltd, Glasgow

To find out more about our authors and books visit www.bloomsbury.com
and sign up for our newsletters.

BRIEF CONTENTS

DETAILED CONTENTS

8. HUMAN RIGHTS — 171

9. FOOD AND AGRICULTURE — 193

10. HEALTH — 215

FEATURES

LIST OF MAPS

IOs IN ACTION

IOs IN THEORY

SPOTLIGHT

ABOUT
THE AUTHOR

John McCormick is Professor of Political Science at the Indianapolis campus of Indiana University in the United States. His areas of interest focus on global studies, comparative politics, environmental policy, and the politics and policies of the European Union. He has held a Jean Monnet Professorship in European Union studies, a Fulbright-Schuman Visiting Professorship at the College of Europe in Bruges, Belgium, and is the author of multiple best-selling textbooks, including *Comparative Government and Politics* (12th edition, 2022), *Introduction to Global Studies* (2nd edition, 2022) and *Understanding the European Union* (8th edition, 2021).

TOUR OF THE BOOK

CHAPTER PREVIEWS

Each chapter begins with a brief preview of what the chapter is about and a list of the contents.

INTERNATIONAL ORGANIZATIONS IN THEORY

Each chapter contains a box that focuses on the core theories relevant to contemporary debates.

INTERNATIONAL ORGANIZATIONS IN ACTION

Each chapter also contains a box that focuses on the aims and effects of particular organizations or provides detail on the practical challenges they face.

SPOTLIGHT

Each chapter contains a spotlight on a key topic relevant to the theme of the chapter.

TABLES AND FIGURES

The text is interspersed with tables and figures that present key numbers or express some of the more complex ideas in visual form. Most are based on the latest data available from the websites of key national and international organizations.

PREVIEW

The goal of this opening chapter is to provide a survey of international organizations: to explain what they are and how they relate to states, to review the varieties in which they are found, and to explain how they have evolved and what they do. The chapter also explains the concept of global regimes and the manner in which IOs fit within these regimes, as well as differences in the depth and reach of regimes. The chapter begins with a review of the system of global governance and its constituent parts, then reviews the motives behind the creation of the earliest international organizations, before discussing the pressures that have led to the construction of the liberal world order since 1945. The

IOs IN THEORY 1

REALISM AND NEOREALISM

Realism has long been the foundational theory in the study of international relations. With a heritage dating back to the ancient Greeks, its main interest lies in understanding and explaining how power is acquired and used by states. It takes the view that because humans are by nature self-centred and competitive, and motivated by rational self-interest, states are encouraged to protect their interests relative to other states and not to trust long-term cooperation and alliances. Realists talk of an anarchic global system in which there is no authority above the level of states that is capable of helping them manage their interactions with one another, and believe that states must use conflict and cooperation to ensure their security through a balance of power among states.

Realists tend to have a limited view of the possibilities of international organizations, arguing that they have the ability neither to constrain the behaviour of states nor – in the final analysis – to prevent war. They point to the example of the League of Nations and its failure to address major security challenges after 1918, or to prevent the outbreak of World War II. They also point to the mixed record of the UN in preventing the many conflicts and wars that have broken out around the world since 1945.

IOs IN ACTION 1

ENVIRONMENTAL TREATY SECRETARIATS

Although most international treaties are housed in and monitored by intergovernmental organizations, some have their own dedicated secretariats, with different degrees of ability to protect and promote the treaties for which they are responsible. Contrasting examples are offered by the records of two dealing with environmental treaties: the climate change convention secretariat based in Bonn, Germany, and the biological diversity convention secretariat based in Montreal, Canada.

The climate change convention secretariat – usually known as UN Climate Change – was established in 1992 to support the UN Framework Convention on Climate Change, which was opened for signature in 1992, came into force in 1994 and now has 198 parties. It has a staff of about 450 (making it bigger than many international organizations) whose job is to coordinate the agreements that have come out of the 1992 convention, to provide technical expertise and to organize the annual Conferences of Parties, which now attract about 25,000 participants (UN Climate Change, 2023). Although the climate change secretariat began life as a limited

SPOTLIGHT 1

IS THERE A LIBERAL WORLD ORDER?

The changes that came to global governance after World War II represent the building of what came to be known as the liberal world order (also known as the liberal international order). This describes a global, open and rules-based system of international cooperation based on international organizations and treaties, and on norms such as multilateralism (see Ikenberry, 2011). Many credit the order with multiple achievements, including the expansion of free trade, the promotion of democracy and human rights, and the encouragement of the peaceful resolution of international disagreements. Others question whether there is – in fact – such an order, or whether it is as orderly as the label implies, and point to its many failures. Pabst (2019), for example, argues that it is both illiberal and undemocratic, intolerant of the cultural values of ordinary people, and that it concentrates power in the hands of Western elites and Western-dominated institutions, fuelling both economic injustice and social fragmentation.

However we understand the liberal world order, there is no question that the world of international organizations has grown in breadth, depth and complexity since 1945, leaving many of the scholars of the subject competing to decide how best to understand and portray that world. Terms such as orchestrated, fragmented, partnerships, networks and layering have all been used, and the world of IOs has even been likened to a bowl of spaghetti (see summary in Barnett et al., 2021). States and intergovernmental organizations still draw the most attention in studies of the liberal world order, but they must work with an expanding range of non-state actors and arrangements, including interest groups, corporations, foundations and communities of experts.

Table 1.1: The core elements of global governance

Element	Features
Institutions	Formal or informal bodies of people working together with a particular purpose in mind, with shared rules and procedures, a hierarchy and internal communication systems.
Rules and laws	Legal agreements drawn up and signed by states, taking the form of treaties, protocols, conventions, or judicial decisions.

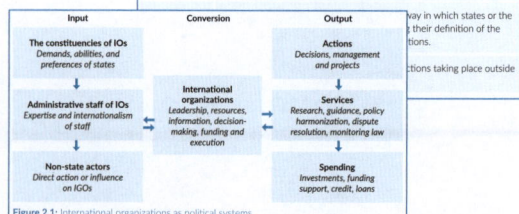

Input	Conversion	Output
The constituencies of IOs *Demands, abilities, and preferences of states*		**Actions** *Decisions, management and projects*
Administrative staff of IOs *Expertise and internationalism of staff*	**International organizations** *Leadership, resources, information, decision-making, funding and execution*	**Services** *Research, guidance, policy harmonization, dispute resolution, monitoring law*
Non-state actors *Direct action or influence on IGOs*		**Spending** *Investments, funding support, credit, loans*

Figure 2.1: International organizations as political systems.

MAPS

Maps of the world, or of particular states and regions, have been placed strategically throughout the book to offer a global view of topics within each chapter, comparing countries on a variety of topics.

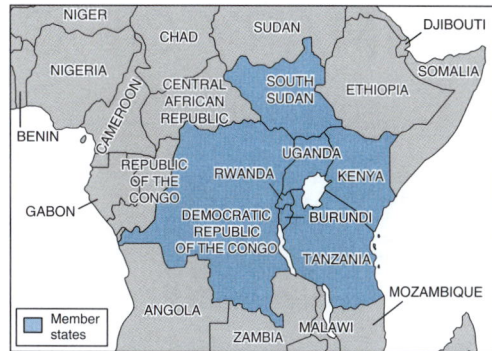

Map 3.1: East African Community.

THINKING POINTS

Each chapter ends with a set of six open-ended and occasionally provocative questions designed to help students think critically about some of the issues raised in the chapter and to suggest topics for further research.

THINKING POINTS

- What are the boundaries (assuming there are any) of the idea of development?
- What are the advantages and disadvantages of formal arrangements such as G7 and G20 relative to the work of formal intergovernmental organizations?
- What (if anything) can or should be done about the dominance of wealthy states from the Global North in the work of the IMF and the World Bank?
- Are multilateral development banks a good idea?
- Are there too many international non-governmental organizations active in the field of development?

IOs RELATED TO THIS CHAPTER

Most chapters end with a list of international organizations referenced in or relevant to the chapter content.

IOs RELATED TO THIS CHAPTER

African Union (AU)

Association of Southeast Asian Nations (ASEAN)

Commonwealth of Independent States (CIS)

Community of Latin American and Caribbean States (CELAC)

East African Community (EAC)

Economic and Monetary Community of Central Africa (CEMAC)

Economic Community of West African States (ECOWAS)

FURTHER READING

Each chapter ends with a short, annotated list of books chosen to provide detailed and current information, and to act as resources for research assignments. The emphasis is on survey texts that provide a good and recent introduction to the topic.

FURTHER READING

DiGiacomo, Gordon, and Susan L. King (eds) (2019) *The Institutions of Human Rights: Developments and Practices* (University of Toronto Press). An edited collection on the human rights regime, with chapters on each of the key international organizations.

McGaughey, Fiona (2021) *Non-governmental Organisations and the United Nations Human Rights System* (Routledge). A review of the place of NGOs in the UN human rights system, and the ways in which NGOs influence that system.

Mégret, Frédéric, and Philip Alston (eds) (2020) *The United Nations and Human Rights: A Critical Appraisal*, 2nd edn (Oxford University Press). An edited collection of studies of the work of the UN on human rights, including chapters on the structure and activities of all its major organs and commissions.

Schabas, William A. (2020) *An Introduction to the International Criminal Court*, 6th edn (Cambridge University Press). A survey of the origins, structure, jurisdiction, procedures and work of the ICC.

Tistounet, Eric (2020) *The UN Human Rights Council: A Practical Anatomy* (Edward Elgar). A survey of the goals and structure of the HRC, including chapters on its major stakeholders, activities and voting procedures.

SUMMARY OF CHAPTERS

1 INTERNATIONAL ORGANIZATIONS AND REGIMES

The goal of this opening chapter is to provide a survey of international organizations: to explain what they are and how they relate to states, to review the varieties in which they are found, and to explain how they have evolved and what they do. The chapter also explains the concept of global regimes and the manner in which IOs fit within these regimes, as well as differences in the depth and reach of regimes. The chapter begins with a review of the system of global governance and its constituent parts, then reviews the motives behind the creation of the earliest international organizations, before discussing the pressures that have led to the construction of the liberal world order since 1945. The chapter then defines the terms *international organization* and *regime*, making a distinction between IOs that are intergovernmental (with states as members) and those that are non-governmental in that they engage non-state actors in the process of global governance. The chapter ends with a review of international law and its place in global governance: how international laws are developed, the areas in which these laws have been agreed and their relationship to the work of international organizations.

2 HOW INTERNATIONAL ORGANIZATIONS WORK

This chapter focuses on the functions of international organizations. It does this by approaching them as political systems, reviewing the rules on which they are based, the manner in which they make decisions, how they are led and how they are funded. The chapter begins by looking at the common characteristics of IOs, including their purposes, their terms of membership, and the methods they use. It then looks at the practical reasons behind the creation and operation of IOs, emphasizing their roles as facilitators and their lack of independent powers or direct powers of enforcement. The bulk of the chapter is devoted to an assessment of the different elements of IOs, including their founding agreements, their leaders, their decision-making systems and their secretariats, asking how each of these elements fit together and assessing the results. It looks at the different pressures and demands that come to bear on IOs, and at the way these are converted into outputs. The chapter ends with a review of the ways in which IOs are funded, contrasting the advantages and disadvantages of mandatory and voluntary funding, and the implications of variations in the share of funding provided by different members.

3 REGIONAL INTEGRATION

Before moving to the specific regimes around which each of the remaining chapters of the book are based, this chapter looks at the more focused work of regional international organizations (RIOs). These are more geographically limited than most IGOs, and yet they are also often more ambitious, and are typically interested in a wider range of policies, including economic cooperation, foreign policy coordination and the development of single markets. Regional integration has become increasingly common since the creation in the 1950s of what is now the European Union (EU). The chapter begins by looking at the underlying motives and dynamics of regional integration, at the structures of the organizations created, and then focuses on the EU as the lynchpin of the idea of integration. It explains the origins of the EU, outlines its constituent institutions, and critiques the different policy areas in which it has been active. The chapter then looks at examples of regional integration in Africa, Asia and Latin America, comparing and contrasting the records of different RIOs in these regions, and the different motivations behind their creation. It ends with a brief review of the role of non-state actors in regional integration.

4 PEACE AND SECURITY

This first chapter focused on a regime deals with international organizations whose work addresses the needs of peace and security. It begins with a discussion about the meaning of terms such as *war*, *peace*, *security* and *human security*, and then looks at the short history of the League of Nations (founded in 1920). The chapter then reviews the creation of the United Nations (UN) and the expansion of the definition of security, before focusing on the work of the UN, the dominating intergovernmental organization of the modern era. The structure and the work of the UN are reviewed, its advantages and disadvantages are discussed, and its peacekeeping activities are assessed. The chapter goes on to look at collective security organizations, prime among them being the North Atlantic Treaty Organization (NATO). The concept of peace through cooperation is then reviewed through the work of IGOs such as the Commonwealth, the Organization of American States (OAS) and the Organization for Security and Cooperation in Europe (OSCE). The chapter ends with a discussion of the activities of non-state actors, mainly international non-governmental organizations interested in the promotion of peace, campaigning for disarmament, providing humanitarian relief and working to influence security policy.

5 FINANCE AND DEVELOPMENT

The second regime addressed revolves around finance and development, although given the control that states prefer to exert over economic policy there is more of a focus on the latter than the former. The chapter begins with a review of the global economic picture, introducing the Human Development Index as a comparative measure. It goes on to look at the Bretton Woods system and its related international organizations, before summarizing changes in the global economic landscape since 1945. The concept of sustainable development is explained and the goals of the UN's Sustainable Development Goals outlined. The chapter then looks at informal arrangements such as the Group of 7 and the Group of 20, before focusing on the work of the International Monetary Fund (IMF). The chapter then moves on to development organizations, headlined by the World Bank and the extensive global network of multilateral development banks. It ends with a review of non-state development actors, looking at a selection of the many international non-governmental organizations (such as Oxfam and BRAC) that have an interest in the fight against poverty. It also notes, though, that development interests overlap with several other fields, such as health care, human rights and refugee assistance.

6 TRADE

The focus of this chapter is on international organizations active in matters related to trade. It begins with a review of the context of global trade, discussing the evolution of approaches to trade and summarizing the domination of the leading trading powers. The chapter goes on to look at the evolution of the global trade regime, emphasizing the rapidity with which it has changed since 1945, and discussing the work of the General Agreement on Tariffs and Trade (GATT). It looks at the nature of international trade law (particularly regional trade agreements) before turning to a focus on the structure and work of the World Trade Organization (WTO). It discusses the strengths and weaknesses of the WTO, and

the impact of its dispute resolution system, before turning the focus to other trade IGOs such as the World Customs Organization (WCO), the World Intellectual Property Organization (WIPO) and the Organization for Economic Cooperation and Development (OECD). It also looks at the unusual example of the Organization of Petroleum Exporting Countries (OPEC). The chapter ends with a review of the role of non-state actors, with an emphasis on the critical influence of multinational enterprises in defining, shaping and operating the global trade system.

7 MIGRATION AND REFUGEES

The focus of this chapter is on IOs concerned with migration and with the welfare of refugees, asylum-seekers and stateless people. It opens with a review of the rapidly changing global migration picture, which has seen a dramatic increase in numbers in just the last few decades. It goes on to look at the halting development of the global migration regime, noting how the work of international organizations has been compromised by the degree to which states control and shape the debate. The chapter then reviews the content and effects of the key pieces of international law on refugees and migrants before turning to the work and the structure of the two key intergovernmental organizations: the International Organization for Migration (IOM) and the UN High Commission for Refugees (UNHCR). The former mainly provides services to migrants and promotes respect for their human rights, while the latter provides help and protection to refugees during emergencies. The chapter continues with an assessment of other IGOs, including UNICEF, before ending with a discussion of the work of non-state actors, including the large number of non-government organizations with an interest in the welfare of migrants and refugees, including Save the Children and the International Rescue Committee.

8 HUMAN RIGHTS

The focus of this chapter is on international organizations that work to promote human rights, as outlined in the Universal Declaration of Human Rights. It opens with a definition of those rights and the threats they face, before reviewing the troubled and controversial efforts made to build a human rights regime after 1945. The struggles of the Commission on Human Rights are discussed, followed by an outline of the major pieces of international human rights law. The chapter then moves on to the current UN human rights regime, revolving around the UN Human Rights Council (HRC) and the Office of the High Commissioner for Human Rights (OHCHR). The structure and goals of both organizations is discussed, along with the challenges they face. The work of other IGOs is then discussed, with a focus on the International Criminal Court (ICC) and on regional human rights courts. Prime among the latter is the European Court of Human Rights (ECHR), whose growing reach and workload contrasts with the difficulties faced by the ICC. The chapter concludes with a review of the non-state actors active on human rights, focusing on the achievements of two international non-governmental organizations: Amnesty International and Human Rights Watch.

9 FOOD AND AGRICULTURE

This chapter addresses the international regime that has evolved around food and agriculture, and more specifically around the so far unmet challenge of ensuring global food security. It opens with a review of the causes of food insecurity and of the dimensions of the problem, asking whether access to food should be considered a human right. It then looks at the evolution of the post-war global food regime, noting that agriculture was barely addressed internationally until after World War II, being given a boost by the first world food crisis in the 1970s (followed by a second in 2007–08). The chapter then discusses the goals and structures of the major agricultural IGOs: the Food and Agriculture Organization of the UN (FAO), the World Food Programme (WFP), the International Fund for Agricultural Development (IFAD) and the Consultative Group on International Agricultural Research (CGIAR). It goes on to review the place in the regime of international commodity bodies such as those concerned with coffee and with tropical timber. The chapter closes with an assessment of the influence of agribusiness multinationals, and the implications of having large elements of global agriculture and food supply being controlled by a small number of large corporations.

10 HEALTH

Cooperation on health, and particularly on controlling the spread of infectious disease, is the focus of the organizations assessed in this chapter. It opens with a review of the challenges posed by such disease and draws attention to the inequalities found in health care around the world. It then outlines the most important steps in the development of the global health regime, underlining the transformations that have come in recent decades. The focus of the chapter is on the World Health Organization (WHO), whose structure is outlined and whose goals are explained before the work of the organization is critically reviewed. Other IGOs involved in health matters are then discussed, notably the UNAIDS joint programme, UNICEF, the World Bank and the UN Population Fund (UNFPA). The chapter then reviews the place of public–private partnerships such as the Global Fund to Fight AIDS, Tuberculosis and Malaria, and the Gavi Alliance that works to promote access to immunization in poorer countries. The chapter assesses the work of non-state actors involved in health, notably the Bill and Melinda Gates Foundation (BMGF) and Doctors Without Borders (MSF), and concludes with a reminder of the key roles played by faith-based organizations and by pharmaceutical companies.

11 ENVIRONMENT AND NATURAL RESOURCES

In this chapter, international organizations are focused on the management of the environment and natural resources, a challenge that has deepened in the wake of climate change and threats to biodiversity. National responses to these problems vary in quality and in quantity, reflected in the slowness with which the foundations of

a global environmental regime were built; it was not until after the 1972 Stockholm conference that the UN Environment Programme (UNEP) was founded, and while there was progress on addressing acid pollution and threats to the ozone later, the story on other problems was less positive. After reviewing achievements in agreeing environmental law, the chapter focuses on the structure and goals of UNEP, noting the failure of efforts to create a World Environment Organization. It then discusses the work of the Global Environment Facility (GEF), and the varied results in building regimes around forests and energy. On the latter, the work of IOs such as the International Energy Agency (IEA) is reviewed. The chapter ends with an assessment of the work of non-state actors, arguing that environmental INGOs have been a source of pressure on governments and IGOs, and noting the impact of changes in the policies of multinational enterprises.

12 SCIENCE AND TECHNOLOGY

This final chapter focuses on a wide range of international organizations engaged in activities with an emphasis on science and technology. It opens with an explanation of the parameters of these two areas, noting that while neither has a broad regime, or a dominating IGO, both have still been the target of important international collaboration. The breadth and depth of this collaboration has grown and changed with advances in scientific knowledge and technological applications. The chapter looks at the work of the UN Educational, Scientific and Cultural Organization (UNESCO) before reviewing the more focused interests of the International Atomic Energy Agency (IAEA), the World Meteorological Organization (WMO) and the European Organization for Nuclear Research (CERN), as well as several scientific INGOs. It then assesses the work of IOs engaged in shipping, aviation and space, including the International Maritime Organization (IMO) and the International Civil Aviation Organization (ICAO). International standards organizations are then reviewed, with a focus on the International Organization for Standardization (ISO) and the chapter ends with a discussion of the complex regime surrounding governance of the internet. Opinion is divided on how best to understand the latter given the prominence of self-regulating and private sector organizations.

ONLINE RESOURCES

International Organizations
by John McCormick

Home
Instructor Resources
Student Resources

International organizations such as the World Health Organization and the United Nations have never been so important in addressing global challenges. This new textbook from bestselling author John McCormick introduces readers to nature, structure and purpose of international organizations. It considers both their historical development and their place in the contemporary world, along with the problems they face and solutions they offer.

This site hosts resources to accompany the book. Please use the links in the sidebar to navigate.

For a freely accessible website containing comprehensive resources for both instructors and students, visit https://bloomsbury.pub/international-organizations

For students

- A media library of videos, primary sources and relevant news articles, which have been carefully selected to illustrate the themes in each chapter.

- Interactive flashcards of key terms in global studies.

For lecturers

Lecturers who adopt the book gain access to a password-protected selection of resources to help plan and deliver their courses.

- Lecturer slides: MS® PowerPoint presentations to accompany every chapter, richly illustrated with photographs, figures and tables from the textbook.

- Testbank of multiple choice and true/false questions for every chapter.

FEATURED INTERNATIONAL ORGANIZATIONS

The following is a list of the major international organizations featured by chapter. For those that have won the Nobel Peace Prize, the years are indicated in brackets.

3

African Union (AU)
Association of Southeast Asian Nations (ASEAN)
Commonwealth of Independent States (CIS)
Community of Latin American and Caribbean States (CELAC)
East African Community (EAC)
Economic and Monetary Community of Central Africa (CEMAC)
Economic Community of West African States (ECOWAS)
European Union (EU) (2012)
Mercosur
South Asian Association for Regional Cooperation (SAARC)
Southern African Development Community (SADC)
Union of South American Nations (UNASUR)

4

Collective Security Treaty Organization (CSTO)
Commonwealth
Eurocorps
Eurojust
Europol
International Campaign to Ban Landmines (ICBL) (1997)
International Campaign to Abolish Nuclear Weapons (ICAN) (2017)
International Committee of the Red Cross (ICRC) (1917, 1944, 1963)
International Crisis Group (ICG)
International Peace Bureau (IPB)
INTERPOL
Islamic Military Counter Terrorism Coalition (IMCTC)
League of Nations (defunct)
North Atlantic Treaty Organization (NATO)
Organization for Security and Cooperation in Europe (OSCE)
Organization of American States (OAS)
Royal Institute of International Affairs
Shanghai Cooperation Organization (SCO)

Southeast Asia Treaty Organization (SEATO) (defunct)
Stockholm International Peace Research Institute (SIPRI)
United Nations (UN) (2001)

5

BRAC
CARE International
European Investment Bank (EIB)
Group of 7 (G7)
Group of 15 (G15)
Group of 20 (G20)
Group of 77 (G77)
Inter-American Development Bank (IADB)
International Monetary Fund (IMF)
Islamic Development Bank (IsDB)
Oxfam
UN Conference on Trade and Development (UNCTAD)
UN Development Programme (UNDP)
World Bank

6

Fairtrade International (FI)
Organization for Economic Cooperation and Development (OECD)
Organization of Petroleum Exporting Countries (OPEC)
World Customs Organization (WCO)
World Economic Forum
World Fair Trade Organization (WFTO)
World Intellectual Property Organization (WIPO)
World Trade Organization (WTO)

7

Global Forum on Migration and Development (GFMD)
International Catholic Migration Commission (ICMC)
International Organization for Migration (IOM)
International Rescue Committee (IRC)
Jesuit Refugee Service (JRS)
Migration Policy Institute (MPI)
Refugees International
Save the Children
UN High Commissioner for Refugees (UNHCR) (1954, 1981)
UN Relief and Works Agency (UNRWA)
United Nations Children's Fund (UNICEF) (1965)

8

African Court on Human and Peoples' Rights (ACHPR)
Amnesty International (AI) (1977)
Anti-Slavery International (ASI)
European Court of Human Rights (ECHR)
Human Rights Watch (HRW)
Inter-American Court of Human Rights (IACHR)
International Criminal Court (ICC)
International Labour Organization (ILO)
Office of the High Commissioner for Human Rights (OHCHR)
UN Human Rights Council (UNHRC)

9

Codex Alimentarius Commission
Committee on World Food Security (CFS)
Common Fund for Commodities (CFC)
Consultative Group on International Agricultural Research (CGIAR)
Food and Agriculture Organization of the UN (FAO)
Global Agriculture and Food Security Programme (GAFSP)
International Coffee Organization (ICO)
International Fund for Agricultural Development (IFAD)
International Tropical Timber Organization (ITTO)
World Food Programme (WFP) (2020)

10

Bill and Melinda Gates Foundation (BMFG)
Gavi Alliance
Global Fund (Global Fund to Fight AIDS, Tuberculosis and Malaria)
International Health Partnership (UHC2030)
Médecins Sans Frontières (MSF or Doctors Without Borders) (1999)
Pan American Health Organization (PAHO)
UNAIDS (UN Programme on HIV/AIDS)
UN Population Fund (UNFPA)
World Health Organization (WHO)

11

Environment Liaison Centre International (ELCI)
Global Environment Facility (GEF)
Greenpeace
Intergovernmental Panel on Climate Change (IPCC)

International Energy Agency (IEA)
International Energy Forum (IEF)
International Union for Conservation of Nature (IUCN)
United Nations Environment Programme (UNEP)
World Business Council for Sustainable Development (WBCSD)
World Energy Council (WED)
World Wide Fund for Nature (WWF)

12

Arctic Council
Antarctic Treaty
European Organization for Nuclear Research (CERN)
European Space Agency (ESA)
InterAcademy Partnership (IAP)
International Atomic Energy Agency (IAEA) (2005)
International Bureau of Weights and Measures (BIPM)
International Civil Aviation Organization (ICAO)
International Maritime Organization (IMO)
International Organization for Standardization (ISO)
International Science Council (ISC)
International Telecommunication Union (ITU)
Internet Corporation for Assigned Names and Numbers (ICANN)
Internet Engineering Task Force (IETF)
Internet Governance Forum (IGF)
UN Educational, Scientific and Cultural Organization (UNESCO)
World Academy of Sciences (TWAS)
World Meteorological Organization (WMO)

ABBREVIATIONS AND ACRONYMS

This list includes only those organizations and concepts that appear in more than one paragraph in the chapters that follow.

ACHPR	African Court on Human and Peoples' Rights
ASEAN	Association of Southeast Asian Nations
AU	African Union
BRICS	Brazil, Russia, India, China, South Africa
CELAC	Community of Latin American and Caribbean States
CERN	European Organization for Nuclear Research
CGIAR	Consultative Group on International Agricultural Research
CHR	Commission on Human Rights
CIS	Commonwealth of Independent States
CO_2	carbon dioxide
CSR	corporate social responsibility
CSTO	Collective Security Treaty Organization
EAC	East African Community
ECHR	European Court of Human Rights
ECOSOC	UN Economic and Social Committee
ECOWAS	Economic Community of West African States
EEC	European Economic Community
EIB	European Investment Bank
EP	European Parliament
EU	European Union
FAO	Food and Agriculture Organization of the UN
FTA	free trade agreement
G7	Group of 7
G20	Group of 20
G77	Group of 77
GATT	General Agreement on Tariffs and Trade
GDP	gross domestic product

GEF	Global Environment Facility
GFMD	Global Forum on Migration and Development
HRC	UN Human Rights Council
IACHR	Inter-American Court of Human Rights
IADB	Inter-American Development Bank
IAEA	International Atomic Energy Agency
ICAO	International Civil Aviation Organization
ICB	international commodity body
ICC	International Criminal Court
ICRC	International Committee of the Red Cross
IFAD	International Fund for Agricultural Development
IGO	intergovernmental organization
ILO	International Labour Organization
IO	international organization
IMF	International Monetary Fund
IMO	International Maritime Organization
INGO	international non-governmental organization
INTERPOL	International Criminal Police Organization
IOM	International Organization for Migration
IPCC	Intergovernmental Panel on Climate Change
ISO	International Organization for Standardization
ITU	International Telecommunication Union
ITTO	International Tropical Timber Organization
IUCN	International Union for Conservation of Nature
LGBTQ+	lesbian, gay, bisexual, transgender, queer
LWO	liberal world order
MDP	multilateral development bank
MNE	multinational enterprise
NATO	North Atlantic Treaty Organization
NGO	non-governmental organization
OAS	Organization of American States
OAU	Organization of African Unity
OECD	Organization for Economic Cooperation and Development
OHCHR	Office of the High Commissioner for Human Rights
OPEC	Organization of Petroleum Exporting Countries
OSCE	Organization for Security and Cooperation in Europe
RIO	regional integration organization
SAARC	South Asian Association for Regional Cooperation
SCO	Shanghai Cooperation Organization

SDG	Sustainable Development Goals
SDR	Special Drawing Rights (IMF)
UDHR	Universal Declaration of Human Rights
UN	United Nations
UNASUR	Union of South American Nations
UNCTAD	UN Conference on Trade and Development
UNDP	UN Development Programme
UNEP	UN Environment Programme
UNESCO	UN Educational, Scientific and Cultural Organization
UNFPA	UN Population Fund
UNGA	UN General Assembly
UNHCR	UN High Commissioner for Refugees
UNICEF	UN Children's Fund
UNRWA	UN Relief and Works Agency for Palestinian Refugees in the Near East
WCO	World Customs Organization
WFP	World Food Programme
WHO	World Health Organization
WIPO	World Intellectual Property Organization
WMO	World Meteorological Organization
WTO	World Trade Organization

ACKNOWLEDGEMENTS

Writing and producing a book is always a team project, dependent on the encouragement of the publisher and the efficiency of the production team. In both regards, Bloomsbury is always perfection to work with. I would particularly like to thank my commissioning editor Milly Weaver, who guided the project from the beginning, and gave me detailed and valuable feedback on all the chapters. My thanks also to Tallulah Griffith and her good work as assistant editor, to Liz Holmes as the production manager and to Dawn Booth for her copy-editing. My thanks and appreciation also to the anonymous reviewers from the UK, the US, the Netherlands and Australia who gave me much valuable feedback on the proposal, the draft manuscript or individual chapters – their suggestions added much to the quality of the finished book. Finally, my love and appreciation as always to Leanne, Ian and Stuart for their work as my essential support team.

INTRODUCTION

On a cool day in the northern spring of May 2023, the Secretary General of the United Nations – António Guterres – took to the stage at the Royal Monastery of Yuste, in the western Spanish region of Extremadura. He was there to receive the Carlos V European Award from the King of Spain in recognition of his commitment to the process of European union. It should have been a time for celebration, but Guterres had a grim message to share. The values of human dignity and freedom that had been enshrined in the UN Charter, he warned, had never before faced such serious threats. Peace remained 'our most precious goal', he noted, but 'we live in a world today in which peace is elusive and fragile'. Wars and humanitarian crises were spreading, sometimes visibly but often far from the spotlight, with causes and effects that were complex and interconnected. 'In a world that is tearing itself apart,' he warned, 'we must heal divisions, prevent escalation and listen to grievances'. Diplomacy – he concluded – should replace rule by the gun, centred around negotiation, mediation, conciliation and arbitration.

The worrying picture painted by the Secretary General was just the latest in a series of warnings issued by leaders and ordinary citizens about the numerous threats facing the world, ranging from war to discrimination, inequality, authoritarianism, polarization, hate speech, misinformation and climate change. The degree of these problems varies from place to place, with some societies faring much better (or worse) than others. The underlying point, though, is that we all live in a global system whose connections have tightened, in which problems and opportunities spread more rapidly, and in which the work of a complex network of international organizations (IOs) must be understood alongside the work of the national and local governments to which we are more immediately connected.

There are now literally tens of thousands of these IOs in existence, most of them founded in the waves of international cooperation that have swept over us since the end of World War II. They now cover almost every field of human activity, from security to economics, trade, migration, agriculture, human rights, health, the environment and technology. The biggest organizations bring together the representatives of governments to address shared concerns, others bring together citizens with the same goals in mind, and yet others take the form of profit-driven international corporations. Although we are all citizens of states, and look to national and local governments to make decisions and address our most immediate needs, our growing interdependence means that none of us is unaffected by changes at the global level, nor by the work of these IOs.

Because of these realities, it is critical that we understand how IOs work: what are they, where are they, what do they do, and how are they structured? Moreover, given the challenges that we now all face, what impact have they had – or are they having, or could they have – on addressing these challenges? These are the kinds of questions asked (and answered) in the chapters that follow. They look at the variety of IOs, the logic behind their creation and development, the range and focus of their interests, the size of their memberships, the degree of their influence, their successes and failures, and the ways in which they interact with the governments of the states in which we live.

Several goals drive this book. The most important is to capture as much as possible of the range and variety of the world's international organizations. This is obviously a tall order when there are an estimated 75,000 IOs in existence (but probably many more, given the difficulties in recording them all, and the problems arising from agreeing the definition of an IO). Even so, the chapters that follow contain more than 120 representative examples. At their heart lie the United Nations (UN) and its specialized agencies and programmes, along with many of the most important non-UN bodies, such as the World Trade Organization, the North Atlantic Treaty Organization and the European Union. Care has also been taken to go beyond the biggest intergovernmental organizations, and those based in and dominated by the world's most powerful states, and to look at IOs based in different parts of the world. Close attention is also paid to non-state actors, including international non-governmental organizations and multinational enterprises.

The second key goal of this book has been to explain the place of IOs within the context of the problems they address, and to explain the legal basis of their work. The book begins with two chapters that look broadly at the work and structure of IOs, and are followed by ten chapters (3–12) dealing with specific regimes (areas of activity), each with the same general structure:

- An outline of the problems and needs addressed by IOs, providing the context for their work.

- A review of the evolution of each regime, explaining its origins and the key steps in its development, finishing with a review of the major pieces of international law related to that regime.

- A discussion of the major international organizations active in each regime, beginning with the most important of those organizations – the UN in the peace and security chapter, for example, and the World Trade Organization in the trade chapter – and moving on to assess the work of other related IOs.

- A review of the activities of non-state actors in each regime, with an emphasis on the work of international non-governmental organizations.

In order to understand the motives behind migration IOs, for example, we need to know something about migration law and patterns of migration, and in order to understand international approaches to health, we need to know something about international health law and the different challenges faced by different parts of the world. It is also important to appreciate the variety of theories used to explain international organizations, a selection of which are addressed in the *IOs in Theory* boxes found in each chapter.

A third goal of this book has been to make international organizations as real and as accessible as possible. With this in mind, the chapters that follow go beyond a recitation of the structure of IOs by offering insights into the personalities and politics involved in their work, providing anecdotes with examples of the work of selected IOs, and using *IOs in Action* and *Spotlight* boxes to answer focused questions and provide more detail on how IOs actually operate in different parts of the world.

Several points will become clear as you read the chapters that follow. First, while the chapters may be organized around regimes, the connections among these regimes are many and complex. The UN, for example, may have been founded mainly to promote peace and security, but its interests have since expanded such that the UN or its specialized agencies and programmes are mentioned in almost every chapter that follows. Similarly, there is a chapter on finance and development that revolves around the work of the International Monetary Fund and the World Bank, but it is difficult to draw clear lines around either finance or development, which are part of the work of IOs in several other chapters. The challenge of easy classification is clearly illustrated by the cross-cutting theme of responses to humanitarian problems, which are closely intertwined with interests such as human rights, security, health care, migration and the welfare of refugees.

Second, it will become clear that a distinction must be made between three core types: international organizations in general, intergovernmental organizations (whose members are states), and a wide array of non-state actors that include international non-governmental organizations and multinational enterprises. Care has been taken throughout the chapters that follow to distinguish between those IOs in which states are members and those in which they are not.

Third, generalizations – while problematic – are also sometimes a necessary evil. In order to understand IOs, we must appreciate that they involve interactions among the 193 member states of the UN, along with numerous additional entities (including *de facto* states, such as Taiwan and Somaliland, that are not generally recognized under international law). Some states are rich while others are poor, some are stable while others are unstable, some are strong while others are weak, some are large while others are small, and some are democratic while others are authoritarian. In order to help us distinguish among these varieties, with their different roles in – and perspectives on – the work of international organizations, the chapters that follow use the labels *Global North* and *Global South*. The former includes the wealthier states of North America and Europe, along with Russia, Japan, South Korea, Australia and New Zealand, while the latter covers Latin America, Africa, most of the Middle East, and most of south and southeast Asia. The terms are controversial, but then so are all the alternatives, using ranking adjectives such as *developed*, *developing*, *underdeveloped*, *emerging* and *industrializing*.

A final point that will soon become clear is that it impossible to write or to talk about IOs without potentially becoming lost in a sea of acronyms. There are dozens of them in the pages that follow, and while they can be distracting and confusing, they are also a necessary evil, and every effort has been made both to offer reminders of what the acronyms mean and to keep them to a minimum. All the major acronyms were listed just before this Introduction and are repeated at the end of each regime chapter.

FURTHER READING

Barnett, Michael N., Jon C. W. Pevehouse, and Kal Raustiala (eds) (2021) *Global Governance in a World of Change* (Cambridge University Press). A collection of studies of the changes that have come to the architecture of the organizations involved in global governance.

Bremmer, Ian (2022) *The Power of Crisis: How Three Threats – and our Response – Will Change the World* (Simon and Schuster). A polemic that argues the importance of sharpening our responses to global health emergencies, climate change and the artificial intelligence revolution before it is too late.

Canton, Helen (2021) *The Europa Directory of International Organizations* (Routledge). An edited encyclopaedia with entries on numerous international organizations.

Lopez-Claros, Augusto, Arthur L. Dahl, and Maja Groff (2020) *Global Governance and the Emergence of Global Institutions for the 21st Century* (Cambridge University Press). A critical review of international organizations, with an emphasis on the United Nations, offering suggestions for reform designed to meet new challenges.

Weiss, Thomas G., and Rorden Wilkinson (eds) (2022) *Global Governance Futures* (Routledge). An edited collection of studies of the key problems faced by global governance, and how actors, mechanisms and resources need to be mobilized.

INTERNATIONAL ORGANIZATIONS AND REGIMES

PREVIEW

The goal of this opening chapter is to provide a survey of international organizations: to explain what they are and how they relate to states, to review the varieties in which they are found, and to explain how they have evolved and what they do. The chapter also explains the concept of global regimes and the manner in which IOs fit within these regimes, as well as differences in the depth and reach of regimes. The chapter begins with a review of the system of global governance and its constituent parts, then reviews the motives behind the creation of the earliest international organizations, before discussing the pressures that have led to the construction of the liberal world order since 1945. The chapter then defines the terms *international organization* (IO) and *regime*, making a distinction between IOs that are intergovernmental (with states as members) and those that are non-governmental in that they engage non-state actors in the process of global governance. The chapter ends with a review of international law and its place in global governance: how international laws are developed, the areas in which these laws have been agreed, and their relationship to the work of international organizations.

CONTENTS

- Understanding global governance
- Building a system of global governance
- International organizations and regimes
- State-driven organizations
- Non-state organizations
- International law

UNDERSTANDING GLOBAL GOVERNANCE

In November 2022, in the Indonesian tourist resort of Bali, leaders from most of the world's leading economies met at the latest summit held under the auspices of the Group of 20, otherwise known as G20. An informal organization that lacks a permanent home or bureaucracy, G20 was formed in 1999 in response to several economic crises, and its leaders have since met every year, either in person or remotely. Vladimir Putin of Russia opted not to attend the 2022 meeting, and Ukrainian leader Volodymyr Zelensky – who made a video speech to the gathering – snubbed Russia (then at war with Ukraine) by referring to the G19 instead of the G20, implying that

Russia should no longer be a member. Meanwhile, President Joe Biden of the US and President Xi Jinping of China used the opportunity of the summit to have their first in-person meeting, Biden announcing afterwards that he saw no prospect of a new Cold War between their two countries (Reuters, 2022).

The meeting of the G20 leaders was just one example of the ongoing process of global governance, a key part of how we define and understand international relations. It was also a reminder – with its focus on the words of national leaders – that while international organizations (even informal ones such as G20) play a key role in that process, the power of making decisions and driving the global agenda still rests with states. While national leaders, or their ministers, or their representatives, frequently gather in the meeting rooms of bodies such as the United Nations (UN), the World Trade Organization (WTO) or the Group of 20, it is still ultimately the interests of states that shape international decisions and that shape the global system as we understand it today. Before coming to grips with the work of international organizations, then, we first need to understand the qualities and dynamics of the state (see Jessop, 2016).

A state is a political and legal entity with five key features:

- A fixed *territory* marked by borders, and control over the movement of people, money and goods across those borders.

- A permanent human *population* of citizens and non-citizens.

- Structures of *government* with the recognized authority to administer and to represent the state in dealings with other governments.

- *Sovereignty*, meaning that states have the sole authority to develop and impose laws and taxes within their borders.

- *Legitimacy*, meaning that states are recognized by their residents and by other states as having jurisdiction and authority within their territory.

If we use the membership of the UN as our point of reference, then there are 193 states in the world. Each has a government consisting of the people, bodies and processes involved in making the decisions needed to run states. They include the courts that protect constitutions, the executives and legislatures that make law and public policy, and the bureaucracies that implement that law and policy. A government differs from a state in the sense that it acts for the state, is more concrete than the abstract idea of the state, and its members are temporary, in contrast to the permanent idea of the state. Meanwhile, *governance* is a looser term than *government*, describing the process by which decisions, laws and policies are made, with or without the input of the formal organizations of government.

Although there are plenty of additional levels of government below the level of the state, reaching down to the smallest and most compact level of local government, there is no government above the level of the state. What we find instead is anarchy, meaning an absence of organized government, and the idea of global governance has emerged to describe the efforts made to provide order above the level of states, whether it is global, transnational, or international (see Finkelstein, 1995). Just how best to understand the dynamics of that process is a matter of debate, one of the oldest and most influential theoretical approaches being realism, which places an emphasis on the self-interest of states; see *IOs in Theory 1*. In later chapters we will see alternative approaches, such as those supported by liberals and neoliberalism; see *IOs in Theory 3*.

Although global governance is far from a new idea, it is mainly a product of events and developments since World War II, the busiest phase of growth having taken place since the end of the Cold War in about 1990. With the reduction in international tensions, the growth in trade, and the greater understanding of challenges such as climate change, there has been a new collective effort by state actors and non-state actors to make the arrangements needed to solve problems, address conflicts, improve efficiency and shape opportunities at a level that transcends state frontiers.

IOs IN THEORY 1

REALISM AND NEOREALISM

Realism has long been the foundational theory in the study of international relations. With a heritage dating back to the ancient Greeks, its main interest lies in understanding and explaining how power is acquired and used by states. It takes the view that because humans are by nature self-centred and competitive, and motivated by rational self-interest, states are encouraged to protect their interests relative to other states and not to trust long-term cooperation and alliances. Realists talk of an anarchic global system in which there is no authority above the level of states that is capable of helping them manage their interactions with one another, and believe that states must use conflict and cooperation to ensure their security through a balance of power among states.

Realists tend to have a limited view of the possibilities of international organizations, arguing that they have the ability neither to constrain the behaviour of states nor – in the final analysis – to prevent war. They point to the example of the League of Nations and its failure to address major security challenges after 1918, or to prevent the outbreak of World War II. They also point to the mixed record of the UN in preventing the many conflicts and wars that have broken out around the world since 1945.

Much like any other theories with the conditional term *neo*, neorealism is an outgrowth of the earlier theory, its major difference being its claims that war is a possibility at any time. In this sense, neorealism takes a more pessimistic view of the international system, placing even more emphasis on its anarchic nature, and insisting that none of the laws, norms, or organizations that are part of the system of global governance are enough to prevent war. It is a prominent school of thought in international relations, being used – for example – by Akdag (2018) to consider the possibilities of a cyberwar breaking out between the US and China. More recently, it was used to help explain the reaction of many states to the Covid-19 pandemic. The pandemic did not lead to war, but – argues Alhammadi (2022) – neorealism is applicable to an understanding of the effects of the closing of international borders, international competition to accumulate Covid vaccines, bans on exports and the protection of their national interests by wealthier states.

As the needs of cooperation have grown, so the character of the global system has become more complex, and so has the character of global governance, which includes elements ranging from the formal to the informal.

Although it can be difficult to neatly categorize all the elements of global governance, at least four stand out (summarized in Table 1.1). First, we need to consider institutions. At the state level and below, government institutions are expected to reach and execute decisions for the good of the community over which they have jurisdiction. This is a process that – in democracies, at least – involves direct public representation and accountability: voters make demands of governments, while governments claim to be responsive to those demands, based on laws. Above the state level, institutions can be found in the form of the intergovernmental organizations (IGOs) that are created when states see opportunities for mutual benefits arising out of cooperation, and of the international non-governmental organizations (INGOs) that encourage cooperation outside the hallways of government. Both types are motivated by identifying problems that are best addressed collectively, and work across borders to achieve their goals. They lack sovereignty, have only as much authority as their members give them, and have no direct political relationship with voters.

The second element in global governance consists of the rules and laws that commit states to work together to achieve shared goals, and that form the body of international law that governs relations between states and the work of international organizations (see Harrington, 2018). International treaties do not have the same reach or effect as national laws, because there is rarely a meaningful mechanism for enforcement, and signatories can opt out of their obligations – or work around them – without much fear of punishment. Even so, they provide a framework within which global governance takes place. As for international non-governmental organizations – which do not have states as members – the rules that govern their work are found in the form of founding charters, articles of incorporation, or contracts.

Table 1.1: The core elements of global governance

Element	Features
Institutions	Formal or informal bodies of people working together with a particular purpose in mind, with shared rules and procedures, a hierarchy and internal communication systems.
Rules and laws	Legal agreements drawn up and signed by states, taking the form of treaties, protocols, conventions, or judicial decisions.
Norms and expectations	Standards of expected behaviour driving the way in which states or the partners in IOs deal with one another, shaping their definition of the kinds of actions that go against those expectations.
Ad hoc agreements	Informal agreements, decisions, events, and actions taking place outside law and government.

Third, and in addition to the formal arrangements set by organizations and treaties, global governance is also based on sets of norms or expectations, or 'soft law'. For example, when a state ratifies a treaty, it is expected to voluntarily respect and adhere to the terms of the treaty. Unlike national laws, which are backed up by governments, courts and police, there are no mechanisms for directly enforcing most international rules. Other examples of norms include the expectation that states with nuclear weapons will not use those weapons, that states are expected not to interfere in the domestic affairs of other states and that it is unacceptable for one state to use violence or assassination against another.

The fourth element in global governance consists of ad hoc agreements or contacts among interested parties. Informality is true at the domestic level and also at the global level, where groups of states will come together periodically at conferences or through ad hoc commissions, without creating institutions. They move close to formality when they meet as the Groups of 7, 20 and 77 (see Chapter 5), or when (at least before the Russian invasion of Ukraine) the emerging powers of Brazil, Russia, India, China and South Africa would coordinate interests as the BRICS. More informally, there are countless decisions, events and actions within the systems and networks that underlie international cooperation. These can be found at work on everything from health care to education, the protection of human rights, police investigations, research, environmental management, the conduct of trade, the alleviation of poverty, the setting of standards, and the technological developments that help us communicate quickly and effectively.

BUILDING A SYSTEM OF GLOBAL GOVERNANCE

As Barnett et al. (2021) summarize it, global governance began to take shape in the mid-nineteenth century, accelerated after World War I and came of age after World War II. Although there is evidence of diplomatic interactions dating back several thousand years, and a long history of agreements being signed between leaders, governments and factions, the history of global governance and international organizations in their modern forms dates back only to the 1815 Congress of Vienna that brought an end to the Napoleonic wars. The major European powers began to assume shared responsibility for encouraging regional peace, and established rules and customs for diplomatic interaction, and a consultation process known as the Concert of Europe, focused on encouraging peace within Europe (in which it mainly succeeded).

Changes in communications and technology were additional incentives for cooperation, sparking the creation of some of the earliest international organizations; see Table 1.2. The oldest still-functioning IGO in the world is the Central Commission for the Navigation of the Rhine, created in 1815 with the practical goal of encouraging cooperation among the countries through which the Rhine flowed: France, Germany, the Netherlands and Switzerland (as well as Belgium, whose ships made up a large segment of the Rhine fleet). In 1865, the International Telegraph Union (now the International Telecommunication Union) was founded to establish international standards and regulations on what was then a new technology, and in 1874 the General

Table 1.2: The world's oldest international organizations: Examples

Name	Founded	Headquarters	Structure
Central Commission for the Navigation of the Rhine	1815	Strasbourg, France	IGO
Anti-Slavery International	1839	London, UK	INGO
International Committee of the Red Cross	1863	Geneva, Switzerland	INGO
International Telegraph Union	1865	Geneva	IGO
Institute of International Law	1873	Geneva	INGO
Universal Postal Union	1874	Bern, Switzerland	IGO
International Council of Women	1888	Paris, France	INGO
International Peace Bureau	1891	Berlin, Germany	INGO
International Olympic Committee	1894	Lausanne, Switzerland	INGO
League of Nations	1920	Geneva	IGO

Postal Union (now the Universal Postal Union) was founded to establish international postal standards. Both bodies had efficient international communication as their main goal, and membership of both is today open to all members of the UN; see Chapter 12.

The first generation of international organizations

For Herren (2016), the period between 1860 and 1865 can be seen as a 'take-off period' for IOs, because a first generation of such bodies emerged that gained a new level of stability and public visibility that was to influence the history of IOs for decades to come. Interconnectedness became an indispensable tool of power not just for governments but also for those outside government. Prominent among the events of that short period was the creation in 1863 of the International Committee of the Red Cross to help care for soldiers wounded in war. Its foundation was prompted by the Swiss businessman Henry Dunant (1828–1910), who had been shocked by what he saw of the lack of facilities and medical aid to help soldiers after the 1859 Battle of Solferino in what is now Italy. In 1901, Dunant became the joint winner – along with the French peace activist Frédéric Passy – of the first award of the Nobel Peace Prize.

In 1864, the Geneva Convention codified – for the first time – the treatment of wounded soldiers, and was followed in 1899 and 1907 by the Hague Conventions on the conduct of war and the definition of war crimes. While these were treaties rather than organizations, they were aimed at reforming the rules of the international system, were based on formal structures for organizing meetings and electing chairs, and included the creation in 1899 of a Permanent Court of Arbitration (PCA) that continues to function today (in The Hague). Less a court than an administrative body that can help with commissions of enquiry and conciliation, the PCA was a prototype for later international courts, such as the International Court of Justice.

At the same time, changes in the dimensions of the international marketplace were encouraging the creation of IOs with a focus on issues such as the regulation of copyright and the standardization of measurements. One of the former was the International Literary and Artistic Association (ALAI), founded in Paris in 1878 by the writer Victor Hugo, which campaigned for the protection of the rights of writers and artists. Its work was behind the agreement of the 1886 Berne Convention, which continues today to be the basis of the protection of copyright for authors, musicians and artists. Meanwhile, the creation of international standards in manufacturing, technology and engineering was promoted by the International Federation of the National Standardizing Associations, founded in 1926. It merged with a similar UN body in 1946 to become the International Organization for Standardization (ISO), headquartered in Geneva (see Chapter 12).

Among the effects of World War I was an end to the Concert of Europe, a new involvement of the US in international affairs, and support for the idea of a new type of body that could help promote security on a worldwide basis; hence the creation in 1919 of the League of Nations, designed to encourage peaceful means for the settlement of disputes. The League, however, had many structural and political problems (see Chapter 4), its greatest failing being that it was unable to prevent the outbreak of World War II. Its work did, though, give new focus to the possibilities of international cooperation: its Assembly laid the foundations for the later work of the UN General Assembly, its Council was the forerunner of the UN Security Council, its High Commissioner for Refugees later evolved into the UN High Commissioner for Refugees, and the International Labour Organization – which still exists – traces its origins back to the work of the League.

The evolution of international organizations was also impacted by initiatives taken outside government, forming the basis of what we now think of as global civil society (see later in this chapter). In an effort to better understand international law, for example, a group of lawyers founded – in Belgium in 1873 – the Institute of International Law. It went on to win the 1904 Nobel Peace Prize for its work in encouraging the peaceful means of settling international disputes. Meanwhile, the International Peace Bureau was founded in Berlin in 1891 to promote international peace, Save the Children was founded in the UK in 1919 (later evolving into one of the pre-eminent international humanitarian organizations; see Chapter 7), the Royal Institute for International Affairs was founded in London in 1920 as one of the first of many think-tanks studying the dynamics of international relations, and the International Rescue Committee was founded in New York in 1933 – at the suggestion of Albert Einstein – to help refugees fleeing Nazi Germany.

Developments since 1945

The sheer breadth and depth of World War II, combined with a widespread horror at the number of people who died or were wounded or displaced by the war, brought a change in attitudes towards international cooperation. Early signs of that change came with the convening of a three-week meeting in July 1944 at the resort of Bretton Woods, New Hampshire, where plans for the post-war world were made by the representatives of 44 states (including China and the Soviet Union, but not Japan or Germany). Most importantly, they agreed on the principles of free trade, non-discrimination, the convertibility of currencies and stable rates of exchange (see Conway, 2014). What came to be known as the Bretton Woods system would be underpinned by the new global strength of the US dollar, and by the creation of two new international organizations: the International Monetary Fund (IMF) would encourage exchange rate stability in the interests of promoting international trade, and the World Bank would help European countries recover from the war – see Chapter 5 for more details. At the same time, the General Agreement on Tariffs and Trade (GATT) was set up to oversee negotiations aimed at the progressive reduction of barriers to trade – see Chapter 6.

The end of the war also moved the US to centre stage in the promotion of global peace, and resulted in the creation in 1945 of a prominent new intergovernmental organization – the UN – within which broad security matters could be addressed. Specialized agencies and programmes of the UN would go on to address more focused matters as diverse as food security, health, civil aviation, tourism, human settlements, education and the environment. Security was enhanced by the work of the UN Security Council, of peacekeeping operations launched and sustained under the auspices of the UN, and of collective security organizations such as the North Atlantic Treaty Organization (NATO). These changes were part of the birth of what came to be known as the liberal world order, which has since been a point of reference for understanding the international system; see *Spotlight 1*.

Along the way, there have since been many changes to the state system and to the place of international organizations within that system:

- The number of independent states has nearly quadrupled, from the 51 that were founding members of the UN to the 193 that are UN members today.

- Regional integration has become a core area of cooperation, spearheaded by the European Union and its equivalents in Asia, Africa and the Americas.

- The number, influence and reach of multinational enterprises has grown.

- New problems have arisen, including international terrorism, the dangers of infectious disease and climate change.

- There have been changes in the patterns and volume of the cross-border movement of people, whether as tourists, migrants, refugees or asylum-seekers.

- Global trade has blossomed, growing in volume by 3,800 per cent between 1950 and 2020, and leading to greater economic interdependence among states.

- The diversity of IOs and their memberships have grown, bringing in a wider range of interests and perspectives.

SPOTLIGHT 1

IS THERE A LIBERAL WORLD ORDER?

The changes that came to global governance after World War II represent the building of what came to be known as the liberal world order (also known as the liberal international order). This describes a global, open and rules-based system of international cooperation based on international organizations and treaties, and on norms such as multilateralism (see Ikenberry, 2011). Many credit the order with multiple achievements, including the expansion of free trade, the promotion of democracy and human rights, and the encouragement of the peaceful resolution of international disagreements. Others question whether there is – in fact – such an order, or whether it is as orderly as the label implies, and point to its many failures. Pabst (2019), for example, argues that it is both illiberal and undemocratic, intolerant of the cultural values of ordinary people, and that it concentrates power in the hands of Western elites and Western-dominated institutions, fuelling both economic injustice and social fragmentation.

However we understand the liberal world order, there is no question that the world of international organizations has grown in breadth, depth and complexity since 1945, leaving many of the scholars of the subject competing to decide how best to understand and portray that world. Terms such as *orchestrated*, *fragmented*, *partnerships*, *networks* and *layering* have all been used, and the world of IOs has even been likened to a bowl of spaghetti (see summary in Barnett et al., 2021). States and intergovernmental organizations still draw the most attention in studies of the liberal world order, but they must work with an expanding range of non-state actors and arrangements, including interest groups, corporations, foundations and communities of experts.

The broadest of the changes in recent decades has been the impact of globalization, or the process by which the links between people, corporations and governments have been integrated through cooperation, trade, communications, investment, technology. It reach has resulted – as Robertson (1992) once put it – in 'both the compression of the world and the intensification of the consciousness of the world as a whole'. The process of globalization is far from new, although just how far back we can reasonably go to find its first steps is debatable. The era of European exploration and colonization may have constituted a first wave, although that title is usually given to the period between 1870 and 1914 with its growth of international trade (Zinkina et al., 2019). The second wave came between 1945 and some time in the 1970s, spurred by the growth in international cooperation and the opening of markets, while the most recent wave (since about 1990) rests on the emergence of digital technologies. Not everyone is convinced by the degree of globalization, though, with sceptics arguing that the world has not changed much over the last century, others pointing to a backlash against globalization, and yet others arguing that its effect has not been to reduce the power of states so much as to change the relationships among them. These are all views that we need to bear in mind as we think about the meaning of global governance.

INTERNATIONAL ORGANIZATIONS AND REGIMES

At the heart of the system of global governance are IOs. Name almost any field of human endeavour – from human rights to environmental management, migration, the alleviation of poverty, the marketing of coffee and the promotion of tourism – and there is likely to be at least one IO serving its interests, but most likely many more. According to data maintained by the Brussels-based Union of International Associations (UIA) (2023), founded in 1907 as an information clearinghouse, there were about 75,000 such organizations in existence in 2022. This represented a notable increase over the previous century, from 220 in 1909, to just under 1,000 in 1951, to 3,600 in 1970 and to 27,000 in 1990 (see Figure 1.1). The growth has been biggest among non-governmental organizations, which are less stable because most rely on public donations and the work of volunteers. Hence, notes the UIA, about 1,200 new organizations are added to its records each year, but just under 44 per cent of the organizations in those records in 2022 were described as dormant.

International organizations

Despite the proliferation in their numbers, the debate about the definition of IOs is far from settled. The narrow view – as found in the 1969 Vienna Convention on the Law of Treaties (sometimes known as the 'treaty on treaties') – limits IOs to bodies with states as members and requires that they be based on founding treaties. While it is true that only states can enter into treaties with one another, a wider definition of an IO would include almost any body that consisted of representatives from multiple states, whether those representatives came from governments or not. Whatever the

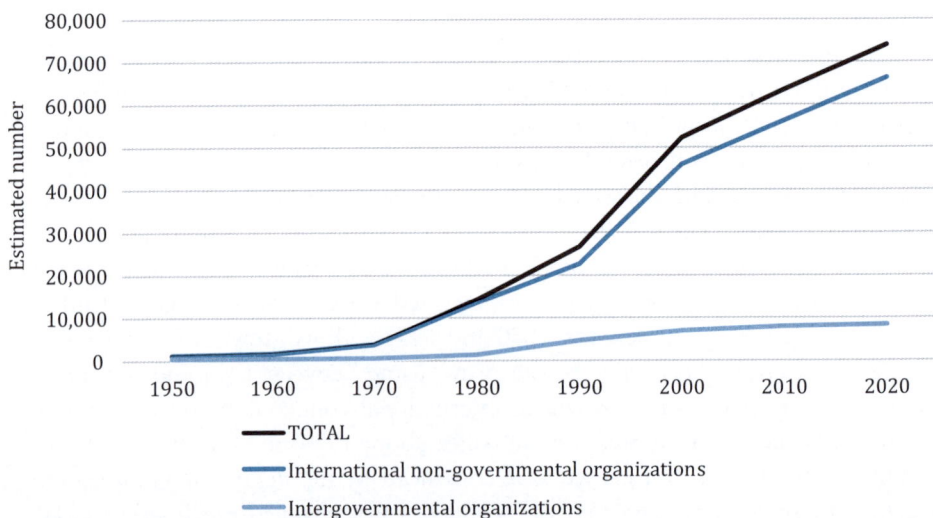

Figure 1.1: The growth of international organizations.
Source: Based on data in Union of International Associations (2023).

questions, most scholars of international relations agree that an IO should be active in at least three states, because the key to the work of IOs is multilateralism, through which multiple countries pursue common goals. This is distinct from the more focused bilateralism that binds organizations with only two members, working on a different dynamic.

Although treaties are important, IOs can also be based on less formal agreements reached by the participating bodies or individuals, or else they can simply come together as a result of more fluid pressures and needs. Most IOs – but not all – will have a permanent secretariat, an executive head and an executive council, perhaps an assembly of some kind, and a salaried staff; see Chapter 2 for details. It is critical to note, though, that while the membership of IOs is voluntary, and while they have shared interests, they have no independent legal authority or direct powers of enforcement.

Beyond these features, IOs come in a wide variety of ages, sizes, interests, reach, capabilities, effectiveness and levels of specialization:

- Some, such as the UN and WTO, are global in scope, with memberships that actually or potentially consist of every independent state in the world.

- Others are regional, focused on the interests of a limited group of states. Because the idea of a region is a political construct, regional IOs come in a wide range of forms. They include geographically-proximate IOs working towards regional integration (such as the European Union), others – such as multilateral development banks – with more focused interests and yet others – such as the Organization for Economic Cooperation and Development – that consist of like-minded (but not necessarily neighbouring) states with shared interests.

- Some (such as the biggest intergovernmental organizations) are overtly political in their structure and objectives, while others (including many international non-governmental organizations) might exist to provide services, and multinational enterprises are driven by production and profit.

- While the oldest IOs date back to the nineteenth century, the vast majority have only been in existence for a few decades.

- Some IOs have relatively broad goals, as in the cases of those that promote peace and security (such as the UN), while others have more focused and task-specific goals (such as Doctors Without Borders).

- IOs have different levels of staffing and financial resources to bring to bear on their tasks. The biggest multinationals have millions of employees and enormous revenues, while most intergovernmental organizations have smaller numbers of staff and smaller budgets; see Chapter 2 for more details.

- Some IOs will be programmatic, meaning that they oversee the setting of rules for their members, while others are operational in the sense that they oversee the implementation of those rules. The International Labour Organization is an example of the first, with its work on setting international labour standards, while the International Atomic Energy Agency is an example of the second because it carries out inspections aimed at ensuring that its member states use nuclear materials only for peaceful purposes.

– IOs have different levels of centralization. With the International Monetary Fund, for example, decisions are centralized, and implementation is overseen by the secretariat. In the Organization of Petroleum Exporting Countries, by contrast, the member states make decisions and also oversee implementation.

The chapters that follow will illustrate this variety, showing clearly that there is no fixed template for international organizations, which come in many different forms.

Regimes

Occasionally, there may be enough organizations, treaties, norms and systems revolving around a given issue as to make it possible to identify a regime. This is a concept defined by Krasner (1983) as consisting of the principles, norms, rules and decision-making procedures around which the expectations of a group of actors converge in a given area of international relations. In other words, a solid regime will consist of a cluster of international organizations (governmental and non-governmental), a body of laws, a set of policies, a set of informal networks and a track record of activity on a given issue, such as security, finance, trade, migration and human rights (see Table 1.3 and Chapters 3–12 of this book are each based around distinct regimes).

As we think about regimes, several key points are worth bearing in mind:

– Not all international issues have an associated regime. When it comes to the global environment, for example (see Chapter 11), there are relatively clear regimes dealing with climate change and biodiversity, but only partial regimes for energy or fisheries, and efforts to build a global maritime regime have not moved far beyond agreements to control pollution at sea.

– Just as there is no fixed template for IOs, so there is no fixed template for regimes. The elements of each change according to how much structured action has been taken (or not taken) on a particular problem, and the degree to which IOs have been formed around that problem.

Table 1.3: International regimes: Examples

Agriculture	Finance	Security
Biodiversity	Health	Technology
Climate change	Human rights	Telecommunications
Development	Migration	Trade
Environment	Nuclear weapons	

– Many problems cannot be neatly placed in a definable box, which means not only that the work of IOs often overlaps but that regimes combine often related interests. The activities of three or more regimes with overlapping interests have resulted in the creation of what Orsini et al. (2013) call 'regime complexes'. Examples include food security, migration and climate change, none of which can be fully understood in isolation.

– The roles of states and international organizations vary from one regime to another. While relatively well-developed state-driven regimes exist on finance and trade, for example (see Chapters 5 and 6), when it comes to migration states have been more resistant to working together through international organizations (see Chapter 7), and the body of international law is modest.

– The influence of participants in different regimes – as in different IOs – is far from equal. Every state will bring its own perspective to the discussion, while the bigger and wealthier member states usually play bigger roles in shaping regimes, and smaller or weaker states can often only express themselves by forming coalitions. Meanwhile, the long-time influence of the US and the major European powers is still evident in many regimes, although this is changing as emerging powers such as Brazil, China and India become more assertive.

Regimes need not be based on specific international treaties (or sets of treaties) or the creation of dedicated organizations, although it gives a regime more focus if they are. Nor are they exclusively driven by the work of states and their governments; the growing complexity of the global system and of the shared issues that have arisen has been accompanied by a growth in the variety of actors involved, ranging from non-governmental organizations to multinational enterprises, private foundations, communities of experts and even sometimes social movements.

STATE-DRIVEN ORGANIZATIONS

International organizations come in two major types (summarized in Table 1.4). The most prominent and influential are those that are based around state actors, meaning that they are created by states and have states as their primary members. As a result, they are usually the forums in which the most substantial agreements are likely to be reached on matters of international concern. Prime among these are intergovernmental organizations (IGOs), which are created through formal treaties or charters, and within which the interests of states are represented by government officials, working in conjunction with the staff of the IGOs. Although IGOs would seem to be venues in which states can pursue their own national interests, they have increasingly been studied and understood as actors in their own right. When it came to Covid-19, for example, the World Health Organization took the lead in drawing attention to the outbreak and spread of the virus, and played a key role in coordinating or shaping the responses of states; see Chapter 10.

The term *intergovernmental* should not always be taken too literally, because most IGOs do not actually bring together the political leaders of governments so

Table 1.4: Types of international organizations

Type	Sub-types	Examples
State-driven	Intergovernmental organizations	United Nations African Union Multilateral development banks
	International courts	International Court of Justice European Court of Human Rights International Criminal Court
	Treaty secretariats	Those for treaties on the status of refugees, the rights of the child and biodiversity
Non-state-driven	International non-governmental organizations	International Committee of the Red Cross Amnesty International Doctors Without Borders
	Multinational enterprises	Walmart, Toyota, Saudi Aramco
	Epistemic communities	Those dealing with standardization, the science of climate change and nuclear arms control
	Social movements	Those targeted on democratic, social and economic change, including movements against racism
	Violent non-state actors	Terrorist groups and organized crime

much as bureaucrats, scientists or experts speaking on behalf of those governments. Also, while governments make the ultimate decisions and pay the financial costs of membership, the positions they take will be influenced and even implemented – as we will see in Chapter 2 – by officials working within the secretariats of IGOs. These officials are international civil servants rather than the representatives of states, play key roles in gathering and analysing information, and as such can have much influence over shaping the work of IGOs and the impact that this work has on the decisions of states.

A particular kind of IGO whose work is intimately related to international law is an international court, of which there are just under two dozen in existence. Alter (2014) identifies three 'critical junctures' in the development of such courts:

- The first was the agreement of the Hague Conventions of 1899 and 1907 that led to the establishment of the Permanent Court of Arbitration discussed earlier in this chapter.

- After World War II, the European Court of Justice was created as part of what is now the European Union (see Chapter 3), while several regional courts focused on human rights.

- The end of the Cold War in 1990 paved the way for new demands for accountability in the wake of war crimes and prompted the creation of the International Criminal Court (see Chapter 8).

Alter (2019) has since identified a fourth critical juncture in which she sees a questioning of the liberal world order of which international courts have been an important part. International courts, she argues, depend on popular support for the rule of law, and if that support continues to erode, and if courts are pushed into directly condemning state actors for their actions, they will find themselves under strain.

IOs IN ACTION 1

ENVIRONMENTAL TREATY SECRETARIATS

Although most international treaties are housed in and monitored by intergovernmental organizations, some have their own dedicated secretariats, with different degrees of ability to protect and promote the treaties for which they are responsible. Contrasting examples are offered by the records of two dealing with environmental treaties: the climate change convention secretariat based in Bonn, Germany, and the biological diversity convention secretariat based in Montreal, Canada.

The climate change convention secretariat – usually known as UN Climate Change – was established in 1992 to support the UN Framework Convention on Climate Change, which was opened for signature in 1992, came into force in 1994 and now has 198 parties. It has a staff of about 450 (making it bigger than many international organizations) whose job is to coordinate the agreements that have come out of the 1992 convention, to provide technical expertise and to organize the annual Conferences of Parties, which now attract about 25,000 participants (UN Climate Change, 2023). Although the climate change secretariat began life as a limited technocratic body, Hickmann et al. (2021) argue that it has loosened its straitjacket and has interacted increasingly with sub-national governments, NGOs and corporations to promote the climate change agenda.

Meanwhile, the secretariat for the Convention on Biological Diversity manages a treaty that was also opened for signature in 1992, coming into force in 1993, but which has not been the subject of quite such fervent or urgent political activity, even though biodiversity is under threat all over the world. It provides many of the same services as the climate change treaty secretariat, but has only about 110 staff and has had to organize fewer CoPs: the fifteenth was held in Montreal in December 2022, shortly after the conclusion of the twenty-seventh climate change CoP held in Sharm el-Sheikh, Egypt. While it may be smaller than the climate change secretariat, and attracts less attention, this can be an advantage: the biodiversity secretariat – argues Siebenhüner (2015) – is more of a facilitator and thus has more influence over how decisions are reached.

Another and more focused kind of IGO whose work is also closely related to international law is a treaty secretariat. This is a body set up to monitor compliance with an international treaty, and to promote negotiations among signatory states, often at meetings known as Conferences of Parties (CoPs). Secretariats may exist in their own right, or may be housed within existing IGOs, and while they have no direct powers of enforcement, and are usually focused on administrative work, Jinnah (2014) argues that they exert influence through the allocation of resources and the way in which they manage interstate cooperation and communication. Their influence also depends on the number of signatories to the treaty they are monitoring, the complexity of the problems and the goals involved, and the amount of progress achieved in implementing treaty goals; see *IOs in Action 1*.

NON-STATE ORGANIZATIONS

The second major type of international organization consists of a more varied community of organizations based around non-state actors, meaning – quite simply – that their participants are not states. The exact definition of a non-state actor is fuzzy (see discussion in Irrera and Charountaki, 2022), and the list of candidates offered as examples ranges from formal organizations to religious groups, armed groups, transnational ethnic groups and even organized criminal networks. In short, they include almost any collectives that work outside government but that are organized at the international level to influence states. At the top of most lists of non-state actors are non-governmental organizations (NGOs), which are private, voluntary, non-profit organizations whose members are individuals or national associations. The term *non-governmental organization* was first used by the American diplomat Dwight Morrow (1919) to distinguish international organizations that had not been created by states from those that had been. It became more widely used after World War II when the UN Charter allowed for membership of NGOs in the UN Economic and Social Council (Grant, 2018), with a focus on bodies that were international in reach.

Since then, the term has been applied more widely, and is now defined by the World Association of Non-Governmentals Organizations (2023) as 'any not-for-profit organization that is not established by a governmental entity or intergovernmental agreement and which is organized on a local, national, sub-regional, regional, or international level'. NGOs are also known as interest groups, pressure groups, or – because they are part of civil society (the arena outside government within which citizens engage with one another to address public problems of shared concern) – as civil society organizations (see Götz, 2019). The latter label, though, is usually used to describe organizations that provide services, in contrast to those that try to influence government. Whatever we call them, NGOs use multiple means to achieve their goals, including lobbying governments, undertaking research, organizing conferences, raising and spending funds, promoting media coverage of the issues they care about, and blowing the whistle on the performance of states, corporations or individuals.

International non-governmental organizations

The biggest NGOs form networks or federations, creating international non-governmental organizations (INGOs) that encourage cross-border cooperation through the work of their national groups, and are part of what has come to be known as global civil society. As we will see in later chapters, INGOs have been particularly active in addressing human rights, humanitarian issues, health and environmental management.

Like IGOs, INGOs vary widely in terms of their age, size, interests, reach, capabilities, effectiveness and level of specialization:

- Some are international because they have offices or member organizations in multiple countries, while others are international because they are active in different parts of the world.

- Some have focused interests, such as assistance to refugees or the protection of nature, while others have a wider range of interests, such as the alleviation of poverty.

- Some use direct action (engaging with the governments, people or organizations they seek to help or influence), while others use more indirect means to achieve change.

In many respects, the existence of INGOs represents the failure of governments to effectively address many international problems. For example, environmental INGOs such as the Swiss-based World Wide Fund for Nature predate the creation of environmental agencies by governments in most countries, and other environmental INGOs – such as Friends of the Earth and Greenpeace – were created because of disappointment at the slow speed with which governments were responding to problems such as air and water pollution; see Chapter 11. Some of these organizations have the advantage of being run by ordinary citizens unconstrained by narrow political agendas, which gives them greater freedom to work with like-minded citizens from other states.

Often, an NGO will be created in one country and will inspire the creation of equivalent national offices in other countries, the network being held together – and kept on the same track – by the creation of an international coordinating office. This is the case, for example, with Save the Children, an organization founded in the UK in 1919 that now has 30 national offices that are active in more than 120 countries; see Chapter 7 for more details. Occasionally, NGOs and INGOs will combine to form transnational advocacy networks (TANs) in which they combine their resources in order to work on achieving their shared goals. These networks are usually motivated, argue Keck and Sikkink (1998) by values rather than by material concerns or professional norms. Recent examples including the international campaigns against land mines, to protect tropical forests, to eradicate poverty and to address the threat of HIV/AIDS.

Kaloudis (2021) argues that the number, strength and reach of INGOs is likely to continue growing, representing what some scholars describe as a 'global associational revolution'. The changes have come for several reasons:

- Changes in technology that have allowed people and communities to connect more easily with one another.

- The globalization of issues such as human rights and the environment.

- The crises of efficiency, legitimacy, identity and equity that have afflicted many national political systems (even in democracies), leaving non-state actors to become voices for the voiceless.

- Efforts by international organizations to cooperate with NGOs as service providers.

- The engagement of NGOs in almost all the issues addressed by the UN system.

INGOs are at a disadvantage compared to their governmental equivalents, for the simple reason that they are mainly excluded from decision-making. At the same time, they do not suffer from the same levels of declining public trust as national governments, and their more direct alignment with the public sphere means that they have a tactical advantage relative to intergovernmental organizations.

Multinational enterprises

A second type of non-state actor is a multinational enterprise (MNE), or a multinational corporation. This is a private for-profit entity that has facilities and income-generating assets in more than one country, managing its global activities from its home state. Just as national businesses – particularly the bigger ones – play a key role in influencing and implementing policy at the state level, so MNEs are an important part of the system of global governance.

Most MNEs are surprisingly young, their number and reach having grown only in recent decades in tandem with trade and globalization. The value of merchandise exports and imports (each of which has closely followed the other) grew by nearly 500 per cent between 1990 and the breaking of the Covid-19 pandemic in 2020 (World Trade Organization, 2020). Meanwhile, the number of MNEs nearly tripled over the same period of time, from about 35,000 in 1990 to about 100,000 in 2020 (United Nations Conference on Trade and Development, 2020). Some are so big that they have become what Khanna (2016) describes as 'metanationals' in the sense that they are truly global, and are no longer headquartered in a single state. For example, corporations such as Walmart, Volkswagen Toyota, and energy giants such as Sinopec, State Grid (both Chinese), Saudi Aramco and BP control such extensive assets and employ so many people that it could be argued that they have become more politically influential than smaller states, leading Khanna to assert that 'the world is entering an era in which the most powerful law is not that of sovereignty but that of supply and demand'.

Multinationals impact global governance in multiple ways:

- Driving international trade.

- Making decisions about foreign investment.

- Controlling often large financial or natural resources.

- Driving the production of goods and services.

- Meeting consumer needs while helping change consumer tastes and choices.

- Influencing the use of energy.

- Impacting environmental policy.

- Leading the way in the development of new technologies.

- Shaping policies on workers' rights.

- Driving the creation of new jobs, the loss of old jobs and the placement of jobs.

- Influencing the economic health of states.

The international influence of MNEs is felt particularly in the fields of trade, agriculture, labour, the environment and technology, while pharmaceutical companies are important to the global health regime, and the labour policies of MNEs has a direct impact on human rights.

Other non-state actors

A third type of non-state actor is found in the form of transnational networks of experts working within what are known as epistemic communities. These are groups of experts with recognized skills and knowledge in a particular area (Haas, 1992) who have been drawn together to share and pass on their knowledge. As the need for information about the causes and effects of international problems has grown, so has the need for informed and workable solutions of the kind that epistemic communities can provide. Their members might come from national government agencies, universities, research institutes and private industry, forming a network driven by the goal of generating and sharing knowledge. For example, hundreds of scientists have participated since 1988 in the work of the Intergovernmental Panel on Climate Change, which produces periodic reports on the state of our understanding of climate change; see Chapter 11. These reports raise public awareness and help guide the decisions of national policymakers. Meanwhile, the Geneva-based International Organization for Standardization – whose goal is to develop international standards on everything from engineering to occupational safety – consists of technical committees made up of experts in their different fields; see Chapter 12.

Where the work of IGOs relies on the cooperation of states, epistemic communities revolve around a consensus reached among specialists or experts. States are still important in their work, but the fact that the activities of epistemic communities derive from their knowledge rather than from political, social or other motives, gives them authority and credibility. Many of the studies of such communities have focused on scientists, but they could as well review networks of economists, lawyers, diplomats or journalists (Cross, 2013).

A fourth type of non-state actor, which is less formal and more transitory than a typical international organization, is a social movement. This is a spontaneous gathering of large numbers of people, inspired to press for social, political or economic change, and working outside the formal structure of the state or international organizations. Just as national NGOs will often work together across borders to create international NGOs, so domestic social movements will often inspire or be inspired by those in other countries, resulting in pressure for change regionally or internationally. Examples include the labour movements that led to the creation of trade unions or socialist political parties, the women's suffrage movements of the late 1800s and early 1900s, the national independence movements of the mid-twentieth century, the feminist and environmental movements of the 1960s and 1970s, the Arab Spring democracy movement of 2010–12, and the Black Lives Matter and #MeToo movements. They tend to come and go, according to levels of popular support and the extent to which their goals are met (or not met), but along the way they will often have a profound impact on global governance, the work of multiple states and the work of IOs.

A final type of non-state actor is one that functions outside rules and law, and resorts to violence and extremism as a way of achieving its goals. Examples would include insurgencies, terror groups and networks, militias, mercenaries, warlords, organized crime and even private security companies (Ezrow, 2017). The activities of such actors are nothing new, and they have long posed a challenge to law and order, but just as the globalization of law and organizations has progressed in recent decades, so has the violent reaction against them. Actors such as ISIS, al-Qaeda and the Taliban have become part of the discussion about the nature of global governance and the work of international organizations; see Chapter 4 for more details.

INTERNATIONAL LAW

At the heart of national government, and also of global governance, is law. Broadly defined, a law is a rule that imposes limits and obligations on people or organizations, and that is enforceable by designated authorities, including courts and the police. At the national level, laws are drawn up and agreed by legislatures (with different levels of input from executives), and anyone caught breaking one can expect to be detained by the police and perhaps punished with a fine or jail time, as determined by the courts.

International law differs in several ways:

– It is drawn up not by legislatures but by national representatives (usually bureaucrats or legal experts) working with one another.

– While elections and the pressures of political parties at the national level can result in changes in the law (in democracies, at least), the same dynamic is absent with international law.

- It is targeted at states rather than at individuals (except in cases of war crimes or crimes against humanity).

- It is not supported by the police or judicial systems that we find in states. Even where there are international courts in which legal cases can be tried, there is no international police force that can monitor application of the law and chase down lawbreakers, and there is no unified system of sanctions that can be used to punish lawbreakers (Shaw, 2021). For a notable exception to these general rules, see the discussion about European Union law in Chapter 3.

International law is usually based either on treaties signed between states or on the terms of membership of an international organization. A treaty (also known as a convention, charter, pact, protocol or covenant) is an agreement voluntarily reached between states or international organizations, holding parties responsible for upholding specified principles or for meeting specified goals and deadlines. It brings participants together to achieve a consensus on their shared goals, and ties them into a policy community where action, achievement and failure are monitored, and the results shared among members of the community. Treaties can be regional or global in scope, may be bilateral (with two parties) or multilateral (three or more parties), cover topics ranging from the broad to the narrow, and can be broadly aspirational or narrow and technical. They usually follow a standard format, beginning with a preamble describing the general goals, a series of articles containing the substance of the agreement and the means for resolving disagreements, and the list of signatories.

There are tens of thousands of treaties in existence, addressing numerous different topics (see Table 1.5 for some examples). Quantity, however, does not necessarily translate into quality, and while many international treaties are both ambitious and respected, others set only general goals, or have resulted in little or limited change, or have attracted too little support to be effective. The achievements of a given treaty depend to a large extent on how the five main steps in the process of treaty-making evolve:

- *Problem recognition*: A problem is defined as needing a treaty response.

- *Negotiation and adoption*: The terms and goals of the new treaty are discussed and adopted. This can be a long and arduous process that can result in a watering down of the original goals.

- *Signature*: A state signs the treaty, indicating that it supports the treaty and agrees to act in good faith not to undermine its goals, but the treaty is not yet in force for the signatory country.

- *Ratification*: A state becomes a party to the treaty, meaning that it consents to be legally bound by its terms, and the treaty usually comes into force once a pre-agreed number of ratifications has been achieved.

- *Substantiation*: Detailed commitments are worked out in meetings of parties to the treaty, often resulting in protocols containing new and more ambitious obligations.

Table 1.5: International treaties: Examples

Title	Opened for signature	Where signed	Chapter of this book
Treaty Establishing the European Economic Community	1957	Rome, Italy	3
Charter of the South Asian Association for Regional Cooperation	1985	Dhaka, Bangladesh	3
North Atlantic Treaty	1949	Washington DC, USA	4
Comprehensive Nuclear Test Ban Treaty	1996	New York, USA	4
No international treaties specific to finance and development regimes			5
Global System of Trade Preference Among Developing Countries	1988	Geneva, Switzerland	6
General Agreement on Trade in Services	1995	Geneva	6
Convention Relating to the Status of Refugees	1951	Geneva	7
Convention on the Protection of the Rights of All Migrant Workers and Members of their Families	1990	New York	7
Convention on the Prevention and Punishment of the Crime of Genocide	1948	Paris, France	8
Convention on the Rights of the Child	1989	New York	8
International Plant Protection Convention	1951	Rome	9
International Tropical Timber Agreement	2006	Geneva	9
Occupational Safety and Health Convention	1981	Geneva	10
WHO Framework Convention on Tobacco Control	2003	Geneva	10
Convention on the Control of Transboundary Movements of Hazardous Wastes and their Disposal	1989	Basel, Switzerland	11
UN Framework Convention on Climate Change	1992	Rio de Janeiro, Brazil	11
Convention on International Civil Aviation	1944	Chicago, USA	12
Convention on Nuclear Safety	1994	Vienna, Austria	12

The steps between problem recognition and ratification can take many years, the outcome depending on the breadth and complexity of the problem being addressed and the number of parties involved. Some agreements – such as the 2017 Convention on the Prohibition of Nuclear Weapons – are mainly symbolic, because the key states involved (the major nuclear powers, in this case) have chosen not to sign. Others – such as the 1996 Comprehensive Nuclear Test Ban Treaty – are sufficiently controversial that they have not achieved enough ratifications to bring them into force (see Zartman et al., 2014). The vast majority of treaties, though, address problems on which there is a broad consensus for action.

Treaties are important, but they are not always a solution to a problem. In his study of global environmental law, for example, Selin (2014) suggests that the negotiation and implementation of environmental agreements 'is a process that encourages and enables, but does not require, cooperation. Treaties can play a constructive role in establishing common rules and standards, but they cannot be the sole problem-solving mechanism.' At the same time, he points out that compliance is not the only measure of effectiveness, and that treaties should also be assessed according to the extent to which they mitigate a problem, change common practices, and shape norms and decisions beyond the confines of the treaty process. This is all assuming, of course, that the problem addressed by a treaty was well-identified to begin with, and that the role of the treaty in mitigating a problem can be teased out from all the other factors that may come into play.

THINKING POINTS

- How well does the term *anarchy* describe the system of global governance?
- What was missing before World War I that encouraged the kind of international cooperation that we have seen since the end of World War II?
- Is there a liberal world order?
- What advantages and disadvantages do non-state actors bring to the process of global governance?
- How valuable is international law given the absence of mechanisms for its enforcement?

FURTHER READING

Barnett, Michael N., Jon C. W. Pevehouse, and Kal Raustiala (eds) (2021) *Global Governance in a World of Change* (Cambridge University Press). An edited collection of studies on how global governance works in areas ranging from climate change to trade, health and conflict.

Cogan, Jacob Katz, Ian Hurd, and Ian Johnstone (eds) (2016) *The Oxford Handbook of International Organizations* (Oxford University Press). An edited collection of studies of the history, forms, functions, structures and activities of IOs.

Davies, Thomas (ed.) (2019) *Routledge Handbook of NGOs and International Relations* (Routledge). An edited collection of studies of the role of NGOs in global governance, including chapters on their work in different policy areas and different parts of the world.

Hosli, Madeleine O., Taylor Garrett, Sonja Niedecken, and Nicolas Verbeek (eds) (2020) *The Future of Multilateralism: Global Cooperation and International Organizations* (Rowman & Littlefield). An edited collection of chapters on the future of IOs in the global system, including chapters on the UN, the World Trade Organization, the IMF and the European Union.

Shaw, Malcolm N. (2021) *International Law*, 9th edn (Cambridge University Press). A popular guide to international law, explaining the underlying principles and including chapters on different areas of law.

HOW INTERNATIONAL ORGANIZATIONS WORK

2

PREVIEW

This chapter focuses on the functions of international organizations. It does this by approaching them as political systems, reviewing the rules on which they are based, the manner in which they make decisions, how they are led and how they are funded. The chapter begins by looking at the common characteristics of IOs, including their purposes, their terms of membership and the methods they use. It then looks at the practical reasons behind the creation and operation of IOs, emphasizing their roles as facilitators and their lack of independent powers or direct powers of enforcement. The bulk of the chapter is devoted to an assessment of the different elements of IOs, including their founding agreements, their leaders, their decision-making systems and their secretariats, asking how each of these elements fit together, and assessing the results. It looks at the different pressures and demands that come to bear on IOs, and at the way these are converted into outputs. The chapter ends with a review of the ways in which IOs are funded, contrasting the advantages and disadvantages of mandatory and voluntary funding, and the implications of variations in the share of funding provided by different members.

CONTENTS

- **The context**
- **The functions of IOs**
- **IOs as political systems I: Inputs**
- **IOs as political systems II: Rules and decision-making**
- **IOs as political systems III: Leaders and staff**
- **The funding of IOs**

THE CONTEXT

Visitors to the Belgian capital of Brussels over the last 20 years cannot have failed to have noticed the almost constant construction that has been going on to the southeast of the city centre, in a suburb now known as the European Quarter. Even as the political leaders of the members states of the European Union (EU) have disagreed among themselves, and have wrestled with challenges as diverse as inflation and the Russian invasion of Ukraine, Belgium's builders and architects have been busy constructing the offices and meeting rooms in which those leaders have met to debate. The most recent addition has been the $320 million Europa Building, a new home for the European Council, the meeting place of the heads of government of the EU member states. The building is designed around a luminous sphere contained within a glass-enclosed box, grafted on to an Art Deco building from the 1920s, the whole standing as a symbol of the supposed transparency of the work that goes on within.

The core purpose of international organizations such as the EU is to bring their members together to cooperate in shaping policy and making decisions on matters of mutual interest or concern. As summarized in Table 2.1, the work of IOs is undertaken voluntarily, using multiple methods, based on a founding document or agreement (sometimes in the form of a treaty) and with few formal powers beyond those given to them by their members or constituents. Most have been created in response to a specific need or an opportunity, and not as part of any wider plan or strategy. Although they have since learned from one another, and have many structural similarities, they come in different forms and sizes, with interests ranging from the narrow to the broad, with differing levels of authority, with different numbers of and combinations of members, and with staff numbers ranging from a few dozen to tens of thousands.

Despite this variety, the structures of most international organizations have at least five features in common:

- A set of goals and rules defining the purpose and performance of the organization and outlining the roles of members.

- Leadership, to guide and drive the work of the organization.

- A decision-making system, through which members can express their opinions and shape the goals of the organization.

- A supporting bureaucracy that can implement the decisions of the organization.

- A source (or sources) of funding to pay for the staff and for the resources they need to carry out their work.

Table 2.1: The characteristics of international organizations

Purpose	To bring members together to cooperate in shaping or influencing policy and in making decisions on matters of mutual interest or concern.
Terms	Voluntary membership, with work based on consent and cooperation.
Methods	To act as facilitators or as venues through which members can negotiate or cooperate with one another. This is done – for example – by gathering information, setting standards, carrying out research, hosting conferences, encouraging states, executing programmes and actions.
Foundation	Most are based on formal agreements that outline the interests, goals, obligations and limits of membership.
Powers	Few formal independent powers, and authority only to do what their members allow them to do.

In the world's most prominent intergovernmental organizations – such as the United Nations (UN), the World Trade Organization (WTO) and the European Union (EU) – these internal structures achieve their highest degree of formality. States are the primary actors, the lines of authority are relatively clear, and the dynamics of decision-making are complex. In the case of international non-governmental organizations, these structures are often just as formal, but the internal dynamics are different given that states are not members. In the case of multinational enterprises, meanwhile, internal structures are more directly based on the legal requirements of running corporations, and the motives behind the work of MNEs are driven more by profits than by politics.

As to whether or not cooperation through international organizations is desirable or effective, opinion is divided. The view of realists, with their argument that humans are self-centred and competitive, and that states are motivated by rational self-interest within an anarchic world, is that the prospects for international organizations are inherently limited (see *IOs in Theory 1*). Interactions among states, they argue, use a combination of conflict and cooperation to ensure state security, and the only exception they might make to this argument would be the value of military alliances as a means of strengthening national security (see Donnelly, 2022). By contrast, liberalism takes a more optimistic view about the possibilities of cooperation (see *IOs in Theory 3*). Liberals agree with realists that we live in an anarchic international system, but they believe that states can work constructively together in the interests of managing or resolving shared or common needs or problems (see Burchill, 2022).

As regards the practical challenges of creating and operating effective and productive international organizations, opinion is also divided. Although some might argue that international cooperation may be the only effective way of addressing many challenges (or, at a minimum, the least worst of the options available), international organizations have different levels of efficiency; see *Spotlight 2*. Some have done a good job in the face of challenging circumstances, others suffer from structural handicaps, and yet others are clearly in need of reform. Against the background of these differences of opinion, this chapter will look in more detail at the structure of IOs, and at how they are operated and managed, offering a general preview of their work within which we can better understand the specific results that are outlined in the chapters that follow.

THE FUNCTIONS OF IOs

As we saw in the last chapter, states exist independently of one another, take the lead in defining their own interests and are self-governing. However, except in the few cases of the most isolated examples, such as North Korea or Turkmenistan, they usually find it helpful to work together in defining, shaping, discussing and managing matters in which they have shared interests, including trade, investment, environmental quality, health and food security. Where once these issues were approached in the belief that states (or kingdoms or empires before them) could and should give priority to their

SPOTLIGHT 2

THE EFFICIENCY OF INTERNATIONAL ORGANIZATIONS

Institutions (or organizations) are created, built and operated by humans, and they are mainly only as efficient and productive as the rules on which they are based and the record of their staff and leadership in managing and running them. Even small organizations have their problems, but the bigger they are, the greater the challenges of efficient management. Just as national government departments are often criticized for inefficiency, waste and a lack of transparency, so are international organizations, whose difficulties are sometimes amplified by the peculiarities of the challenges they face. In the most extreme cases, states might decide to leave the IOs they have joined, or IOs might be closed down altogether: a study by Eilstrup-Sangiovanni (2020) found that of the 561 IGOs created between 1815 and 2006, 216 (about 40 per cent) have since ceased to exist (having perhaps lost political support or been replaced).

Davies (2002) argues that the core problem with IOs originates from the management structure through which member states exercise their control. IOs must often undertake large and sometimes demanding jobs with limited resources (including small budgets), and the hierarchical structure of IOs can allow senior administrators to avoid taking responsibility for their shortfalls. There is also a tendency for micro-management by national government representatives who do not always fully understand the administrative complexities of IOs. 'There is an overall lack of transparency,' Davies notes, 'processes are not always respected, accountability is poor and democratic dialogue between staff and management is sometimes conspicuous by its absence.' To these problems, notes Lall (2017), can be added the propensity of states to use IOs to promote narrow national interests rather than broader regional or global goals.

IOs also vary in terms of their sheer vitality: the degree to which they are active and actually doing their jobs. Gray (2018) points out the mistake of assuming that once an organization is founded, it will fulfil the goals and obligations of its founding charter, or will be reorganized if it does not. In her study of 70 international economic organizations, she noted a problem with organizational drift, and identified three levels of vitality:

- Some organizations were alive and functioning at the time of her study. This described 52 per cent of the sample, including the EU, the Association of Southeast Asian Nations and Mercosur.

- Others had effectively died because of exits or abandonment. This described 10 per cent of the sample, including the Central Asian Economic Union, which functioned from 1994 to 1998, and the Eurasian Economic Community, from 2001 to 2013.

- Yet others – which she labelled zombies – still existed but were not achieving much. This described 38 per cent of the sample, including the Arab Maghreb Union, a North African trade IO founded in 1986 but which did little between 1994 and 2013.

In short, the world of international organizations is one of considerable variety, ability, efficiency and capacity.

own interests, the practical need to cooperate within a system of global governance has grown, with international organizations being the core actors in that system.

There are several practical reasons for creating and operating international organizations:

- Identifying and helping address cross-border challenges.

- Collecting and sharing knowledge about the causes and effects of these challenges.

- Spreading the cost and burden of addressing these challenges.

- Providing forums for debates, bargaining and settling disputes.

- Providing mechanisms for the development, application and adjudication of international rules.

- Encouraging the redistribution of resources and opportunities.

- Encouraging the agreement of shared goals and targets.

In working to do all this, it is critical to understand that IOs are mainly facilitators, rarely have independent powers or direct powers of enforcement, and can only (formally) do as much as their member states or constituents allow them to do. Also, it is important to remember that the membership of IOs is voluntary, and members can opt to leave (or not to join) those IOs with whose goals or activities they disagree. In some cases they can even be denied entry, or suspended or expelled for failing to respect the obligations of membership (although it is more usual for states to go unpunished for violations of the rule of IGOs). By one count (Borzyskowski and Vabulas, 2019), there were 95 instances of suspensions from IGOs between 1945 and 2019. For example, Fiji was suspended from the Commonwealth in 2009 for breaches of civil liberties and judicial independence, Niger was suspended from the African Union in 2010 after a military coup in that country, and Venezuela was suspended from Mercosur in 2017 for delayed elections and the jailing of opposition activists. In 2022, the Council of Europe expelled Russia after years of human rights violations, capped by its invasion of Ukraine (see Chapter 8).

It is revealing that the founding agreements of IGOs refer less to their *powers* (a term that implies the ability to achieve a given objective) than to their *function*s. For example:

- The Food and Agriculture Organization of the UN (FAO, see Chapter 9) has multiple functions outlined in Article I of its constitution that include collecting, analysing, interpreting and disseminating information relating to food and agriculture. It is also stated that FAO 'shall promote, and where appropriate, shall recommend national and international action' with respect to a variety of topics, including scientific research, and the conservation of natural resources. The emphasis here is clearly on responsibilities rather than powers.

- The World Health Organization (WHO, see Chapter 10) has a similar set of functions listed in Article 2 of its constitution, including 'to act as the directing and coordinating authority on international health work', and 'to promote and conduct research in the field of health'. Again, the latter is more a responsibility than a power, and the capacity of the WHO to conduct research is restricted by the amount of funding it receives from its member states.

Even in the cases of IGOs whose founding agreements use terms such as *power* to explain what they can and cannot do, there are practical limitations to the expression of that power. In the case of the International Criminal Court, for example (Chapter 8), Article 1 of its constitution boldly asserts that it 'shall have the power to exercise its jurisdiction over persons for the most serious crimes of international concern'. However, not only have 70 states opted not to become full members of the court, but when it comes to the enforcement of its judgements, the court has several practical limitations. Prime among them is that the court has neither the power nor the resources to apprehend criminals for prosecution, nor to imprison them after

IOs IN THEORY 2

INTERGOVERNMENTALISM AND SUPRANATIONALISM

One of the core sets of explanatory theories for intergovernmental organizations is found in the contrast between intergovernmentalism and supranationalism. While the former argues that national interests lie at the heart of the work of IGOs, with governments making all the key decisions, the latter argues that once intergovernmental organizations are created, they can develop capabilities that exist above the level of their member states. With the former, the new cooperative bodies are more clearly the servants of their members, while in the case of the latter they may develop something of a life of their own.

Intergovernmentalism is underpinned by realism, and sees intergovernmental organizations mainly as a meeting place in which representatives from the member states negotiate with each other in an attempt to achieve a consensus, protecting state interests while paying less attention to the broader interests of the international community. In theoretical terms, intergovernmentalism looks at the costs and benefits to states of their participation in the work of IGOs, protecting national interests while also looking at the extent to which cooperation results in more efficient decision-making. The main criticism directed at this idea is that decisions among governments cannot be treated in isolation, because governments are subject to economic and social forces that either encourage them to cooperate or discourage them from cooperating.

Supranationalism is a concept very much associated with regional integration (particularly in its European form – see Chapter 3). Sometimes portrayed as the opposite end of a continuum that begins with intergovernmentalism, it broadly refers to administration taking place above the level of participating states. It means that decision-making is delegated to an institution working above the level of the states involved, and involving some degree of loss of sovereignty by the states involved. One of the arguments made by neofunctionalists – see *IOs in Theory 4* – is that because supranational institutions have their own political agenda, they are likely to see national interests being replaced over time with a focus on supranational interests.

successful prosecution; states must volunteer to accept them, and these states can attach conditions to the terms of their acceptance (Koomen, 2019).

An interesting question about the dynamic of cooperation within intergovernmental organizations concerns the degree to which their structure – and the interests they represent – are truly intergovernmental, or whether they rise above the level of the states involved to become supranational; see *IOs in Theory 2*. As we will see in Chapter 3, several of the institutions of the EU have become supranational in that they clearly work in the interests of the EU as a whole, rather than acting as forums for the defence of national interests.

At the global level, we can ask which IGOs are fundamentally international in nature (that is, based on the interactions between sovereign states), and which have evolved to become 'world organizations', or organizations with a global view and a global set of responsibilities. As we will see in Chapter 6, for example, the World Trade Organization is less a body that makes intergovernmental decisions than one that works to administer the global trading system of which all of its member states are a part. Meanwhile, Geiger and Koch (2018) argue that the International Organization for Migration (Chapter 7) is less engaged as a vehicle for relations between states (in the manner of a typical IO) and is instead more embedded in the societies in which it works, and interacts not just with states but with other IOs and NGOs involved in migration politics.

IOs AS POLITICAL SYSTEMS I: INPUTS

One way to understand how IOs work is to approach them as political systems. To adapt the classic work of the political scientist David Easton (1953), this means understanding them as the interactions through which decisions are made for the communities of actors or interests that are brought together by the formation and work of international organizations. Political systems, Easton argued, consist of a series of inputs (demands or pressures) that are converted or transformed into a series of outputs (actions or responses); see *IOs in Theory 12* for more on systems theory. In order to understand IOs, then, we need to look at the sources of the demands that are made of them, and at how the demands are converted (or fail to be converted) into results. (See summary in Figure 2.1.)

The primary inputs come from the core constituencies of IOs. In the case of IGOs, these are the governments of the member states, including national executives, legislatures and courts, whose preferences and policies are channelled to IGOs through national representatives. States are far from consistent as a source of such demands, a key distinction being between the underlying views of individual states, on the one hand, and – on the other – the changing views of those states under different leaders and political parties. Most European states have a modern tradition of support for multilateralism and for the work of IOs, for example, that does not much change regardless of which leaders or parties are in power (Telò, 2023). By contrast, the US has been consistently a champion of international

Input	Conversion	Output
The constituencies of IOs *Demands, abilities, and preferences of states*		**Actions** *Decisions, management and projects*
↓	**International organizations** *Leadership, resources, information, decision-making, funding and execution*	↓
Administrative staff of IOs *Expertise and internationalism of staff*		**Services** *Research, guidance, policy harmonization, dispute resolution, monitoring law*
↓		↓
Non-state actors *Direct action or influence on IGOs*		**Spending** *Investments, funding support, credit, loans*

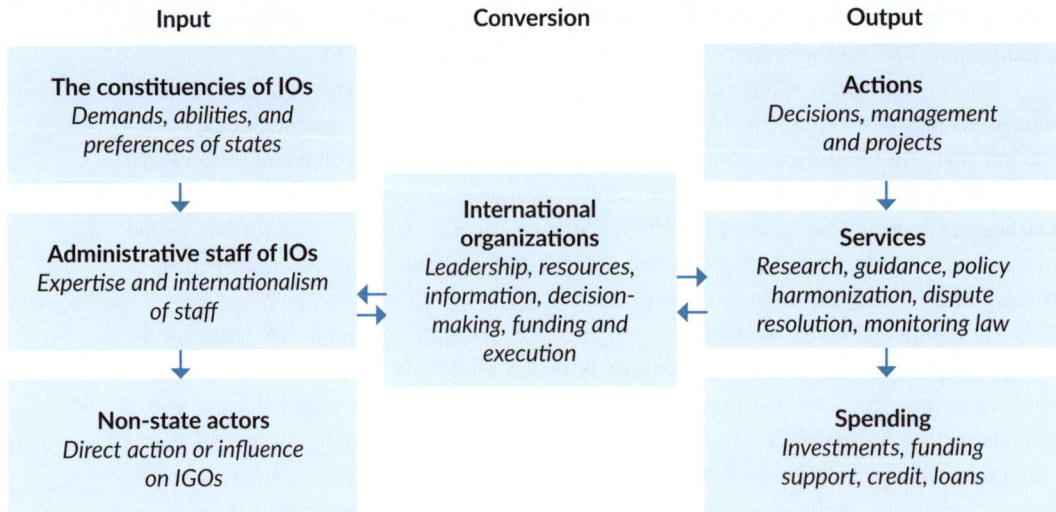

Figure 2.1: International organizations as political systems.

cooperation since 1945, but its enthusiasm has blown hot and cold with changing administrations. Although Republicans and Democrats both mainly believe in the value of multilateralism, notes Inboden (2012), the former tend to emphasize sovereignty and freedom of action, while the latter tend to emphasize legitimacy and interdependence (see *Spotlight 9*).

Meanwhile, the balance of opinion within IGOs has changed with the rising influence of emerging states (and Chatin and Gallarotti, 2018). Although the BRICS (Brazil, Russia, India, China and South Africa) are usually quoted as exemplifying this trend, the picture is more nuanced than the acronym suggests, not least because of the distrust often shown towards IGOs by Russia and China. It is also important to avoid generalizing about the Global South, or emerging states, or rising powers; whichever term we use. Their policies, interests and preferences vary, just as is the case with the more powerful and influential states. The latter still take the lead in mobilizing cooperation, and are usually the major sources of fundings for IGOs, but rising powers, argues Weiss (2016), have long desired to play a greater role, and are unwilling to be mere 'rule-takers', instead aspiring to be 'rule-makers'. Emerging states also have different views about international cooperation depending on the topic under debate. They will largely be more supportive, for example, of the work of IGOs that provides them with assistance and opportunities (in the fields of investment, development, health care and agriculture) than of the work of IGOs that imposes limitations (such as initiatives on climate change, migration or human rights).

National governments will also bring different capabilities, capacities, and priorities to the work of IGOs. The wealthiest member states are usually the most influential actors because they are more globally connected and have the most capacity to respond to problems, whether through the provision of economic assistance, investments, or knowledge. Poorer member states, meanwhile, are often less globally connected, have more restricted abilities to respond to international problems, and have less influence in the meeting rooms of IGOs. The inequalities in influence are most clearly reflected – as we will see later in this chapter, and in subsequent chapters – in the financial contributions that different states make to the work of IGOs. Different states also have distinctive values and priorities, while the priorities and capacities of wealthier and poorer states, and of democratic and authoritarian states, will also differ.

A second source of inputs into the work of IOs is their administrative staff. Strictly speaking, they are international bureaucrats whose job – like bureaucrats everywhere – is to execute the decisions of leaders. However, they bring advantages to their work that gives them informal influence: they work full-time on IO business, and are often experts in their fields, sometimes making them better informed than either the leadership or the membership of IOs. Littoz-Monnet (2017) notes that they can act as autonomous and independent actors, and despite the fact that the member states of IOs define their mandates and pay their salaries, the staff of IOs are adept at building on their autonomy by emphasizing their value to governments. The more deeply international organizations have been studied, note Knill and Stienebach (2023), the more the role of their permanent staff has been understood as a system within a system. Directly or indirectly, they can influence the setting of agendas, the gathering and provision of data, the shaping of decisions, and the implementation of those decisions. They are also more likely to be champions of the idea of international cooperation, and so will bring perspectives to the work of IGOs that might be different from those of member states that are more resistant to cooperation.

In Chapter 5, we will see that the conditions for loans made by the World Bank are shaped to a large degree by the Bank's own staff rather than by the member states. In addition, Rittberger et al. (2019) provide several examples of important inputs to the work of IOs from administrative staff:

- Providing planning documents for military operations by NATO.

- Undertaking field visits to verify the proper implementation of policy by the IMF.

- Policy on climate change being informed by reports produced by the Intergovernmental Panel on Climate Change.

- New EU laws being drafted by the several thousand employees of the EU's main bureaucracy, the European Commission.

The third key source of inputs into the work of IGOs lies in the activities of non-state actors. International non-governmental organizations (INGOs) are, of course, IOs in their own right, with processes, structures, goals and agendas that parallel those of IGOs. Many have been created because of a failure on the part of governments to cooperate effectively on international issues, and in some ways they have been more effective (or active) than IGOs; this is particularly true in the fields of human rights, migration, humanitarian aid and the environment. At the same time, NGOs need access to the work of IGOs and governments if they are to achieve their maximum level of influence. For their part, IGOs often value INGOs for the information and expertise they can provide, their specialist knowledge of the situation in the field, and their sometimes complementary work.

The most formal channels for non-state influence are found where arrangements are made for such actors to take part in the decision-making of IGOs. One example is offered by the International Labour Organization, which allows the representatives of employers and trade unions to vote on its proposals; see Chapters 7 and 9. Meanwhile, NGOs play a consultative role in the United Nations through the work of its Economic and Social Committee (ECOSOC). The latter has allowed thousands of NGOs to attend official meetings, submit oral or written statements, take part in debates and organize parallel events. Questions, though, have been raised about the quality of NGO input into the work of ECOSOC (Mowell, 2021). Similar questions have been raised about the input of NGOs into the work of the European Economic and Social Committee (EESC), which links NGOs with the institutions of the EU. In an article titled 'Is anybody listening?', Hönnige and Panke (2016) argue that EU legislators rarely read the opinions submitted by the EESC, which tends to be heard only when it proactively organizes seminars or when its members take part in formal hearings.

For the most part, non-state input into the work of IGOs tends to be informal and often indirect, as it is with the work of non-state actors at the national level. Much of that input comes through lobbying: exerting influence via government representatives or administrative staff, providing information to IGOs, or by using the media and public opinion to shape the decisions of IGOs. While epistemic communities of experts can have formal input into the work of IGOs, other non-state actors – such as social movements – will have more informal and less structured or predictable inputs.

IOs AS POLITICAL SYSTEMS II: RULES AND DECISION-MAKING

Having looked at the influences on the work of IOs, we now need to focus on how inputs are converted into actions and results. All organizations – whether national or international, whether governmental or non-governmental, whether public or private – need to address three administrative functions: leadership, decision-making and execution. The larger the organization, the more complexity there will be in how these functions are defined and divided, and the more difficult it can sometimes be to identify responsibilities. This becomes more clear as we review the internal structure of IOs (summarized in Table 2.2).

Founding agreements

All formal IOs are based on founding agreements that – much like the constitutions of states – outline their aspirations, structures, responsibilities and terms of membership. Strictly speaking, these are not constitutions, because they are not part of an organized legal code supported by a constitutional court, dealing with entire and self-contained systems of government. Instead, they might be treaties, charters, statutes, articles or agreements reached among members on the purposes of an organization, and on the terms of membership. They can all typically be changed or expanded by protocols. For

Table 2.2: The structural elements of international organizations

Element	Features	Primary function
Founding agreement	The founding document of an IO, often in the form of a treaty, statute or charter, sometimes with subsequent amendments.	Outlines purposes, goals and rules
Assembly	Gathering place for the membership of an IO as a whole, to discuss options and make decisions.	Decision-making
Courts and tribunals	A (relatively rare) option through which IOs give judicial backing to their decisions.	Judicial
Executive head	The chief administrator.	Leadership
Executive council	The executive body of an IO, tasked mainly with supervising the secretariat and overseeing the execution of decisions of the assembly.	Executive
Secretariat	The full-time administrative staff of an IO, tasked with supporting the work of the leadership and the membership.	Administrative

multinational enterprises, meanwhile, the functional equivalent of a constitution is a set of articles of incorporation, which includes details on the purpose and structure of an MNE, the number and types of shares it issues, and the process of electing a board of directors. Whatever the name, though, and however the details differ, these foundational documents have the same general purpose and effect.

The United Nations Charter (1945) offers an example. Signed by 50 countries in San Francisco on 26 June 1945, at the end of the conference convened to discuss the terms and goals of the new UN, and coming into force on 24 October 1945, it includes the following:

– A Preamble explaining the underlying goals of the UN, including 'to save succeeding generations from the scourge of war … and to reaffirm faith in fundamental human rights'.

– Opening articles on the purposes of the UN, including 'to maintain international peace and security … [and] to achieve international co-operation in solving international problems of an economic, social, cultural, or humanitarian character'.

– Articles on the terms of membership, which is open to all 'peace-loving states which accept the obligations contained in the present Charter and, in the judgment of the Organization, are able and willing to carry out these obligations'.

– Several chapters on the structure and responsibilities of the major organs of the UN, including the General Assembly, the Security Council, the International Court of Justice and the UN Secretariat.

- Chapters dealing with the peaceful settlement of disputes, and the definition of threats to peace or breaches of the peace.

- A chapter outlining the process of amending the Charter, requiring the support of two-thirds of the membership of the General Assembly and nine of the 15 members of the Security Council.

Elsewhere, founding documents contain levels of detail and ambition that vary according to the goals of different organizations, and according to how much (or little) the members of IOs have been able to agree on the terms of operation. Some are only a few pages long and have not been much changed since they came into force, while others are longer and more complex and have undergone greater change. The seven treaties underlying the work of the EU are a good example of the latter; see Chapter 3.

Assemblies

Since IGOs are based on the principle of the sovereignty of states, they need organs in which the representatives of the member states can gather in plenary sessions (meetings of the whole) to make decisions. The bigger an IGO, and the more ambitious its purposes, the more need there will be for such a body. This is partly why 13 of the 19 specialized agencies of the UN have their own assemblies, the exceptions being the International Monetary Fund and the five bodies that make up the World Bank Group (see Chapter 5). At the core of the UN system lies the UN General Assembly (UNGA), which Karns (2016) describes as 'the place to set the agendas of world politics, to get ideas endorsed or condemned, to have actions taken or rejected'. As such, she argues, it has come closer 'than any other international body to embodying what today is often called the "international community"'.

At the same time, the power and reach of the UNGA should not be overstated. It has (or shares with the Security Council) the power of appointment or election to other UN bodies, to amend the UN Charter, to make non-binding recommendations and to hold emergency debates on threats to international peace. As we will see in Chapter 4, though, the Security Council of the UN is more substantial and authoritative when it comes to debating matters of international security. Also, the membership of the UNGA is big and diverse, and it struggles (and often fails) to bring together the views of rich and poor states, of the Global North and the Global South, of democracies and authoritarian regimes, and of competing regional interests. Even so, it is a global meeting place, and the one body where different views from around the world can be aired and debated on a wide variety of issues.

While the UNGA consists of national diplomats, other assemblies might consist of technical experts, and they will vary in terms of their size and authority. The frequency of their meetings will range from as often as once annually to once every four or five years, and their voting systems will also vary: some (such as the Parliamentary Assembly of NATO; see Chapter 4) make decisions on the basis of a consensus (effectively giving each member the power of veto), while others – such as the UN General Assembly – use a simple majority, and yet others use a weighted voting system. The latter is used in the Council of the EU, which includes among its voting options a qualified majority which requires the support of 55 per cent of the member states, containing at least 65 per cent of the population of the EU. A proposal for a weighted voting system in the UN General Assembly was rejected during the drafting of the UN Charter because of the inequalities it would have created, as a result of which all 193 member states of the UN – whether they have populations that number in the thousands or the millions – work in the UNGA based on one state, one vote.

The most powerful international assembly in the world is the European Parliament (EP), which plays a key role in making laws and policies for the EU, and derives most of its power from the fact that it is directly elected by voters in the EU member states (see Servent, 2018). There are a few other international parliaments – such as the South African-based Pan-African Parliament and the Panama-based Latin American and Caribbean Parliament – but none are elected by voters. Although the EP lacks many of the standard powers of a national legislature (such as the ability to draw up and propose legislation), it has used its moral advantage as the only elected EU institution to win more powers for itself, holding the other institutions politically accountable for their work. It can influence the shaping of proposals for new EU laws and has committees of specialists that debate and amend those proposals.

In addition to assemblies, IOs may periodically convene conferences at which members will discuss and take broader strategic decisions, or focus on a particular problem. The UN has been particularly active on this front, convening conferences that have – among other results – generated international treaties on climate change and biodiversity. A series of UN-sponsored global summits between 1992 and 2012 debated (with declining enthusiasm and political commitment; see Chapter 11) issues related to the environment and development. Few IOs have been quite such productive conveners of conferences, though, as the EU: it was born in the 1950s out of conferences held in Paris and Rome, it convened later conferences in cities such as Amsterdam and Lisbon to develop its treaties and goals, and along the way has held more focused conferences dealing with topics ranging from education to human rights and employment.

Courts and tribunals

Courts are a relatively unusual part of the structure of IOs. Some, such as the United Nations and various regional IGOs, have courts that are part of their organizational structure, while several courts are free-standing IGOs in their own right; see Table 2.3. Despite their rarity, courts are a key part of the network of international organizations, representing either a defined and critical need in the case of IGOs where the defence of their constitutions or founding treaties is a key part of their work, or a model that other IOs might want to consider or avoid, depending on the views of their members.

The structure and power of these bodies – perhaps better known by the more all-encompassing description of 'international adjudicative bodies' (Giorgetti, 2016) – varies, ranging from the relatively powerful and structured to more ad hoc

Table 2.3: International courts: Examples

Name	Founded	Associated IO
Permanent Court of Arbitration	1899	Free-standing
Central American Court of Justice	1907–1918, 1994	Central American Integration System
International Court of Justice	1945	United Nations
European Court of Justice	1952	European Union
European Court of Human Rights	1959	Council of Europe
Andean Tribunal of Justice	1979	Andean Community
International Tribunal for the Law of the Sea	1982	Free-standing
African Court on Human and Peoples' Rights	1987	African Union
International Criminal Court	2002	Free-standing
Caribbean Court of Justice	2005	Caribbean Community

bodies and arbitrating tribunals. They can all issue decisions that are binding on the parties at which the decisions are directed, the subjects of which range from the broad to the specific. The most significant courts – because they have a permanent judiciary and a supporting administrative structure – include the International Court of Justice and the European Court of Justice. Less significant are tribunals that are convened more infrequently to rule on disputes under the terms of membership of an IO or the terms of an international treaty. The International Tribunal for the Law of the Sea, for example, has jurisdiction over a single international treaty, the 1982 UN Convention on the Law of the Sea. It has 21 members elected by the parties to the treaty, and, while the tribunal meets in Hamburg, only the president of the tribunal is resident there; the others travel to Hamburg as needed. As of 2023, only 31 cases had been submitted to the tribunal (International Tribunal for the Law of the Sea, 2023).

IOs AS POLITICAL SYSTEMS III: LEADERS AND STAFF

IOs may not have much direct power as the term is usually understood, but they still need leadership to guide and support their work. If decisions are made by the membership meeting in assemblies, responsibility for the administration and execution of those decisions lies with executive heads, executive councils that meet between meetings of assemblies and the full-time staff of the secretariats of IOs.

Executive heads

Every large organization has a leader. Much like the president or prime minister of a state, or the mayor of a city, the executive head of an IO is not only the most public face of the organization but also the person responsible for providing direction and overseeing the execution of policy. They are not all equal, though, their functions varying not just in terms of the formal responsibilities of the office but also in terms of the skills that officeholders bring (or fail to bring) to the job. Formally, executive heads exist in what Chesterman (2016) describes as a curious limbo: they are entrusted to lead organizations that may employ thousands of people with budgets that run to billions of dollars, and yet their ability to operate independently of the member states of these organizations is usually severely constrained by the terms of their office and the limits placed on spending.

Whatever their title (see Table 2.4), executive heads are usually appointed or elected to their jobs by the assemblies of IOs, and to a limited number of terms: typically, a maximum of two four-year or five-year terms. Some of the appointments – as in the case of the Secretary General of the UN – are made by all members of the organization, with each having one vote. Other appointments are made by a sub-group of members, as with the Director General of the International Labour Organization; the officeholder is appointed by the Governing Body of the ILO, bringing together representatives from 28 of the ILO's 186 member states, along with the representatives of employers and workers (see Chapters 7 and 9). Two exceptions

Table 2.4: Executive heads of international organizations

Title	Examples
Administrator	UN Development Programme
Director General	Food and Agriculture Organization of the UN, International Labour Organization, International Organization for Migration, UNESCO, World Health Organization, World Trade Organization
Executive Director	UN Environment Programme
High Commissioner	Office of the High Commissioner for Human Rights, UN High Commissioner for Refugees
Managing Director	International Monetary Fund
President	European Commission (part of the EU), International Criminal Court, UN Human Rights Council, World Bank
Secretary General	Association of Southeast Asian Nations, Commonwealth, International Maritime Organization, North Atlantic Treaty Organization, Organization of American States, United Nations

to the general rules are the International Monetary Fund (IMF) and the World Bank; in the former, the managing director is appointed by the Executive Board, while in the latter the president is nominated by the US (as the largest shareholder) and confirmed by the Bank's 25 Executive Directors (see Chapter 5).

Once in office, executive heads blend political and administrative responsibilities. Politically, they are expected to promote the goals of the organization by brokering agreements among the members and negotiating with national leaders and other IOs. Administratively, they are expected to manage their organizations via setting goals, making appointments, organizing and chairing meetings, and managing budgets. There is much that can trip them up, though. Davies (2002) notes that management practices in IOs are amalgams of the national cultures from which the managers come, making it sometimes difficult for them to shape a clear and accepted management culture of their own. Also, they need to wield their political influence carefully; they are not elected, their authority is limited, and they need to consider the views of the leaders of the states or organizations with whom they negotiate.

The tenures of different secretaries general of the UN illustrate some of the difficulties at the intergovernmental level. While Dag Hammarskjöld of Sweden (1953–61) and Kofi Annan of Ghana (1997–2006) had mainly positive records and continue to be held in high regard, different reputations attach to Kurt Waldheim of Austria (1972–81), whose service in the army of Nazi Germany was exposed after he left office, and Boutros Boutros-Ghali of Egypt (1992–96), whose appointment to a second term was vetoed by the US against the background of charges that he had failed to reform the UN. Various other controversies were also associated with the tenure of Amadou-Mahtar M'Bow at UNESCO, Edouard Saouma at FAO, Jacques Attali at the European Bank for Reconstruction and Development, and Hiroshi Nakajima at the WHO.

In some IGOs, the appointment of executive heads is influenced by an understanding – whether formal or informal – that member states should take turns holding the top job. With the Association of Southeast Asian Nations (ASEAN), for example, the job of Secretary General rotates alphabetically through the ten member states, while the job of President of the European Commission (a key part of the EU) is decided by trade-offs among the leaders of the EU member states, often resulting in the appointment of the least controversial candidate (see McCormick, 2020). Appointments to other IGOs have been driven by an agreement *not* to have a rotation: the leadership of NATO and the IMF, for example, has traditionally been held by a European, while the leadership of the World Bank has traditionally been held by an American.

Demands have grown in recent decades for more diversity in appointments to the executive positions of the major global IGOs. Many of them were founded in Europe or North America, and spent their early decades being led by white men. It was not until 2011 that the IMF had its first female Managing Director, for example, or until 2017 that the World Health Organization had its first African Director General, or until 2021 that the World Trade Organization had its first female and African Director General. Meanwhile, several IGOs have yet to appoint any women as executive heads; among them are the Food and Agriculture Organization of the UN, NATO, the Organization of American States and the International Labour Organization.

Executive councils

The executive councils of IOs are usually smaller than their assemblies, meet more often than assemblies (some, in fact, are in almost year-around session), and are tasked with both supervising the secretariat of the IO and overseeing the implementation of decisions made by the assembly of the IO. Not all IOs have executive councils (the World Trade Organization, for example), and there is no fixed template for the work they do; they all have executive functions, while some have legislative functions, and some – thanks to the increased need for technical expertise rather than just political input – even have independent governing functions (Wessel, 2016). Whether they go by the title *executive board*, or *executive council*, or *governing body*, their members are usually elected by the assembly, sometimes on the basis of a formula designed to provide fair geographical representation. In the case of the 47 national members of the UN Human Rights Council, for example, there is a regional quota ranging from 13 for Africa to six for Eastern Europe. In the case of the Executive Board of the IMF, there is a more informal agreement that groups of states will pre-agree to combine their voting shares to give themselves more influence.

The UN Security Council is an unusual example of an executive council, in the sense both that it does not have the same agenda as the UN General Assembly (it deals only with issues pertaining to international peace and security), and that it has five permanent members and ten non-permanent members, half of whom are elected each year by the General Assembly for a two-year term. Geography again comes into play with the ten non-permanent members, ranging from three from Africa to one from Eastern Europe.

Secretariats

All IOs have a secretariat, or a body of full-time staff whose role is to advance the work of the IO by supporting both the leadership and the membership. They do this through multiple means:

- Providing advice and information to the leadership of their IO.

- Overseeing and ensuring consistency in the implementation of the rules and goals of their IO.

- Organizing meetings of the membership.

- Representing the work of their IO to outside parties, including other IOs and members of the media.

- Undertaking research and generating data related to the work of their IO.

- Helping manage IO budgets and undertaking field trips to monitor the implementation of IO policy.

- In more specialized cases, monitoring the implementation of international treaties, and organizing meetings of parties to the treaties.

The international equivalent of national government departments, the staff of these secretariats – sometimes known as international public administrations (IPAs) – are international bureaucrats; see *IOs in Action 2*. Much like their national equivalents, they are responsible for the administration of an organization and the execution of its goals. Where the assemblies and the executive councils are dominated by and made up of the representatives of member states, and act mainly in the interests of their states, IPAs provide the organizational infrastructure (Knill and Stienebach, 2023). They can be easily (and wrongly) thought of as the IO itself, when in fact their role is usually to support the work of the leadership and the assembly of an IO, where the main decisions are made. It is also important to appreciate that, unlike the members of IO executive councils or assemblies, the staff in secretariats are not national representatives, but are instead expected to work in support of the broad goals of an IO. They are accountable not to the member states, but to the IOs for which they work.

IOs IN ACTION 2

THE IMPORTANCE OF LOCATION

Unlike national government departments, whose offices are mainly based in national capitals, the secretariats of IOs are spread all over the world, with some having a global reach and others focused on regional interests. Although most of the oldest IOs are headquartered in Europe or North America, the variety of their locations has grown as the number of IOs has grown. This has not always gone down well with staff members, though, as reflected in the phenomenon of 'hardship pay' that must sometimes be offered in order to encourage staff to take postings at IOs situated in some of the less desirable cities of the world. In the case of Brussels, records Gray (2018), there is no hardship pay because the city is globally connected, has good housing and schools, and hosts many of the main administrative structures for the EU, as well as the headquarters of the North Atlantic Treaty Organization. By contrast, 25 per cent hardship pay is offered for large and crowded cities such as Jakarta, site of the secretariat of the Association of Southeast Asian Nations, and for Georgetown, Guyana, site of the headquarters of Caricom, while 50 per cent is offered for Freetown, Sierra Leone, site of the headquarters of the Mano River Union (a modest regional economic IO).

If there is a single city that could be designated as a global 'capital' of international organizations, it might be Geneva, the second-biggest city in Switzerland. How is it that so many IGOs and INGOs have chosen it as their base? The historical neutrality of Switzerland has helped, as has its long record as a centre of diplomacy and banking. It is also geographically located at the heart of Europe, and early developed a record as the location of key IOs, such as the International Committee of the Red Cross (1863), the International Telegraph Union (1865), the International Labour Organization (1919) and the League of Nations (1920). Since 1945, it has been chosen as the site of the headquarters of the World Health Organization, the World Meteorological Organization, the UN Conference on Trade and Development, the World Trade Organization, the UN High Commissioner for Refugees, the International Organization for Migration, the UN Human Rights Council, the Office of the High Commissioner for Human Rights and the Intergovernmental Panel on Climate Change, among others.

THE FUNDING OF IOs

Among the most telling influences on the work of any organization (or any system of government or governance, for that matter) is its budget: how much revenue does it have (or need), what are the sources of that revenue, what are the costs of the tasks it addresses, how well (or badly) does it use its financial resources and what are the limitations placed on its spending? Of course, not all problems can be solved by spending money, and many problems are actually created or worsened by spending money badly, or in the wrong places, or on the wrong projects. Also, the sheer size of an organization's budget is not necessarily an indicator of the size or importance of its task; the World Trade Organization, for example, is one of the behemoths of the global IGO community, and yet its 2022 budget was about one-sixth the size of that of the International Organization for Migration (IOM); see Table 2.5. The WTO was

Table 2.5: Budgets of international organizations: Examples

Organization	Membership	Annual budget 2022	Revenue formula
United Nations	193	$3.12 billion	Contributions determined by General Assembly using formula based on wealth of individual member states.
World Trade Organization	164	$212 million	Mainly national contributions based on shares of international trade.
North Atlantic Treaty Organization	32	$2.48 billion	National contributions based on wealth of individual member states.
European Union	27	$182 billion	Based on complex formula of national contributions, customs duties and value added tax.
International Monetary Fund	190	$1.2 billion (administration only)	National contributions using quotas based on size and position of each state in world economy.
International Committee of the Red Cross	192 national societies	$3 billion	Voluntary contributions from states, national societies, other IOs and public sources.
Asian Development Bank	68	$730 million	Revenue from loans, investments and borrowing.
International Organization for Migration	174	$1.2 billion	Voluntary contributions.

able to function with much less because it is a forum for debate rather than an IGO – like the IOM – that pursues hands-on activities in the field.

In terms of revenues, most IOs look to one or more of three different sources. First, members might make mandatory fixed contributions based on the terms of membership. Occasionally, all members will contribute equal amounts, as in the cases of the Association of Southeast Asian Nations (ASEAN) or the Organization of Petroleum Exporting Countries (OPEC). More commonly, members will make different contributions based on the principle of 'capacity to pay', usually based on different levels of national income, or different degrees of activity in the work of an IO. In the case of the United Nations, where assessments are regularly reviewed and adjusted, the share of contributions to the budget has recently ranged from highs of 22 per cent (US), 15 per cent (China), 8 per cent (Japan) and 6 per cent (Germany), to lows of 0.001 per cent for the smallest and/or poorest member states, including Belize, the Central African Republic, Nauru and Somalia (United Nations General Assembly, 2023). A failure by a member to pay their dues might result in sanctions, including a withdrawal of voting rights.

Second, IOs might depend wholly or partly on voluntary contributions from members. This is the case with many specialized agencies or programmes of the UN, including the World Health Organization (WHO), the UN Development Programme and the UN Environment Programme. There are no obligations on the part of contributors, the amounts of the contributions can change, and some of the contributions might be earmarked for particular projects, creating uncertainty and planning problems for IOs. As donors rather than contributors, members or supporters of organizations also exert more influence over the work of IOs; in the view of Cogan (2016), organizations that rely mainly on voluntary contributions 'no longer act as true multilateral institutions with collective principals' but instead 'as the delegated agents of multiple principals'. There is also a degree of competition involved with voluntary contributions as IOs chase limited amounts of funds and occasionally have to rely on philanthropy. The WHO may be the world's pre-eminent international organization dealing with often critical health issues, and yet – as we will see in Chapter 10 – it has recently had to rely heavily on donations from the Bill and Melinda Gates Foundation.

The third source of financial support is self-funding through charges for services, investments or sponsorships. For example, both the World Intellectual Property Organization (Chapter 6) and the International Atomic Energy Agency (Chapter 12) charge for the services or materials they provide to users, while some of the multilateral development banks discussed in Chapter 5 earn interest on their loans, or have revenue from investments, the issuance of bonds or borrowing from capital markets. Meanwhile, IOs active on issues that have a wider public appeal than the kinds of mainly political questions dealt with by the UN or the EU can attract sponsorships. For example, UNICEF (the UN Children's Fund) has been adept at setting up partnerships with corporations and with other IOs, and at running public fund-raising appeals. It signed an agreement in 2006 with Barcelona Football Club by which the club's Barça Foundation made an annual donation to UNICEF of €1.5 million, in return for which the UNICEF logo appeared on the shirts of the team's players. In 2023, the UNICEF logo was replaced on those shirts with the logo of the UN High Commissioner for Refugees.

The variety of influences on the work of IGOs is most clearly reflected in the different financial contributions made by member states, where the old adage that who pays the piper calls the tune is clearly in effect. We will see the impact of this most clearly in the work of the North Atlantic Treaty Organization in Chapter 4, and in the work of the International Monetary Fund and the World Bank in Chapter 5. When the US accounts for 16 per cent of the budget of NATO, has multiple military bases in Europe and is also the world's biggest producer of weapons, it clearly has much more influence over NATO decisions than NATO's smaller members. In the hallways of the IMF and the World Bank, meanwhile, the wealthiest economies account for the biggest shares of the budgets of the two organizations, giving them considerable influence over shaping international financial and development policy.

At the same time, changes in the way that international organizations have been funded has altered the balance of influence between states and non-state actors. In her study of funding trends in IGOs, Graham (2017) identified two important changes over the course of the twentieth century. First, funding rules were altered in order to give states greater control over their contributions, notably by allowing more earmarking of those contributions (designating them to be spent on particular projects or areas). The result was to undermine traditional ideas about multilateral governance. Second, the rules were altered in order to extend eligibility to non-state actors, who – as they became bigger donors – had more ability to demand earmarks, giving them greater influence over the work of IGOs to non-state actors.

The steps taken in the evolution of the global system have resulted in most IGOs not only being headquartered in the wealthier states of the world, but also being dominated by those states in terms of their management and budgets. Because of this, there has been an effort by emerging states to create new IOs to offset the powers of the older ones. An example of this – see Chapter 5 – is found in the new multilateral development banks created in Latin America and the Islamic world to offset the influence of the older banks, which – despite their regional focus – are dominated by the Western powers. There has also been an effort, argues Bower (2017) by coalitions of middle-power states and international non-governmental organizations to negotiate legal agreements in the face of opposition from some of the bigger powers; he uses the cases of the anti-personnel mine treaty (see Chapter 4) and the International Criminal Court (see Chapter 8) to illustrate his point.

THINKING POINTS

- Could we manage without international organizations?

- In terms of understanding IOs, what is the difference between a function and a power?

- Is the typical structure of international organizations logical, given the need to keep members engaged and content, or is it excessively complex?

- How much opportunity is there for IOs to provide leadership?

- Does the location of the headquarters of IOs matter?

FURTHER READING

Fröhlich, Manuel, and Abiodun Williams (eds) (2018) *The UN Secretary-General and the Security Council: A Dynamic Relationship* (Oxford University Press). An edited collection of studies of secretaries general of the UN, analysing the leadership qualities of each and their changing place within the structure of the UN.

Harrington, Alexandra R. (2018) *International Organizations and the Law* (Routledge). A detailed study of the structure of IOs from a legal perspective, including chapters on membership, leadership and voting rights.

Littoz-Monnet, Annabelle (ed.) (2017) *The Politics of Expertise in International Organizations: How International Bureaucracies Produce and Mobilize Knowledge* (Routledge). An edited collection of studies of the influence that international bureaucrats have over the organizations in which they work.

Lopez-Claros, Augusto, Arthur L. Dahl, and Maja Groff (2020) *Global Governance and the Emergence of Global Institutions for the 21st Century* (Cambridge University Press). An assessment of the architecture of global institutions, with an emphasis on the UN, and on the need to reform them in light of new challenges.

Xu, Yi-Chong, and Patrick Weller (2018) *The Working World of International Organizations: Authority, Capacity, Legitimacy* (Oxford University Press). An assessment of the structure of IOs, including chapters on their members, executive heads, secretariats and funding.

REGIONAL INTEGRATION

PREVIEW

Before moving to the specific regimes around which each of the remaining chapters of the book are based, this chapter looks at the more focused work of regional international organizations (RIOs). These are more geographically limited than most IGOs, and yet they are also often more ambitious, and are typically interested in a wider range of policies, including economic cooperation, foreign policy coordination and the development of single markets. Regional integration has become increasingly common since the creation in the 1950s of what is now the European Union (EU). The chapter begins by looking at the underlying motives and dynamics of regional integration, at the structures of the organizations created, and then focuses on the EU as the lynchpin of the idea of integration. It explains the origins of the EU, outlines its constituent institutions and critiques the different policy areas in which it has been active. The chapter then looks at examples of regional integration in Africa, Asia and Latin America, comparing and contrasting the records of different RIOs in these regions, and the different motivations behind their creation. It ends with a brief review of the role of non-state actors in regional integration.

THE CONTEXT

Like many sub-Saharan African states, Ethiopia is home to numerous ethnicities: as many as 80, depending on how the distinctions are defined. Among them are the Tigrayans who live in the northern part of the country, and whose Tigray People's Liberation Front (TPLF) ruled Ethiopia for 27 years until ousted in 2018. When Ethiopian Prime Minister Abiy Ahmed tried to distance Ethiopia from its ethnic nationalism by merging the country's parties into a new national coalition, the TPLF resisted, and fighting broke out in November 2020 between the TPLF and the government. Among the efforts made to bring peace to Ethiopia was one led and brokered by the African Union (AU), a regional organization that counts conflict resolution and the maintenance of peace on the continent among its goals. The AU's initiative in Ethiopia was the latest of several other peace missions run by the AU, including those in Burundi, Somalia and Sudan, indicating some of the ways in which the AU was designed to offer African solutions to African problems, rather than depending on external actors (Glas, 2018).

The AU is just one of a growing number of examples from all over the world of international organizations whose goals go beyond cooperation and move into the deeper realms of regional integration. This involves collective action by a group of states that goes beyond the usual level of international cooperation and involves the building of deeper ties, perhaps even the pooling of sovereignty, and the creation of shared administrative institutions and laws. Although the initial motivation for most of these regional integration organizations (RIOs) has been economic cooperation, several have found that this has created a spillover effect: economies cannot be integrated, or barriers to trade brought down, without cooperation in a variety of other policy areas, ranging from agriculture to education, energy, the environment, finance, migration, security, technology, transport and even external relations.

In the most ambitious of these exercises – the European Union (EU) – the degree of cooperation has gone well beyond that typically found in an international organization. The EU is based on treaties that look much like a constitution, it has institutions – including an elected parliament and a Court of Justice – that look much like their equivalents at the state level, and 19 of its 27 member states have adopted a single currency (the euro). While the EU has stopped short of becoming a United States of Europe, its work has long implied the controversial goal of creating a political union among its members. It is doubtful that the EU can even any longer be called an international organization, as the term is usually defined, although there has been no agreement yet on how it is best understood (see debate in McCormick, 2021).

It is important to make a distinction between groups of states interested in the collective goal of free trade (discussed in Chapter 6) and those interested in the more ambitious idea of integration. Once the former go beyond the initial focus on free trade, they often start to move into the realms of open markets and common policies, overseen by shared administrative bodies. While there are numerous free trade agreements in force, regional integration is a rarer phenomenon: one estimate (Panke, 2020) put the number of RIOs active between 1945 and 2015 as 76, although at least five closed down during that time, and several others were reinvented and reformulated. The potential for success varies from one group of states to another (see *Spotlight 3*), as illustrated by the experience of two examples. The East African Community fell apart in 1977 before being reborn in 1999 with expanded ambitions and membership, while the Union of South American Nations was founded in 2008, only to have most of its members leave in the wake of political divisions, and to regroup in 2019 as the Forum for the Progress and Integration of South America.

The key difference between conventional international cooperation and regional integration can be found in the difference between the kind of intergovernmentalism and supranationalism reviewed in *IOs in Theory 2*. In the case of the former, states that are members of an IGO cooperate among themselves, and all the key cooperative decisions are made as a result of negotiations among representatives of those states.

SPOTLIGHT 3

THE POTENTIAL OF REGIONAL INTEGRATION

Stubbs (2019) argues that it is difficult to assess the success or failure of regional organizations, given the lack of a framework with which to evaluate and compare their work. It is important to appreciate that they often have different goals, expectations and potential, and that they vary by economic size and structure, and by population, culture and external connections. At the same time, we can fall back on what Nye (1970) once described as integrative potential, suggesting that there is a mix of economic and political factors that will determine whether or not an RIO will last. These factors include the following:

- The economic equality and compatibility of the states involved. In the case of the South Asian Association for Regional Cooperation, for example, the overwhelming dominance of India has long been a problem for smaller states. In the case of the EU, meanwhile, it has long been important that Germany and France – potentially dominating states – are both there to offset each other. If one or the other was to leave the EU, the balance would be upset.

- The extent to which the elite groups that control economic policy in the member states think alike and hold the same values.

- The presence and the extent of interest group activity in the member states; their absence makes integration more difficult.

- The capacity of the member states to adapt and respond to public demands, which depend in turn on levels of domestic stability and the capacity – or desire – of decision-makers to respond.

It can also help if the states involved in regional integration face a common 'enemy' or challenge. In the case of the African Union, for example, a key handicap faced by most of its states is their disadvantaged place in the global system, and they can potentially express themselves more effectively if they work together in the face of that challenge. The most committed supporters of regional integration find themselves joining multiple RIOs, as we will see later in this chapter, while only a small handful of states have never joined an RIO; Haiti, Israel, North Korea and Timor-Leste come to mind.

In the case of the latter, states within an RIO create new shared institutions that have more legal authority than is the case with standard IGOs, and there is a transfer of authority to these new institutions. Where intergovernmental bodies represent the interests of the member states, supranational bodies represent the collective interests of all the member states.

In all the remaining chapters of this book, the focus is on the building of global regimes based around international organizations with a global or near-global reach. In this chapter, the focus is on the narrower phenomenon of regional regimes based around regional IOs. While they are more geographically focused, though, RIOs usually have a wider set of interests and goals than IGOs, and have often achieved a deeper degree of cooperation. In other words, they are the most advanced form of international cooperation, some even holding out the possibility of eventual political union among their members. At the same time, RIOs have different structures, different sets of goals, and we have to be careful to distinguish between their aspirations and their achievements.

BUILDING REGIONAL INTEGRATION REGIMES

Regional integration as we understand it today was little known before World War II, although there were some in Europe who thought that it might be an effective means of encouraging peace in a part of the world that was often disturbed by war (see Heater, 1992). This was particularly true during the tumult that followed the French Revolution and the Napoleonic wars. For example:

- The British philosopher Jeremy Bentham, in *A Plan for an Universal and Perpetual Peace* (1789), wrote of his ideas for a European assembly and a common army.

- In his *Perpetual Peace: A Philosophical Essay?* (1795), the German philosopher Immanuel Kant included the idea of a 'federation of free states' as one of his suggestions for the achievement of world peace.

- In his 1814 pamphlet *The Reorganization of the European Community*, the French theorist Comte de Saint-Simon argued in support of a federal Europe with common institutions, but within which national independence would be maintained and respected.

In Latin America, following the era of the wars of independence (1808–25), there were some who thought that the danger of American or British imperialism in the region might be neutralized if the new states and provinces of the region could form defensive confederations. Among the proponents of this idea was the Venezuelan political and military leader Simón Bolívar (1783–1830), who was briefly able to unite the northwest corner of South America (present-day Colombia, Ecuador, Panama and Venezuela) into the state of Gran Colombia. He fell far short, though, of the idea proposed by his predecessor Francisco de Miranda of uniting all of Spanish America into an independent empire (see Parent, 2011).

While such ideas did not go far in practice, there are multiple examples from history of a different kind of integration: separate political units building ties that were close enough to lead to political union. They include the blending of 13 former British colonies in North America into a brief and unsuccessful confederation, followed by the creation in 1789 of the federal United States of America. In Europe, meanwhile, the German confederation was formed in 1815, incorporating 39 independent states, and was followed in 1834 by the German Customs Union (the *Zollverein*), an economic union that included most German states. Both fed into the unification of Germany in 1871 under Prussian leadership. Elsewhere, separate colonies under mainly British control ultimately led to the creation of the Confederation of Canada in 1867, the Commonwealth of Australia in 1901 and the Union of South Africa in 1910.

Each of these initiatives had unique circumstances, the groundwork for political union was often laid in advance and the logic of political union was usually clear. They rarely, however, involved the creation of international organizations, but were instead political or economic agreements among participating states. Where IOs existed, as in the case of the Congress of the Confederation in the US, or the Federal Convention in Germany, they were more like proto-governments than intergovernmental organizations. It was not until the end of World War II that the climate started to change in favour of the idea of creating deeper ties among independent states, but with the idea of political union often being discussed as a distant goal rather than a short-term objective.

Developments since 1945

Panke (2020) defines a regional integration organization as one in which at least three states cooperate in a formalized arena with a permanent headquarters or secretariat, focusing on more than one narrowly defined issue, with membership based on geographical criteria. The template for regional integration organizations was provided by what is now the European Union. This was born in 1952 as the more modest European Coal and Steel Community, evolving in 1958 into the European Economic Community (EEC). The key underlying goals of both were to encourage peace in Europe and to support efforts at economic and political construction after World War II. For Jean Monnet, the French businessman and bureaucrat often acclaimed as one of the founders of the EU, intergovernmental solutions to international problems had failed, and 'cooperation between nations, however important it may be, does not resolve anything. What one has to seek is a fusion of the interests of European people, not just to preserve a balance among those interests' (Monnet, 1978).

The EEC had many teething troubles as its founding member states worked to understand the mechanics and the implications of integration. Despite this, governments in other parts of the world began to take notice, and new RIOs were created in South America, the Caribbean, West Africa, South Asia and the Pacific (see Table 3.1 for examples). They all had their own sets of challenges and problems, but several made progress toward encouraging their member states to work together on issues of mutual interest, notably internal trade. In the Arab world, meanwhile, there was a notable lack of progress. Despite the common history, language, religion and culture of the region, RIOs such as the Council of Arab Economic Unity, the Gulf Cooperation Council and the (now mainly dormant) Arab Maghreb Union have all been handicapped by political and religious divisions (Oumazzane, 2021). The Caribbean has also been unable to make much progress, despite its states having much in common, including history and the structure of their economies.

If there is a logical progression to the process of regional integration (and it is debatable whether or not it can be reduced to the same steps in every situation), then it might run as follows:

1. Agreement of *free trade area* with the easing of internal barriers to trade (such as tariffs and border restrictions) while maintaining a common external tariff against non-member states.

2. The creation of a single market (otherwise known as a common market) with the removal of internal barriers to the free movement of people, capital, goods and services.

3. Efforts to promote monetary union, where national currencies are tied to one another, and efforts are made to replace them with a single currency.

4. Ultimately, perhaps, a political union in which the member states combine into a new federal system in which the former national governments become sub-national governments, and new institutions are created to govern the whole.

Most of today's RIOs are still at either Stage 1 or 2, and many are better understood as free trade agreements (FTAs, see Chapter 6) than as more fully developed exercises in integration. These FTAs may have secretariats, as in the case of the headquarters of the Andean Community in Lima, Peru, or the headquarters of

Table 3.1: Regional integration organizations: Examples

Region	Name	Founded	Membership
Europe	European Union	1952	27, including France, Germany, Greece, Poland, Spain and Sweden
Asia	Association of Southeast Asian Nations (ASEAN)	1967	10, including Indonesia, Malaysia and Thailand
	South Asian Association for Regional Cooperation (SAARC)	1985	8, including Afghanistan, India and Pakistan
Africa	East African Community	1967–77, 2000–	7, including Democratic Republic of Congo and Kenya
	Economic Community of West African States (ECOWAS)	1975	15, including Côte d'Ivoire, Ghana and Nigeria
	Southern African Development Community (SADC)	1980	16, including Angola, Democratic Republic of Congo and South Africa
	African Union	2002	55: every African state
The Americas	Caribbean Community (Caricom)	1973	15, including the Bahamas, Guyana and Jamaica
	Latin American Integration Association (ALADI)	1980	13, including Argentina, Brazil, Chile, Mexico and Venezuela
	Community of Latin American and Caribbean States (CELAC)	2011	30, including Argentina, Chile, Mexico and Peru

the United States-Mexico-Canada Agreement (USMCA) in Washington DC, but their interests are mainly focused on trade. Although several aspire to build single markets and move to Stage 2, few have done so. Despite its name, for example, the 21-member Common Market for Eastern and Southern Africa (COMESA, headquartered in Lusaka, Zambia) has not yet moved much beyond free trade. In some parts of the world, states have achieved Stage 3 – the creation of a single currency – without having first built free trade or single markets. Examples include the seven states that use the Eastern Caribbean dollar (adopted in 1965 as a successor to the British West Indies dollar), and the clusters of eight and six African states that use, respectively, the West and Central African CFA (African Financial Community) francs introduced by France in 1945; see later in this chapter.

The only RIO so far to have moved fully through Stages 1, 2 and 3 is the European Union, where 12 member states in 2002 replaced their national currencies with a single currency – the euro – and have since been joined by seven more. Although the single market was the core goal of the European Economic Community, it took another 35 years before most of the key elements of the single market were finally in place, showing that even a cluster of countries with much in common might have to struggle to achieve a key goal of regional integration. Some of the theoretical explanations behind this process are outlined in *IOs in Theory 3*.

One example of a regional body that worked backwards, in the sense that it began at Stage 3 before collapsing and beginning again at Stage 1, is the East African Community (EAC) (see Map 3.1). It was founded in 1967 out of three states that had long been governed in tandem as British colonies: Tanzania (independent in 1961), Uganda (1962) and Kenya (1963). They inherited a common currency, a customs union, a common external tariff on all goods coming into the three countries, and common transport and communications systems, including a shared East African Airways. The Community collapsed in 1977 following concerns that Kenya was

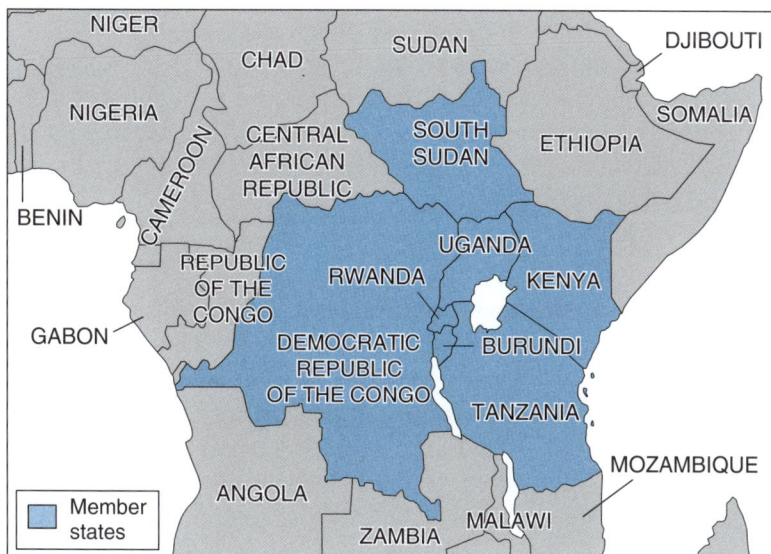

Map 3.1: East African Community.

IOs IN THEORY 3

FUNCTIONALISM AND ITS VARIATIONS

Regional integration – particularly in its European form – has inspired several related theories about its dynamics and about the roles played by international organizations. The oldest of these is functionalism, credited mainly to the Romanian-born British social scientist David Mitrany, who sought to move away from what he considered to be a 'fixation' with the role of states in international relations. The best way of bringing about peace, he argued, was not through alliances and agreements among governments, but by setting up a network of functionally specific international institutions dealing with relatively non-controversial matters such as postal services or the harmonization of weights and measures, and managed by bureaucrats (Mitrany, 1966). This way, he thought, regional integration would develop its own internal dynamic, and peace could be achieved through the creation of a web of interstate ties without the need for grand intergovernmental agreements.

His arguments were not so much a theory as a suggested course of action, spelling out what should be done to achieve peace rather than explaining the conditions needed to make his scheme succeed (Mattli, 1999). This shortcoming was addressed in 1958 by the American political scientist Ernst Haas, who asked how cooperation in specific economic policy sectors could lead to deeper economic integration in Europe specifically, and then to political integration. Questioning the core ideas of realism (see *IOs in Theory 1*), Haas wanted to understand how and why states voluntarily cooperated with their neighbours while developing new techniques for resolving conflict (Haas, 1958). He concluded that in addition to the cooperation that would arise from functional links, integration would need to be deliberately encouraged by political and economic actors pursuing self-interest. Thus was born neofunctionalism.

Neofunctionalism was criticized for not adequately explaining the role of governments in the process of integration, or for showing how the preferences of subnational and supranational actors would translate into political action. Then came a series of economic and political crises in the European Union, encouraging Hooghe and Marks (2009) to propose – with postfunctionalism – that European integration had become more politicized, that the preferences of voters and parties had come to play a more important role, and that identity had come to be a critical part of debates about the direction being taken by regional integration.

benefitting at the expense of Uganda and Tanzania, and pressures from the different economic directions being taken by Kenya and Tanzania. The EAC was revived in 1999 against the background of improved political and economic circumstances, with a new customs union and common system of tariffs, plans for a single market and a single currency, and even talk of an East African Federation (see Trouille, 2021). The three founding members have since been joined by Burundi, the Democratic Republic of Congo, Rwanda and South Sudan.

RIOs vary in size, in their goals, in the stability of their histories and in their prospects, and routinely experience political differences about the directions in which they should be heading. They also have different structures, but the most advanced will usually include the following institutions:

- *Executive bodies.* These are bodies responsible for guiding the organization and overseeing the implementation of its policies. These include the European Commission (in the EU), the Commission of the African Union and – in the more modest examples of the Association of Southeast Asian Nations (ASEAN) and the South Asian Association for Regional Cooperation – Councils of Ministers or secretariats that also organize regular summits of head of government. The EU and the AU also both have an institution in which the heads of state or government of the member states meet to make the broad decisions affecting both organizations; in the case of the EU it is the European Council, and in the case of the AU it is the Assembly of Heads of State and Government.

- *Assemblies.* Several RIOs have assemblies responsible for guiding or making decisions on proposals for new laws. The best-known of these is the European Parliament (part of the EU), whose elected members have a full-fledged legislative function, while the AU has a Pan-African Parliament whose appointed members have an advisory and consultative role. Meanwhile, the Latin American Parliament was founded in 1964, again with an advisory role, and discussions are under way that might result in it becoming part of the Community of Latin American and Caribbean States.

- *Courts.* Several RIOs have courts designed to protect and interpret their founding treaties. The European Union, the East African Community and the Caribbean Community each has a Court of Justice, and while the African Union had plans to follow suit, it was decided instead to create an African Court on Human and People's Rights (see Chapter 8).

- *Specialized agencies.* Several RIOs have created bodies to deal with focused policy interests. The EU has again gone the furthest, creating more than 40 such agencies to address everything from food safety to border control, disease prevention, gender equality and police cooperation.

- *Peacekeeping.* With their interest in security, the EU and the AU have gone furthest in setting up and providing peacekeeping and advisory operations, with the former having committed out-of-area missions to Iraq, Libya, Mali, Somalia and Ukraine (among others), and the latter – as noted earlier in the chapter – to Burundi, Ethiopia, Somalia and Sudan. See Chapter 4 for more details about peacekeeping.

The process of regional integration has been far from trouble-free: all RIOs have faced challenges in achieving their goals, in building political and public support for those goals, in designing workable administrative institutions, and in deciding the best mix of authority between themselves and their member states. Even so, the sheer number of RIOs in existence, and their repeated efforts to fine-tune their work, suggests that in spite of the doubts, we can expect to continue to see and feel the growing effects of regional integration.

Regional integration law

Unlike most treaties covered in later chapters of this book, which are usually global in scope, those related to regional integration organizations (see Table 3.2) are more geographically limited, often have a more ambitious set of requirements, focus on a wider set of policy issues, and are sometimes backed up by the work of regional courts. In some cases, notably the European Union, they have taken on some of the qualities of constitutions (see Schütze, 2015). What this means is that unlike most standard treaties, which – as we saw in Chapter 1 – do not have the same reach or effect as national laws, and lack a direct enforcement mechanism, regional integration treaties have stronger enforcement arrangements. This is certainly true in the case of the EU, whose treaties are protected and monitored by the European Court of Justice, and it is also potentially true with other less advanced RIOs whose structures include courts. For example:

– The Tanzania-based African Court on Human and Peoples' Rights is partly responsible for reviewing cases arising out of the Constitutive Act of the African Union.

– The Trinidad-based Caribbean Court of Justice is responsible for interpreting and applying the treaties at the foundation of the Caribbean Community.

– The Nicaragua-based Court of Justice is responsible for interpreting and applying the founding Protocol of the Central American Integration System.

Table 3.2: Regional integration agreements: Examples

Signed	Type	Place	Result
1951	Treaty	Paris, France	European Coal and Steel Community
1957	Treaty	Rome, Italy	European Economic Community
1967	Declaration	Bangkok, Thailand	Association of Southeast Asian Nations
1973	Treaty	Chaguaramas, Trinidad and Tobago	Caribbean Community
1975	Treaty	Lagos, Nigeria	Economic Community of West African States
1980	Treaty	Montevideo, Uruguay	Latin American Integration Association
1983	Declaration	Dhaka, Bangladesh	South Asian Association for Regional Cooperation
1991	Protocol	Tegucigalpa, Honduras	Central American Integration System
1999	Treaty	Arusha, Tanzania	East African Community
2000	Constitutive Act	Lomé, Togo	African Union

Even so, the idea of enforcement must be approached with caution. While states have multiple means for enforcing law, using courts, the police, fines and imprisonment, regional courts (in those RIOs that have them) can only issue judgments, and are not backed up by a criminal or civil justice apparatus. It is left up to the courts and governments of the member states to follow through with enforcement when cases involve individuals, corporations or local government within those states. When cases involve the states themselves (and there have been many times in the European Union when a member state has been challenged by another member state, or an EU institution), enforcement is based more on the idea of honouring the rules of membership. In some cases, funding to a state from an RIO can be withheld, as happened in September 2022 when the European Union proposed suspending €7.5 billion in funding to Hungary in the wake of charges of government corruption.

THE EUROPEAN UNION

During the response in 2022 to the Russian invasion of Ukraine, the European Union was highly visible in condemning the invasion, coordinating the sanctions imposed on Russia and helping with the resulting refugee crisis. It closed its airspace to Russian aircraft and its ports to Russian vessels, prohibited a wide range of imports from Russia, gave billions of euros in military assistance to Ukraine, ostracized Russian banks, froze the assets of Russian leaders, made it more difficult for Russians to obtain visas for visits to the EU, worked with the leaders of EU member states to phase out imports of fossil fuels from Russia, and coordinated its activities closely with the military, economic and political responses of the US. It even went so far as to fast-track future membership of the EU for Ukraine. Individual EU member states had their own responses as well, but the coordinated response of the massive EU marketplace was always going to be more telling and was a clear example of some of the effects of regional integration.

The European Union is the most prominent and evolved example of regional integration in the world (see McCormick, 2021). Tracing its roots back to the early 1950s, it began as a modest effort to coordinate the coal and steel industries of its six founding member states: France, West Germany, Italy, Belgium, Luxembourg and the Netherlands. This then expanded in the 1960s into an effort to build a single market. In order to complete that market, member states found themselves developing common or shared policies on a wide range of topics, including agriculture, asylum, competition, education, the environment, external relations, immigration, security, terrorism and trade. Meanwhile, membership expanded, taking its most significant leap in 2004–07 when multiple mainly Eastern European states joined, including Estonia, Latvia and Lithuania, all three of which were former republics of the Soviet Union.

Just as the EU is ambitious, so it is demanding when it comes to applying for membership; it is both more difficult to join the EU, and to leave, than is the case with most intergovernmental organizations. According to the Copenhagen conditions, agreed in 1993, aspirant members must be democracies, must have free-market economies, must be willing to meet the requirements of all existing EU laws and policies, and must adapt their administrative structures to meet the necessary conditions for integration. Applications must be considered and approved by the key EU institutions, at which point negotiations are opened on the terms of membership. These can take several years to complete, depending on how many adjustments the applicant country must make.

The EU today has 27 members (see Map 3.2), a population of nearly 450 million people, and the third biggest economy in the world after the USA and China. The member states are still legally independent, and still retain a high degree of control over domestic policy; there is no European tax or military, for example, and members can leave if they choose to do so (as did the UK in 2020). Most EU states have adopted a single currency (the euro), most of the rest are set to adopt the euro over the next few years, and several other countries have been accepted as candidates for future membership of the EU.

The EU has no constitution as such, and has instead been built on a series of treaties that have each expanded the reach and the definition of integration. The first was the 1951 Treaty of Paris, which created the European Coal and Steel Community. The 1957 Treaty of Rome created the more ambitious European Economic Community (EEC), while a significant change of direction was taken by the 1992 Treaty on European Union. The change of name was accompanied by agreement on

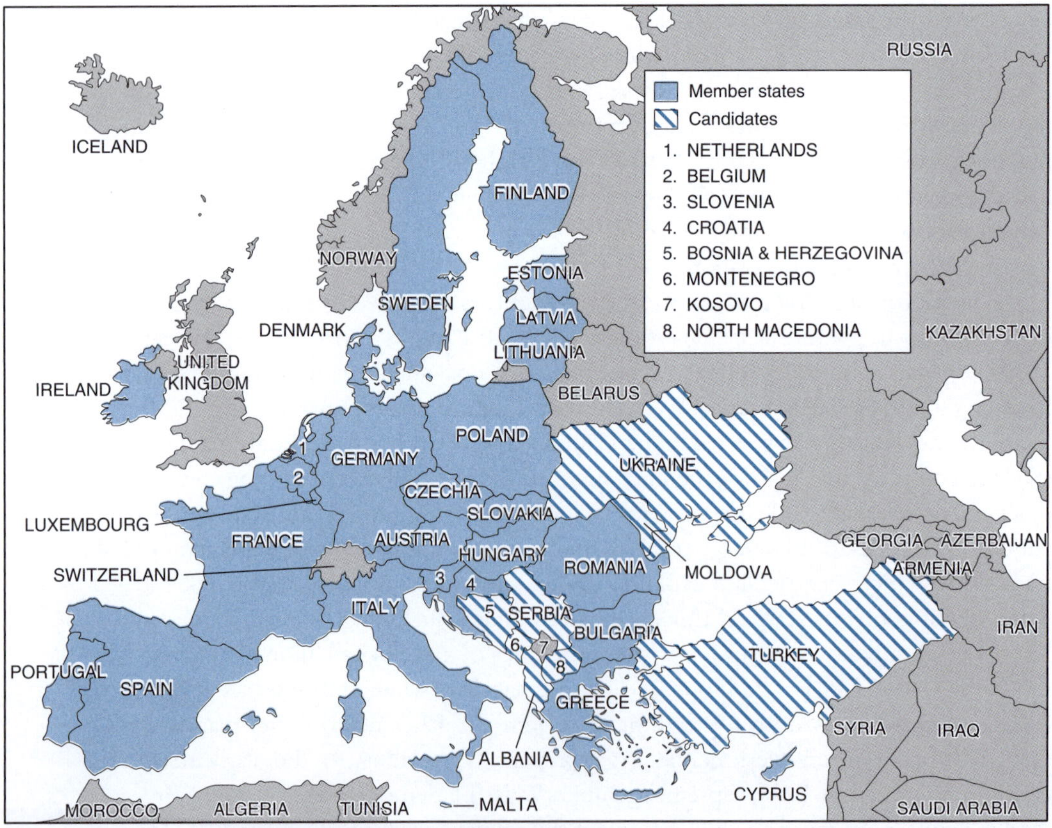

Map 3.2: European Union.

common security and defence policies (see Chapter 4), and new responsibilities in policy areas such as consumer protection, industry, education, and social matters. In 2007, the Treaty of Lisbon revised some of the rules of the EU institutions, gave the EU new policy responsibilities, and gave the EU a single legal personality, designed to strengthen its negotiating powers on the international stage (Ashiagbor et al., 2012).

Along the way, the EU has created and built on a network of administrative institutions (based mainly in Brussels, Belgium) with powers that mainly go well beyond their equivalent institutions within other international organizations addressed in other chapters; see the summary in Table 3.3. They still amount to a system of governance rather than a European government, but they have moved more towards the latter than has been the case with any other IO.

- The *European Commission* is the executive body of the EU. It consists of one Commissioner from each of the member states, headed by a President appointed by the leaders of the member states, and supported by about 24,000 full-time EU civil servants. The Commission provides direction to the EU by developing proposals for new laws and policies, and then overseeing their implementation in the member states.

- The *European Parliament* is the assembly of the EU, and the only directly elected legislature in the world. It has 705 members, elected to five-year terms, and divided among the member states on the basis of population (Germany has 96 members, for example, while Cyprus, Luxembourg and Malta have just six each). Committees of the Parliament meet in Brussels while plenaries (meetings of the whole) are held in Strasbourg, France. The Parliament shares powers with the Council of the EU over discussing and adopting new EU laws and the EU budget.

- The *Council of the EU* (often known as the Council of Ministers) consists of the national government ministers of the member states, and shares legislative and

Table 3.3: European Union institutions, summarized

Institution	Function	Location	Quality
European Commission	Executive	Brussels, Belgium	Supranational
European Parliament	Legislative	Strasbourg and Brussels	Supranational
Council of the European Union	Quasi-legislative	Brussels	Intergovernmental
European Council	Steering	Brussels	Supranational and intergovernmental
European Court of Justice	Judicial	Luxembourg	Supranational
European Central Bank	Monetary	Frankfurt, Germany	Supranational and intergovernmental

budgetary powers with the European Parliament. The configuration of ministers depends on the topic being discussed: agriculture ministers will meet to discuss new proposals on agriculture, environment ministers to discuss environmental proposals and so on. The member states of the EU take turns of six months each holding the presidency of the Council, guiding its work and chairing its meetings during their time at the helm. The Council uses a qualified majority voting system, giving each member state a set number of votes in proportion to its population, and requiring support from at least 55 per cent of member states, containing at least 65 per cent of the EU population.

- The *European Council* is a steering committee for the EU, consisting of the heads of government (and sometimes the heads of state) of the member states, who meet at least four times annually to take the broad decisions on the direction of the EU. The Council is chaired by a President elected by the Council for a maximum of two terms of two and a half years each.

- The *European Court of Justice* is the judicial body of the EU, consisting of one judge for each of the member states, appointed for six-year renewable terms of office. Its job is to interpret the treaties of the EU and to issue judgments in legal disputes involving EU institutions, member states and individuals affected by EU law. It is headed by a President elected to three-year renewable terms by the judges from among their members, and is helped by a lower General Court that is the first point of decision on less complicated cases.

- The *European Central Bank* is responsible for managing the euro, setting interest rates in the euro zone, monitoring national budgets and supervising the euro zone's largest banks. It has a Governing Council consisting of the central bank governors of the 19 euro zone states, and an Executive Board consisting of a President, a Vice-President, and four other members, all appointed by the governments of euro zone states to eight-year non-renewable terms. It is the most powerful international bank in the world, with more independence than many national central banks.

- The EU has an expanding body of *specialized agencies* that are responsible for different areas of policy, with different powers and roles, and often looking like government agencies at the national level.

- The work of the EU is paid for by a combination of national contributions from the member states, and by what are known as 'own resources'. The national contributions are based on the size of national economies, with Germany and France paying the most, while the own resources include revenues from value added tax (a consumption tax used in Europe) and a percentage of duties collected on imports from non-EU states. The EU is not allowed to run a debt, so income and spending must be balanced.

While the single market has been a popular idea (see *IOs in Action 3*), European integration has been far from uncontroversial, particularly with those who worry that the process is undermining national sovereignty and that open borders mean

IOs IN ACTION 3

THE EUROPEAN UNION AND THE SINGLE MARKET

We saw earlier in this chapter that the development of a single market was one of the core goals of European integration from the outset. This involved the removal of all the internal barriers to the free movement of people, capital, goods and services so that the frontiers among Europe's states no longer stood as a limitation to free trade and movement. It took decades to achieve this goal, but it has arguably been the major achievement of the European Union.

The single market has meant changes on a host of policy fronts:

- Almost all internal customs and border checks have been removed, except for mainly cursory inspections of passports for travellers arriving by air or by train.

- Tens of thousands of different technical regulations and standards have been harmonized and standardized so that products sold in one EU country can be sold in others, and professionals and students trained in one country can have their credentials recognized in others.

- Trans-European highway, rail, telecommunications and energy supply networks have been built so as to help integrate the European marketplace.

- European corporations have engaged in active programmes of mergers and acquisitions across borders, while investments have also been made in smaller businesses.

- The EU has built an effective competition system aimed at preventing the creation of large monopolies, even to the point where the European Commission has fined large companies such as Nintendo, Microsoft and Google for abusing their dominant market positions.

The combined effect of all these changes has been to create one of the three largest marketplaces in the world (the others being the US and China) and to help transform the character and dimensions of European economies.

more migration. A backlash against the idea has been brewing since at least the early 1990s, feeding into the rise of right-wing anti-immigrant and anti-EU political parties in many EU member states, and a groundswell of opinion in favour of reforming or even – in some countries – leaving the EU. Particularly strong shockwaves were caused by the Brexit vote in Britain in 2016 to leave the EU, which it finally did in 2020. It was clear, though, that many of those British voters who supported Brexit did not fully understand how the EU worked or the potential costs of leaving, and there have since been signs of buyer's remorse in the UK (Collins et al., 2022).

OTHER REGIONAL IGOs

While the EU is the most advanced example of a regional integration organization, in terms of both the depth and the breadth of its impact, there are many other RIOs, all at different stages of development. As noted earlier with the concept of integrative potential (*Spotlight 3*), they all have different degrees of motivation to integrate, and different prospects for success. Some have made steady progress, others have floundered and a few have even collapsed from inertia or political disagreement.

African integration

If judged by the sheer number of RIOs founded on the continent, Africa is a global leader in efforts to encourage regional integration. The numbers, though, tell us little about hard achievements and African RIOs face numerous challenges. Prime among these are the varied political records of African states, which range from the democratic achievements of Botswana and South Africa to the internal strife of Somalia and Sudan. The economies of African states also vary widely in size and structure.

One of the earliest regional organizations in sub-Saharan Africa was the Customs and Economic Union of Central Africa (UDEAC), created in 1964 with the goals of creating a customs union and a free trade area. Among its members were some of the poorest countries in the world, including the Central African Republic, Chad and Gabon, and progress on achieving its goals was slow. It was eventually superseded in 1999 by the Economic and Monetary Community of Central Africa (CEMAC), headquartered in Bangui, the capital of the Central African Republic, and designed to promote economic integration among the six countries using the Central Africa CFA franc (see Map 3.3). It has achieved most of the requirements of Stages 1, 2 and 3 of regional integration, but implementation of common external tariffs is incomplete.

The Economic Community of West African States (ECOWAS), headquartered in Abuja, the capital of Nigeria, was founded in 1975 with an emphasis on economic and trade integration. The goals outlined in its founding Treaty of Lagos included an economic union for West Africa, the establishment of a single market and even the eventual adoption of a single currency. Its problems, though, have been myriad: they include economic and political differences among its 11 members, competing interests from actors outside the region, civil conflicts in several of its member states (notably Côte d'Ivoire, Mali and Sierra Leone), and different experiences stemming from the heritage of colonialism and military rule (Balogun, 2022). Five of its member states – Guinea-Bissau, Liberia, Mali, Niger and Sierra Leone – rank among the poorest countries in the world, while Nigeria accounts for 60 per cent of its gross domestic product (GDP) and just over half its population. Three members – Burkina Faso, Guinea and Mali – were under military government in mid-2022, complicating efforts needed to achieve the agreements required to move the organization forward.

Further south, the Southern African Development Coordination Conference was formed in 1980 as a way of encouraging cooperation among what at the time were called the Frontline States that bordered apartheid South Africa. It was transformed in 1992 into the Southern African Development Community (SADC), which now has 16 member states, a free trade area and even organizes a periodic multi-sport event in the form of the SADC Games, first held in 2004. Its members do not have the same degree of political and economic differences as do the members of ECOWAS (the Democratic Republic of Congo being the major outlier), making it – in the view

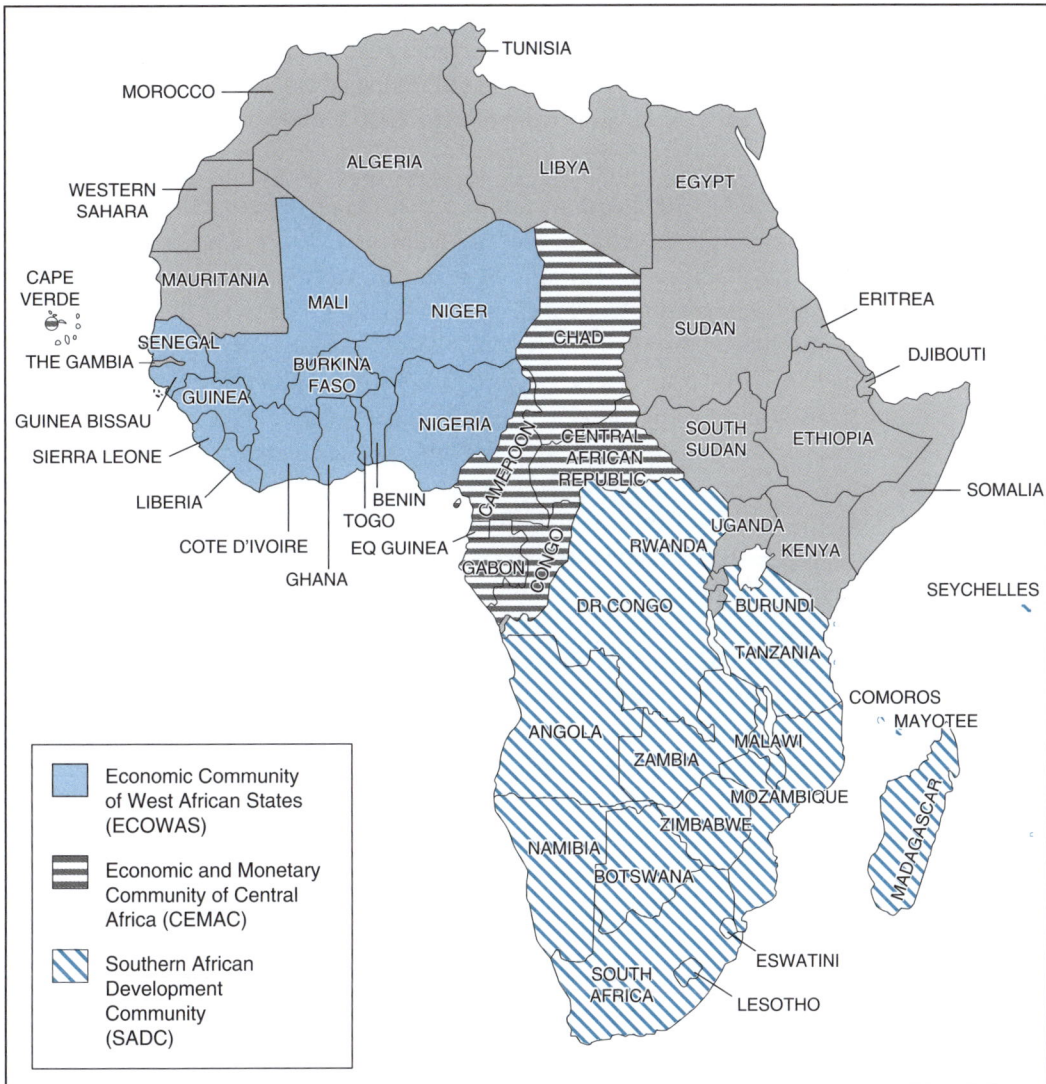

Map 3.3: Integration in sub-Saharan Africa.

of Muntschick (2018) – one of the more promising examples of regional integration in Africa. The headquarters of the SADC are situated in Gaborone, the capital of Botswana.

Several other African international organizations have less ambitious goals, and are better understood – for now, at least – as free trade agreements. Two examples:

– The Economic Community of Central African States (ECCAS) was founded in 1983 to promote economic stability, but has been inactive for several years because of financial problems and conflicts in several of its member states.

– The Common Market for Eastern and Southern Africa (COMESA) was founded in 1994, has attracted 21 member states, declared a free trade area among nine of its members in 2000 and launched a customs union in 2009. However, a recent study of COMESA by Gondwe (2021) concludes that while it has helped encourage trade among its members, their manufacturing capacities are lagging and they need to diversify their exports away from raw materials and semi-processed products.

Turning to the most ambitious RIO in Africa (and the world), the African Union (AU) was launched in 2002 with institutions that closely mirror those found in the European Union: the Assembly of the AU reflects the European Council, the Pan-African Parliament reflects the European Parliament, and the AU Commission reflects the European Commission. It goes at least as far as the EU in terms of its aspirations: in its Constitutive Act, adopted in July 2000, the AU included among its objectives the achievement of 'greater unity and solidarity' among its member states, an acceleration of 'the political and socio-economic integration of the continent', and the promotion and defence of 'African common positions on issues of interest to the continent and its peoples'.

Headquartered in Addis Ababa, Ethiopia, the AU replaced the Organization of African Unity (OAU), founded in 1963 in the midst of the wave of ambition and optimism that accompanied the decolonization that was then sweeping the continent. Although the goals of the OAU were noble, and included the defence of the independence of African states, the eradication of colonialism and the promotion of human rights, it had no powers to directly enforce or act upon its decisions. Military governments were all too common in sub-Saharan Africa during the early decades of the tenure of the OAU, which was often derided as being generous with rhetoric but less so with tangible action and results. It coordinated pressure on the apartheid regime in South Africa and was behind the creation of the African Development Bank (see Chapter 5), but the pressure began to grow in the 1990s for an organization with more substance and the OAU was disbanded in 2002.

Even if the African Union has higher ambitions than the OAU, it continues to face many hurdles. Not least among these are the considerable differences among its member states in terms of their wealth, their political standing (some are democracies but many are authoritarian states), their population size (ranging from nearly 220 million people in Nigeria to fewer than 100,000 in the Seychelles) and their internal stability; most of the states that rank as least stable on the Fragile States Index (Fund for Peace, 2023) are in sub-Saharan Africa. Many are also divided by ethnicity and religion, leading at best to civil unrest and at worst to military government or civil war. Even so, Tieku (2021) argues that the AU's main executive body – the Commission – has a stronger record than is often appreciated, and that it has often been at the heart of agenda-setting, decision-making, rule creation and policy development.

Asian integration

In contrast to most of Africa, where slow economic growth is not unusual, much of Asia is booming. Four of the ten biggest economies in the world are found there (China, Japan, India and South Korea), along with multiple emerging economies, including Bangladesh, Cambodia, Indonesia, the Philippines, Thailand and Vietnam.

Whether the size and the growth of economies offer opportunities and a strong logic for regional integration, though, varies from one state to another. China alone has an economy that is bigger than that of the 27-member European Union, and has its own ideas about economic and political priorities; its ideas about regional integration do not go much beyond free trade. At the same time, the sheer power and reach of China has been enough to provide a motivation for some of its neighbours to work together to experiment with integration (see Map 3.4).

Prime among them are the ten members of the Association of Southeast Asian Nations (ASEAN), founded in 1967. Together, they account for nine per cent of the world's population but a modest three per cent of global GDP. With the exception of Myanmar, they are all fast-emerging economies with mainly strong democratic records and a geopolitical importance to the world's major powers. With a small headquarters in Jakarta, Indonesia, and nothing like the extended institutional structure of the European Union, ASEAN emphasizes regional economic cooperation. It established a Free Trade Area in 1992 and an Economic Community in 2015 that made it look more like the European Economic Community of the 1960s. Its approach to cooperation has come to be known for the 'ASEAN Way', describing an informal and non-confrontational way of building a consensus on policy. Despite its achievements, Stubbs (2019) notes that opinion on the effectiveness of ASEAN is divided, with proponents and sceptics differing over how much it has helped bring peace and stability to the region, provided a forum for resolving conflicts, helped manage relations with the major powers, or helped promote the economic development of the region.

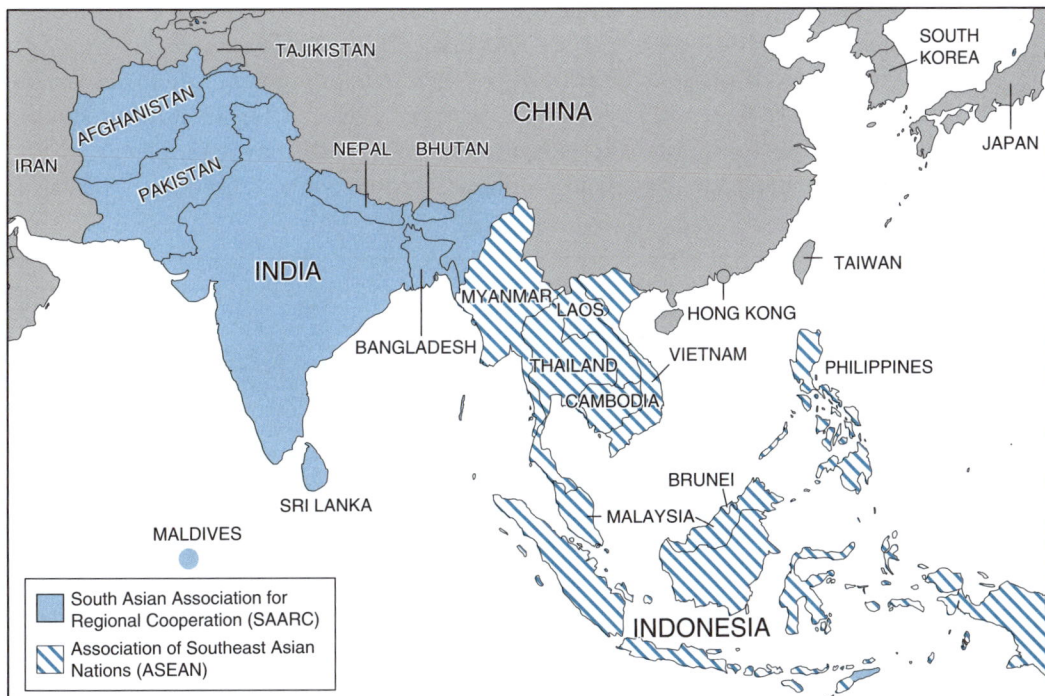

Map 3.4: Integration in South and Southeast Asia.

Meanwhile, the South Asian Association for Regional Cooperation (SAARC) was founded in 1985 and is notable not just for the massive presence among its eight members of India (which accounts for 74 per cent of the population and 78 per cent of the GDP of the group), but also for the political problems of Afghanistan and Pakistan, and the limited economic prospects of Bhutan and Nepal. The biggest handicap faced by SAARC is the rivalry between India and Pakistan (both nuclear powers), which has undermined the principle in the founding Charter of having its members work together 'in a spirit of friendship, trust, and mutual understanding'. The rivalry has even resulted in the cancellation of summit meetings among SAARC leaders, undermining the implementation of the organization's programmes and policies (Bishwarkama and Hu, 2022). The headquarters of the SAARC are situated in Kathmandu, the capital of Nepal.

To the north and west, nine Asian and European states are members of the Commonwealth of Independent States (CIS), a unique variation on the model of a regional integration organization. Created in 1991 as a successor to the Soviet Union, and headquartered in Minsk, Belarus, it brings together all the Soviet successor states except Estonia, Georgia, Latvia, Lithuania, Turkmenistan and Ukraine (see Map 3.5). Although it includes a free trade area, and was a progenitor of the Collective Security Treaty Organization (discussed in Chapter 4), it was born less as an effort to bring independent states together than to preserve ties among newly independent states created by the end of the USSR. It was soon regarded as a failure, Kubicek (2009), for example, noting that few member states participated in its work, its institutional machinery was weak and Putin's Russia tended to favour bilateral relationships over multilateral institutions. Georgia left the group in 2009 following the Russo-Georgian war, and Ukraine left in 2018, although it had stopped participating in the CIS several years earlier.

While one of the goals of most RIOs has been to promote peace and democracy, the CIS is today better regarded as an example of what Libman and Obydenkova (2018) describe as authoritarian regionalism. In other words, it is a regional organization founded by autocracies (Russia in particular) to preserve and promote autocracy. It

Map 3.5: Commonwealth of Independent States.

does this mainly through redistributing resources and providing legitimacy to weaker authoritarian states, and even through military interventions to suppress revolution. Libman and Obydenkova go on to argue that the creation of authoritarian regional organizations (another example being the Shanghai Cooperation Organization discussed in Chapter 4) projects the idea of high status and global power for the member states, and emphasizes what countries such as Russia see as the division of the world into blocs competing for dominance and control. They also provide focal points where authoritarian leaders can regularly meet and learn from one another under the guise of international cooperation.

Latin American integration

Another part of the world that would seem to have potential for regional integration is Latin America, whose states have an intertwined history (much like those in Europe) and have at least one critical feature in common: a desire to build independence from the US. The record, though, has not been strong, and despite multiple initiatives (see Table 3.4), RIOs in the region have typically been fraught by disagreements, and have struggled to achieve their original goals. The challenges, note Merke et al. (2021), range from domestic polarization and economic struggles to ideological differences, personal rivalries and antagonism among the region's leaders, democratic backsliding, a lack of leaders willing to champion regional cooperation and declining intraregional trade. The result has been regional governance mechanisms that often seem to be paralyzed, even as Latin America faces multiple challenges, including organized crime, environmental degradation, migration and anaemic economic growth.

The depth of the challenges is illustrated by the short life of the Union of South American Nations (UNASUR). Founded in 2008 as a Latin American alternative to the Organization of American States (see Chapter 4), it was championed in particular by left-wing governments (notably those of Brazil and Venezuela) supporting a distancing from US influence. It had little economic potential, however, notes Burges (2018), because transport and infrastructure links among its members were not strong enough to support large trade volumes, and it lacked the integrated value chains that have driven groupings such as the EU or ASEAN. Instead, UNASUR was founded on politics, and particularly a desire by Brazilian president Luiz Inácio Lula da Silva for South American countries to solve their own problems rather than asking the US or Europe for assistance.

UNASUR was soon strained by international tensions as centre-right governments were elected in several of its member states, creating political differences that were hard to resolve. Twelve countries joined initially, but Brazil and Venezuela began jockeying for influence in the organization (Merke et al., 2021), while political crises in both countries added more problems. This led six member states – including Argentina, Brazil and Chile – to suspend their membership pending a reorganization of UNASUR's structure. By 2019 it had just four remaining members: Bolivia, Guyana, Suriname and Venezuela. That same year, a new Forum for the Progress and Integration of South America (PROSUR) was launched on the initiative of the leaders of Chile and Peru. It was dismissed by *The Economist* (2019) as a right-wing response

Table 3.4: Latin American and Caribbean regional integration organizations

Name	Founded	Headquarters	Membership	Status
Latin American and Caribbean Parliament	1964	Panama City, Panama	23	Consultative role only
Latin American Integration Association (ALADI)	1980	Montevideo, Uruguay	11	Trade bloc with longer-term goal of a single market
Mercosur (Southern Common Market)	1991	Montevideo, Uruguay	5 (but Venezuela suspended) and 7 associate members	Trade bloc with goal of a single market
Central American Integration System (SICA)	1993	San Salvador, El Salvador	7, with one associate member	Includes parliament and court of justice
Community of Latin American and Caribbean States (CELAC)	2011	Caracas, Venezuela	33	Brazil suspended its membership 2020–23
Union of South American Nations (UNASUR)	2011	Currently open	4	Aspirations to follow EU, but most founding members have left
Forum for the Progress and Integration of South America (PROSUR)	2019	Currently open	7	Replacement for UNASUR

to UNASUR, and as 'far from being an answer to regional disunity', instead looking more like 'a restatement of the problem: that in Latin America regional institutions have become hostage to ideology and ephemeral political alignments'.

The widest regional initiative in the Americas (in geographical terms) came in 2011 with the creation of the Community of Latin American and Caribbean States (CELAC), which includes most of South America and the Caribbean. It was founded on the initiative of Venezuelan President Hugo Chavez as yet another alternative to the Organization of American States, with a headquarters in Caracas, Venezuela. It continued to be championed subsequently by Mexican President Andrés Manuel López Obrador, who proposed modelling it more overtly on the European Union (see Kilroy, 2022). In January 2020, Brazil – where conservative populist Jair Bolsonaro had been elected as president a year earlier – suspended its participation in CELAC, once again showing how integration in Latin America has so often been unable to move past ideological divisions between the governments of the countries involved. It returned in 2023 under the presidency of Luiz Inácio Lula da Silva, taking its membership to 33; see Map 3.6.

Map 3.6: Latin American integration.

In 1991, the Southern Common Market – usually known as Mercosur – was created with five members: Argentina, Brazil, Paraguay, Uruguay and Venezuela. Mercosur is interesting in part as an example of the motives and possibilities behind cooperation between RIOs; in particular, it has strong connections with the European Union, one described by Arana (2017) as the most important relationship that the EU has with another regional integration organization. The EU is the biggest foreign investor in Mercosur, and the two organizations in 2019 signed a trade agreement that was designed to open up the Mercosur market to EU corporations and to encourage the two blocs to work together in shaping global trade rules. The EU market is almost ten times the size of Mercosur in GDP terms, however, and Brazil accounts for 90 per cent of Mercosur's GDP, leaving the prospects for the bloc heavily dependent on political and economic trends in its biggest member state.

NON-STATE REGIONAL ACTORS

Although regional integration can only be formally achieved by states, it has also engaged the interests and activities of a variety of non-state actors. Prominent among these have been multinational enterprises that have exploited the opportunities created by more open markets. This has been particularly true in Europe, where businesses were once focused mainly on domestic markets, and discouraged from pursuing cross-border mergers by different tax laws and legal systems. Regional integration has changed the landscape by encouraging mergers and acquisitions, resulting in the growth of pan-European and international corporations such as the pharmaceutical company GlaxoSmithKline, the brewing company Anheuser-Busch InBev, and large telecommunications and energy companies. Similar opportunities might well arise in other parts of the world currently at an earlier stage in the process of integration.

Regional integration has also encouraged (and been encouraged by) a range of transnational advocacy networks with an interest in international cooperation or federalism, as well as epistemic communities generating understanding and sharing knowledge about the implications of regional integration. Examples (again with a focus on Europe) include the following:

- The Brussels-based Union of European Federalists – founded in 1946 – campaigns for a federal Europe by lobbying political leaders, working for reforms of the EU, and encouraging public awareness of European federalism. It has national sections in nearly two dozen countries.

- The Brussels-based European Movement International (EMI) – founded in 1948 – was involved in the creation in 1949 of the Council of Europe (see Chapter 8) and of the College of Europe, a Belgian and Polish-based graduate school offering courses in the study of European integration. The EMI promotes regional integration in Europe and has national offices in 26 countries.

- The US-based European Union Studies Association (founded in 1988) brings together scholars from all over the world interested in promoting and sharing ideas about the EU and its relevance to other exercises in regional integration.

There are also multiple think-tanks focusing on European integration, including the European Policy Centre, the Centre for European Reform, Friends of Europe and the Centre for European Policy Studies. While most are based in Brussels, their interests are pan-European and they often network with national organizations.

There are few equivalents of think-tanks and advocacy networks on regional integration outside Europe, mainly because no other regional integration organizations have evolved as broadly or as deeply as the European Union. In the case of Latin America, for example, Merke and Pauselli (2015) note that there has been a rapid growth of interest in civil society in Latin America, underlying the work of organizations such as the Argentine Council for International Relations, the Brazilian Centre for International Relations and the Mexican Council for International Relations.

However, these bodies rarely focus on regional integration, and they mainly lack the same incentives or resources as their European or North American equivalents, leaving them to follow rather than to challenge government agendas. For now, at least, most of the studies of regional integration outside Europe continue to emanate from research organizations based in Europe and North America.

THINKING POINTS

- How does regional integration differ from international cooperation?
- Using the concept of integrative potential, is there more cause to be optimistic or pessimistic about the future of regional integration?
- To what extent is the model of the European Union transferable (or not) to other parts of the world?
- Is the African Union admirably ambitious or an unrealizable dream?
- Why have Latin American states had so much difficulty achieving regional integration?

IOs RELATED TO THIS CHAPTER

African Union (AU)

Association of Southeast Asian Nations (ASEAN)

Commonwealth of Independent States (CIS)

Community of Latin American and Caribbean States (CELAC)

East African Community (EAC)

Economic and Monetary Community of Central Africa (CEMAC)

Economic Community of West African States (ECOWAS)

European Union (EU)

Mercosur

South Asian Association for Regional Cooperation (SAARC)

Southern African Development Community (SADC)

Union of South American Nations (UNASUR)

FURTHER READING

Acharya, Amitav (2021) *ASEAN and Regional Order: Revising Security Community in Southeast Asia* (Routledge). A summary survey of the origins, institutions and work of ASEAN, speculating on how its future will be impacted by changes in the region.

Briceño-Ruiz, José, and Andrés Rivarola Puntigliano (eds) (2021) *Regionalism in Latin America: Agents, Systems and Resilience* (Routledge). An edited collection of studies of the record with integration in Latin America and the Caribbean, and its resilience in the face of multiple crises.

Closa, Carlos, and Lorenzo Casini (2016) *Comparative Regional Integration: Governance and Legal Models* (Cambridge University Press). A comparative study of the way in which regional integration organizations are structured and organized.

McCormick, John (2021) *Understanding the European Union*, 8th edn (Red Globe Press). A summary survey of the origins, institutions and work of the European Union.

Tieku, Thomas Kwasi (2017) *Governing Africa: 3D Analysis of the African Union's Performance* (Rowman & Littlefield). A review of the origins, goals and performance of the AU, placing it within the context of understandings about international organizations.

PEACE AND SECURITY

4

---PREVIEW---

This first chapter focused on a regime deals with international organizations whose work addresses the needs of peace and security. It begins with a discussion about the meaning of terms such as *war*, *peace*, *security* and *human security*, and then looks at the short history of the League of Nations (founded in 1919). The chapter then reviews the creation of the United Nations (UN) and the expansion of the definition of security, before focusing on the work of the UN, the dominating intergovernmental organization of the modern era. The structure and the work of the UN are reviewed, its advantages and disadvantages are discussed and its peacekeeping activities are assessed. The chapter goes on to look at collective security organizations, prime among them being the North Atlantic Treaty Organization (NATO). The concept of peace through cooperation is then reviewed through the work of IGOs such as the Commonwealth, the Organization of American States (OAS), and the Organization for Security and Cooperation in Europe (OSCE). The chapter ends with a discussion of the activities of non-state actors, mainly international non-governmental organizations interested in the promotion of peace, campaigning for disarmament, providing humanitarian relief and working to influence security policy.

CONTENTS

- The context
- Building a global security regime
- The United Nations
- Collective security organizations
- Peace through cooperation
- Non-state security actors

THE CONTEXT

One of the effects of the February 2022 Russian invasion of Ukraine was to give new energy to the work of the North Atlantic Treaty Organization (NATO). Founded in 1949 as a collective security body, NATO's mission during the Cold War had been clear: to discourage a Soviet invasion of Europe. With the end of the Cold War, though, and the end of the Soviet threat, the organization's purpose changed, and – for the first time – it engaged in offensive manoeuvres by taking part in military actions in the Balkans and Libya. With the Russian invasion of Ukraine, security was back at the top of its agenda; NATO forces were committed to the defence of the Baltic states, Ukraine was provided with defensive weapons, and steps were taken to expand NATO membership as Finland and Sweden applied to join the organization.

In few areas of international cooperation has there been a longer or more motivated history of activity than in building peace and security. Communities and states have long fallen out or gone to war with one another, or have lived on the edge of war, and they have long made collective efforts to protect themselves and their resources from threats, to offset or neutralize aggression, and to avoid war. Ironically, despite the fascination that humans seem to have with war, the frequency with which they have fought each other over the centuries, and the extent to which the causes and effects of war have been studied, we have failed to develop a clear definition of the meaning of either war or security.

If we use Common Article 2 of the 1949 Geneva Convention as our source, then interstate armed conflict is defined as 'declared war or any other armed conflict which may arise' between two or more contracting parties of the convention, even if the state of war is not recognized by one of them. However, a five-year study of the meaning of war, launched in 2005 by the International Law Association, concluded that that not every engagement by armed groups could be considered an armed conflict, which it defined as intense armed fighting between organized groups (see O'Connell, 2012).

On the other side of the coin, the definition of peace – and, by implication, of security – has been even harder to pin down. At its most basic, it means the absence of war, a phenomenon defined by the Norwegian sociologist Johan Galtung as negative peace. By contrast, positive peace – and meaningful security – is achieved through sustained efforts to avoid conflict through the building of structures promoting the constructive resolution of disagreements, and ensuring equal access for all to opportunities and resources. Critics ask, however, how it is possible for states to achieve a positive peace when so many of them maintain armies and have the capacity to wage war; as Albert Einstein argued, 'You cannot simultaneously prevent and prepare for war' (quoted in Nathan and Norden, 1960). The best hope for real security would come once we achieved a condition of perpetual peace, described by the German philosopher Immanuel Kant (1795, 2009) as the absence of the conditions that can lead to war. These include the abolition of standing armies, an action taken by fewer than two dozen states, including Costa Rica, Grenada, Iceland, Mauritius and Panama.

Security, though, goes beyond its association with war and peace. In its *Human Development Report* for 1994, the United Nations Development Programme (1994) argued that security had for too long been understood to mean the defence of territory from foreign aggression, or the protection of national interests. Although war and violence are still unfortunate realities of human existence, relatively few people experience them directly, and far more people experience the challenges to human security arising from the worries of daily life. New attention was drawn to this broader problem in the 1980s, when several authoritative reports – including the Brandt Commission (1980 and 1983) on international development, and the Brundtland Commission (1987) on environment and development – shifted the focus to human concerns. In a resolution adopted by the United Nations General Assembly (2012), human security was defined as an approach to 'identifying and addressing widespread

Table 4.1: The dimensions of security

Community	Food	Political
Corporate	Health	Regional
Cyber	Home	Religious
Economic	Maritime	Resource
Energy	National	Social
Environmental	Personal	Terrestrial

and cross-cutting challenges to the survival, livelihood and dignity' of people. The resolution also noted that human security did not entail the threat or use of force, and did not replace state security. As Hough (2018) has since put it, security is a human condition, and a security issue should be seen as one which threatens, or appears to threaten, our security as humans. Its different dimensions are listed in Table 4.1.

In understanding the work of IOs active on security, then, we need to look not just at those dealing most obviously with war and peace, but also at those addressing new (and not so new) threats to security from other sources. We also need to appreciate, as Wakefield (2021) argues, that global risks and threats are becoming more complex, and that the international systems of institutions, regulations and mechanisms developed after World War II need to adapt to accommodate the changes. It could be argued that all the IOs covered in all the chapters in this book are dealing in their own ways with security issues, because they are all working to help us avoid problems that would undermine our quality of life. Before we look at them, though, we need to begin with an assessment of responses to the threats posed by the promise or use of violence, which has – sadly – been the oldest theme in the definition of insecurity.

BUILDING A GLOBAL SECURITY REGIME

It was the threat of war and conflict that was behind the creation after World War I of the first international organization with something approaching a global perspective. This was the League of Nations, founded in January 1920 with a headquarters in Geneva, Switzerland. Its charge, as outlined in its founding covenant, was to 'promote international co-operation and to achieve international peace and security' based on 'open, just and honourable relations between nations'.

While these were fine goals, the League was handicapped from the outset by the limitation of its founding membership to the five Allied signatories of the 1919 Treaty of Versailles and the 13 countries that had remained neutral during the war. This encouraged cynics to describe the new body as a 'League of Victors' of the war, a view that was given further substance when the five Allies were given permanent membership of the new executive Council of the League. Another blow was struck to its credibility when isolationists in the US Senate refused to ratify the Covenant of the League, as a result of which the US never became a member. To make matters worse, Germany joined in 1926 but left in 1933, Japan withdrew in 1933 after its invasion of Manchuria, and the Soviet Union joined in 1934 but was expelled in 1939 following its invasion of Finland. At its peak, the League's membership included 58 of the more than 70 independent states of the world. Although it all but ceased to function in September 1939, it was not formally wound up until April 1946.

The League's primary failure was its inability to ease the tensions that led eventually to World War II. These included ongoing great power competition, the reparations demanded of Germany after 1918, limitations on the German military, political instability in Germany, Japanese militarization, and the imperial aspirations of Germany and Japan (see Overy, 2017). Economic problems were added to the list with the Great Depression, which broke in the US in October 1929, spread to all the world's major economies and brought a sharp decline in international trade. The problems continued to build in stages to the outbreak in September 1939 of a war that was more truly global than World War I, involving most of Europe and its empires, the Middle East, the US, China and Japan.

Another effect of the League, argues Pedersen (2015), was to offer a channel through which the efforts of the great powers to maintain their authority could be challenged for the first time, setting the scene for changes that would come after 1945. The League also set some of the institutional foundations of the post-1945 global security regime, as reflected in its major components:

- *Secretariat and executive head.* The Permanent Secretariat of the League in Geneva came under the direction of the Secretary General (a job held for most of the short life of the League by the British diplomat Sir Eric Drummond), and was divided into sections of experts dealing with issues ranging from politics to communications, disarmament and health. This was something entirely new, argues Pedersen (2015): 'a truly international bureaucracy, structured by function and not by nationality, loyal to an international chatter, and capable of managing a complex programme'.

- *Assembly.* The Assembly of the League was made up of representatives of all member states, each of which had a single vote, and which had the collective authority to discuss issues pertaining to the Covenant, to propose amendments to the Covenant, and to make decisions on admitting new members to the League.

- *Executive council.* The Council of the League acted as an executive body of the Assembly, with four founding permanent members (France, Italy, Japan and the UK) and four non-permanent members.

- *Court.* The Permanent Court of International Justice, with 11 judges elected by the Assembly and the Council, had the power to hear and decide international disputes.

- *Other elements.* The International Labour Organization was an autonomous body set up to promote workers' rights, and which survives today; see Chapters 7 and 8.

With the benefit of hindsight we can look back on the weaknesses of the League of Nations and consider the many ways in which its structure and rules could have been improved, and perhaps better assured international security. We have to remember, though, that it was the first international organization of its kind and reach, and its mistakes were not forgotten as governments thought about how to replace it after World War II.

Developments since 1945

In 1945, representatives from 50 countries met at a conference in San Francisco to create a new global organization that would build on some of the principles of the League of Nations while avoiding its handicaps. They agreed the Charter for a new UN, whose goal was – once again – to encourage international peace and security. The UN began life with 51 member states, the roster growing as Europe's empires were dissolved. Membership was open to all 'peace-loving states which accept the obligations contained in the [UN] Charter and, in the judgment of the Organization, are able and willing to carry out these obligations' (Article 4). Membership had grown to 99 members by 1960, to 154 members by 1980, and today stands at 193. The last new member was South Sudan in 2011.

At the time of its creation, the interests of security revolved mainly around the kind of war and conflict associated with states and their militaries. The reach of the UN, though, soon expanded far beyond the League of Nations, as a host of specialized agencies and programmes were created to address matters as varied as food security, health, civil aviation, development, tourism and the environment. The UN also inherited pre-existing IGOs, such as the International Telecommunication Union and the International Labour Organization, and launched its first peacekeeping operation in 1948, in the early stages of the First Arab Israeli War. That operation has been in place ever since as the UN Truce Supervision Organization, and peacekeeping has been a major part of the work of the UN.

The UN has been far from the only organization involved in security matters, as the work of IGOs involved in police cooperation shows; see *IOs in Action 4*. The management of cross-border crime has been given new urgency with the rise of domestic and international terrorism. Understood as the threatened or actual use of violence against property or people, designed to generate fear and encourage policy change, it is far from a new problem: history is sprinkled with examples of groups using violence to achieve their political ends, and the term *terrorism* was first used during the Reign of Terror in France in 1793–94. It has achieved a new prominence since the 1960s and 1970s, with terrorist groups working to achieve political independence, or making statements against capitalism or in favour of other causes. By the 1980s and 1990s it had become an international problem, with, for example, the rise of al-Qaeda in Afghanistan and Iraq, of the Taliban in Afghanistan in 1994, of ISIS after 1999 in Iraq and Syria, and of Boko Haram in West Africa from 2002.

The definition of security has been further expanded in recent decades with the need to provide cybersecurity in order to prevent attacks on computers or computer networks. The number of examples of serious cyberattacks to date has been small:

IOs IN ACTION 4

INTERPOL, EUROPOL AND POLICE COOPERATION

National security is not just a military matter, but is also a police matter. The first international organization with police cooperation as its goal was the International Criminal Police Organization, otherwise known as INTERPOL. Headquartered in Lyon, France, INTERPOL dates back to 1923, and was substantially reorganized in 1956. It is not a police force or enforcement agency, and has no powers to make arrests, but it instead provides liaison support to national police forces as they pursue cross-border criminal activity. Its targets include terrorism, cybercrime, organized crime, crimes against humanity, drug trafficking, child pornography and white-collar crime. It also maintains international databases of criminals, containing information not usually accessible by national forces. It has 181 member states, and is run by a president working with an Executive Committee, a General Secretariat and a General Assembly.

A similar organization, and the only regional police cooperation body in the world, is Europol, which is part of the European Union (EU). Based in The Hague, it oversees an EU-wide system of information exchange targeted at helping national police forces combat serious forms of international crime, including those dealt with by INTERPOL as well as clandestine immigration networks, and money forging and laundering. In recent years it has helped break up an organized crime ring involved in facilitating illegal immigration, helped break up another ring involved in money laundering and selling fake clothing and footwear, and helped break up a network illegally distributing pay-tv channels across Europe using legally established Internet Service Provider companies. Europol coordinates operations among the national police forces of the EU, and can ask these forces to launch investigations.

The EU has gone a step further by working internationally to improve investigations and prosecutions involving two or more EU member states. It does this through Eurojust (its Judicial Cooperation Unit), working from headquarters in The Hague. This has the authority to ask national authorities to launch an investigation or to start a prosecution, coordinates the work of multiple national authorities, sets up joint investigative teams and provides supporting information. Meanwhile, the work of Europol and Eurojust is complemented by the European Judicial Network, set up in 1998 in order to encourage judicial cooperation in criminal matters across the EU. (For a study of Europol and Eurojust, see Kaunert et al., 2015).

examples include possible Russian interference in the 2016 Brexit vote in the UK and the US presidential election; attacks in 2017 on banks, government departments and media outlets in Ukraine; and a hack of US government departments and corporations during 2020, most likely by Russia. The potential, though, is substantial, and states have found themselves poorly prepared. The problem is still dealt with mainly at the national level, but international cooperation has grown as malware and denial-of-service attacks have become more common, and as the importance of the internet to political, economic and social interactions has deepened. Tightening cybersecurity is complicated, though, as Nye (2020) points out, by several challenges: the role of non-state actors in cyberspace, the existence of multiple transnational networks (many of them privately owned) and the role of many large companies in shaping technology. (See Chapter 12 for more details.)

International security law

Because security can now be defined so broadly, it is not easy to tie down the body of relevant international law; it runs the gamut from the use of force to the conduct of war, controls on the spread of weapons, the use of sanctions, the right of self-defence, humanitarian intervention and peacekeeping operations. For Simma et al. (2012), international security requires 'a transformation of international relations so that every State is assured that peace will not be broken, or at least that any breach of the peace will be limited in its impact. International security implies the right of every State to take advantage of any relevant security system, while also implying the legal obligations of every State to support such systems.'

In later chapters we will look at bodies of international law dealing with security as it relates to development, migration, human rights and the environment. For now, a brief survey of international law as it relates to nuclear weapons gives us insights into how that law has evolved. Nuclear weapons have been the subject of several treaties, beginning with the 1963 Partial Test Ban Treaty that ended all atmospheric

Table 4.2: International security treaties: Examples

Opened for signature	Where signed	Subject
1963	LMW	Partial Nuclear Test Ban Treaty
1967	LMW	Outer Space Treaty
1968	LMW	Treaty on Non-Proliferation of Nuclear Weapons
1972	LMW	Biological Weapons Convention
1993	Paris	Chemical Weapons Convention
1996	New York	Comprehensive Nuclear Test Ban Treaty
1997	Ottawa	Anti-Personnel Mine Convention
2005	New York	Convention for the Suppression of Acts of Nuclear Terrorism
2008	Oslo	Convention on Cluster Munitions
2013	New York	Arms Trade Treaty
2017	New York	Treaty on the Prohibition of Nuclear Weapons

LMW = London, Moscow, Washington DC

nuclear tests, reducing the amount of radiation in the atmosphere. A non-proliferation agreement followed in 1968, and a Comprehensive Test Ban Treaty in 1993, but the latter was not enough to stop India, Pakistan or North Korea from continuing with their tests, and it is still eight ratifications short of the number needed to bring it into force; neither China, Iran, nor the US have ratified. Meanwhile, the 1967 Outer Space Treaty prohibits the use of nuclear weapons in outer space, as well as establishing that space can be freely but peacefully explored by all states. Other treaties prohibit the use of biological or chemical weapons, anti-personnel mines and cluster munitions, and regulate trade in conventional weapons; see Table 4.2.

THE UNITED NATIONS

It can sometimes seem as though every day in the year has been designated as a day of celebration or recognition for someone or something, whether it is for fathers, mothers, national independence, the environment, jazz or indigenous people. In 2013, the UN added to the list by declaring 20 March to be the International Day of Happiness, as recognition – according to its web site – of 'the relevance of happiness and well-being as universal goals and aspirations in the lives of human beings around the world'. Setting aside the question of exactly how happiness is defined and quantified, and the reality that everyone has a different idea about what makes them happy, the launch of the day ushered in the publication of an annual 'World Happiness Report', using global survey data. Recent editions have produced few surprises, with the wealthiest and most stable countries (including Finland, Norway, Switzerland and New Zealand) ranking high, and the poorest and most unstable countries (including Afghanistan, Lebanon, Zimbabwe and Rwanda) ranking low.

Celebrations and reports of this kind give us some narrow insight into the larger questions about security and peace that have lain at the heart of the work of the UN since its foundation in 1945. Its goals are summarized in the two opening articles of the UN Charter (with the key phrases italicized here for emphasis):

– Article 1.1: 'To maintain *international peace and security*, to take effective *collective measures* for the prevention and removal of threats to the peace, and for the *suppression of acts of aggression* or other breaches of the peace, and to bring about by *peaceful means*, and in conformity with the principles of *justice and international law*, adjustment or settlement of international disputes or situations which might lead to a breach of the peace'.

– Article 2.1: The UN 'is based on the *principle of the sovereign equality* of all its Members'.

Article 2 goes on the stipulate that the terms of membership include support for the peaceful resolution of disputes, and an agreement by member states not to use (or threaten to use) force in the conduct of their relations with other states. (Both of these principles were ignored by Russia in its 2022 invasion of Ukraine, as they had been many times before by multiple members of the UN that had launched invasions or wars against other members.) Although Articles 5 and 6 of the Charter allow for the suspension or expulsion of UN members for persistent violations, this ultimate sanction has never been used. As a result, the UN must work to encourage the principles of the organization against the background of multiple handicaps, including a frequent lack of consensus brought on by the different perspectives and priorities of its member states (see Mingst et al., 2022). It works to do this via these major organs:

- *Secretariat and executive head.* The headquarters of the UN are based in New York, with subsidiary regional offices in Geneva, Vienna and Nairobi. The Secretary General is the main administrative officer, appointed to the job for a maximum of two five-year terms by the General Assembly, based on a nomination by the Security Council. Most officeholders have been compromise candidates from smaller countries, and none so far have been women.

- *Assembly.* The General Assembly is the main deliberative and policymaking organ of the UN. Reflecting the work of the Assembly of the League of Nations, it is where all 193 member states are equal and have the authority to discuss and pass resolutions. It also appoints the Secretary General and the non-permanent members of the Security Council, and is responsible for the UN budget.

- *Executive council.* The Security Council reflects the work of the old Council of the League of Nations: it has 15 members, made up of five permanent members that were the victors of World War II (China, France, Russia, the UK and the US, each with veto power), along with ten rotating members: three from Africa, one from Eastern Europe, and two each from Asia, Latin America and the Caribbean, and from Western Europe and 'Others'.

- *Court.* The International Court of Justice is the successor to the Hague Conventions and the Permanent Court of International Justice, responsible for settling disputes between states (but only if they so consent). Based in The Hague (the Netherlands), it has 15 judges elected from different countries by the General Assembly to renewable nine-year terms.

- *Other elements.* An extensive family of specialized agencies and programmes (several dealt with in detail in later chapters) deals with a variety of more focused issues; see Table 4.3. Specialized agencies have independent legal identities and operate autonomously under the umbrella of the UN, with their own governing bodies, rules, memberships and budgets. Programmes, by contrast, have less autonomy, report directly to the UN General Assembly, and mostly rely on voluntary donations for their budgets.

- The *UN Economic and Social Council* (ECOSOC) coordinates the economic and social activities of the UN, particularly in the work of the specialized agencies and programmes.

- *Budget.* The UN relies on a combination of mandatory and voluntary contributions from its member states, the total budget in 2022 being just over $3.1 billion. Assessments are based on the capacity to pay as measured by the size of national economies; hence the five biggest economies in recent years – the US, China, Japan, Germany and the UK – have also been the biggest contributors. The peacekeeping budget (just over $6 billion in 2021–22) is set separately.

Table 4.3: Specialized agencies and programmes of the UN

Name	Acronym	Founded	Headquarters	Chapter of this book
Specialized agencies				
Food and Agriculture Organization	FAO	1946	Rome, Italy	9
International Civil Aviation Organization	ICAO	1947	Montreal, Canada	12
International Fund for Agricultural Development	IFAD	1977	Rome	9
International Labour Organization	ILO	1919	Geneva, Switz	7
International Maritime Organization	IMO	1948	London, UK	12
International Monetary Fund	IMF	1945	Washington DC, USA	5
International Telecommunication Union	ITU	1865	Geneva	12
UN Educational, Scientific and Cultural Organization	UNESCO	1945	Paris, France	12
UN Industrial Development Organization	UNIDO	1966	Vienna, Austria	
UN World Tourism Organization	UNWTO	1974	Madrid, Spain	
Universal Postal Union	UPU	1947	Bern, Switzerland	
World Bank Group	WBG	1945	Washington DC	5
World Health Organization	WHO	1948	Geneva	10
World Intellectual Property Organization	WIPO	1974	Geneva	6
World Meteorological Organization	WMO	1950	Geneva	12
Funds and Programmes				
Office for the Coordination of Humanitarian Affairs	OCHA	1991	New York, USA	
UN Capital Development Fund	UNCDF	1966	New York	

UN Conference on Trade and Development	UNCTAD	1964	Geneva	5
UN Development Programme	UNDP	1965	New York	5
UN Environment Programme	UNEP	1972	Nairobi, Kenya	11
UN Population Fund	UNFPA	1969	New York	10
UN Centre for Human Settlements	UNCHS-HABITAT	1978	Nairobi	
UN Children's Fund	UNICEF	1946	New York	7
UN Relief and Works Agency for Palestinian Refugees	UNRWA	1949	Amman, Jordan	7
UN Volunteers	UNV	1978	Bonn, Germany	
World Food Programme	WFP	1961	Rome	9
Related organizations				
International Atomic Energy Agency	IAEA	1957	Vienna	12
International Organization for Migration	IOM	1951	Geneva	7
UN High Commissioner for Refugees	UNHCR	1951	Geneva	7

Opinion is divided on the value of the UN, which is frequently criticized for its actions, amid repeated calls for reform of its structure (see Müller, 2021, for example). On the positive side of the ledger:

- It is a global forum for the discussion of major problems and differences.
- It has helped keep the peace in most parts of the world since 1945.
- UN resolutions often give support to international action.
- It has a strong record in promoting international peacekeeping; see *Spotlight 4*.

   On the negative side of the ledger:

- The UN has no direct powers of enforcement. While the Security Council can make legally binding demands of member states, and can authorize sanctions and the use of military operations, it is left to the member states to apply these measures.

– It tends to be dominated by the Security Council, which has an outdated voting system.

– Like most large organizations, the UN suffers from waste, bureaucracy, inefficiency and a failure of the parts always to communicate effectively with one another.

– It must rely on political support and budgetary contributions from countries that often disagree with each other and with the directions taken by the UN.

In spite of its problems, the UN is an essential part of the system of global governance. It is arguably the best kind of institution that can be achieved given the ways in which states protect and promote national interests, and that fact that it has no direct powers of enforcement reflects the dominance of states rather than being an inherent weakness of the UN. Also, as we will see in later chapters, many of its specialized agencies and programmes have provided essential leadership in a variety of areas of need.

SPOTLIGHT 4

INTERNATIONAL PEACEKEEPING

Even while the UN has its critics, in at least one area – international peacekeeping – the work of the UN has arguably proved indispensable and superior to most alternatives (see Koops et al., 2015). Based on the idea of preventive diplomacy, peacekeeping involves brokering agreements among the parties involved in actual or potential conflicts, committing multinational military forces as a buffer, and launching multi-dimensional missions involving state-building activities and even, in some cases, offensive operations. Peacekeeping has been undertaken by the UN as well as a variety of other international organizations, including the European Union and the African Union.

Usually lightly armed or unarmed, and wearing distinctive blue helmets or berets, with vehicles painted white so as to be clearly seen and to make no pretence at subterfuge, UN peacekeepers have been active in more than 70 operations around the world since 1948. These have included Angola, Burundi, Cambodia, Croatia, Cyprus, Ethiopia and Haiti, India, Pakistan and Rwanda. The personnel involved are contributed by UN member states, with Bangladesh, Nepal, India, Rwanda and Ethiopia having contributed the most, while more than 70 countries – mainly the smaller and/or poorer ones, or those without militaries – have contributed none.

In 1988, UN peacekeeping forces won the Nobel Peace Prize for their efforts in 'preventing armed clashes and creating conditions for negotiations'. Not all has been well in the record, however. Thanks mainly to limits on its rules of engagement, typically allowing it to use force only in self-defence, it suffered two dramatic failures in the 1990s: the UN Assistance Mission for Rwanda (1993–96) was unable to prevent the Rwandan genocide, which resulted in an estimated 500,000–660,000 deaths, while UN peacekeeping forces in Bosnia in 1995 failed to prevent the fall of the town of Srebrenica, allowing Bosnian Serb forces to massacre more than 8,300 Bosniak Muslim men and boys.

COLLECTIVE SECURITY ORGANIZATIONS

While the UN operates at a global level, there are several regional IOs that are underpinned by more focused and committed obligations to military security. Where they were once either bilateral or regional in scope, were mainly found in Europe and rarely resulted in the creation of new supervisory agencies, there has been a shift of focus since 1945 as alliance-making has often been based on the concept of collective security. Under this, states sign an agreement and set up an IGO based on the principle that the security of one of them is the security of all, and that an attack on one of them is an attack on all.

The North Atlantic Treaty Organization

Prime among these bodies is the North Atlantic Treaty Organization (NATO), founded among Western allies in 1949 in order to send a signal to the Soviet Union that it should not invade Western Europe (Sayle, 2019). Its objectives are most clearly reflected in Article 5 of the founding North Atlantic Treaty:

> The Parties agree that an armed attack against one or more of them in Europe or North America shall be considered an attack against them all and consequently they agree that, if such an armed attack occurs, each of them, in exercise of the right of individual or collective self-defence recognised by Article 51 of the Charter of the UN, will assist the Party or Parties so attacked by taking forthwith, individually and in concert with the other Parties, such action as it deems necessary, including the use of armed force, to restore and maintain the security of the North Atlantic area.

In May 1955, the Soviets responded by creating the Warsaw Pact (formally the Treaty of Friendship, Co-operation and Mutual Assistance), designed to send a similar message about the consequences of a NATO attack, and confirming the Cold War division of Europe. However, while NATO was a democratic organization in which membership was voluntary, the Warsaw Pact was an extension of Soviet control over Eastern Europe, and was even used in 1968 to put down a democratic uprising in Czechoslovakia. While several Western European states opted not to join NATO (including Austria, Ireland and Switzerland), only Yugoslavia and (after 1968) Albania remained outside the Warsaw Pact. Not everyone agrees with the standard analysis of Soviet dominance in the Warsaw Pact, though, with Crump (2015), for example, arguing that it may have inadvertently helped its non-Soviet members to assert their own interests and to emancipate themselves from Soviet control.

NATO has the following structure based on a combination of civilian and military functions:

- *Secretariat and executive head.* At its headquarters in Brussels, Belgium, the staff of NATO is made up of national delegations consisting of civilians and military officers. The executive head is the Secretary General, nominated by member governments for four-year renewable terms to chair the North Atlantic Council and other key bodies, and to act as a spokesperson for NATO. The post has traditionally been held by a European.

Map 4.1: European members of the North Atlantic Treaty Organization.

- *Assembly.* The Parliamentary Assembly consists of 274 legislators from NATO's 32 members (see Map 4.1) and associate members, and meets twice annually to set broad strategic goals for the organization.

- *Executive council.* The North Atlantic Council is the major civilian part of NATO, with the key responsibility of decision-making. It consists of permanent representatives from the member states (or national ministers of foreign affairs or defence, or even heads of government if they choose to attend), and it meets at least weekly to make major policy decisions. Action is agreed by consensus, with no voting.

- *Military Committee.* This is composed of senior military officers from the member states, tasked with advising the North Atlantic Council on military strategy, with decisions again made by a consensus. The Chair of the Committee – traditionally a senior non-US officer – is NATO's senior military officer and military advisor to the Secretary General.

- *Allied Command Operations* (ACO) is responsible for all NATO military operations. It is commanded by the Supreme Allied Commander Europe (SACEUR), who is always an American.

- The *NATO Response Force* (NRF) consists of land, air sea, and special forces units from the member states that are capable of being deployed quickly in the face of security threats. Commanded by SACEUR, the NRF had 40,000 troops in early 2022, and was activated for the first time following the Russian invasion of Ukraine, which also prompted a plan to increase the total to 300,000.

- *Budget*. NATO is funded through a combination of direct contributions designed to support its general work, using a cost-share formula based on the gross national income of member countries, and voluntary indirect funding in the form of the costs of committing troops and equipment. A decision was made in 2006 that all NATO members would spend at least two per cent of their gross domestic product on defence, but only seven countries – Croatia, Estonia, Greece, Latvia, Poland, the US and the UK – have so far met that target.

The end of the Cold War in 1989–90 altered the military landscape of Europe: the Warsaw Pact was dissolved on 1 July 1991, and, with no immediate threat of a Russian invasion, NATO evolved into a transatlantic crisis management body that went beyond defence to include military operations outside the borders of its members. The first 'out of area' operations were in the Balkans in 1992, when NATO oversaw a no-fly zone and an arms embargo. It was active after 2003 in helping build new security forces in Afghanistan, enforced a no-fly zone over Libya in 2011 (under a UN mandate) and participated in anti-piracy operations off the Horn of Africa in 2008–16. Then, in 2022, it had to regroup in the wake of the Russian invasion of Ukraine.

Other collective security organizations

In December 1991, just five months after the dissolution of the Warsaw Pact, Russia and eight other former Soviet states formed the Commonwealth of Independent States (CIS), a new IGO – as we saw in Chapter 3 – that was designed to encourage economic and political cooperation among its members. In May 1992, most members of the CIS signed the Collective Security Treaty, which – much like the North Atlantic Treaty – committed them to help each other in the event of external aggression. Although nine states signed the treaty, three of them – Azerbaijan, Georgia and Uzbekistan – withdrew in 1999. In 2002, the Collective Security Treaty Organization (CSTO) was formed as a regional military structure along the lines of NATO, with a headquarters in Moscow and six members – see Map 4.2 and Table 4.4. It long existed mainly on paper, notes Weitz (2018), and is clearly a Russian-led organization designed to promote Russian influence in the former Soviet Union. Repeated efforts by Russia to organize CSTO–NATO joint operations to fight terrorism and drug trafficking were rebuffed by NATO, the prospect of cooperation disappearing following Russia's annexation of Crimea in March 2014. Since few of its members face the realistic threat of invasion, it is a far cry from either NATO or the Warsaw Pact.

An example of a failed collective security IGO is offered by the Southeast Asia Treaty Organization (SEATO). A product of the 1954 Southeast Asia Collective

Map 4.2: Collective Security Treaty Organization.

Table 4.4: Collective security organizations: Examples

Name	Acronym	Founded	Number of members	Headquarters
North Atlantic Treaty Organization	NATO	1949	32	Brussels, Belgium
Southeast Asia Treaty Organization (defunct)	SEATO	1955–77	8	Bangkok, Thailand
Collective Security Treaty Organization	CSTO	2002 (with origins in 1992)	6	Moscow, Russia
Islamic Military Counter Terrorism Coalition	IMCTC	2015	41	Riyadh, Saudi Arabia

Defence Treaty, or the Manila Pact, SEATO was part of an effort by the US to check the spread of communism in the region and was modelled on NATO. Created in 1955, its members included Australia, France, New Zealand, Pakistan, the UK and the US, and just two countries from the region: the Philippines and Thailand. Most of its members contributed little to the organization in practical or political terms, involvement in the conflicts in Laos and Vietnam was opposed by France and the UK, and the main rationale behind the body was justification for Australian and US involvement in the Vietnam war. In the wake of Pakistan's withdrawal in 1972 and the defeat of South Vietnam in 1975, SEATO was dissolved in 1977.

Meanwhile, in a different part of the world, the Islamic Military Counter Terrorism Coalition (IMCTC) was founded in 2015 to fight terrorism. It is an example of what Miller and Cardaun (2020) describe as a multinational security coalition, formed under the leadership of Saudi Arabia to bring combinations of mainly Arab and/or Muslim states together to address regional threats. Unlike traditional security alliances, the IMCTC is informal in structure, and is notable for excluding major external powers, and for being led by a local middle-ranking power. It has a Secretary General, a military commander and a headquarters in Riyadh, but it is a new and mainly untested species of IO, and its informality has led to criticisms that it is more a coalition on paper than in reality. Although it had 41 members in 2022, ranging from western African states to Indonesia, they all have Sunni Muslim-dominated governments; those with Shia-dominated governments, such as Iran, Iraq and Syria, have not joined.

Security cooperation of yet another kind is found in the European Union, whose Common Security and Defence Policy is focused on peacekeeping and conflict prevention (see Schmidt, 2020). Although the EU states together have a large military budget, large numbers of personnel (more than 1.4 million), and enormous resources in the form of military aircraft and naval vessels, the EU's military ambitions have mainly been shaped within the context of NATO (although four EU member states – Austria, Cyprus, Ireland and Malta – have not joined NATO). Another notable initiative to come out of Europe has been the efforts made since 1992 by Belgium, France, Germany, Luxembourg and Spain to build a multinational military force known as Eurocorps. Seen by some as a potential foundation for a future EU military, the force – headquartered in Strasbourg, France – has about 900 troops, and Eurocorps has been active in peacekeeping missions in Afghanistan, Bosnia, the Central African Republic and Mali. Although its achievements may be modest, there has been much to learn from one of the world's few formal multinational military forces.

PEACE THROUGH COOPERATION

Security is not just concerned with the avoidance of war and conflict. Looking at the broader interests of human security, and using a liberal approach to international relations (see *IOs in Theory 4*), peace and security can also be encouraged by the work of international organizations focused on bringing states and their citizens together through cooperation, using soft means (cultural, social and economic) rather than hard military means. Two regional IOs – both of which have their origins in efforts by major powers to sustain their influence in other parts of the world – offer examples of this idea at work.

The first of these is the Commonwealth, which is a legacy of the British Empire. Often wrongly labelled the British Commonwealth (the word *British* was dropped from its title in 1949), it was based originally around the dominions of Australia, Canada and New Zealand. It grew and became increasingly diverse in the 1950s and 1960s as Britain's African, Caribbean, Asian and Pacific colonies won their independence. It even attracted three countries that had never been under British control: Mozambique, Namibia and Rwanda. It now has a membership of 56 countries with a collective population of 2.6 billion people (nearly one-third of the world total).

IOs IN THEORY 4

LIBERALISM AND NEOLIBERALISM

In contrast to the pessimistic (or realistic) view of realists, an alternative understanding of the work of international organizations is offered by liberalism, a theory that emphasizes the possibilities of peace through international cooperation. Liberalism traces its roots back to the idealist philosophy that was a product mainly of World War I, suffered reduced credibility in the years leading up to World War II and was supplanted during the Cold War by realism. It remains a strong alternative to realism, though, contrasting the realist focus on matters as they are (the reality) with a view of matters as they should or could be (the ideal).

Liberals, like realists, acknowledge the anarchic nature of the international system, but have a different view about the prospects of cooperation. While realists think in zero-sum terms (an advantage or a win by one side is a disadvantage or a loss for the other), liberals think more in terms of mutual gains. They emphasize the importance of international organizations in driving the relations among states, and point to the lessons of democratic peace theory, which suggest that democracies are unlikely to go to war with one another. Liberals also prefer multilateralism over unilateralism. If the latter is understood as a willingness by a state to go it alone and rely on its own resources to achieve change, then multilateralism means a belief in approaching problems in concert and cooperation with other states.

Neoliberalism (otherwise known as liberal institutionalism, and not to be confused with economic neoliberalism) takes the argument further by suggesting that international cooperation is both feasible and sustainable. It is based on the idea that international organizations are important because they can influence states by encouraging rules-based behaviour or promoting shared values. They do this by making the commitments of states more credible, by encouraging reciprocity and the building of coalitions, by establishing points of coordination and by providing information.

A loosely structured and voluntary organization, it has a Secretariat in London. Although the British monarch is the titular head of the organization (as well as also being head of state in 15 member states, including Australia, Canada and several Caribbean states), the executive head is a Secretary General nominated and approved by Commonwealth leaders for a maximum of two four-year terms. Biennial summits are held for the Commonwealth heads of government, and every four years the Commonwealth Games bring together athletes from the member states in a mini-Olympics.

The interests of the Commonwealth focus mainly on education, economic assistance and cultural exchanges, and on the management of regional investment funds designed to encourage trade within the Commonwealth. Its economic interests are heavily influenced by the perspective of the relatively poor African and Asian states that make up much of its membership. As a result, its priorities tend to be driven by issues such as poverty, economic development, trade and aid to underdeveloped countries. The Commonwealth also has a cultural role in the world thanks in part to its use of English as the sole official language, and in part to the contribution it makes to the promotion of diplomatic ties among its member states.

It was once described (see Shaw, 2007) as 'a slightly anachronistic, somewhat hidden, but nevertheless important actor in global governance'. Its importance, though, is debatable, and by 2022 the news weekly *The Economist* was arguing that the Commonwealth was 'struggling for relevance'. While it has a record for holding its members to the obligations of upholding democracy and human rights, and sanctions them if needed, it has sometimes been defined more by what divides it than by what unites it. For example, while the Commonwealth has suspended Fiji, Nigeria and Pakistan in the wake of military coups in those countries, it prevaricated on the issue of Zimbabwe. Britain led efforts to suspend it in the wake of the authoritarian policies of President Robert Mugabe in 2001–02, but the African members of the Commonwealth fell out with non-African members over the issue. Zimbabwe took matters into its own hands in December 2003 by withdrawing from the Commonwealth, to which it has not since returned (although it has been trying since 2018).

If the Commonwealth was founded on British global influence, then the Organization of American States (OAS) was founded on American regional influence. It traces its origins to the creation in 1890 of the Washington DC-based International Union of American Republics, the goal of which was to arbitrate in the case of disputes, and to encourage trade among its members. It became the Pan American Union in 1910, and the OAS in 1948. Still headquartered in Washington DC, its membership today includes 35 North and South American states, the only exception being French Guiana, considered to be part of France.

It began its new life in 1948 as a collective security organization designed to offer a unified front against communism, and was used throughout the Cold War as an instrument of US foreign policy, helping the US isolate Cuba and supporting anti-communist dictatorships in countries such as Grenada, Guatemala and Panama. With the end of the Cold War, its focus switched to resisting authoritarianism, promoting democracy and human rights, election monitoring and encouraging free trade. It has also continued helping resolve disputes, including one in 2008 between Belize and Guatemala. For Cooper and Legler (2006), the work of the OAS can be summarized as 'intervention without intervening', but there were still enough questions about US influence in the organization in 2010 to encourage President Hugo Chávez of Venezuela to launch the Community of Latin American and Caribbean States (CELAC; see Chapter 3) as an alternative to the OAS (Kilroy, 2022).

Another variation on the idea of security cooperation is found in the form of the Organization for Security and Cooperation in Europe (OSCE), which has 57 members straddling the old divisions of the Cold War: it includes most European states, most former republics of the Soviet Union (including Russia), along with the US, Canada and Turkey. It traces its origins back to the convening in 1973 of the Conference on Security and Cooperation in Europe (CSCE), which met as part of the process of détente (relaxation of tensions) during the Cold War. This resulted in the signature in 1975 of the Helsinki Final Act (otherwise known as the Helsinki Accords), an agreement on topics such as sovereign equality and the peaceful resolution of disputes. With the end of the Cold War, the CSCE was given its new name, the hope being that it could become the main pillar of a new post-Cold War order. This idea faded as divisions widened between an enlarged EU and NATO on the one side, and Russia on the other (Russell, 2021).

With a secretariat and a Secretary General based in Vienna, a Ministerial Council, a Permanent Council, and a Parliamentary Assembly, the OSCE takes what it likes to call a comprehensive approach to security (Galbreath, 2019), incorporating its political, military, economic, environmental and human aspects. It uses consensus decision-making on a politically binding – but not legally binding – basis. Emphasizing soft over hard security, its interests run the gamut from human rights to conflict prevention, arms control, education, border management, democratization, cybersecurity and policing. It is probably best known for election monitoring in countries such as Albania, Kosovo and Montenegro (an offer to send observers to the 2012 election in Texas and other US states was not received well) and developed a reputation in 2022 as a reliable source of information on the conflict in Ukraine.

Meanwhile, changes in Chinese and Russian foreign policy have encouraged a review of another IGO – the Shanghai Cooperation Organization (SCO) – that claims to be interested mainly in soft security, but where all is not as it seems. Its origins lie in an earlier body known as the Shanghai Five, founded in 1996 as a collective security agreement involving China, Kazakhstan, Kyrgyzstan, Russia and Tajikistan. In 2001, the leaders of these countries and of Uzbekistan met in Shanghai to announce the SCO, the Charter for which was signed in 2002 and entered into force in 2003. Membership expanded to eight in 2017 when India and Pakistan joined. Headquartered in Shanghai, the SCO is governed by a Council of Heads of State and a Council of Heads of Government that both meet at annual summits, while foreign ministers of the member states hold regular additional meetings.

The SCO describes its main goals as 'strengthening mutual trust and neighbourliness among the member states; … making joint efforts to maintain and ensure peace, security, and stability in the region; and moving towards the establishment of a democratic, fair, and rational new international political and economic order' (Shanghai Cooperation Organization, 2022). What was once known as the 'Shanghai Spirit' – emphasizing the principles of sovereignty, territorial integrity and non-interference – was claimed to be the cornerstone of the SCO's work. However, Freire (2018) notes that Russia's plans to use the organization to promote regional stability, with an emphasis on security, was only partly successful prior to the Ukraine invasion, given the growing economic weight and preferences of China. For MacHaffie (2021), meanwhile, the SCO lacks the kind of cohesive collective identity needed to move it forward, a problem made deeper once India and Pakistan joined, weakening Chinese and Russian efforts to shape that identity. Not only is it still too early to know how the SCO will evolve, but the fallout from the Russian invasion of Ukraine will also need time to be understood and absorbed.

NON-STATE SECURITY ACTORS

In most of the chapters that follow, we will find varied communities of non-state actors involved in global governance, and in the shaping of domestic and international policy. As such, they hold a key position in our understanding of the dynamics of international organizations. In this chapter, non-state actors are less prominent, for the simple reason that military security has been dominated by intergovernmental cooperation, leaving most non-state actors on the margins of that process. If we expand our focus to human security, though, then we find INGOs more active; as we will see in several chapters that follow, INGOs are prominent in humanitarian, human rights, poverty and environmental issues.

The work of non-state actors – specifically INGOs – in security regimes can be found in four main areas (summarized in Table 4.5). The first consists of groups interested in the promotion of peace. Probably the world's oldest international peace federation is the International Peace Bureau, founded in 1891, winner of the 1910 Nobel Prize for Peace, and headquartered in Geneva until it moved to Berlin in 2017. It brings together about 300 organizations in 70 countries, using education, conferences and public events to help coordinate their efforts to encourage a reduction in military spending and to support nuclear disarmament. Meanwhile, the Stockholm International Peace Research Institute (SIPRI) – funded mainly by the Swedish government – generates data and authoritative information on conflicts, military budgets, nuclear arsenals and the global arms industry, for use by governments, media and researchers.

The second area consists of groups active in campaigning for disarmament. Here, note Benjamin-Britton et al (2019), a loose coalition of small and medium-sized states, humanitarian agencies and advocacy group have made headway in helping conclude treaties on several topics. Prime among the involved INGOs is the International Campaign to Ban Landmines (ICBL), a coalition of national NGOs founded in 1992

Table 4.5: Security INGOs: Examples

Type	Examples	Founded	Headquarters
Peace groups	International Peace Bureau	1891	Berlin, Germany
	Stockholm International Peace Research Institute	1966	Stockholm, Sweden
Disarmament groups	International Campaign to Ban Landmines	1992	Geneva, Switz
	International Campaign to Abolish Nuclear Weapons	2005	Geneva
Humanitarian/ relief groups	International Committee of the Red Cross	1863	Geneva
	International Rescue Committee (see Chapter 7)	1933	New York, USA
Think tanks	Royal Institute of International Affairs (aka Chatham House)	1920	London, UK
	International Crisis Group	1995	Brussels, Belgium

and headquartered in Geneva, with the goal of achieving a ban on anti-personnel landmines and cluster munitions (see Rutherford, 2011). The campaign and its founder, an American political activist named Jody Williams, jointly received the Nobel Peace Prize in 1997 for their efforts to achieve the signature of the 1997 Ottawa Treaty on prohibition of landmines. The latter currently has 164 parties, but they exclude China, Russia and the US. Inspired by the model of the ICBL, the International Campaign to Abolish Nuclear Weapons (ICAN) was founded in 2005, also with headquarters in Geneva, and helped champion the signing and implementation of the 2017 Treaty on the Prohibition of Nuclear Weapons. The treaty was resisted – and has not been signed – by all the major nuclear powers (including China, France, Russia, the UK and the US), but ICAN has helped encourage nearly 70 states to ratify, and it too won the Nobel Peace Prize (in 2017).

The third area consists of groups providing humanitarian relief during and after conflict, their missions often crossing over from security to peace, health care, human rights and caring for refugees. (See Chapter 7 for a discussion of refugee INGOs, Chapter 8 for human rights INGOs and Chapter 10 for health care INGOs.) The most famous and oldest humanitarian agency is the International Committee of the Red Cross (ICRC), which is notable for its special role in holding states accountable for violations of humanitarian law under the terms of the Geneva Conventions. It was founded in 1863 with the original purpose of improving the treatment of soldiers wounded on the battlefield, since when it has broadened its interests to cover relief for the victims of epidemics, natural disasters and conflict (Dromi, 2020). It has won the Nobel Peace Prize three times (1917, 1944 and 1963), and is part of the International Federation of Red Cross and Red Crescent Societies; the name *Red Crescent* was adopted on the insistence of leaders of the Ottoman Empire in 1906 for programmes of the Red Cross in Muslim countries.

The fourth group of NGOs working on security issues includes those working to influence policy, taking the form of multiple national and international think tanks. Prime among these is one of the oldest, the London-based Royal Institute of International Affairs (usually known as Chatham House after its headquarters building), which was founded in 1920. A newer body is the International Crisis Group, founded in 1995 in response to the wars and occurrences of genocide in Bosnia, Rwanda and Somalia. Headquartered in Brussels, it gives advice to governments on conflict prevention, operates a CrisisWatch global tracker that provides updates on conflicts and crises (it had more than 70 listed on its web site in mid-2022), carries out field research, and publishes reports aimed at shaping national and international policy.

Another and entirely different area in which non-state actors are active on security matters is in creating insecurities by turning to violent means to achieve their ends. Ezrow (2017) argues that the long focus of international security studies on the behaviour of states has encouraged us to overlook the role and effects of violent non-state actors, including the following:

– Insurgencies aimed at challenging states through armed struggle, as with the example of the Tamil Tigers, which fought between 1976 and 2009 for an independent homeland for the Tamil minority of northern Sri Lanka.

- Terrorist organizations and networks, whose structures, tactics, recruitment and funding have all changed, posing greater threats to national and human security. Examples include al-Qaeda in Afghanistan and Iraq, the Taliban in Afghanistan, ISIS in Iraq and Syria, and Boko Haram in West Africa.

- Warlords and marauders whose activities have been a cause and effect of the weakening of such states as Afghanistan, Somalia and Sudan.

- Organized crime and gangs, including drug cartels and the Mafia, who often control politicians and cause disruption that encourages migration, spreading disruption to neighbouring countries (Catino, 2019).

- Private security companies and paramilitary units motivated by profit, and used as an extension of state policy in recent years in Afghanistan, Colombia and Iraq.

States may dominate the definition and shaping of security, making intergovernmental organizations more prominent than non-state actors. The work of the latter, though, and the accumulation of citizen action in favour of peace in numerous countries and situations, means that the work of INGOs plays a key role in numerous facets of human security. This will become more clear in the chapters that follow, notable those dealing with development, human rights and the environment.

THINKING POINTS

- What is the difference between war and peace?

- How could the structure of the UN be improved?

- To what extent has NATO helped keep the peace in Europe since 1949?

- What are the relative advantages and disadvantages of collective security and peace through cooperation?

- Is there more potential for non-state actors to play a role in security issues?

IOs RELATED TO THIS CHAPTER

Collective Security Treaty Organization (CSTO)

Commonwealth

Eurocorps

Eurojust

Europol

International Campaign to Ban Landmines (ICBL)

International Campaign to Abolish Nuclear Weapons (ICAN)

International Committee of the Red Cross (ICRC)

International Crisis Group (ICG)

International Peace Bureau (IPB)

INTERPOL

Islamic Military Counter Terrorism Coalition (IMCTC)

League of Nations (defunct)

North Atlantic Treaty Organization (NATO)

Organization for Security and Cooperation in Europe (OSCE)

Organization of American States (OAS)

Royal Institute of International Affairs

Shanghai Cooperation Organization (SCO)

Southeast Asia Treaty Organization (SEATO) (defunct)

Stockholm International Peace Research Institute (SIPRI)

United Nations (UN)

FURTHER READING

Ezrow, Natasha (2017) *Global Politics and Violent Non-State Actors* (SAGE). A study that looks at the threats posed to global security by violent non-state actors, including terror groups and organized crime.

Hough, Peter (2018) *Understanding Global Security*, 4th edn (Routledge). A textbook summary of the global security matters, ranging from the traditional (war and deterrence) to non-military threats such as famine, crime and disease.

Jackson, Ben, and Harriet Lamb (2021) *From Anger to Action*: *Inside the Global Movements for Social Justice, Peace, and a Sustainable Planet* (Rowman & Littlefield). A study of the methods, achievements and failures of citizen movements and civil society.

Mingst, Karen A., Margaret P. Karns, and Alynna J. Lyon (2022) *The United Nations in the 21st Century*, 6th edn (Routledge). A textbook study of the UN, including chapters on its origins and evolution, and the different issue areas in which it is active.

Sayle, Timothy Andrews (2019) *Enduring Alliance: A History of NATO and the Postwar Global Order* (Cornell University Press). An assessment of the origins, evolution and work of NATO, arguing that leaders and diplomats kept it alive and strong even in the face of crises and evolving challenges.

FINANCE AND DEVELOPMENT

5

PREVIEW

The second regime addressed revolves around finance and development, although given the control that states prefer to exert over economic policy there is more of a focus on the latter than the former. The chapter begins with a review of the global economic picture, introducing the Human Development Index as a comparative measure. It goes on to look at the Bretton Woods system and its related international organizations, before summarizing changes in the global economic landscape since 1945. The concept of sustainable development is explained, and the goals of the UN's Sustainable Development Goals outlined. The chapter then looks at informal arrangements such as the Group of 7 and the Group of 20, before focusing on the work of the International Monetary Fund (IMF). The chapter then moves on to development organizations, headlined by the World Bank and the extensive global network of multilateral development banks. It ends with a review of non-state development actors, looking at a selection of the many international non-governmental organizations (such as Oxfam and BRAC) that have an interest in the fight against poverty. It also notes, though, that development interests overlap with several other fields, such as health care, human rights and refugee assistance.

THE CONTEXT

While speaking at an event on the sidelines of the UN General Assembly meeting in New York in September 2022, David Malpass – the Donald Trump-nominated President of the World Bank – was asked if he accepted the scientific consensus that the burning of fossil fuels by humans was implicated in climate change. Malpass initially avoided a direct answer, instead talking about World Bank projects focused on climate change, then arguing that the mission of the Bank was 'powerful', and finally saying that he did not know, and that he was not a scientist (Gelles and Rappeport, 2022). Although Malpass subsequently tried to retract his comments, admitting to poorly chosen words, climate activists were quick to criticize him, and called on President Biden to take steps to have Malpass removed from his post. A possible impasse was avoided when Malpass resigned in February 2023 to 'pursue new challenges', and was succeeded by Ajay Banga, the Indian-born former CEO of Mastercard.

While small, the incident emphasized the importance to climate change policy of the leadership provided by international organizations such as the World Bank, which has made much in recent years of the centrality of such policy to its decisions. The World Bank, in turn, is part of a system of international organizations designed to improve or coordinate global economic governance. They include formal IGOs such as the World Bank and the International Monetary Fund, less formal intergovernmental fora such as the Group of 7 and the Group of 20, and multilateral development banks. So crowded is the field, in fact, that the international approach to economic matters has been criticized for lacking the kind of coordination that might have helped prevent the global financial crisis of 2007–09, and the struggles today to address the fallout from the Covid-19 pandemic. For Moschella (2016), the problem has been a combination of power politics (involving mainly the leading state members of financial IOs) and the autonomous activities of these many IOs.

States continue to guard their powers over the core drivers of economic activity, including taxes and money supply, leaving international organizations to play a role in helping define and shape just three parts of the bigger economic picture. The first of these is trade, which is a big enough issue to merit its own chapter, so we will look at the work of trade IOs in Chapter 6. The second part is finance, and more specifically the matter of exchange rates and monetary cooperation. The normally stable exchange rates that most of the world once experienced came to end in 1971 when the US cut the last ties between the US dollar and gold, since when there has been more volatility and more need for a coordinated international response to that volatility.

The third part is development, meaning the improvement of the economic and social wellbeing of peoples, communities or states. The term is typically used in the context of poorer or emerging states, but it has wider application, and in fact has come to be so broadly defined that the web-based Directory of Development Organizations (Wesselink, 2020) lists nearly 70,000 organizations that are active on the topic, including NGOs, labour unions, faith-based bodies and indigenous peoples' movements. Although the discussions about development were once led almost exclusively by economists, the application of the term has since expanded to include health, human rights, gender and the environment. In fact, there is little that cannot be defined as a development issue, and – as a result – the sources of (and solutions to) developmental problems can be hard to tie down.

The global economic picture is further shaped by the differences that exist among states in their levels of wealth and productivity, and hence in the degree of their economic influence. Productivity is usually expressed using the measure of gross domestic product (GDP), referring to the total value of all goods and services produced by a country in a year, converted to US dollars. The numbers tell us that the two biggest economies are the US and China, with a GDP in 2022 – respectively – of

$23 trillion and $17 trillion. The smallest economies, meanwhile, have productivity levels that are measured in the tens of millions of dollars. Although there has been a rapid growth in global GDP in recent decades, the distribution of that growth has been skewed: the wealthiest states have become wealthier, the poorer states control less of the wealth, and the degrees of influence over finance and development vary in tandem.

Some of the differences are reflected in the Human Development Index, maintained by the UN Development Programme (UNDP). This rates most of the states of the world on a combination of economic, health and educational measures, rating them as either Very High, High, Medium or Low; see Table 5.1 for examples. Almost all states have improved over the last three decades, while – on a scale of zero to 1 – the global score grew from 0.6 in 1990 to 0.74 in 2019 before falling slightly as a result of Covid-19. However, relative levels of development have remained notably static: few states have substantially improved their situation relative to others, or have had a significant fall relative to others, or have moved from one rank to another. It was hardly encouraging that the *Human Development Report 2021–22* was subtitled *Uncertain Times, Unsettled Lives*, and opened with the observation that 'We live in a world of worry' before going on to note that while uncertainty was nothing new, its dimensions had begun to take 'ominous new forms' as environmental problems and polarization worsened (United Nations Development Programme, 2022).

Table 5.1: The Human Development Index

Very High	High	Medium	Low
1 Switzerland	73 Sri Lanka	116 Philippines	161 Pakistan
2 Norway	76 Iran	117 Botswana	163 Haiti
3 Iceland	79 China	120 Venezuela	163 Nigeria
4 Hong Kong	86 Mexico	121 Iraq	170 Senegal
5 Australia	87 Brazil	123 Morocco	172 Sudan
19 Japan	91 Algeria	132 India	175 Ethiopia
21 USA	97 Egypt	137 Honduras	180 Afghanistan
35 Saudi Arabia	109 South Africa	146 Zimbabwe	185 Mozambique
42 Chile	114 Indonesia	150 Syria	189 Niger
52 Russia	115 Vietnam	152 Kenya	191 South Sudan

Source: UN Development Programme (2022). Numbers indicate rank out of 191.

At the heart of the global system of economic governance lie three key international organizations: the World Trade Organization (WTO), the International Monetary Fund (IMF) and the World Bank. These are all IOs that trace their roots back to the Bretton Woods conference in 1944 (see Chapter 1), and their work has since been dominated by a handful of the world's biggest economies: mainly the US, China, Japan, Germany, France and the UK. The three IOs were once described by Peet (2009) as an 'unholy trinity' of powerful institutions that operated undemocratically and promoted a particular kind of neoliberal capitalism. Their dominance has come under increased scrutiny as the reach of emerging economies has expanded, and as charges have been laid that the influence of the older economies is a form of neo-imperialism. This chapter focuses on the work of the IMF and the World Bank (covering the WTO in Chapter 6), while also looking at several related organizations, including – most importantly – multilateral development banks and the large community of INGOs involved in development issues.

BUILDING GLOBAL FINANCE AND DEVELOPMENT REGIMES

In the nineteenth and early twentieth centuries, the global economic system was dominated by the major powers of Western Europe. At the time, China, Japan and Russia were no more than regional powers, while most of the rest of world either existed on the margins of the global economy or was under colonial control. The picture began to change after World War I with the rise of the US, the earliest signs of demands for independence in India and other parts of the world, and the tensions in Europe that would lead to World War II.

Even before the war was over, the major allied powers had begun to make plans for their vision of a post-war global economic order. To this end, they convened the Bretton Woods conference, the result was the agreement of a post-war system of economic recovery that was designed to avoid the mistakes of the peace negotiated after World War I. There were three pillars to this system, built on the work of a cluster of new intergovernmental organizations:

- Economic development, helped by the World Bank (formally the International Bank for Reconstruction and Development) whose charge has been to provide loans aimed at helping postwar reconstruction and development. Its focus was initially on Europe, but it later became a global institution.

- Stable exchange rates, encouraged by the International Monetary Fund, whose task has been to support economic policies that promote financial stability and monetary cooperation.

- Free trade, which was to have been encouraged by a new International Trade Organization. Following a US veto of this idea, a mechanism known as the General Agreement on Tariffs and Trade (GATT) was instead agreed, under which negotiations took place with the goal of lifting restrictions on trade.

Although the World Bank and the IMF are specialized agencies of the UN, they have long had almost complete functional autonomy, and as such have played a special role in defining the system of global economic governance.

Developments since 1945

On the back of the work of these IGOs, and against a background of the deepening tensions of the Cold War, and of the accelerating process of decolonization that began in the late 1940s, the global economic picture underwent major changes. The US confirmed its position as an economic and military superpower, the global role of Western Europe began to decline as it struggled to recover from war and face the end of colonialism, Eastern Europe was absorbed within the Soviet sphere, and the Middle East began to build influence because of its oil resources.

The US largely had its own way on financial matters in the 1950s as its economy grew and as its allies fell in behind the overwhelming military umbrella offered by the US in the face of threats posed by the Soviet Union. By 1960, the US accounted for about 40 per cent of global GDP, a position that gave it considerable influence within the meeting rooms of the World Bank and the IMF. Even so, another round of changes had already begun to emerge.

- Western Europe in the 1960s was recovering from war and accounting for a growing share of global GDP. It was also – as we saw in Chapter 3 – taking the first steps in the development of what would eventually become the European Union.

- The first indications began to be seen of the emerging economic influence of Asian and Latin American states. Japan's exports were beginning to find their way to most corners of the world, and while China was still a poor, rural, and unstable society, by the late 1970s it had begun to modernize its economy.

- The troubles of many sub-Saharan African states were becoming more evident as they struggled to grow and compete in economic terms, and as many suffered the effects of military government or civil war.

At the heart of global and national governance on development questions since the 1980s has been the concept of sustainable development (Sachs, 2016). This traces its roots to earlier ideas about the conservation of nature and natural resources, but was given new life with the publication of the 1987 report of the UN-sponsored World Commission on Environment and Development (often named the Brundtland report after the chair of the commission, Norwegian prime minister Gro Harlem Brundtland). The report defined sustainable development as 'development that meets the needs of the present without compromising the ability of future generations to meet their own needs' (Brundtland Commission, 1987). At the 1992 Rio Earth Summit (see Chapter 11), nearly 180 countries agreed to Agenda 21, a plan of action based on the idea of encouraging sustainable development.

This evolved in 2000 into an agreement by the member states of the UN to adopt a more strategic approach to development, to which end they agreed eight Millennium

Development Goals. These ranged from cutting extreme poverty rates in half to achieving universal primary education, promoting gender equality, and combatting HIV/AIDS, malaria, and other diseases, all by 2015. The goals had the effect of encouraging and coordinating the work of governments and non-governmental organizations, and were acclaimed by UN Secretary General Ban Ki-Moon as 'the most successful anti-poverty movement in history' (United Nations, 2015).

There was only limited political will to act on the goals, however, with the result that poverty persisted, it was concentrated in the same parts of the world, women were still often denied the benefits of progress in economic development and health care, the differences between rural and urban areas widened, and the environment continued to face serious threats. With these concerns in mind, the UN in 2015 launched an Agenda for Sustainable Development, with 17 Sustainable Development Goals (SDGs) to be met by 2030. The problems of poverty and hunger again featured prominently in the list, which was heavily weighted towards economic goals such as full employment and sustainable growth, and towards environmental goals such as clean water, clean energy, resource conservation and climate change. (See United Nations Department of Economic and Social Affairs, 2023.)

Meanwhile, the global economy had gone through yet more changes:

- The relative power of the US declined with rise of the 'Asian tigers' (Hong Kong, Singapore, South Korea, and Taiwan) and of emerging Latin American economies, a phenomenon that in 2001 spawned the acronym BRIC to summarize the new influence of Brazil, Russia, India, and China. South Africa was added later.

- The break-up of the Soviet Union and Yugoslavia in 1991-92 created 23 new states and released six Central European states to participate more fully in the global economy (as well as to join the European Union and NATO).

- The European Union grew to the point where its economy was equal in size to that of the US.

- The world was shaken in 2007-09 by the breaking of a global financial crisis that was the worst such challenge to the global economy since the Great Depression of the 1930s. It was shaken again in 2020-22 by the Covid-19 pandemic that challenged multiple IGOs as well as disrupting national economies and global financial and trading connections.

In addition to the work of formal IGOs, informal arrangements had also been agreed along the way among clusters of states within which those states could pursue their interests collectively. They are informal in the sense that none has a permanent secretariat or staff, and their meetings are instead organized through a presidency or chair that rotates through the membership of each group. The most influential is the Group of 7 major economies, or G7. Founded in 1975 as the Group of 6 (France, West Germany, Italy, Japan, the United Kingdom, and the US), it became G7 in 1976 when Canada joined, and became G8 between 1998 and 2014 when Russia was admitted, being expelled following its annexation of Crimea. The leaders of G7 meet annually at summits to discuss pressing issues – mainly of an economic or security nature – and to coordinate their responses. Two representatives of the EU also attend, giving all 27 members of the EU some voice in its work. Despite being the most exclusive and powerful club in the world, it has had only a mixed record in helping address global financial challenges. Its share of global GDP has also been declining (down from a peak of 68 per cent in 1988 to 44 per cent in 2022), and two of its critics (O'Neill and Terzi, 2018) have argued that it 'no longer has a reason to exist [in its current formulation], and it should be replaced with a more representative group of countries'.

The Global South had tried to offset the global influence of the wealthier states by creating the Group of 77, or G77, in 1964. So named because it had 77 African, Asian and Latin American members of the UN, it worked to enhance their negotiating capacity in the UN, and its membership has since expanded to more than 130 states. It has faced internal divisions, though, and the voice of Southern states has been expressed more effectively by the Group of 15 that was created in 1989 and now has 17 Southern members, including Brazil, India, Iran, Mexico and Nigeria. The interests of G7 and G77 are meanwhile straddled by the work of the Group of 20, formed in 1999 to bring together finance ministers from the world's biggest economies regardless of their political positions; it includes the G7 along with the European Union and 13 of the world's foremost emerging economies (see Map 5.1), has a diverse set of interests (ranging from trade to health, climate and economic matters), and accounts for about 85 per cent of global GDP and three-fifths of the world's population. It was also behind the creation in 2009 of the Financial Stability Board (FSB), a Swiss-based IGO whose job is to monitor and to make recommendations on the global financial system.

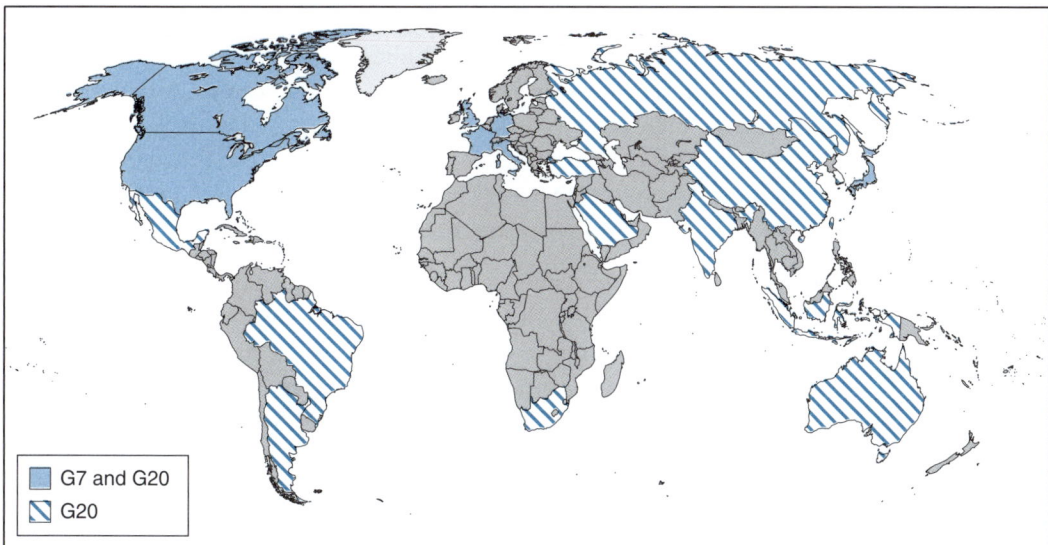

Map 5.1: The Group of 7 and the Group of 20.

THE INTERNATIONAL MONETARY FUND

Few countries have undergone such dramatic economic chaos in recent years as Zimbabwe. A country with considerable human capital and natural resources, it should by all rights be one of sub-Saharan Africa's success stories, but years of economic mismanagement and corruption under the regime of President Robert Mugabe (in office 1980–2019) left Zimbabwe with debt and often with hyperinflation; the inflation rate peaked at an eye-popping 80 billion per cent *per month* in 2008. Since Mugabe's removal from power, and his replacement by a more responsible – but still authoritarian – government, the country's economic policies have been carefully monitored by the International Monetary Fund (IMF), which has welcomed the changes it has seen but has also warned that it could not provide financial support until Zimbabwe's unsustainable levels of debt were addressed. Annual inflation in mid-2023 was still running at close to 200 per cent – a big improvement on the years of hyperinflation but still much too high.

The IMF is the primary IGO focused on helping encourage financial stability and monetary cooperation. It does this by monitoring the international monetary system, undertaking health checks of the economic and financial policies of its member states, identifying risks, and providing loans to any of its member states that might be actually or potentially experiencing balance of payments problems. Its actions are designed to help troubled states stabilize their currencies, rebuild their reserves of foreign currencies and continue to do business with one another. These are all critical goals, because monetary instability can interfere with investment, trade and development, and can lead to (or be caused by) political instability.

A core product of the Bretton Woods conference, the IMF is a specialized agency of the UN with the following components:

– *Secretariat and executive head.* Headquartered in Washington DC, the IMF is overseen by a Managing Director who is appointed by the Executive Board of the IMF for renewable five-year terms. The post has traditionally been held by a European, while the president of the World Bank has most often been an American; these are habits that are increasingly questioned as the place of Southern states in the global economy changes. The first woman appointed to the post was Christine Lagard from France, in 2011. She left in 2019 to become the first woman to be President of the European Central Bank.

– *Assembly.* The nearest equivalent that the IMF has to an assembly is its Board of Governors, which consists of one governor for each of the 190 member states of the IMF (among the few non-members are Cuba and North Korea). The governors are usually the heads of the central bank for their states, or their ministers of finance, and each governor is given a share of votes in proportion to the size of the contributions (called Special Drawing Rights) made by each member state. The Board meets once annually and is the highest decision-making body of the IMF.

– *Executive council.* The Executive Board consists of 24 directors elected by member states, along with the Managing Director. It meets multiple times each week to

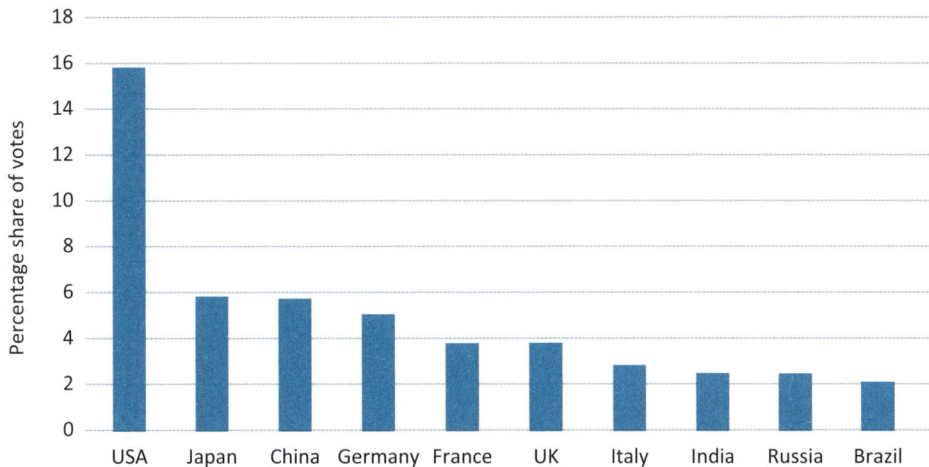

Figure 5.1: The ten biggest shareholders in the International Monetary Fund.
Source: Based on data in International Monetary Fund (2023).

conduct the day-to-day business of the IMF. Some of the Directors represent groups of states, who pre-agree to combine their voting shares to give themselves more influence. One Director in 2022, for example, represented a group of 13 Asian countries with a combined voting share of 4.33 (slightly more than France alone).

- *Budget.* The IMF is funded by its members, using quotas based on the size and position of each state in the world economy (see Figure 5.1), and determined by the Board of Governors. The quotas are regularly reviewed to account for changes (a super-majority of 85 per cent of the voting power of members is required to change quotas), and the IMF in mid-2022 had about $1 trillion to lend.

Despite the critical nature of its work, and its reputation for having a tight management structure that allows it to respond quickly in cases of immediate need, many questions have been asked about the global influence of the IMF. Among the more common criticisms directed at its work are:

- It is the product of a Western-dominated post-war world.

- There is not enough transparency in the way that it works.

- It has helped address problems in some parts of world but not others.

- There are too few clear standards by which to assess its work.

Dembele (2007) once questioned the 'disastrous' record of the IMF and the World Bank in Africa, pointing to the continued deterioration of the economic and social situation in countries subjected to their programmes. Numerous additional questions have also been asked about whether or not the work of the IMF has gone beyond the technicalities of monetary stability, and has strayed into influence over the domestic policies of states, particularly poorer states.

For their part, Bird and Rowlands (2016) warn that care must be taken with assessments of the IMF. They note that for many years after its creation it was not the subject of much academic study, but that this did not stop observers developing opinions about its work: those on the right criticized it for bailing out countries that had been badly mismanaged, while those on the left saw it as causing problems by imposing austerity measures that had a negative impact on economic growth. The analysis was often grounded in ideology rather than objective analysis, claims and counter-claims being made with only passing or selective reference to evidence. Even though there has been more research on its work in recent decades, and rhetoric still features in the analysis of that work, much more is today understood about its structure and policies, even if that understanding has emerged just as the world has gone through dramatic economic change.

IGOs such as the IMF have more power than those of many others because they control considerable funds, and – like all lending institutions – will attach conditions to their loans. These conditions are designed to make sure that the money borrowed will be used wisely, but while they might be seen as representative of the power of the big IGOs, a study by Reinsberg et al. (2021) asks if IMF conditions are unimplementable by design; area departments within the IMF will draft the initial conditions, but they might be amended by functional departments within the organization (such as those responsible for finance or communications) to include policy conditions that they care about, leading to over-ambitious sets of requirements. The number of conditions imposed, found Reinsberg et al., was directly related to the likelihood of programme failure.

Concerns have also been expressed about the extent to which the institutional structure of the IMF gives its biggest shareholders more influence over its operations than smaller states (Heinzel et al., 2020). The founding agreement of the IMF includes the requirement that the leadership of the IMF 'shall owe their duty entirely to the Fund and to no other authority … shall refrain from all attempts to influence any of the staff in the discharge of these functions' (Article XII, Section 4c). (A similar requirement appears almost verbatim in the founding agreement of the World Bank.) How far this applies in practice, though, is questioned. More of an effort has been made recently to make the IMF more reflective of the new global balance of economic power, for example giving China a bigger quota of shares and its own seat on the Executive Board, and making changes in the wake of Covid-19; see *IOs in Action 5*. Despite that, the BRICs went ahead in 2014 and launched a New Development Bank that some saw as offering a challenge to both the IMF and the World Bank (see later in this chapter). By mid-2022, the percentage share of votes controlled by the four BRICs was just over 13.5 per cent, or three points less than that of the US.

THE WORLD BANK

Development has always been a part of organized human society, but the concept began to be applied differently – and globally – with the end of the colonial era in the period 1945–70. With numerous countries winning independence, they were faced with the challenge of building their economies and competing with the older established

IOs IN ACTION 5

THE INTERNATIONAL MONETARY FUND AND COVID-19

Once described as 'the world's controversial financial firefighter' (Masters et al., 2021), the International Monetary Fund (IMF) has been at the heart of multiple recent economic crises, not least among them being the Asian financial crisis of 1997-98, the global financial crisis of 2007–09, and the European sovereign debt crisis that broke in 2010. It had to step up once again to help countries address the economic problems wrought by the breaking of the Covid-19 pandemic in 2020. The Special Drawing Rights (SDRs) used by the IMF are a form of internal currency that member states can exchange with one another for hard currencies such as dollars or euros. In the event of crises, the IMF can change its allocation of SDRs, as it did during the global financial crisis. In 2021, it went much further by allocating $650 billion in SDR, the largest amount in its history and more than twice the amount allocated during the 2007–09 global financial crisis.

Because of the way in which IMF quotas work, wealthier countries received most of the allocations, the resulting criticism prompting the IMF to encourage wealthier countries to share their allocations, which most of them did. Health and social spending moved to the top of the IMF agenda during the pandemic, the response prompting IMF Managing Director Kristalina Georgieva to declare that 'these are the times for which the IMF was created' (quoted in Gallagher and Carlin, 2020).

Just how far IMF action helped countries weather the problems of Covid-19 is hard to say, not least because much of the fallout from the pandemic continued in the form of disrupted supply chains. The waters were then muddied by the effects of inflation in many countries, to which were added the disruptions to energy supplies caused by the 2022 Russian invasion of Ukraine. While wealthier countries were able to cushion the economic effects of Covid-19 with massive and unprecedented injections of fiscal and financial support, note van der Hoeven and Vos (2022), developing states lacked the same capacity. Among the reforms they suggested was an increase in Special Drawing Rights as a way of leveraging additional development finance in the event of future crises.

economic powers. It was assumed at first that open markets and economic planning would transform societies, but it soon became clear that many former colonies were in a disadvantaged situation, and that more investment was needed. The picture was further complicated by the way in which some newly independent states performed relatively well, leaving poorer states even more marginalized.

The first truly global development IGO was the World Bank, which – like the IMF – was a product of the Bretton Woods conference, but whose focus was at first on Europe, a charge reflected in its full name: the International Bank for Reconstruction and Development (IBRD). The emphasis on the *reconstruction* in its title soon shifted to an emphasis on *development*, its European focus being replaced by a global interest in promoting economic growth and ending poverty in less developed countries. By the

Table 5.2: The World Bank Group

Organization	Founded	Functions
International Bank for Reconstruction and Development	1945	Provides loans, credits and grants, with a focus on development.
International Finance Corporation	1956	Promotes the private sector by investing in companies, advising business and governments, and mobilizing capital from other lenders.
International Development Association	1960	Provides zero- to low-interest loans and grants to the world's poorest countries.
International Centre for Settlement of Investment Disputes	1966	Helps arbitrate international investment disputes.
International Investment Guarantee Agency	1988	Provides political risk insurance to encourage foreign direct investment into poorer states.

early 1970s, the Bank had adopted the twin goals of accelerating economic growth and reducing poverty. Much like the IMF, it provides loans, credits and grants, its focus on development complementing the focus of the IMF on monetary cooperation. It invests in areas as diverse as agriculture, education, health, industry, transport and the environment, and has evolved over the decades into a group of IGOs with specialized roles – see Table 5.2.

There are many structural similarities between the IMF and the World Bank. Both are specialized agencies of the UN, and almost all members of the UN are also members of the World Bank and the IMF. In fact, to become a member of the World Bank a state must first join the IMF. The structure of the bank – a near-mirror image of that of the IMF – is as follows:

- *Secretariat and executive head.* Headquartered in Washington DC, the Bank is overseen by a President who is usually nominated by the US (the Bank's biggest shareholder) and confirmed by the Executive Directors for a renewable term of five years. Except for Kristalina Georgieva of Bulgaria (who held the job only for two months in 2019 in an acting capacity), all presidents to date have been men and US citizens (although James Wolfensohn (1995–2005) was born in Australia, Jim Yong Kim (2012–19) was born in South Korea and Ajay Banga (2023–) was born in India).

- *Assembly.* Like the IMF, the nearest equivalent that the Bank has to an assembly is its Board of Governors. There is one for each of the five elements of the World Bank Group, each consisting of one governor for each of the 189 World Bank member states (the same list as for the IMF with the sole exception of Andorra). As with the IMF, the governors are usually the heads of the central bank for their states, or their ministers of finance, and they serve five-year renewable terms. Each governor is given a share of votes in proportion to the size of the contributions made by each member state. The Boards meet once annually and are the senior decision-makers of their respective agencies.

- *Executive council.* The Bank has 25 Executive Directors, one each from the six biggest shareholders (US, Japan, China, Germany, France and the UK), and the balance of 19 shared among the rest of the membership, with each director representing a constituency of multiple member states.

- *Budget.* The Bank is funded by its members, based on the number of shares that each country holds. Shares are allocated differently in each of the World Bank organizations, but the voting powers in the World Bank itself reflect the quotas used by the IMF: the US had the biggest percentage share of votes in 2022 (15.7 per cent), with Japan second (7.4 per cent) and China third (5.8 per cent). The Bank in 2022 had $220 billion in assets.

Also like the IMF, the World Bank attracts competing opinions about its influence. In order to safeguard their positions, all IGOs need to demonstrate their impartiality, meaning that they must work to avoid being seen to have interests that align with those of certain member states (Heinzel et al., 2020). The popular view is that because of the sheer size of the presence of the US in both the IMF and the World Bank, the conditions they set for loans and other help will favour US interests, offering a good example of principle-agent theory at work; see *IOs in Theory 5*. Exactly how this happens in the World Bank has long been something of a mystery because of limitations on the availability of data, but a study by Clark and Dolan (2021) suggests that the conditions are shaped in the World Bank less by states than by the Bank's own staff. In other words, those staff tend to design programmes because they consciously wish to please the largest financier of their organization, and unconsciously share the biases of the US.

A related but more focused development IGO is the UN Conference on Trade and Development (UNCTAD), founded in 1964 and headquartered in Geneva. Its purpose is to help developing and emerging countries achieve better access to the global economy through analysis, technical help, economic diversification and attracting investment. With a small budget and a small secretariat, it has a more limited purview than some of its UN peer organizations, much of its work revolving around the convening of conferences among its member states every four years. It is notable for the fact that all its secretaries-general until 2021 – when the Belgian politician Isabell Durant was appointed to the position – were from the Global South. Despite its long experience and its agenda, UNCTAD has mainly failed to resolve disagreements between its wealthier and poorer members.

A final UN body with a focus on development is the United Nations Development Programme (UNDP), the focus of which is on poverty reduction. Founded in 1965

IOs IN THEORY 5

PRINCIPAL-AGENT THEORY

With its origins in economic theory, principal-agent (PA) theory is concerned with the conflict in priorities that can arise when a person or group (the principal) is represented by another person or group (the agent). The relationship can work when both parties are well coordinated in their thinking and communicate well, but problems arise when the two parties have different priorities, incentives, preferences or levels of information. It applies to numerous different situations, including the retention of a lawyer to represent a client, for example, or the relationship between voters and their legislative representatives.

It has also been applied to international relations to theorize the manner in which the national representatives in IOs might have interests that differentiate them from the preferences of the citizens they represent, who are mainly much less engaged in the work of IOs than in the work of national or local governments. In looking at the case of the IMF, Copelovitch (2010) has taken the idea further by proposing a 'common agency' theory. By this, he means that the IMF is best understood as being dominated by its five largest members (the US, Japan, Germany, France and the UK) and the control they exercise over its Executive Board. While they act as a collective political principal, he suggests, the staff of the IMF acted as the agent. This theory could help explain why the IMF has been so inconsistent in the amounts it is prepared to lend to different states and the variations in the conditions it attaches to its loans.

One of the concerns about both the IMF and the World Bank has been the effect of what is known as the Washington Consensus. This is a philosophy – shaped by the wealthier members of both organizations – regarding the conditions imposed on borrower states by the IMF and the World Bank. Among other things, it requires trade liberalization, privatization, deregulation, improved records on democracy and human rights, and other policies aimed at opening up national markets. Although these might be projected as sensible changes aimed at maximizing the effects of borrowing, they are also strongly criticized by many Southern states as representing efforts to promote the economic agendas of the US and its Western allies (Verbeek, 2022). The rise of China and its growing role in the IMF and the World Bank has changed the balance in both the IMF and the World Bank, however; as the third-largest shareholder in both IOs, China is now able to exert increased influence over their policies.

with a headquarters in New York, the UNDP provides expert advice to developing countries, the goal being to help them attract investment. Describing itself on its web site as 'the UN's development agency', the UNDP – like many UN bodies – subsists on the voluntary monetary contributions of member states; in 2022, the five biggest contributors (in order) were Germany, Japan, Argentina, Sweden and the US. Its first four administrators were from the US, while the four since then have come from the UK, Turkey, New Zealand and Brazil. As well as producing the annual *Human Development Report*, the UNDP was also coordinator of the production of the Sustainable Development Goals.

MULTILATERAL DEVELOPMENT BANKS

Alongside the IMF and the World Bank, with their global reach, there exists an extensive network of multilateral development banks (MDBs) that have each been set up within a given part of the world, pooling contributions from their shareholders to mainly help low- and middle-income countries; see Table 5.3. There are two main types: the biggest and best-known (including the European Investment Bank and the Inter-American Development Bank) make long-term low- or no-interest loans and grants to their poorer members, while others (such as the Caribbean Development Bank) have been founded by the governments of poorer states that can then borrow collectively via the bank at more favourable rates. Some loans will be directed at infrastructure projects (including highways, power plants, port facilities and dams) or at social projects (including health and education initiatives), while others will be directed at changing policies, including reforms to agriculture or urban development.

Table 5.3: Multilateral development banks: Examples

Name	Founded	Headquarters	Member states
Regional			
European Investment Bank (EIB)	1958	Luxembourg	27
Inter-American Development Bank (IDB)*	1959	Washington DC, USA	48
African Development Bank (AfDB)*	1964	Abidjan, Cote d'Ivoire	81
Asian Development Bank (ADB)*	1966	Manila, Philippines	68
Islamic Development Bank (IsDB)	1973	Jeddah, Saudi Arabia	57
European Bank for Reconstruction and Development (EBRD)*	1991	London, UK	73
New Development Bank (NDB)	2014	Shanghai, China	9
Asian Infrastructure Investment Bank (AIIB)	2015	Beijing, China	105
Sub-regional			
Development Bank of Latin America (CAF)	1968	Caracas, Venezuela	17
Caribbean Development Bank (CDB)	1969	Kingston, Jamaica	28
West African Development Bank (WADB)	1973	Lomé, Togo	8
Eurasian Development Bank (EDB)	2006	Almaty, Kazakhstan	6

* The Big Four.

The earliest MDBs were created as part of post-war efforts to support reconstruction, while later banks resulted mainly from dissatisfaction with the lending policies of the World Bank, and as part of an effort to break away from the Western domination of the original banks. There are now at least 30 MDBs, with a growing number focusing on (and based in) the Global South (Bazbauers and Engel, 2021). Unlike commercial banks, they do not look to maximize profits for shareholders so much as to address poverty and inequality. Their core rationale, quite simply, is to bring a multilateral approach to bear on problems that are too complex to be addressed by conventional bilateral or national approaches. This opens up new options to borrowing countries, while giving donor countries new opportunities to promote their interests and influence (Delikanli et al., 2018).

The first MDB – the Inter-American Bank – was proposed in the late 1930s, and although it was halted by the outbreak of war, it can be seen as a precursor to the banks that were to follow. The oldest (and the biggest) of these is the European Investment Bank (EIB), founded in 1958 and headquartered in Luxembourg. It describes itself as the long-term lending arm of the European Union, with funds coming mainly from subscriptions from EU member states, and its loans going mainly to long-term projects involving capital assets such as land, buildings and other structures. Its single biggest project was the Eurotunnel that runs under the English Channel between England and France. Opened in 1994 after centuries of speculation and failed plans, the tunnel cost about $15 billion to build (nearly twice the original estimate) and had to wait until 2007 before returning its first annual profits. More recently, the EIB helped convert athletes' apartments in London's Olympic Village into affordable housing, renovate large parts of the ageing sewer system of Brussels, and helped develop a microinsurance scheme for small business owners in developing countries.

The giant among development banks, with more than twice the assets of the World Bank, the EIB is managed by a board of governors consisting of representatives of the EU member states (usually their finance ministers), who decide policy and appoint a decision-making board of directors (one for each member state along with a representative from the European Commission) to five-year renewable terms, and a nine-member management committee to six-year renewable terms. The latter – consisting of the president and the eight vice-presidents of the Bank – is its main executive body, overseeing day-to-day operations and drafting decisions on spending for the consideration of the board of directors.

A study by Mertens and Thiemann (2019) argues that the EIB has become the centre of gravity of 'long-standing political attempts to increase the investment firepower of the European Union'. Recent economic problems in the EU, they argue, have combined with the goals of the European Commission's Investment Plan for Europe (launched in 2015) to draw new attention to the economic role of state-owned development banks. This network has expanded since the 1980s, creating what they call a European investment state whose reach and stability deserves more attention.

A year after the creation of the EIB, the first of what might be termed the Big Four regional MDBs – the Inter-American Development Bank (IADB) – was founded with headquarters in Washington DC, motivated at least in part by US concerns about the potential spread of communism in Latin America (Babb, 2009). It now has 48 members, including China, Japan, South Korea and most European states, even though all its borrowing members are in Latin America and the Caribbean. In 1964, the African Development Bank was founded as part of an effort by newly independent African states to encourage regional cooperation, followed two years later – for similar reasons, and on the initiative of Japan – by the Asian Development Bank. In 1991 the European Bank for Reconstruction and Development (EBRD) was founded in London as part of an effort to help Central and Eastern European countries with their post-communist economic *and* political transition. (Its democracy-building intent made it unusual among MDBs.) Each of these original MDBs is independent, and is owned by its shareholder countries.

The original MDBs, argue Bazbauers and Engel (2021), played a key role in building the post-World War II financial order, and have been key players in the

SPOTLIGHT 5

THE NORTH–SOUTH IMBALANCE IN GLOBAL GOVERNANCE

The vast majority of international organizations are either located in the Global North and/or dominated by the voting and budgetary powers of their Northern member states, particularly those in Europe and North America. The former point is clear throughout this book, with the large number of examples of IOs headquartered in cities such as Geneva, New York, London, Paris and Rome. The latter point is illustrated most immediately in this chapter with the structure of the World Bank and the IMF, both of them dominated by the voting power of wealthy Northern states. This phenomenon of new (that is, smaller or less powerful) actors being given nominal roles in institutions that mainly serve the interests of dominant actors was described by Wade (2011) as hegemonic incorporation. He went on to argue that in order for actors from the Global South to have a more influential role, they needed to form their own Southern-led institutions.

A study by Ray and Kamal (2019) uses two Southern multilateral development banks – the Development Bank of Latin America and the Islamic Development Bank – to ask whether or not South–South cooperation can compete with the influence of the big multilateral institutions such as the World Bank and the Inter-American Development Bank. They conclude that both banks have successfully challenged the hegemony of the bigger Northern-dominated banks, play a key role in harnessing global capital to finance projects important to borrowers (such as infrastructure) and offer borrowers more representation on their boards than do Northern-based equivalents. However, they also point out that neither bank has shareholder countries with the highest AAA credit ratings, a reality that undermines their own ratings. The two banks also take a conservative position on lending requirements (not unlike the bigger global banks and IOs), and neither are as strong as Northern banks in imposing environmental and social safeguards on the projects they fund.

The influence in global governance of the emerging economies of the South is clearly growing, in tandem with the size and reach of their economies. However, 13 of the world's 20 biggest economies (when measured by GDP) are still in the North, and even the two biggest southern economies (China and India) still have low per capita GDP figures: $13,000 and $2,500 respectively in 2023. It is clear that more still needs to be done before southern countries can convert their size and wealth into global influence.

multiple debt crises the world has faced in recent years, including the 1982 developing world debt crisis, the 1997–98 Asian financial crisis, and the 2007–08 global financial crisis. They all follow the template of the World Bank, and they have helped shape thinking about what development means. At the same time, and despite their regional focus, the wealthier states of the Global North (particularly the US) have long dominated the Big Four regional banks, raising concerns among many of the recipients of their aid about the impact of Northern influence over their work and priorities; see *Spotlight 5*.

As a result of these imbalances, there have been efforts in other parts of the world to create new regional and sub-regional banks without the input of states from the Global North, making an important statement about the importance of regional responses to regional needs. One of the first of these new banks was the Islamic Development Bank (IsDB), which was founded in 1975 at the encouragement of Saudi Arabia, which hosts the bank's headquarters and accounts for nearly a quarter of its capital. For now, at least, banks such as these are handicapped by having access to fewer funds and resources. The difference was particularly clear in 2021, when the European Investment Bank had 20 times the assets of the IsDB while the Asian Development Bank had six times the assets (see Figure 5.2).

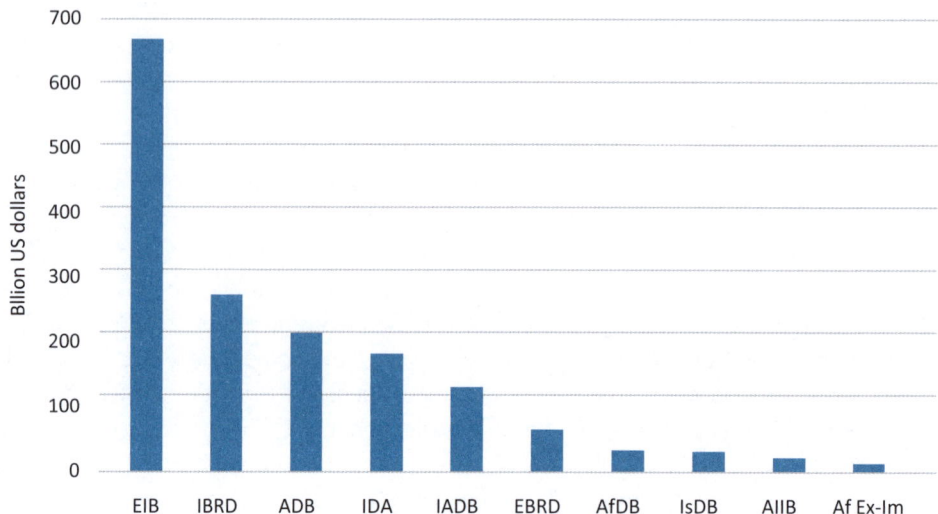

Figure 5.2: Assets of the ten biggest multilateral development banks.
Source: Based on data in Columbia Center on Sustainable Investment (2021).

EIB – European Investment Bank
IBRD – World Bank
ADB – Asian Development Bank
IDA – International Development Association
IADB – Inter-American Development Bank
EBRD – European Bank for Reconstruction and Development
AfDB – African Development Bank
IsDB – Islamic Development Bank
AIIB – Asian Infrastructure Investment Bank
Af Ex-Im – African Export–Import Bank

Two of the most recent attempts by the Global South to express its rising influence came with the creation in 2014 of the BRICS Development Bank (since renamed the New Development Bank), and the creation in 2016 of the Asian Infrastructure Investment Bank (AIIB). Both are still small, with combined assets only 12 per cent of those of the World Bank, but they promise more as emerging states continue to grow. The AIIB was proposed by Chinese President Xi Jinping, not least to help China build infrastructure in Asian and African countries as part of its Belt and Road Initiative of trade routes. The US tried to discourage major US allies – such as Australia, South Korea and the UK – from joining the AIIB, but failed (Dollar, 2015).

NON-STATE DEVELOPMENT ACTORS

Development – and particularly the fight against poverty – has been at the heart of the work of a large and expanding world of NGOs and INGOs. In fact, when the acronym NGO is used in developing countries, it is as often as not associated with bodies focused on development, although the term *development* can be applied to everything from famine relief to emergency assistance, health services, finance, human rights and refugee assistance. Some have come to play such an important role in international development and humanitarian relief, notes Yanacopulos (2019), that 'they are the first names people think of in order to get information they may see on the news, [or] to donate money to a particular emergency appeal'. Behind the first impressions, though, she continues, 'are highly sophisticated, multinational organizations with complex systems, embedded in extensive political networks with a wide global reach'. Many originated in the Global North, often in response to a particular crisis, but they have since broadened their interests, and have often moved elements of their head office functions to the countries on which they are most active. Their work – and their definition of development – is also being challenged by the rise of the BRICS and their different priorities.

Having said all this, the biggest and best-branded INGOs are only a small part of the development NGO sector, as reflected in the data collected by Schnable (2021). Looking just at the US, she reports that while there were just over 1,000 international aid organizations registered with the US Internal Revenue Service in 1990, more than 1,300 new such organizations were created in 2010 alone, and by 2015 the total number had reached 13,030. Many of these are small and focused, though, and are often the personal projects of amateur individuals rather than long-term organizations run by seasoned experts; hence the choice of *Amateurs Without Borders* as the title of Schnable's book. The bigger INGOs, such as CARE International and World Vision, are much fewer in number (see Table 5.4), but the data on the small organizations are worth remembering as an indication of the appeal of helping poorer societies.

Most of today's biggest development INGOs were founded in the Global North by committed individuals with 'an idealistic mission and a strong volunteer spirit' (Jayawickrama, 2011), and usually raised their funds in the North while spending on field programmes in the Global South. When NGOs first became active in development issues, note Lewis et al. (2021), they appealed to different sections of the

Table 5.4: Development INGOs: Examples

Name	Founded	Headquarters
Oxfam	1942, UK	Nairobi, Kenya
CARE International	1945, USA	Geneva, Switzerland
World Vision	1950, USA	London, UK
BRAC	1972, Bangladesh	Dhaka, Bangladesh
ActionAid	1972, UK	Johannesburg, South Africa
Islamic Relief	1984, UK	Birmingham, UK

development community because – compared to often bureaucratic and ineffective government-to-government aid – they provided an alternative, more flexible, and more cost-effective funding channel with a higher chance of local-level implementation and grassroots participation. They have also been subject to criticism, though, not least because of their role in offering public services without direct lines of accountability to local people. Being mainly based in the North, they can also seem to be elite-driven bodies removed from the grassroots world of the poor. In contrast to the praise that development NGOs once attracted, conclude Lewis et al., there is today a more realistic view about what they can and cannot achieve, and a more nuanced understanding of their role in global governance. Despite the claim made by UN Secretary General Kofi Annan that the twenty-first century might be 'the era of NGOs' (quoted in Lang, 2013), development NGOs have come under increased scrutiny.

Among the more prominent is CARE International, which was founded in the US in 1945 as a temporary consortium of charities – the Cooperative for American Remittances to Europe – whose objective was to deliver food aid to war-torn Europe. CARE packages, as they were known, were initially US Army surplus rations (controversially including cigarettes), and were later replaced by a variety of packages more suited to different recipient countries. CARE expanded its reach in the late 1940s to Asia, began providing non-food aid and by the late 1950s had switched its focus to developing countries. In the 1970s and 1980s, CARE offices were opened in several countries (including Canada, Germany, the UK, Australia and Japan), and CARE International was created in 1982 with a small secretariat in Geneva. While food aid continued to be part of its agenda, it took a broader interest in poverty alleviation and development, including efforts to address social exclusion and discrimination, to provide small loans, to promote the empowerment of women (CARE International, 2022).

Parts of the story of Oxfam are similar, in that it was a product of World War II, had an initial focus on famine relief in Europe, and later broadened its interests and reach. Founded in 1942 by a group of British Quakers and academics as the Oxford

Committee for Famine Relief, it began to be joined by national affiliates in the 1960s and 1970s, and today has 21 national affiliates headed by a small Oxfam International secretariat based in Nairobi, Kenya. Its web site headlines the ending of poverty and responses to emergencies as its primary goals, with 'extreme inequality', gender justice, women's rights and climate change as specific interests. Despite the effects of a 2011 scandal involving the exploitation of prostitutes in Haiti (some of them underage) by staff members of the UK office, Oxfam remains one of the leading and best-known of development INGOs.

Much like IGOs, one of the persistent characteristics of development INGOs is that they are mainly founded and located in the Global North while targeting problems and challenges in the Global South. One of the most notable exceptions is BRAC, an NGO founded in Bangladesh in 1972 to offer relief in the wake of the Pakistan civil war that resulted in the independence of Bangladesh. Initially named the Bangladesh Rehabilitation Assistance Committee, it later changed its name to Building Resources Across Communities, but typically goes simply by its acronym. Headquartered in Dhaka, and active in a dozen Asian and African countries, it claims to be one of the world's largest development INGOs, and describes its mission as being 'to empower people and communities in situations of poverty, illiteracy, disease and social injustice' (BRAC, 2023). The work of BRAC is symbolic of the effect of the rise of INGOs based in the Global South, resulting in increased demands from donors and INGOs alike that INGOs work with their southern partners (Yanacopulos, 2019).

Reflecting the changing assumptions about the locations and the targets of the major development INGOs, two of them – ActionAid and Oxfam – have moved their secretariats to the Global South: ActionAid, a British NGO founded in 1972, moved its headquarters from London to Johannesburg in 2003, and Oxfam moved its headquarters from Oxford to Nairobi in 2014. These actions, suggests Forsch (2018), might be seen as part of transformational changes undertaken by INGOs as they turned increasingly towards working with their target populations than for those populations. In the case of Oxfam, he concludes, the move was reflective of changes in global fundraising opportunities, with Southern countries becoming wealthier and more influential. However, Forsch concluded, while the two relocations sent a strong political message with potentially positive spin-offs, they had limited scope and impact, and carried costs and risks.

A recent report (Baiden et al., 2022) looking at the future of development INGOs, and based on interviews with the leaders of many of those INGOs, raised many questions about the prospects for these organizations. Their effectiveness is being more closely examined, competition for funding is growing, and there are increased calls for these INGOs to be localized and 'decolonized', while the capacity of local actors to manage them is also questioned. The legitimacy of INGOs is increasingly being called into question, noted the report, whether as a result of local actors highlighting what they see as the paternalistic behaviour of INGOs, or concerns about the 'colonial' nature of global aid. Whether the necessary changes can be achieved, though, continues to be a matter of debate.

THINKING POINTS

- What are the boundaries (assuming there are any) of the idea of development?

- What are the advantages and disadvantages of formal arrangements such as G7 and G20 relative to the work of formal intergovernmental organizations?

- What (if anything) can or should be done about the dominance of wealthy states from the Global North in the work of the IMF and the World Bank?

- Are multilateral development banks a good idea?

- Are there too many international non-governmental organizations active in the field of development?

IOs RELATED TO THIS CHAPTER

BRAC

CARE International

European Investment Bank (EIB)

Group of 7 (G7)

Group of 15 (G15)

Group of 20 (G20)

Group of 77 (G77)

Inter-American Development Bank (IADB)

International Monetary Fund (IMF)

Islamic Development Bank (IsDB)

Oxfam

UN Conference on Trade and Development (UNCTAD)

UN Development Programme

World Bank (UNDP)

FURTHER READING

Bazbauers, Adrian Robert, and Susan Engel (2021) *The Global Architecture of Multilateral Development Banks: A System of Debt or Development?* (Routledge). A survey of multilateral development banks, explaining their origins, structure and goals.

Develtere, Patrick, Huib Huyse, and Jan Van Ongevalle (2021) *International Development Cooperation Today: A Radical Shift Towards a Global Paradigm* (Leuven University Press). An assessment of the changing nature of development, looking at the growing number of actors involved and the changing definition of development.

Eichengreen, Barry (2019) *Globalizing Capital: A History of the International Monetary System*, 3rd edn (Princeton University Press). A survey of the international monetary system, beginning with the gold standard and taking the story through Bretton Woods to the recent era of global and regional crises.

Lewis, David, Nazneen Kanji, and Nuno S. Themudo (2021) *Non-governmental Organizations and Development*, 2nd edn (Routledge). An assessment of the roles played by NGOs in development, including chapters on their history, work and relationship to globalization and humanitarian action.

Vitterbo, Annamaria (2019) *International Monetary Fund*, 3rd edn (Kluwer Law International). A review of the IMF, including chapters on its origins, purposes and structure, and its relationship with its member states and other IGOs such as the World Bank.

TRADE

6

PREVIEW

The focus of this chapter is on international organizations active in matters related to trade. It begins with a review of the context of global trade, discussing the evolution of approaches to trade and summarizing the domination of the leading trading powers. The chapter goes on to look at the evolution of the global trade regime, emphasizing the rapidity with which it has changed since 1945, and discussing the work of the General Agreement on Tariffs and Trade (GATT). It looks at the nature of international trade law (particularly regional trade agreements) before turning to a focus on the structure and work of the World Trade Organization (WTO). It discusses the strengths and weaknesses of the WTO, and the impact of its dispute resolution system, before turning the focus to other trade IGOs such as the World Customs Organization (WCO), the World Intellectual Property Organization (WIPO) and the Organization for Economic Cooperation and Development (OECD). It also looks at the unusual example of the Organization of Petroleum Exporting Countries (OPEC). The chapter ends with a review of the role of non-state actors, with an emphasis on the critical influence of multinational enterprises in defining, shaping and operating the global trade system.

CONTENTS

- **The context**
- **Building a global trade regime**
- **The World Trade Organization**
- **Other trade IGOs**
- **Non-state trade actors**

THE CONTEXT

At a small shop in the central English city of Leicester, a family with Indian origins has become locally famous for sourcing and importing food with the needs of the Indian diaspora in mind (Shah, 2022). Sweet and savoury goods are on sale, many of them imported from south Asia and bearing the labels of producers in Mumbai and Delhi, designed for the tastes of first-generation immigrants, the native-born descendants of immigrants, and anyone who has developed a taste for the rich and multiple cuisines of India. The shop may be small, with just 15 staff and a growing online presence, but it is representative of a growing worldwide trade involving small businesses and designed to cater to the demands of diasporas all over the world; Turks in Germany, Algerians in France, Greeks in Scotland, Mexicans in the US, Pakistanis in the Gulf states and more. These are not big businesses, but all big businesses had small beginnings, and global trade has long been driven by the work of small entrepreneurs such as these.

Few topics are so central to the idea of global governance as trade, which – by definition – is international in character. Involving the buying, selling or exchanging of goods and services, trade has been part of the human experience since the emergence of organized society. When one person, or community, has had access to a resource that another person or community lacks, arrangements and agreements will usually emerge by which the two parties trade what they have for what they lack. As humans moved further from their homes over time, their needs and tastes changed, the variety of goods and services that were traded grew, trade routes expanded and widened, and the nature of trade became more complex. Once large corporations became involved, and the state system emerged and expanded, the complexities of trade deepened even further.

Although most trade is arranged and carried out between individuals and companies, states have been key actors in policy, pursuing variations on the theme of two options:

- *Protectionism* has involved efforts to protect home markets and industries, using trade controls such as tariffs, subsidies and embargoes. Although governments might convince themselves that national interests are being protected in the process, barriers to trade can lead to international tensions and even trade wars.

- *Liberalism* holds that open markets are best for everyone, that competition is good for production and invention, and that we should work to reduce or remove trade barriers. The downside of this view, however, is that it can be a matter of the survival of the fittest, with rich states and corporations becoming richer and more powerful.

The prevailing view in most quarters since the nineteenth century has been that free trade is typically best, and hence much of the focus of global trade governance has been on the reduction or removal of trade barriers. This effort has involved the negotiation and signature of free trade agreements (FTAs) designed to bring down those barriers while controlling the movement of people and capital. More advanced goals, as we saw in Chapter 3, include the creation of single markets within which there is free movement of people, capital, goods and services, and even of monetary union and the creation of single currencies; both options, though, are far more ambitious and relatively rare.

Meanwhile, the desire to manage international trade is behind the work of the World Trade Organization, one of the behemoths among international organizations. Its members include all of the world's major economies (most of the WTO's non-members are small island states in the Caribbean and the Pacific) and the decisions reached under its auspices impact almost everyone. In turn, the WTO and the global trade regime is dominated by a small group of powerful actors, notably China, the European Union and the US, which among them account for about 40–45 per cent of the total volume of world trade; see Table 6.1. The balance of trading power is changing, though, as new competitors emerge. Shaffer (2021) notes the irony in how

Table 6.1: The world's major trading powers

Merchandise				Services			
Exports	%	Imports	%	Exports	%	Imports	%
European Union	29	European Union	28	European Union	23	European Union	21
China	15	USA	13	USA	17	USA	12
USA	8	China	12	UK	8	China	11
Japan	3	Japan	3	China	6	UK	6
South Korea	3	UK	3	India	4	Japan	4
Total share	58		59	Total share	58		54

Source: World Trade Organization (2023a). Measured in US dollars, figures rounded out.

the global trading system was largely designed by the US, and criticized by emerging states for unfairly restraining their economic development, but is now defended by emerging powers while the US becomes one of its major critics. Brazil, China and India – he notes – have led the way in those challenges by using the legal channels created by the WTO to make new demands on their own terms.

This is not the only change faced by that regime. Elsig et al. (2019) argue that it is also challenged by its reliance on trade deals that were mainly agreed in the 1990s, by ongoing changes in technology that are impacting jobs and production methods, by widespread public dissatisfaction with globalization and international trade agreements, and by questions about how to address the effects of climate change. It is also worth noting that this list was compiled before the Covid-19 pandemic, the economic and trade effects of which are still being worked out.

BUILDING A GLOBAL TRADE REGIME

Governments, corporations and economists have long debated the most effective approach to trade, asking how best to balance the benefits brought by exports with the potential harm caused by imports and competition. The earliest modern thoughts on these questions date back to the era of mercantilism in Europe of the seventeenth and eighteenth centuries, when arguments were made by Jean-Baptiste Colbert and others that the core goal of trade policy should be a balance of trade surplus in which the value of exports exceeded the costs of imports. Mercantilists supported government actions aimed at achieving this goal, overlooking the reality that not every country could have a surplus at the same time.

This was an anomaly understood by the Scottish economist Adam Smith, whose book *The Wealth of Nations* (published in 1776) argued that specialization was the key to economic growth: all states could specialize in what they did best, he suggested, exporting those goods or services in return for imports to cover their needs. Smith was also a critic of government intervention in trade, such as taxes on imports (designed to make them more expensive) and subsidies to domestic producers (designed to reduce the prices they charged for exports). Later, economists were to develop the idea of comparative advantage, suggesting that countries should focus on exporting those goods and services that they could offer more cheaply than other countries.

Removing or reducing barriers to trade is often easier said than done, however, because corporations or states may be looking to protect themselves from competition, and opinion is divided on how best to promote free trade. Some states have chosen to unilaterally lift restrictions without expecting reciprocal action from other states, while others prefer to take a bilateral or multilateral approach by reducing trade barriers in concert with other states. The more states, corporations or industries that are involved in this process, the more complex become the challenges.

Protectionism was long popular in many parts of the world, probably feeding into – and extending – the Great Depression of the 1930s. Irwin (2018) argues that the passage in the US 1930 of the Tariff Act (otherwise known as the Smoot–Hawley Act after its two primary Congressional authors) is often rightly blamed for the onset of the depression. Duties on numerous imports were increased, encouraging other countries to retaliate by increasing tariffs on US goods, feeding into such a dramatic decline in world trade that the ghosts of Reed Smoot and Willis C. Hawley continue to haunt anyone arguing for higher trade barriers even today. The proliferation of restrictions helped cause the volume of world trade to fall by 25 per cent between 1929 and 1932 (Eichengreen and Irwin, 2010).

Developments since 1945

The most active era of free trade promotion has come since 1945, at least initially as part of the Bretton Woods system. The two major institutional products of that system were – as we saw in Chapter 5 – the International Monetary Fund and the World Bank. A third new IGO would have been an International Trade Organization (ITO) that would have functioned as the trade agency of the new United Nations (UN). However, the US was opposed to the restrictions that would have been imposed by the ITO, so governments instead opted for the General Agreement on Tariffs and Trade (GATT). A treaty rather than an organization, GATT was agreed in 1947 as a process through which participating states could negotiate the reduction of barriers to trade. Although only nine countries joined immediately, membership had expanded to 37 by the end of 1960 and to 76 by the end of 1970.

Prompted by questions arising out of the terms of GATT, several European countries met during the late 1940s to discuss rules on customs arrangements, and in 1950 they signed the Convention Establishing the Customs Cooperation Council (CCC). The CCC was headquartered in Brussels, and its job was to develop new agreements on customs rules, as well as rules on the classification of commodities, the collection of customs revenue, the security of supply chains, and controls over cross-border transfers of illegal drugs and weapons. In 1994 it was decided to change its name to the World Customs Organization (WCO), although its tasks remain the same.

GATT had been charged with overseeing rounds of international negotiations aimed at reducing barriers to trade. These rounds were usually named after the country or city in which they began, producing the Geneva round (1956), the Tokyo round (1973–79), the Uruguay round (1986–93), and – in honour of the assassinated US president – the Kennedy round (1962–67). These negotiations resulted in staged reductions in tariffs, focused at first on industrial goods and later adding services. The rounds varied in length from as little as five months to as long as several years, and each resulted in a new set of trade agreements. The GATT era also saw numerous changes in the global trading landscape, greatly complicating the demands made on the trade regime:

- The US was already a major trading power before World War II, but its economy grew rapidly after the war, and it was willing to invest heavily in the reconstruction of Western Europe and Japan, ultimately creating new competition for itself.

- Many new countries entered the trading system with decolonization in the 1950s and 1960s. At first, they often took the view that they needed to protect their economies from competition from the older and more powerful industrialized powers, but they made little headway, and most eventually followed the lead of more open economies such as South Korea (Bhagwati et al., 2016).

- Western Europe began the process of regional integration that would lead eventually to the European Union, launching the model of new regional IOs that would eventually spread to much of the rest of the world, as we saw in Chapter 3.

- China – after years of instability and isolation – began to modernize its economy in the 1970s, investing in industry, creating special export zones, attracting foreign investment and making big investments in other parts of world.

- The number of multinational enterprises grew rapidly, with many of them developing a global reach, weaker association with individual countries, and a critical role in shaping trade decisions and patterns of trade.

- The ways in which goods and services were made, transported and sold were transformed, with increased automation and the capacity to move goods more quickly and in larger quantities. The use of containers began to take hold in the 1950s, and more than 90 per cent of packaged cargo is now moved in containers. Delivery options have also broadened, giving more business to couriers such as FedEx and DHL, while bricks-and-mortar stores are being steadily replaced by online shopping, creating a global digital mall.

- Along the way, the volume of global trade increased by a factor of 3,800 per cent between 1950 and 2020; see Figure 6.1.

- At the same time, many of the financial and economic imbalances found within states were transmitted globally; see *IOs in Theory 6*.

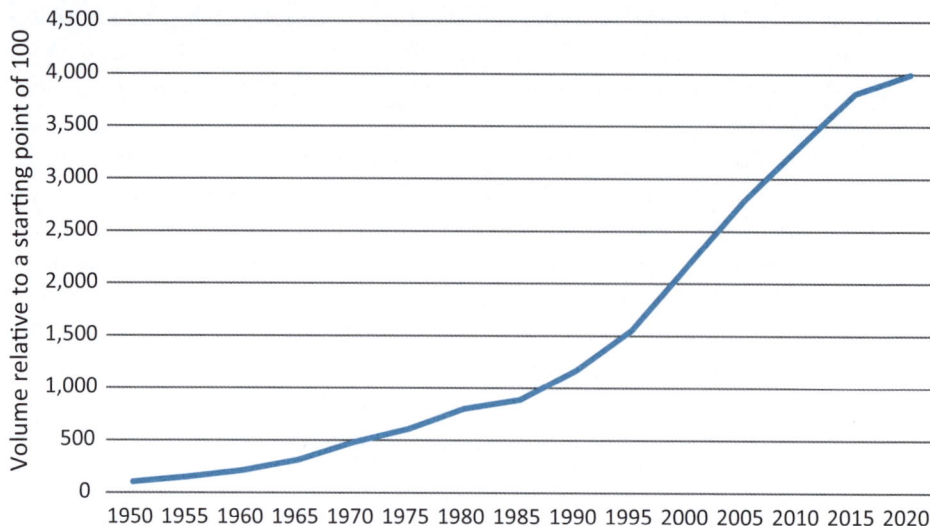

Figure 6.1: The growth of global trade.
Source: Based on data in World Trade Organization (2023a). Based on volume for 1950 being expressed as 100.

Another change came with the addition to the global trading regime of an interest in protecting intellectual property: intangible inventions and creations of the human mind, such as designs, copyrights, trademarks and patents. Treaties on the protection of patents, literary works and trademarks date back to the nineteenth century, but it was not until the 1960s, and the rise of the information economy, that a more structured approach began to be taken to address the threats posed to intellectual property. With a new emphasis on the production and management of information, and the increased ability of buyers of information and designs to replicate and sell such property, new depth of action was needed. In 1967 the World Intellectual Property Organization (WIPO) was created, becoming a specialized agency of the UN in 1974. Later, trade in services achieved a new prominence with the entering into force in 1995 of a new General Agreement on Trade in Services.

Although GATT had helped bring barriers to trade down to historic lows, the sheer volume and complexity of international trade had pushed the process far beyond the capacity of its original design. When a new round of trade negotiations began in Uruguay in 1986, the conversation included the need for a new and updated arrangement, which led to the creation of the World Trade Organization (WTO). This would not only oversee the GATT process (with its early emphasis on trade in goods), but would also oversee agreements on trade in services, intellectual property rights and trade-related investment, and would also provide a forum in which trade disputes could be negotiated and settled. The existing 75 members of GATT, along with what was then the European Community, became founding members of the WTO on 1 January 1995, with the signature of the Marrakesh Agreement.

Although the Uruguay around was successfully concluded in 1994, the first round negotiated under the auspices of the new WTO was also the first to fail. Launched

IOs IN THEORY 6

MARXISM

Marxism describes a set of economic, political and social theories deriving from the work of the German philosopher Karl Marx (1818–83) and his collaborator Friedrich Engels (1820–95). To summarize what Marx argued in a few sentences is not easy, but at the core of his ideas was the principle that class conflict is behind the development of human societies, and that – under capitalism – this conflict manifests itself in tensions between the working class (the proletariat) and the ruling class that controls the means of production (the bourgeoisie). Marxism prioritizes historical explanations for inequalities, the dominant role of economic influences in explaining political relationships, and the manner in which capitalism has shaped production. Marx predicted that class tensions would lead to the destruction of capitalism and its replacement by a new classless communist society.

As applied to the international system and to the manner in which global governance works, Marxist theory suggests that international organizations – particularly the World Trade Organization, the IMF and the World Bank – reflect and promote the interests of global capitalism: the hierarchical structure of the system gives some states, groups and interests an advantage over others, and the class struggle that was – in the view of Marx – so much a feature of revolutions within states has been expanded to the global level. Developments of the core ideas of Marx are broadly known as neo-Marxism, and among these are the ideas of Antonio Gramsci, former leader of the Italian Communist Party. Gramsci focused on the idea of hegemony: the dominant class has power over the subordinate class, using coercion and consent to convince the proletariat that they benefit from the system.

In turn, neo-Gramscian ideas were developed (notably by Cox (1983)) to argue that this hegemonic dynamic could be found at a global level. An alliance of social classes in different countries has used its advantages and the work of international organizations (created by hegemonic states) to promote universal norms or world values in order to support its hegemony, to co-opt the global proletariat and to impose a world order that suits its interests. In other words, the US and its major Western allies have used international organizations to project their hegemony internationally.

in Doha, the capital of Qatar, in November 2001, it broke down seven years later following a disagreement between the US and the EU over agricultural subsidies, and disagreements between the North and the South over agricultural trade, industrial tariffs and non-tariff barriers to trade. The North–South disagreements were reflective of the rising negotiating influence of the Global South. Efforts to revive Doha failed, and it had been all but abandoned by the end of 2015, casting a pall over the future of the global trading system. Within a matter of years, the WTO was being described by many as an organization in crisis, and as in urgent need of reform and modernization (see Van den Bossche and Prévost, 2021, for example).

Many of the problems can be ascribed to the changing context of international trade: there has been a reaction to many of the old assumptions about the international trading system, and – despite the lessons that should have been learned from the 1930s – there has been a rise both of economic nationalism and of protectionism. For Van den Bossche and Zdouc (2022), there are three main explanations for this:

– Populist political leaders and parties have built a following based on the fears and frustrations of those who have felt most threatened by globalization, and worry about job security, supporting the need for protection from the competition posed by imports.

– The confrontation between the US and China has been deepening, as the former strives to protect its economic position and to address the competition from China. The effects have spilled over into US and Chinese trade relations with other countries.

– There have been growing concerns about the environmental, social and economic sustainability of globalization, and about the expansion of trade.

While the world trade map is always changing, the most notable and important trend today is the growing share of emerging economies, particularly the fastest growing economies of Asia and Latin America: as their share of exports and imports grows, so the shares of the wealthiest states decline, and the balance of power within the WTO changes. This is already having – and will continue to have – a critical impact on global trade governance.

International trade law

When it comes to grasping international trade law, the main point to bear in mind is that there are relatively few global agreements, and that those few tend to be highly technical; examples include the conventions on coding systems and customs procedures monitored by the World Customs Organization. At the same time, there are numerous more focused trade agreements connecting almost every part of the world. These are either bilateral (involving two states), regional (involving three or more states in a contained region) or – to use WTO terminology – plurilateral (bringing together a limited number of states with a focused interest). In the particular case of the WTO, a multilateral agreement would be one to which all WTO members are a party, while a plurilateral agreement would be one in which WTO members would have the choice on whether or not to sign on a voluntary basis. Examples of the latter include the 1980 Agreement on Trade in Civil Aircraft (with 33 signatories) that eliminates import duties on civilian aircraft (along with their parts and engines), and the 2011 treaty setting up a free trade agreement among members of the Commonwealth of Independent States (led by Russia).

According to data from the World Trade Organization (2023b), there were just over 350 regional trade agreements in force in January 2022 (see Table 6.2 for some

Table 6.2: Regional trade agreements: Examples

Date in force	Name	% share of global GDP	Membership
2022	Regional Comprehensive Economic Partnership (RCEP)	30.5	15 Asian and Australasian states
2020	United States Mexico Canada Agreement (USMCA)	28	Canada, Mexico and USA
1958	European Union (EU)	19	27 European states
2019	African Continental Free Trade Area (ACFTA)	2.9	43 African states
1991	Southern Common Market (Mercosur)	2.4	Argentina, Brazil, Paraguay and Uruguay
1960	European Free Trade Association (EFTA)	1.4	Iceland, Liechtenstein, Norway and Switzerland

examples), with another 442 reported as no longer active. The numbers have been growing most actively since the early 1990s (when there were only about 50–60 in force). The biggest economies – including Australia, Canada, China, Europe, India, Japan, New Zealand and South Korea – are members of the greatest number of such agreements, while African and Middle Eastern states are members of the fewest. Measured by share of global gross domestic product (GDP), the biggest agreement in the world is also one of the newest: the 15-member Regional Comprehensive Economic Partnership (RCEP) that came into effect in 2022, involving Australia, China, Japan, New Zealand, South Korea and the ten member states of ASEAN (see Chapter 3). It would have been even bigger had India not withdrawn over concerns about competition from China.

As far as international law and the WTO are concerned, the rulebook agreed under the terms of membership of the WTO now runs to more than 30,000 pages and includes multiple separate treaties and agreements. The main treaty is the Agreement Establishing the WTO, signed in Marrakech, Morocco, on 15 April 1994, which outlines the role, structure and powers of the WTO. Subsequent agreements were signed to deal with the three broad areas of trade covered by the WTO (goods, services and intellectual property), to outline the dispute settlement process and to cover reviews of national trade policies by WTO member states. Rulings by the WTO, meanwhile, have generated an extensive body of trade law designed – at least in theory – to prevent restrictive trade measures, to provide consistency, to encourage equity and to protect consumers, workers and the environment (see Van den Bossche and Prévost, 2021).

THE WORLD TRADE ORGANIZATION

At a conference in Geneva in mid-2022, ministers from the member states of the World Trade Organization (WTO) met for the first time in five years against a background of concerns about the health of the organization. It had been struggling in the wake of the hostility of the Trump administration to its work, a shortage of judges on its appeals court and questions over how it should respond to climate change. As if this was not all challenging enough, nearly 30 years had passed since the WTO had successfully concluded its last round of negotiations aimed at loosening barriers to trade.

The ministers at the Geneva meeting were able to reach agreement on several proposals, including protection of the world's rapidly declining fish stocks, opening up the market for generic Covid-19 vaccines and addressing food insecurity problems in the wake of the Russian invasion of Ukraine. The fact that they were able to reach any agreements at all was hailed as a milestone and, despite the modesty of the agreements, the meeting was generally considered to be a success (Wagner, 2022). Smiles and congratulatory hugs accompanied the closing of the meeting, and delegates returned to their home states with a sense that the organization had recovered some of its lost momentum. The concerns, though, have not all gone away.

The overall goal of the WTO is to help make trade as free and as equitable as possible, and to protect trade rules. It does this by being a forum for negotiations among its members on new trade rules, monitoring national trade policies and the application of trade agreements, and conducting research and maintaining data on trade. It also operates a dispute resolution mechanism by which members engaged in a trade dispute can make their cases before the WTO, which then issues a judgement (see Palmeter et al., 2022).

These all sound well and good in theory, but the goals face multiple practical challenges. The monitoring of national trade policies, for example, is only as good as the quality of reporting from member states, many of which fail to comply with the reporting requirements built into WTO agreements (Van den Bossche and Prévost, 2021). Also, the WTO has no powers of enforcement, the understanding being that membership comes with an obligation to follow the organization's rules. Trade is ultimately about quid pro quo, and governments usually want to avoid harmful, costly and time-consuming trade disputes or wars. A country that failed to honour WTO rules could soon find itself and its companies suffering from the imposition of tariffs on its exports and limitations on its companies doing business abroad. At the same time, though, most countries want to avoid trade wars, so there is a limit to how far they will take their resistance. Conversely, there is no procedure for suspending or expelling members, and even if a country was being considered for expulsion, it would be unlikely to happen given that the WTO members make decisions on the basis of a consensus.

The structure of the WTO is as follows:

– *Secretariat and executive head.* From its headquarters in Geneva, the WTO is headed by a Director General (DG) who is appointed by the Ministerial Conference of the WTO for a maximum of two four-year terms. Since WTO decisions are made by the member states, the director general has fewer powers than most executives of IOs, playing a mainly managerial role. Even so, the selection process for the job can be lengthy and contentious, and involves the whittling down of a list of proposed candidates to the person attracting the consensus support of WTO members. Past DGs have come from Ireland, Italy, New Zealand, Thailand, France and Brazil. In 2021, Ngozi Okonjo-Iweala – the former Nigerian Minister of Finance – became the first woman and the first African appointed to the position. The director general is supported by a small secretariat, charged with providing technical and other support to the other WTO members, to monitor trends in world trade, and to gather and provide information on trade.

- *Assembly.* The Ministerial Conference consists of representatives from all WTO member states, is the highest authority of the WTO, and meets for just a few days every two years. It has the power to make decisions on all WTO business, including the interpretation and amendment of agreements, giving waivers to member states, making decisions on new applications for membership, and appointing the Director General. With 164 members, the WTO is a multilateral organization rather than a universal organization in the style of the UN. Most of its non-members are in the Middle East and North Africa, and include Algeria, Iran, Iraq and Sudan, with Belarus and North Korea further afield.

- *Executive functions.* The WTO is unusual in the sense that it does not have a permanent executive body with a limited number of members to take care of business between meetings of the larger bodies. It has a General Council that consists of all WTO members, and that meets every two months (and also functions as both the Dispute Settlement Body and the Trade Policy Review Board). Otherwise, all WTO bodies consist of the entire membership of the organization, a situation that makes negotiations difficult, and encourages informal meetings among the most important WTO members, or those with a specific interest in the problem being discussed (Van den Bossche and Prévost, 2021).

- *Courts and tribunals.* The Dispute Settlement Body (DSB) makes decisions on trade disputes based on reports generated by small panels of experts chosen by the DSB in consultation with the states involved in a dispute. Appeals can be submitted to a permanent Appellate Body, whose seven members are appointed for four-year terms. Meanwhile, the Trade Policy Review Board meets to review the trade policies of member states when questions are raised about them.

- *Other elements.* The WTO also has numerous permanent and ad hoc bodies that meet to discuss and decide more focused trade questions, such as regional trade agreements, the environmental effects of trade and subsidies.

- *Budget.* Because most of its expenses are related to the operation of its secretariat, the budget of the WTO is fairly small: about $220 million in 2022. Contributions from members are based on a formula driven by shares of international trade, leaving the US and China as the biggest contributors in recent years, followed by Germany, Japan, France and the UK; see Figure 6.2.

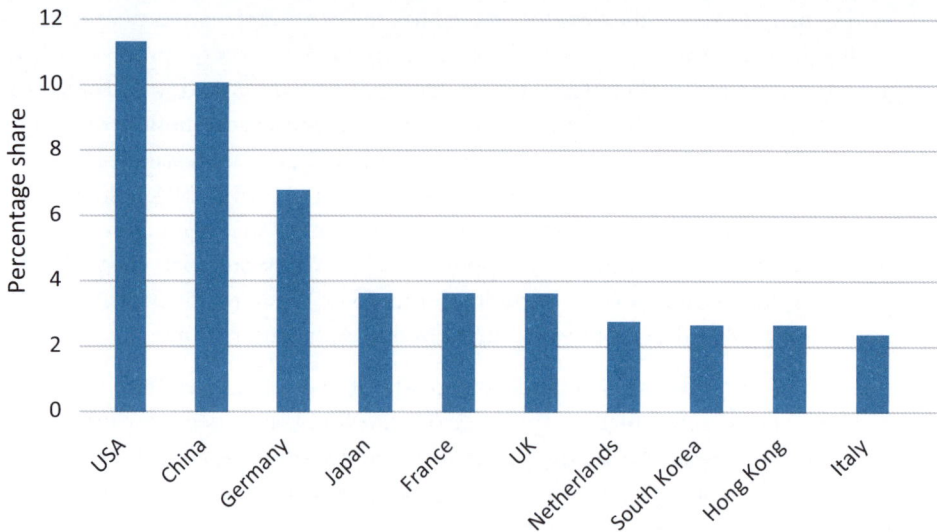

Figure 6.2: The ten biggest contributors to the WTO budget.
Source: Based on data in World Trade Organization (2023a).

Countries can become members of the WTO in two ways. First, the members of GATT had the option of becoming founding members of the WTO simply by accepting the terms of the WTO Agreement. The second option, for post-GATT members, has been to apply for membership and then negotiate terms, including acceptance of the WTO Agreement, and taking steps to ensure that all its national laws and regulations conform with WTO obligations. The process can be less or more difficult depending on how applicants and existing members receive one another. Although it only took two years for Kyrgyzstan to be accepted in 1998, for example, negotiations with China took 15 years and those with Russia took 18 years. Both were long kept out because of a lack of openness in their economies, with China eventually joining in 2001, and Russia – several years after achieving the required recognition as a market economy from the EU and the US – in 2012.

One of the WTO's most important responsibilities is to act as a forum in which trade disputes can be heard, argued and hopefully resolved. While GATT included a weak dispute settlement procedure, the WTO has a stronger and binding system that has been used frequently: a total of 606 disputes were brought to the WTO between 1995 and 2021 (World Trade Organization, 2023a). Cases can only be brought by members (and not by NGOs or corporations), and most disputes have been resolved and have cleared the way for more open trade or for a tighter definition of rights and responsibilities. Others, though, have been more troublesome and have taken longer to resolve; see *IOs in Action 6*. Perhaps not surprisingly, the bigger trading powers have been the most active in either lodging complaints or being the target of complaints, although China has been less active than its size might suggest and has brought many fewer complaints than have been brought against it.

The dispute resolution system has come under new pressure in recent years (Van den Bossche, 2021) thanks to a combination of the increased workload involved,

IOs IN ACTION 6

THE WORLD TRADE ORGANIZATION AND CIVILIAN AIRCRAFT

The world's biggest trade dispute by value has been one between the US and the European Union over subsidies to their respective major civilian aircraft manufacturers: Boeing and Airbus. The dispute dates back to 2004, and to charges by Boeing that Airbus (which was jointly owned at the time by Germany, France, Spain and BAE Systems of the UK) benefitted from government subsidies to develop new aircraft models. Airbus countered that Boeing benefitted from tax breaks and US government defence contracts. The stakes were huge, because we live under a virtual global duopoly in which most of the world's largest civilian aircraft are made by these two corporations, which between them have about a 90 per cent market share. The balance of mainly smaller aircraft are made by Embraer of Brazil (which Boeing tried to acquire in 2018) and Bombardier of Canada (in which Airbus has a majority stake).

In an on-going series of tit-for-tat cases and accusations that continued for 17 years until a truce was finally declared in 2021, the WTO ruled that both sides had unfairly subsidized their respective aircraft manufacturers: the European Union had supported Airbus with subsidized loans, for example, while the US government had supported Boeing with generous contracts and tax breaks. In 2019, the WTO ruled that the US could impose tariffs on imports from the EU worth $7.5 billion, and in 2020 it ruled that the EU could impose tariffs worth $4 billion on US goods.

In March 2021, both sides agreed to a four-month suspension of their tariffs on each other, later extending the suspension to a period of five years. The key concern for both sides was they would be hurting each other instead of cooperating in the face of the growing threat of competition from China and its state-owned Commercial Aircraft Corporation (Comac). While this had only a small market share in 2022, and made most of its sales domestically, it has been developing a new plane – the C919 – that is a direct rival to the best-selling Airbus A320 Neo and the Boeing 737 Max. Comac has also been working to develop a partnership with the United Aircraft Corporation of Russia on a larger, wide-body passenger aircraft.

the growing size and complexity of trade disputes, and the problems faced by the WTO General Council in challenging decisions by the Appellate Body. Its problems worsened with accusations by the Trump administration in the US that judges on the body were engaged in judicial activism and that the WTO was not sufficiently demanding of China. Trump blocked appointments to the body, which by December 2019 had just one member instead of seven. The Biden administration moved only slowly to respond, reflecting a bipartisan consensus in the US about the slowness of the Appellate Body to act on China for its unfair trading practices and about overreach on the part of some of the body's members.

Opinion more broadly on the work and the impact of the WTO has been divided, with criticism from both the left and the right of the political spectrum. Its supporters credit it with promoting global economic growth and raising living standards by making trade easier and more open, with reducing the barriers to protection, and with promoting healthy competition. Meanwhile, Reinsch (2018) clusters the source of its challenges into four types:

- The criticisms of those on the political right who charge the WTO – like IOs more generally – with reducing the sovereignty of its members by limiting their freedom of action.

- The criticisms of those on the political left who believe that the WTO encourages a 'race to the bottom' by weakening worker safety and environmental standards as jobs are moved from wealthier countries to poorer countries with less stringent worker rights and environmental quality.

- The damage done by countries such as India, China and the US that pay lip service to WTO principles while blocking progress on new agreements or sometimes even ignoring WTO rules.

- The division between (a) the rich countries that created and sustained both GATT and the WTO, but where political support for WTO rules is declining, and (b) the emerging economies that have benefitted from the world trade system but are resistant to providing the sustenance it now needs.

Against a background of these problems, the changing balance of global trade and the failure of the Doha round, the WTO undoubtedly faces stormy weather ahead.

OTHER TRADE IGOs

Few international organizations play such a prominent role within in a global regime as the World Trade Organization. Despite its problems, it is the body to which states turn for reference on the rules of trade, or – if needed – to address and hopefully resolve conflicts. Its prominence, though, should not distract us from the work of other IOs with an interest in more focused aspects of trade.

The World Customs Organization

The oldest trade IGO is the World Customs Organization (WCO), established in 1952 as the Customs Cooperation Council, and adopting its current name in 1994. Headquartered in Brussels, the WCO is an intergovernmental body that – according to its web site – 'develops international standards, fosters cooperation, and builds capacity to facilitate legitimate trade, to secure a fair revenue collection and to protect society'. It helps national customs administrations coordinate their efforts to block imports of illegal drugs and hazardous substances, to protect national products from unfair competition and fraud, and to collect the duties and taxes that – for many poorer countries – are a significant part of national income (Allende, 2022).

The WCO has 184 members (more than the WTO), representing about 98 per cent of world trade and including the entire membership of the UN except for North Korea and several Caribbean and Pacific island states. It is headed by a Secretary General appointed for five-year terms by the membership, supported by a

Secretariat of about 150 staff. The major decision-making body of the WCO is the Council, which brings the membership together at annual meetings to make decisions on policy. The WCO also administers a large body of treaties on different aspects of customs work, including a 1988 treaty designed to build a harmonized system of descriptions and codes for traded commodities. More than 5,000 commodity groups have been identified, and each has been given a six-digit code designed to make it easier for customs administrations to identify the nature of imported goods, and to collect import duties and taxes. Recent questions addressed by the WCO include whether high-fat cream cheese is cheese or dairy spread, whether smart watches are communication devices or wristwatches, and where to draw the line between motor vehicles designed to carry passengers and those designed to carry goods (World Customs Organization, 2023).

The World Intellectual Property Organization

Another IGO with a focus on trade is the World Intellectual Property Organization (WIPO), founded in 1970 in response to concerns about the need to protect inventions and creations of the mind, including works of art, computer programs, designs, copyrights, trademarks and patents (and books like this one). Although relatively new, its origins date back to three treaties in Paris (1883), Berne (1886) and Madrid (1891) on the protection – respectively – of industrial property, literary and artistic works, and trademark registration. The United International Bureaux for the Protection of Intellectual Property was founded in Switzerland in 1893, and was eventually replaced by WIPO, which became part of the UN in 1974, with the following structural elements:

- *Secretariat and executive head.* From its headquarters in Geneva, WIPO is headed by a Director General working with a Coordination Committee.

- *Assembly.* All members of the UN are also members of WIPO, which is governed by a General Assembly that consists of representatives from all member states (each with one vote) and that meets biennially to oversee the work of the organization while also making decisions on the budget.

- *Other functions.* Detailed functions are carried out by multiple specialist committees, assemblies and working groups that are coordinated by the secretariat. The committees use consensus to make decisions and accredited NGOs (most of them trade organizations) can sit in as observers at meetings. WIPO also runs an Arbitration and Mediation Centre that can be used by parties engaged in disputes over patents or trademarks.

- *Budget.* WIPO is a self-funding IGO, its revenues coming from the fees it charges to help applicants looking for patent protection for their inventions, and looking to register trademarks and industrial designs.

China has been a particular focus of international concern in recent years, with charges by the US and the EU about its lack of protection of intellectual property rights, and accusations that it has failed to live up to international agreements (while, ironically, making active use of the international patent application system; see Chapter 12). There were reports in 2020 (Fung and Lam, 2020) that it was campaigning to take over leadership of WIPO, although it ultimately failed when a decision was made to appoint Daren Tang from Singapore as the new Director General. Nonetheless, the campaign was seen as an indication that China was working to pursue its interests within multilateral bodies that had traditionally been dominated by the West. At the time, Chinese nationals headed four of the 15 specialized agencies of the UN: the International Civil Aviation Organization, the International Telecommunication Union, the Food and Agriculture Organization, and the UN Industrial Development Organization.

The Organization for Economic Cooperation and Development

Moving to a different part of the trade landscape, the Organization for Economic Cooperation and Development (OECD) is not solely a trade organization, but instead acts as a forum within which its 38 member states work to encourage free trade, democracy and open markets. Headquartered in Paris, its founding convention lists its aims as helping to achieve sustainable economic growth and employment, to maintain financial stability and to contribute to economic expansion. It also charges the organization with contributing 'to the expansion of world trade on a multilateral, non-discriminatory basis in accordance with international obligations'. The latter task was always dominated by GATT and then by the WTO, but there is no question that the OECD has helped promote the liberalization of trade and finance among its member states.

Described as elusive, ethereal and often neglected (Woodward, 2009), and as one of the least understood of all international organizations (Schmelzer and Leimgruber, 2017), the OECD does not draw news headlines, political attention or scholarly study as much as it deserves given how much ground it covers. It has something of a reputation as an exclusive club for rich countries, but its membership and its interests have expanded, and it has long been a primary source of data and analysis relating to its members, addressing issues as diverse as education, health care, employment, the environment, investment and migration.

Like many other IOs, the OECD traces its origins back to a more modest body set up to address European issues: the Organization for European Economic Cooperation (OEEC) was founded in 1948 to help administer the Marshall Plan, the post-war US programme to help rebuild Western Europe. The members of the OEEC learned to work with one another and to identify solutions to shared problems, an idea that was expanded upon when it was decided in 1961 to reform the OEEC as the OECD. Membership was opened up to a wider array of states, beginning with Canada and the US, and later expanding to include Japan, Australia, Mexico, Chile, Israel and most of Eastern Europe. Accession talks were opened with Russia in 2007 and stopped in 2014 following Russia's invasion of Crimea. Ukraine applied for membership in 2022, and Argentina and Brazil are prospective members.

The OECD's main decision-making body is its Council, consisting of ambassadors from the member states, and chaired by the Secretary General. The latter is appointed for renewable five-year terms by the Council, and heads a secretariat of about 3,300 people, consisting of a community of economists, lawyers, scientists, political analysts and statisticians. There have only been six secretaries general to date, the first three being from Europe (Denmark, the Netherlands and France) and the last three being from Canada, Mexico and Australia. Fitting with the slightly mysterious nature of the OECD, holders of the post do not become public figures of the same stature as, for example, some of the leaders of the World Bank or the European Union. The work of the OECD is spread among more than 300 specialist committees and working groups, covering the same policy issues as national government ministries (and, to different degrees, overlapping with almost every other regime discussed in this book except security). Recent declarations by the OECD have included an emphasis on the importance of open trade, a level global playing field and sustainable economic development.

The Organization of Petroleum Exporting Countries

A trade IGO of a different kind – focusing on a single export commodity – is the Organization of Petroleum Exporting Countries (OPEC). Its major aim, according to Article 2 of its governing statute, is 'the coordination and unification of the petroleum policies of Member Countries and the determination of the best means for safeguarding their interests, individually and collectively. The Organization shall devise ways and means of ensuring the stabilization of prices in international oil markets with a view to eliminating harmful and unnecessary fluctuations' (Organization of Petroleum Exporting Countries, 2023). What this has meant, in practice, is that it has worked to control the exports of oil from its member states in order to maintain world prices, earning its members greater profits at the expense of oil-importing countries. Whether or not this makes OPEC a cartel (the typical emphasis of which is market control) is a matter of debate.

OPEC was founded in Baghdad in 1960 by five countries (Iran, Iraq, Kuwait, Saudi Arabia and Venezuela), and has been headquartered since 1965 in Vienna, even though Austria is not a member. The five founders have been joined by eight other member states – Algeria, Angola, Congo, Equatorial Guinea, Gabon, Libya, Nigeria and United Arab Emirates. Along the way, three others – Ecuador, Indonesia and Qatar – have joined and then left. Any country can join OPEC provided that it is a substantial net exporter of crude oil, has similar interests to those of existing members and is accepted by a three-fourths majority of existing members, including all five founding members. In 2016, a new group called OPEC+ was formed in order to exert more control of the global oil market, bringing ten new countries into the picture, including Mexico and Russia (see Map 6.1). OPEC+ states voluntarily adapt policies to those of OPEC and can attend its meetings as non-voting observers.

The five founding states were major producers of oil and yet they did not control that oil; for at least 20 years before its formation, the global oil industry was

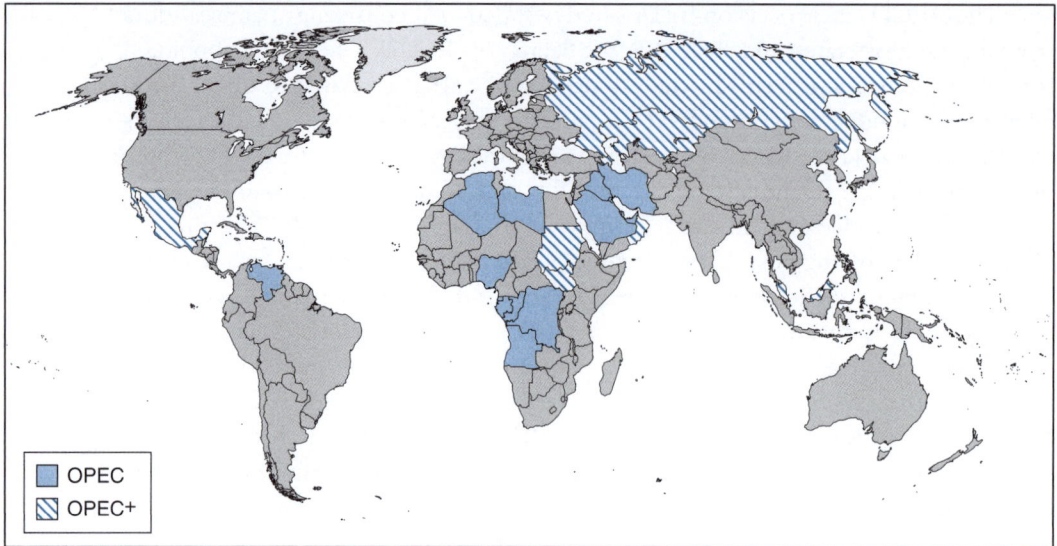

Map 6.1: Organization of Petroleum Exporting Countries.

dominated by the American and European oil companies known collectively as the 'Seven Sisters'. The effect of the work of OPEC – the first international organization formed in the Global South – was to transfer more influence over oil to the major producing countries. In the view of Garavini (2019), this gave OPEC a role that went far beyond the realm of oil politics, helping petrostates such as Iran, Nigeria, Saudi Arabia and Venezuela to become key regional actors. It also helped them to cooperate despite their wide political differences, which in the cases of Iran, Iraq and Kuwait involved going to war with one another. Despite this, OPEC has never reached the same heights of global influence as it achieved in 1973 with its role in setting off a worldwide energy crisis by engineering a quadrupling in the price of oil. Among other effects, the crisis sparked the creation in 1974 of the International Energy Agency to help improve the quality of data and advice on global energy; see Chapter 12.

Colgan (2021) describes the 1973 energy crisis as the 'largest peaceful transfer of wealth across borders in all of human history', noting how OPEC helped turn the tables on the Seven Sisters and their home states. Fifty years later, he argues, oil and energy continue to lie at the heart of international relations, and the story of OPEC still does not fit the standard template of how world politics works: that the most powerful countries set up and sustains the rules of the international order after winning a major war. The example of OPEC, he continues, suggests that the international order is not a single order, but that it operates in parts and often changes during peacetime. Perhaps, he concludes, this example offers lessons as we try to better understand global governance as it faces an array of new challenges, ranging from the deepening rivalry between the US and China to climate change and nuclear proliferation.

OPEC currently faces its own challenges as a growing number of countries and industries work to wean themselves off oil. There are about 100 countries that produce crude oil, with the current members of OPEC accounting for about 44 per cent of the total and for about 82 per cent of the world's proven oil reserves (United States Energy Information Administration, 2023). However, the world's biggest oil producer (the US, with a 20 per cent share), along with other major producers Canada, Brazil and Norway are not members of OPEC. Even though global oil consumption remains high, the problems caused by energy disruptions in the wake of the 2022 Russian invasion of Ukraine have encouraged new efforts to move to renewable sources of energy, which does not augur well for oil producers or for OPEC.

NON-STATE TRADE ACTORS

This chapter opened with the story of a small business in northern England that had identified a local need and was a modest participant in the complex world of international trade. Despite the achievements of millions of similar small businesses all over the world, the most important non-state actors in the field of trade are the much bigger multinational enterprises, their critical role arising simply from the fact that most trade takes place between individuals or companies, and not between states. For Foley et al. (2021), the multinationals are 'the global goliaths of modern times … , collectively responsible for large portions of world production, employment, investment, international trade, research, and innovation'. As we saw in Chapter 1, they take the lead in the development of new technology, in decisions about investment and the creation of jobs, and in shaping trade flows and supply chains. They also play a critical role in shaping national trade policies (being likely to support and lobby for trade liberalization), in driving economic growth and in transmitting economic shocks across borders. To a large extent they have taken the initiative on trade out of the hands of governments, emphasizing once again the declining reach of states.

Just as the location of the biggest intergovernmental organizations tells us much about the balance of political power in the world, the location of the biggest MNEs tells us much about the changing balance of economic and financial power in the world. Where most were once headquartered in Europe and North America, there has been a rise in the number of MNEs based in the Global South, notably in China. In 2005, just 18 of the world's 500 biggest corporations listed in the *Fortune* Global 500 were Chinese. By 2022, the Chinese share had grown to 145. Between 2001 and 2022, meanwhile, the number of North American companies on the list fell from 215 to 136; see Table 6.3 for examples.

An INGO that promotes the interests of multinationals – as well as, for some, representing and upholding the liberal world order – is the World Economic Forum. Founded in Switzerland in 1971 as the European Management Forum, and changing to its current name in 1987, it has a membership of nearly 1,000 corporations. They each pay substantial membership fees, and most take part in the invitation-only annual meeting held in the Swiss resort town of Davos. The meeting is often the site of key announcements on the direction in which Forum members see the global economy heading, and it often attracts political leaders, as when Xi Jinping in 2017 became the first Chinese president to attend the meeting. For Garsten and Sörbom (2018), the forum wields a 'discreet power' that allows it – without a formal mandate – to broker

Table 6.3: The ten biggest multinationals

Rank	Name	Country	Industry	Revenue (billion US dollars)
1	Walmart	USA	Retail	573
2	Amazon	USA	Internet services and retail	470
3	State Grid	China	Energy	461
4	China National Petroleum	China	Petroleum	412
5	Sinopec Group	China	Petroleum	401
6	Saudi Aramco	Saudi Arabia	Energy	400
7	Apple	USA	Technology	366
8	Volkswagen	Germany	Vehicles	296
9	China State Construction Engineering	China	Construction and engineering	294
10	CVS Health	USA	Health care	292

Source: Fortune (2023).

ideas and to extend its reach through its membership and associated individuals. While this opens up novel ways of dealing with urgent problems, they conclude, it also challenges core democratic values.

Multinationals also have an important impact on international relations through the opposition they have sparked towards the nature of the international trade order, which is seen by many of its critics to be unbalanced and exploitative. Take, for example, the phenomenon of dumping, which involves the export of polluting industries or activities to poorer countries with weaker (or less stringently enforced) environmental regulations and cheaper labour. This allows those industries to manufacture goods more cheaply for export back to their home markets. Consider, more specifically, the problem of toxic colonialism, meaning the export from the North to the South of materials (including waste) that are illegal or undesirable in their source countries. One of the effects of such exploitation has been to feed into anti-globalization social movements and to spark the foundation of new INGOs such as the World Social Forum. Playing on the name of the World Economic Forum, it was founded in Brazil in 2001 and has since held annual meetings of NGOs, social groups, and individuals with the common theme of opposition to globalization.

One recent development in international trade has been the rise of digital MNEs, or those that are active mainly on the internet. They include platforms such

SPOTLIGHT 6

FAIR TRADE VERSUS FREE TRADE

When we think about trade, we think mainly about the biggest trading powers, the expanding reach of multinationals, and the kinds of goods and services that are most often exported and imported. The disruptions caused by Covid-19 taught many of us about the nature of supply chains, and emphasized once again how supply and demand are intimately linked. As we buy more from other countries, we might have become more aware not only of those supply chains, but also of the inequalities built into the global trading system, benefitting consumers and corporations at the expense of workers and the producers of raw materials.

Since at least the 1960s, and attracting more attention since the 1990s, there have been more efforts to inform consumers about the maldistribution of profits, and to encourage new approaches to fair trade: the idea that producers in poorer countries should earn a bigger share of the profits from the sale of their commodities, such as coffee, chocolate, cocoa, cotton and fruit. The logic behind this is that fair trade will help offset some of the inequalities created by globalization, and that giving producers a fairer price, or a bigger share of the profits, is the most effective way of helping poorer states to develop.

In 1989, the International Federation of Fair Trade (now the World Fair Trade Organization, or WFTO) was founded with the goal of giving fair trade more consistency. Headquartered in the city of Culemborg (near Utrecht) in the Netherlands, it is an INGO with more than 400 organizations as members. Their business models are verified by the WFTO, at which point they are allowed to use the WFTO product logo in their operations, confirming their commitment to the principles of fair trade. A related INGO is Fairtrade International (FI), founded in 1997 and based in Bonn, Germany, which manages a similar certification scheme. With national organizations in nearly 20 countries, it develops fair trade standards – focusing on bananas, cocoa, coffee, flowers, sugar and tea – and helps producers win and maintain certification for their products.

Despite the work of IOs such as these, questions continue to be asked about fair trade and its efficacy. There has been pushback from producers in the form of fair washing (when producers claim to engage in fair trade without actually doing so), certification schemes are not enough to bring transformative change to the heart of the capitalist system, and the real change must come from governments and the way they negotiate free trade agreements (Bennett, 2020). Recognizing this, the WFTO and FI cooperated in 2004 to launch the Fair Trade Advocacy Office (based in Brussels) to monitor national laws and to encourage more international cooperation.

as Alphabet and Meta, solutions such as PayPal and Nasdaq, digital content providers such as Netflix and Viacom, and e-commerce enterprises such as Amazon and Alibaba. The UN Conference on Trade and Development (2022) recently reported that they were growing 'at breakneck speed' and promised to change the nature of global trade and investment. While sales of traditional MNEs had remained largely unchanged between 2016 and 2021, those of digital MNEs had grown by nearly 160 per cent.

Their inherent dynamism, UNCTAD reported, had led to significant changes in the list of the biggest such MNEs as new enterprises arrived, replacing others that were acquired or had been overtaken. The ranking of the biggest MNEs was geographically concentrated, with more than 70 per cent of these companies located in the US and Europe, but – just as has been happening with traditional MNEs – companies from China, Southeast Asia and Latin America have been catching up.

THINKING POINTS

- Is trade more (or less) important to the work of international organizations than security?

- How does the influence of the Global South in the global trade regime compare to its influence in other regimes?

- How could the structure of the World Trade Organization be improved?

- Does OPEC have much of a future?

- Is the global trade regime better understood by studying the activities of multinational enterprises than by studying the work of trade IGOs?

IOs RELATED TO THIS CHAPTER

Fairtrade International (FI)

Organization for Economic Cooperation and Development (OECD)

Organization of Petroleum Exporting Countries (OPEC)

World Customs Organization (WCO)

World Economic Forum

World Fair Trade Organization (WFTO)

World Intellectual Property Organization (WIPO)

World Trade Organization (WTO)

FURTHER READING

Claes, Dag Harald, and Giuliano Garavini (2020) *Handbook of OPEC and the Global Energy Order* (Routledge). An edited collection of studies of OPEC, its relationship to states and energy companies and its place in global energy governance.

Colgan, Jeff D. (2021) *Partial Hegemony: Oil Politics and International Order* (Oxford University Press). An analysis of the potential future of global governance using the case of OPEC to illustrate the challenges faced by the global order.

Foley, C. Fritz, James R. Hines, and David Wessel (eds) (2021) *Global Goliaths: Multinational Corporations in the 21st Century Economy* (Brookings Institution). An edited collection of studies of the role of multinationals in the global economy, including their impact on trade, jobs and the digital economy.

Shaffer, Gregory (2021) *Emerging Powers and the World Trading System* (Cambridge University Press). An assessment of the ways in which emerging economies such as Brazil, China and India are asserting themselves in the global trading system.

Van den Bossche, Peter, and Werner Zdouc (2022) *The Law and Policy of the World Trade Organization: Text, Cases, and Materials*, 5th edn (Cambridge University Press). Although mainly a book about trade law, this includes chapters on the work and structure of the WTO, and on its dispute resolution system.

MIGRATION AND REFUGEES

PREVIEW

The focus of this chapter is on IOs concerned with migration and with the welfare of refugees, asylum-seekers, and stateless people. It opens with a review of the rapidly changing global migration picture, which has seen a dramatic increase in numbers in just the last few decades. It goes on to look at the halting development of the global migration regime, noting how the work of international organizations has been compromised by the degree to which states control and shape the debate. The chapter then reviews the content and effects of the key pieces of international law on refugees and migrants before turning to the work and the structure of the two key intergovernmental organizations: the International Organization for Migration (IOM) and the United Nations High Commissioner for Refugees (UNHCR). The former mainly provides services to migrants and promotes respect for their human rights, while the latter provides help and protection to refugees during emergencies. The chapter continues with an assessment of other IGOs, including UNICEF, before ending with a discussion of the work of non-state actors, including the large number of non-government organizations with an interest in the welfare of migrants and refugees, including Save the Children and the International Rescue Committee.

CONTENTS

- The context
- Building a global migration and refugee regime
- The UN migration and refugee regime
- Other migration and refugee IGOs
- Non-state migration and refugee actors

THE CONTEXT

During their attempts to cross the Rio Grande between Mexico and the US in August 2022, two groups of would-be migrants from Guatemala ran into trouble in the dangerous undercurrents that are often found in the river. In one group, a 5-year-old girl was swept out of her mother's arms and drowned, while in another group a 3-year-old boy was drowned, and an infant was rescued but had to be admitted to hospital in critical condition. These fatalities were just the latest impacting the stream of people desperate to escape the poverty and instability of countries such as Honduras and

Guatemala. Data gathered by the International Organization for Migration (IOM) indicated that drowning was the second highest cause of death for migrants crossing the US–Mexico border. Meanwhile, the IOM's Missing Migrants Project had between 2014 and mid-2023 recorded more than 55,000 deaths of migrants worldwide, although the project also admitted that the numbers were incomplete and the locations of the deaths not always precise. The greatest number of deaths (more than 26,000) were in the Mediterranean region, while nearly 7,000 had died in the Americas (International Organization for Migration, 2023a).

Migration is as old as human history, but the numbers – and the dangers posed to many migrants – have grown dramatically in just the last few decades. For centuries, the scale of migration was determined by a combination of economic, geographic, and resource factors: in order to move, people needed the motivation, access to transport, and the means to support their migration. As states asserted their authority and protected their borders, political barriers were added to the mix, but even then it remained relatively easy for people with the financial means to move across borders. In some cases, mass migrations were even organized and encouraged, as with the examples of European migration to North America, Brazil, and Australia.

Over the last century, the causes and patterns of migration have become more complex, while increased mobility has made it easier for people to travel and to move across borders, and the number of migrants has grown thanks to a variety of new opportunities and pressures. At the same time, migration has become more difficult. In his study of international migration law, Chetail (2019) notes that the idea of free movement climaxed in the nineteenth century, after which states pursued the codification of the right to admission, introduced immigration controls, and eventually engaged in tighter inter-state cooperation on migration. Passport controls began to be implemented after World War I, and were joined later by tighter visa restrictions, limiting the amount of time that travellers to different countries were allowed to stay.

Although the term *migrant* has not yet been clearly defined under international law, the International Organization for Migration (2023b) offers this general definition: 'a person who moves away from his or her place of usual residence, whether within a country or across an international border, temporarily or permanently, and for a variety of reasons'. The IOM definition includes formal migrants as well as migrant workers, smuggled migrants, and international students. On this basis, the IOM makes the following estimates about the number of people involved:

- There were about 281 million international migrants in the world in 2020, an increase of nearly 235 per cent over the number in 1970; see Figure 7.1.

- The estimated proportion of the world's population who are emigrants grew from 2.8 per cent in 2000 to 3.6 per cent in 2020.

- In addition, 59 million people had been displaced within their own countries as of 2023, usually because of conflict, violence, or disasters. The most seriously affected countries included Colombia, the Democratic Republic of Congo, Iraq, Syria, and Ukraine.

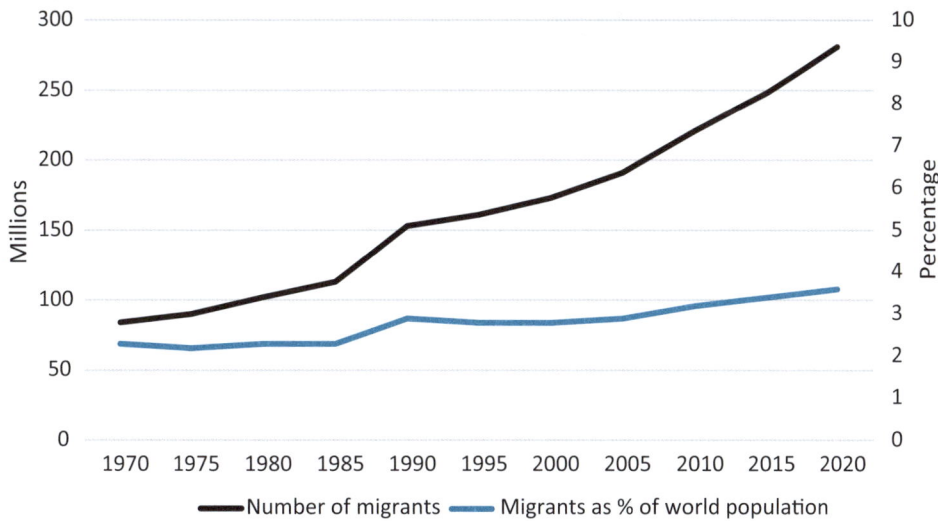

Figure 7.1: Growth in the number of international migrants.
Source: Based on data in United Nations Department of Economic and Social Affairs (2021).

The vast majority of migrants are legally documented, but there are also large numbers of migrants – variously known as undocumented, clandestine, unlawful, non-compliant, irregular, or unauthorized – who have moved across borders without permission. Because it is by definition covert, the exact scale of this phenomenon is hard to gauge, but it certainly runs into the tens of millions. For example, the Migration Policy Institute (2023) estimates that there are as many as 11 million undocumented migrants in the US, while the European Union and India both estimate their respective numbers as being in the low millions (Eurostat, 2023; Shamshad, 2017).

Another element of migration concerns the challenges faced by the growing number of asylum-seekers requesting permanent residence in another country out of fear for their safety if obliged to return home. There was a 600 per cent increase in such claims in the period 2015–18 alone, in the wake of the Syrian civil war. Migration policy must also address the needs of refugees, defined by the 1951 Geneva Convention on the Status of Refugees as people located outside their home country as a result of 'well-founded fear of persecution for reasons of race, religion, nationality, membership of a particular social group or political opinion' or being stateless and unable to return to the country of their former habitual residence. As of 2022, there were estimated to be about 100 million refugees in the world, many of them coming from Afghanistan, South Sudan, Syria or Venezuela (United Nations High Commissioner for Refugees, 2022a).

To the complexity of this picture we need to add the different motivations for migration, which range from the political to the economic and educational (see Table 7.1), and each of which presents its own challenges in terms of a response. Meanwhile, migration is often thought of as a phenomenon of the Global North, the assumption being that people from the Global South are drawn by the attractions of jobs and other opportunities in wealthier countries. The picture, though, is not

Table 7.1: Causes of migration

Cause	Features
Political	Escaping persecution, instability or war.
Economic	Escaping poverty, seeking work or following career opportunities.
Social/cultural	Seeking a better quality of life or following family.
Environmental	Moving away from regions suffering environmental problems.
Educational	Seeking to study in another country.

that simple, and not only must we consider a combination of pull factors and push factors (people being drawn to a new home or repelled from an old home), but we must also consider the variety of sources and targets of migration: about 56 per cent of the world's migrants live in the North, but about 58 per cent of them originated somewhere else in the North, while about 89 per cent of the migrants in the South came from somewhere else in the South (United Nations Population Division, 2020). South–South flows of migration are growing faster than South–North flows, as with the examples of workers chasing jobs in the oil fields of Saudi Arabia or the goldfields of South Africa.

BUILDING A GLOBAL MIGRATION AND REFUGEE REGIME

As a mainly global phenomenon, migration is something that would seem to lend itself naturally to international cooperation, and to be a core component of global governance. However, it is both a controversial and a politically charged issue, and states jealously guard their right to control the flow of migrants across their borders. The debate over migration, argues Chetail (2019), has been taken over by 'mass hysteria', the topic often depicted in media and public debates 'in alarming and emotional terms as an unstoppable massive influx threatening national values, identity, and security'. As a result of different national preferences, and of a desire by states to retain control, international organizations have played a relatively modest role in shaping a global regime. The steps taken towards that regime have, in consequence, been taken only hesitantly (see Table 7.2), the body of migration IGOs and international law being relatively modest, leaving more room – as with human rights (see Chapter 8) – for the input of non-state actors.

When it comes to the more specific question of refugees, though, there is a more tightly defined global regime. States have found themselves obliged to address refugee problems with a greater sense of urgency, and have had to work with one another in either a bilateral or multilateral fashion, often relying on INGOs to provide core services. Refugee crises were, for example, a consequence of World War I, the Russian revolution, and the break-up of the Austro-Hungarian and Turkish empires.

Table 7.2: Key events in building the global migration and refugee regime

Year	Event
1921	League of Nations creates office of High Commissioner for Refugees
1930	League of Nations creates Nansen International Office for Refugees
1933	Convention Relating to the International Status of Refugees signed
1946–52	International Refugee Organization active
1949	UN Relief and Works Agency for Palestinian Refugees in the Near East created
1950	United Nations High Commissioner for Refugees created
1951	International Organization for Migration created Convention Relating to the Status of Refugees signed
2003	Geneva Migration Group created
2003–05	Global Commission on International Migration active
2006	Global Migration Group created
2007	Global Forum on Migration and Development created
2018	United Nations Network on Migration created Global Compacts on refugees and migration adopted

These events combined to create displacements that were behind the creation by the League of Nations in 1921 of an office of High Commissioner for Refugees. The first officeholder was the Norwegian scientist and explorer Fridtjof Nansen, who had been active in the exchange of prisoners of war between Russia, Germany, and what was now Austria, for which he was awarded the 1922 Nobel Peace Prize. That same year, governments meeting at a conference in Geneva accepted the idea of an identity certificate that would help stateless individuals cross borders; it soon became known as a Nansen passport.

When Nansen died in 1930, the League of Nations named its newly created International Office for Refugees (IOR) in his honour. Replacing the office of the High Commissioner, its goal was to resolve the European refugee problem by 1938, at which point it would be closed down. Although the Nansen IOR went on to win the 1939 Nobel Peace Prize, a new refugee problem had by then begun to grow as a result of events in Nazi Germany, prompting the creation in 1933 of a new position with the cumbersome title of 'High Commissioner for Refugees (Jewish and Other) Coming from Germany'. (See Frank and Reinisch, 2017, for background.)

Developments since 1945

The refugee problem created by World War II was even greater than that created by World War I, making governments more receptive after 1945 to the idea of a more structured approach to international cooperation (on refugees, at least). Even before the war had ended, the US-dominated UN Relief and Rehabilitation Administration (UNRRA) was founded, to be soon superseded – again on the basis of US leadership, and with funding coming mainly from the US – by a new International Refugee Organization (IRO), which was operational between 1946 and 1952.

It was also at this time that the longest and most intractable refugee problem in the world was born with the creation of Israel in May 1948, and the resulting displacement of numerous Palestinians. In 1949, the UN Relief and Works Agency for Palestinian Refugees in the Near East (UNRWA) was founded, charged with providing relief and work programmes for refugees. Based at first in Beirut, it was intended to be only a temporary IO, but it has never stopped work. With a move to Vienna in 1978, and then to the Gaza Strip in 1996, it has managed 59 refugee camps in Gaza, Jordan, Lebanon, Syria, and the West Bank, and 5.6 million Palestinian refugees are today registered with the agency. The vast majority of them have known nothing but life in the camps, and there is no sign that the Arab-Israeli problem – and the Palestinian refugee problem – will be resolved any time soon.

In 1950, the office of the UN High Commissioner for Refugees (UNHCR) was created, headquartered in Geneva, modelled to some degree on its League of Nations predecessors and inheriting the work of the International Refugee Organization. It was followed in 1951 by the creation of a provisional organization that would eventually evolve into the International Organization for Migration (IOM). Also based in Geneva, it began life with a focus on Europe, but later expanded and evolved to become the major IGO promoting an understanding of migration issues. It finally became part of the UN system in 2016.

With the number of migrants nearly doubling between 1985 and 2010, the pressures for more meaningful international cooperation grew. In the spirit of similar commissions on international development (see Chapter 5) and on the environment and development (see Chapter 11), it was decided at the turn of the new millennium to convene a Global Commission on International Migration to take a broad view of the state of the issue. With 20 members, the Commission first met in 2003 and reported in 2005, its work providing an example of the kind of shaping of ideas found in constructivist approaches to global governance; see *IOs in Theory 7*. It concluded that the international community had failed to meet the challenges associated with international migration, and lacked the capacity to develop and implement effective migration policies. It also argued that states needed to show greater respect for the commitments they had made to international agreements, particularly those dealing with human rights, and needed to work more closely together. Finally, it identified the need for better coordination between the different IOs working on migration, which often competed with one another and suffered from a lack of coherence in national migration policies. There was room, the Commission concluded, for improvement at every level, from the national to the regional and the international (Global Commission on International Migration, 2005).

IOs IN THEORY 7

CONSTRUCTIVISM

Given the importance of beliefs and cultural practices in shaping the behaviour of individuals, states and other actors, constructivist theory (or social constructivism as it is often known) has increasingly been used as a theoretical approach to global governance. It focuses on the historical and social origins of political structures, including international organizations, arguing – as Knutsen (2016) puts it – that neither states nor state identities are static, that they both evolve, and that the distinctions between domestic politics and international relations become more tenuous as a result. While realists approach the interests and identities of states as a given, constructivists see them as socially constructed, and therefore as subject to change brought on by changes in culture, norms, and international interactions. For example, multiple countries – including the US and Germany – changed their views about international cooperation after World War II, moving from isolationism or unilateralism to engagement and multilateralism.

Pinning down constructivism is not easy, because it is used and understood in different ways. Even so, it has been applied to understanding global governance by focusing on the role of socialization and learning in the construction of global approaches to problems. Put another way, constructivism moves us away from a focus on what are sometimes described as rational studies of institutions and intergovernmental relations to a more ideologically driven focus on what motivates people to act the way they do. Constructivism argues that we need to look at the context within which decisions are made (including the social environment) and that we need to appreciate that interests change over time.

In looking at international organizations, constructivists are interested in understanding the norms that shape them, and in understanding how IOs in turn shape the interests of the states and other actors with which they work, including individual policymakers. IGOs in particular, argue Barnett and Finnemore (2005), play an important role because they help construct the social world in which cooperation and choice take place, helping define the interests that states and other actors come to hold. Just how far migration IOs have gone in helping shape interests is as yet unclear, but the changing structure of global migration governance shows states moving slowly to at least reviewing their approaches to migration in similar ways.

One of the Commission's recommendations was the creation of a Global Migration Group (GMG), which was established in 2006 as recognition of the institutional complexity of the migration regime. It succeeded a smaller body – the Geneva Migration Group, founded in 2003 – and was designed to bring together at regular meetings representatives from ten IGOs involved in migration; these included the IOM, the International Labour Organization, the UNHCR, the World Bank, and the UN Development Programme. The GMG was replaced in turn in 2018 by the UN Network on Migration, coordinated by the IOM and open to any UN body that wanted to join and whose remit included migration. Its main job is to monitor and promote the implementation of the Global Compact for Migration (see later in this section). As of 2023, it had almost 40 UN members, ranging from specialized agencies such as the World Bank and the World Health Organization, to the five regional UN economic commissions (United Nations Network on Migration, 2023).

In a recent assessment of the challenges faced in building a coherent system of global migration governance, the International Organization for Migration (2018) pointed to the following:

- Many states are concerned about the effect of cooperation on their national sovereignty. Any kind of cooperation, they argue, must be based on the recognition of the sovereign rights of states.

- Migration is often a contested issue in domestic politics, with public opinion divided on whether it is a problem or an opportunity.

- International cooperation requires states to consider the interests of other states, which is difficult when states are internally conflicted about migration policy. States of origin, transition and destination will all have different views about how to manage migration.

- There is an asymmetry among states, with destination states often being the biggest or wealthiest, with more influence in international negotiations. Origin states are often both poorer and weaker.

- Unlike global regimes on finance and development, for example, migration is more visibly and directly about people, and for the global migration regime to work, the people being regulated must be involved in improving migration laws and IOs. This is difficult, though, given that it is not always clear who can best represent their interests.

Although there has been a positive trend in the development of the UN migration and refugee regimes in recent decades, it has also been clear – as IOs have learned more about the needs of migration and the possibilities of international agreement – that much still remains to be done.

International migration and refugee law

In contrast to several other areas of global governance covered in other chapters, the body of international law dealing directly with migration is modest, and focuses more on refugees than on migrants more broadly defined; see Table 7.3. At the same time, notes Chetail (2019), migration has featured in a significant and eclectic set of superimposed norms scattered through overlapping fields that range from human rights to trade law, humanitarian law, labour law, criminal law and beyond. Approaches to migration have been further broadened by the need to look at the more particular needs of documented and undocumented migrants, refugees, asylum-seekers and migrant workers.

The first major international treaty of note was the 1933 Convention Relating to the International Status of Refugees, promoted by the League of Nations. It codified basic rights for refugees and became the first agreement to guarantee the right to 'non-refoulement': the principle that no-one should be returned to a country where

Table 7.3: International migration and refugee treaties: Examples

Opened for signature	Where signed	Subject
1933	Geneva, Switzerland	International Status of Refugees (defunct)
1951	Geneva	Status of Refugees
1954	New York, USA	Status of Stateless Persons
1961	New York	Reduction of Statelessness
1990	New York	Migrant Workers and Members of their Families
2018	Marrakech, Morocco	Global Compact for Migration (non-binding)
2018	New York	Global Compact on Refugees

they would run the risk of persecution, a right in international refugee law ever since. Only nine countries became parties to the 1933 treaty (including Britain and France), although many of the non-signatories followed its principles in practice.

After World War II, with Europe facing another major refugee crisis, with most governments more receptive to the idea of reaching agreement on the management of the crisis, and on the back of Article 14 of the Universal Declaration of Human Rights (everyone has the right to seek and enjoy asylum from persecution), work began on a new treaty. The Convention Relating to the Status of Refugees was signed in Geneva in 1951, with a 1967 protocol later removing its focus on post-war Europe. The treaty gave a definition to the term *refugee*, set out the rights of individuals who had been granted asylum, and won enough support to eventually attract 146 parties, entering into force in 1954. The US was one of the notable non-signatories, but once it signed the 1967 Protocol it opted to respect most of the obligations listed in the original treaty. Other non-signatories include Cuba, India, Indonesia, North Korea, Pakistan, Saudi Arabia and Vietnam.

In 1954, the Convention on the Status of Stateless Persons was opened for signature, aimed at addressing the needs of people who were not nationals of a state, and thus were living in legal limbo and being denied basic rights. Once again, it is based on the spirit of the Universal Declaration of Human Rights, Article 15 of which notes that everyone has the right to a nationality, and that no-one should be arbitrarily deprived of the right to that nationality or denied the right to change nationalities. The treaty has attracted mixed support, though, with fewer than 100 states (mainly from Europe and Latin America) becoming parties. Neither the US nor Canada have signed, and nor have most African or Asian countries. The obstacles have been summarized by Chetail (2019) as a combination of misconceptions about the content of the treaty, the financial and administrative costs of its implementation, its incompatibility with domestic law, and – above all – a lack of political will. 'For many politicians,' he notes, 'ratifying a treaty devoted to the protection of migrant workers would put them at risk of losing votes in the politically sensitive context surrounding migration.'

Despite UN estimates that there are about ten million stateless people in the world (United Nations High Commissioner for Refugees, 2022b), the 1961 Convention on the Reduction of Statelessness has been welcomed even less than its 1954 predecessor: it did not come into force until the mid-1970s, and statelessness was seen mainly as a technical problem until the 1990s when the break-up of the Soviet Union and Yugoslavia greatly increased the number of stateless people in the world (Baluarte, 2019). Even so, the treaty by 2014 had just 61 state parties, encouraging the UN High Commissioner for Refugees (UNHCR) to launch a Campaign to End Statelessness in 10 Years. Eight years later, only 14 more countries had become parties.

With the early focus of international law on refugees specifically, rather than on migrants more broadly, it was not until 1990 that the Migrant Workers Treaty was agreed. Formally the International Convention on the Protection of the Rights of All Migrant Workers and Members of Their Families, the goal of the agreement is to foster respect for the human rights of migrant workers, but it has met with limited levels of political enthusiasm because of the widespread resistance to migrant workers in many countries. It was not until 2003 that the treaty had won enough support to enter into force, and only 57 states had signed and ratified by 2022, with 36 additional countries having signed but not ratified. Most of the ratifying states are those that are sources of migrant workers (including most of Latin America – except Brazil – and most of West and North Africa). Almost none of the target countries of migrant workers (including all members of the EU, Australia, Canada, the Gulf states, and the US) have either signed or ratified. According to one study (Western et al., 2019), states that ratify are less interested in protecting the rights of immigrants than in strengthening their relationship with emigrants, among the major values of which are the remittances they send home to their families. When the benefits of migration are large and the costs of potentially providing rights are small, they conclude, states are more likely to ratify the treaty.

In addition to treaties, migration has also been the subject of 'soft law' that is not legally binding but has still often been controversial. The 2018 Global Compact for Safe, Orderly and Regular Migration was an attempt to pull all the dimensions of international migration into a single document and to encourage a common approach. It includes 23 objectives for the improved management of migration, including accurate data, the eradication of human trafficking, using detention only as a last resort, efforts to prevent discrimination against immigrants, and providing migrants with basic services. The US, Israel and three Eastern European countries voted against the compact, mainly over concerns about its impact on their national sovereignty and capacity to control their own borders, even though the compact explicitly points out that states retain the sovereign right to make their own immigration policies. Critics have charged that the compact could eventually be used to press governments into hard legal commitments.

Similar concerns were directed at the 2018 Global Compact on Refugees, drafted by the UNHCR, and intended to improve the global response to refugees.

It has won slightly greater support, with 181 states voting in favour, and the US again being almost alone in voting against. A core part of the compact is the Global Refugee Forum, which met for the first time in 2019 and was designed to meet every four years as a way of helping ease the pressures on countries hosting refugees by sharing best practices and providing financial support. Opinion on the compact and the forum have been mixed, with Chimni (2018), for example, describing the compact as one step forward and two steps back. While it addresses the root causes of refugee flows, he argues, it fails to mention the responsibility of interventions by third states – particularly Western states – for many of those flows. It also emphasizes the importance of easing pressures on host countries rather than the obligations of source countries, and may lead to the erosion of the rights of refugee women and children.

THE UN MIGRATION AND REFUGEE REGIME

Few countries in the world have a bigger refugee problem than Sudan. Not only must it host more than 1.1 million refugees from the conflict in neighbouring South Sudan, but it must also reckon with helping nearly four million of its own people who have been internally displaced by strife in the western and central provinces of Darfur and West Kordofan, and by civil conflict that broke out in April 2023. It must do all this against the background of being one of the poorest countries in the world, as well as one of the most authoritarian. As if these were not challenging enough, it has found itself facing living costs that were growing in the wake of the Covid-19 pandemic, the war in Ukraine, food shortages, and inflation. The response to the Sudanese refugee problem was being supported by the UN High Commissioner for Refugees (UNHCR). While long understood to be the leading international refugee organization, it found itself in September 2022 having received barely one-third of the $350 million in funding needed to deliver an effective response to the Sudanese crisis (United Nations High Commissioner for Refugees, 2022c).

Challenges of this kind are all too common for the UNHCR, which is one of the two key IGOs involved in global refugee and migration matters, the other being the International Organization for Migration (IOM). Although they have different relations with the UN, and although IOM takes a global approach to migration that contrasts with the focus of the UNHCR on refugees, they are together – says Chetail (2019) – 'the centre of gravity around which the institutional architecture of migration evolves', and cannot be understood in isolation from one another. To a lesser degree, the International Labour Organization (ILO) can also be considered part of the UN migration regime, with its focus on the needs of migrant workers as part of a broader agenda on workers' rights.

The International Organization for Migration

Founded in 1951 with the lumbering title of the Provisional Intergovernmental Committee for the Movement of Migrants from Europe (PICMME), the International

Organization for Migration (IOM) was at first a temporary logistics organization outside the UN, with a focus on Europe and just 16 member states. It went through several changes of name before adopting its current name in 1989. In the wake of the new attention being paid to migration in the 1980s, it also adopted a more global agenda with an expanding membership, and joined the UN as a so-called 'related organization' in 2016. This means that it has a cooperation agreement with the UN and retains much of its former autonomy, but does not have the political status or funding predictability of a UN specialized agency. A proposal made in 2003 by UN Secretary General Kofi Annan that it become a specialized agency failed to win the necessary support.

The membership of the IOM has grown to 175 members and eight observers, leaving it ten short of the full membership of the UN; among the states that have chosen not to join are Indonesia, Iraq, North Korea, Oman and Saudi Arabia. Although it has grown to become one of the largest of all IGOs, with more than 400 field locations and nearly 13,000 staff, it has been suggested by Bradley (2020) that it has thrived 'by serving as a compliant executor for states looking to have their migration dirty work done by a partner that won't talk back about principles'. She also questions just how far it has been able to meaningfully shape the governance of migration and how much it is primarily a humanitarian IO.

Formally, the IOM describes its job as being one of facilitating 'the orderly and humane management of international migration' by – for example – providing services to migrants who need help, promoting respect for the human rights of migrants, offering advice and technical cooperation to governments and NGOs, contributing to the economic and social development of states in ways that maximize the benefits of migration, and being a primary source for information on migration. It has undertaken health and background checks of migrants on behalf of governments, recruited migrant workers for wealthier and emerging states, and has helped manage the return and reintegration of undocumented migrants and rejected asylum-seekers (Geiger and Koch, 2018). Its structure is as follows:

- *Secretariat and executive head.* Headquartered in Geneva, the IOM is headed by a Director General who is elected for a maximum of two five-year terms by a two-thirds majority of the IOM Council and is answerable to the Council. All ten of the directors general of the IOM and its predecessors to date have been white men, and most of them from the US (with just two Europeans).

- *Assembly.* The Council, the main governing body of the IOM, consists of representatives from the member states (each with one vote), and meets annually (or more often as needed) to review the work of the organization and to set priorities.

- *Executive council.* The nearest equivalent the IOM has to an executive council is the Standing Committee on Programmes and Finance, which normally meets only twice annually. It reviews policies and the budget, advises the Director General, and can make urgent decisions between meetings of the Council. Membership is open to all IOM member states.

- *Other elements*. There are nine *regional offices* and a network of *country offices* that oversee IOM activities within their regions, implement IOM projects and gather information. See *IOs in Action 7* for an example.

- The IOM has promoted a Migration Governance Framework since 2015 as a set of best practices in helping migrants, and also publishes an annual *World Migration Report* that is the authoritative summary of the global migration situation.

- *Budget*. The IOM's budget comes entirely from voluntary contributions, and amounted to $1.19 billion in 2022. This was a doubling in the size of the budget in eight years, with the biggest sources of funding being the US (40 per cent of the total), Germany (15 per cent), Canada (7 per cent), Australia (5 per cent) and Bangladesh (4 per cent). (All data from International Organization for Migration, 2021.)

IOs IN ACTION 7

THE INTERNATIONAL ORGANIZATION FOR MIGRATION IN HAITI

Few countries in the world have suffered quite so dramatically from human-made and natural disasters in recent decades as Haiti. Despite being independent since 1804 – longer than any other Caribbean or Latin American state – Haiti has struggled to find a workable political form and a functioning economy. Just since 2000 it has suffered political rebellions, the biggest earthquake in 200 years, an outbreak of cholera traced back to UN peacekeeping forces, the assassination in 2021 of its president, a second large earthquake and gang warfare. Little surprise, then, that Haiti has long been a source country of migrants, creating a large Haitian diaspora in neighbouring states, and being a particular focus for the work of the IOM.

The IOM has been active in Haiti since the 1970s, its interests deepening following the 1991 coup that removed the government of President Jean-Bertrand Aristide, engaging in efforts that were widely seen at the time (Bradley, 2020) as being on behalf of US interests. These included collecting data on Haitian asylum-seekers, transporting asylum-seekers to other countries and managing migration movements with the neighbouring Dominican Republic. The IOM was also at the heart of the international humanitarian response in Haiti following the 2010 earthquake, when it distributed shelters, managed refugee camps, built emergency water and sanitation facilities, collected data on camp residents and responded to the cholera outbreak. The work also had implications for the development of the IOM, many of whose staff were shaped by their experiences in Haiti, influencing the way in which the organization has since worked in other parts of the world.

Unfortunately, the IOM's contributions have not brought sustained change to the deeply troubled country, which has seen multiple foreign interventions, including UN peacekeeping operations in 1993–2001 and again in 2003–17. More interventions were being called for in 2022–23 as the government in Haiti collapsed, armed gangs controlled towns and cities, and the Dominican Republic responded to the new refugee crisis by pursuing a programme of mass arrests and deportations of those they believed to be undocumented migrants of Haitian origin. No end seems to be in sight to Haiti's troubles.

Geiger and Koch (2018) portray the IOM as less bureaucratic and centralized than many other IGOs, noting that it delegates comparatively high levels of discretion and autonomy to its individual field and country missions. This makes it, in their view, less an international organization as the notion is usually understood, and more the kind of world organization discussed in Chapter 2. It still remains well short, though, of the kind of World Migration Organization that was suggested as early as 1992 by the Indian-American economist Jagdish Bhagwati. The world, he argued at the time, badly needed enlightened immigration policies, and the spread and codification of best practices, a job that could at least be begun by a truly world body (Bhagwati, 1992). Others (see Trachtman, 2009) have since made similar arguments, pointing – for example – to the model of the World Trade Organization with its strong secretariat and responsibilities in law making and dispute resolution – see Chapter 6.

The United Nations High Commissioner for Refugees

The second IGO involved in migration affairs is the office of the UN High Commissioner for Refugees (UNHCR). Based on the model of the High Commissioner created in 1921 by the League of Nations, it was founded in 1950, and began work in 1951 with a three-year mission to address the European refugee crisis. While its work earned it the 1954 Nobel Peace Prize, it soon became evident that it had to keep working beyond 1954. As a result, and much like the IOM, it was reshaped as a more global body, taking on new responsibilities for stateless people, for asylum-seekers, and more recently for the humanitarian effects of climate change. The number of refugees and internally displaced people (IDPs) that have come under its mandate has accordingly grown; see Figure 7.2. In contrast to the somewhat ambiguous 'related organization' status of the IOM, the UNHCR is more firmly situated within the UN as a subsidiary body of the UN General Assembly.

The organization describes itself on its web site as 'The UN Refugee Agency' and has been described as the 'guardian' of the 1951 Status of Refugees Convention (International Organization for Migration, 2018) in the sense that it promotes and monitors compliance with the agreement. In practical terms, it delivers aid and protection – including shelter, food, water and medical care – to refugees during emergencies, it helps refugees to reach safety and works to ensure that they are not returned to situations where their lives could be at risk, it provides cash transfer or vouchers in situations where they are more practical or cost-effective than rations, and it advocates for the rights and physical security of people forced to leave their homes.

The UNHCR is structured as follows:

- *Secretariat and executive head.* With headquarters in Geneva, the High Commissioner is elected to the position for renewable five-year terms by the UN General Assembly, and answers to both the General Assembly and to the UN's Economic and Social Committee (ECOSOC). The UNHCR in 2023 had a staff of nearly 18,000 people, mostly working in the field in the countries most actively experiencing the effects of the refugee crisis.

- *Executive council.* The Executive Committee (ExCom) consists of 107 members chosen to ensure wide geographical representation and working with a smaller Standing Committee that meets three times each year. ExCom meets annually to review the work of the Standing Committee and to establish the work programme for the following year.

- *Other elements.* The Inspector General's Office is an independent body that monitors the work of the UNHCR, with the goal of improving efficiency and deterring fraud. Honouring Fridtjof Nansen, the UNHCR oversees the award of the annual Nansen Refugee Award to the person, group or organization that has contributed the most to refugee protection. Past winners have included US Senator Edward Kennedy, the opera singer Luciano Pavarotti and the humanitarian INGO Médecins Sans Frontières.

- *Budget.* The budget of the office comes almost entirely from voluntary contributions from governments, topped up with donations from individuals and corporations. With the growing global refugee problem, the budget grew from $1 billion in the late 1990s to nearly $9 billion in 2022 (United Nations High Commissioner for Refugees, 2022d). In 2022, the biggest donors to UNHCR were the US (40 per cent of the income total) and the European Union (31 per cent, of which about one-third came from Germany).

Although the origins of High Commissioners have been more diverse than is the case with the International Organization for Migration, the higher status of the post is reflected in the political backgrounds of some of its holders. Poul Hartling, for example, entered the post in 1978 after serving as foreign minister and prime minister of Denmark, Ruud Lubbers became High Commissioner in 2001 after serving as prime minister of the Netherlands, and António Guterres – a former prime

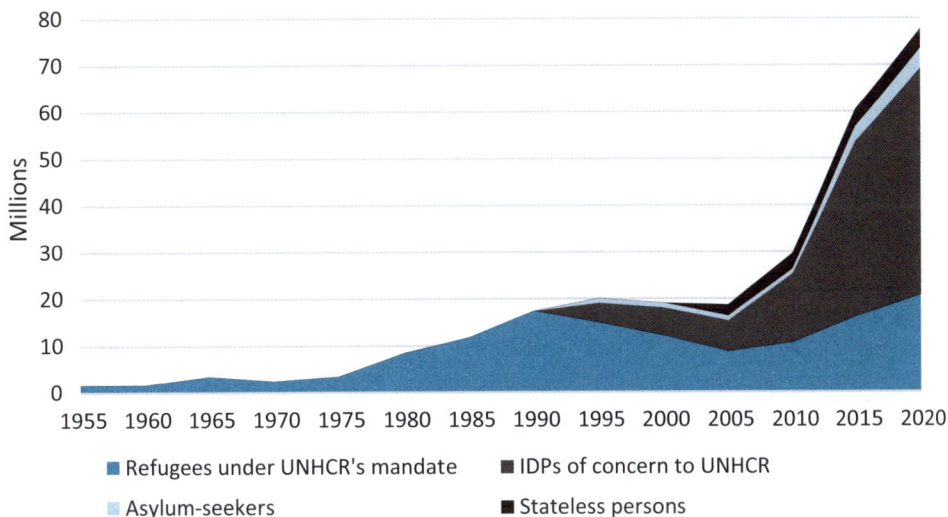

Figure 7.2: The changing numbers of refugees.
Source: Based on data in United Nations High Commissioner for Refugees (2022e).

minister of Portugal – served ten years in the post (2005–15) before becoming the ninth Secretary General of the UN in 2017. Only one woman, the Japanese academic Sadako Ogata, has so far been elected to the post (in 1990), and except for her and Sadruddin Aga Khan of Iran, all Commissioners have been European men.

The mission, budget, and reach of the UNHCR have changed, expanded, and broadened since its creation, it won the Nobel Peace Prize (again) in 1981, and it has made efforts to bolster the international refugee regime through its work on the Global Compact on Refugees and the Global Refugee Forum. However, argues Crisp (2020), it faces major problems. Not only has the international environment become increasingly hostile to the concept of refugee protection, but there is also a wider disregard for international law, a disdain for multilateral cooperation, and a humanitarian system that has been stretched to its limits by major emergencies and the Covid-19 pandemic. The UNHCR may have 'gained a degree of international visibility that is the envy of many other UN agencies', Crisp notes, but governments feel 'increasingly free to flout the norms and standards enshrined in international refugee law'. Furthermore, many of the world's refugees are now in countries such as Pakistan and Bangladesh that are not parties to the 1951 Convention. The US – once the mainstay of the international refugee regime, and still the biggest contributor to the UNHCR budget – has become less receptive to the task of refugee protection, while the European Union has adopted increasingly restrictive refugee and migration policies.

The International Labour Organization

Although it is mainly a human rights IGO (see Chapter 8), no discussion of the UN migration regime would be complete without a mention of the International Labour Organization (ILO). Founded in 1919 as part of the League of Nations, it survived the demise of the League to become the first specialized agency of the UN in 1946, charged mainly with the job of promoting workers' rights. Despite this, the ILO contributed to the evolution of global governance on migration, mainly through its role in the development and agreement of the 1990 Migrant Workers Convention. Headquartered in Geneva, the ILO has had to define a place for itself working with new bodies such as the IOM and the UNHCR, against a background of the growing urgency and complexity of migration issues. Piper and Foley (2021) argue that the relationship between the ILO and the IOM has only really begun to take shape since the mid-2000s, and that the result has been an 'uneasy alliance' in which the two bodies have ended up competing with one another, and have only recently years moved more toward what they describe as a partnership.

OTHER MIGRATION AND REFUGEE IGOs

Although migration is a global phenomenon, some parts of the world feel its effects more than others: most migrants come from countries with political and economic problems, and head for those countries with the greatest opportunities. As a result,

Geddes et al. (2019) argue that migration as a matter of international governance lends itself to being addressed by regional cooperation. The result, though, has been less the creation of regional IOs than the pursuit of informal cooperation among governments, to some extent using existing regional organizations such as those discussed in Chapter 3.

One example of an interesting *absence* of a regional migration IGO is the European Union (EU). One of the two major targets for migrants and asylum-seekers (along with the US), the EU has built a network of administrative organizations and an extensive family of specialized agencies that manage to skirt the issue of migration. The tasks of these agencies include providing advice, running EU operations, and acting as clearinghouses for information, all of which could be applied to migration. However, while EU agencies deal with everything from intellectual property to workplace safety, police cooperation, disease prevention, and gender equality, the EU member states have not yet seen fit to agree to set up a European migration or refugees agency. There is an EU Agency for Asylum – headquartered in Valletta, Malta – whose task is to help EU member states apply the EU's Common European Asylum System. However, reflecting the degree to which migration and asylum issues remain the purview of the member states, the web site of the agency (European Union Agency for Asylum, 2023) goes to some lengths – using boldface for emphasis – to explain that the agency 'acts as a **resource**' for EU member states, and '**does not replace** the national asylum or reception authorities'. The job of the agency is to instead help the member states reach a point where their asylum practices are **harmonized** (again in boldface) so that an application by an individual to any EU member state will be treated in the same way.

Although it is an informal and non-binding forum rather than an IGO, the Global Forum on Migration and Development (GFMD) must be included in any discussion about intergovernmental activities in the field of migration. Founded in 2007 at the suggestion of UN Secretary General Kofi Annan, it works outside the UN but its membership is mainly the same as that of the UN. It meets every year as a venue for policymakers to discuss and share policies and best practices, and to influence the global migration agenda. Despite its informality, and lack of a permanent budget or secretariat (it has a Geneva-based support unit that provides administrative services), it has some of the trappings of a formal institution, as follows:

- A Chair-in-Office, held by a country for one year.

- A Troika (group of three) formed by the incumbent Chair together with its immediate predecessor and successor.

- A Support Unit to help the Chair.

- A Steering Group designed to give the Forum some continuity.

- A consultative Friends of the Forum consisting of all member states and observers of the UN.

- A network of National Focal Points whose job is to maintain links between the Forum and participating governments.

For Chetail (2019), the Forum is a talking shop that achieves little, that lacks transparency and that suffers from being outside the UN. Much has also changed since it was founded, particularly as the IOM has become bigger and expanded its reach, leaving questions about the ongoing value of the format of the GFMD, and the duplication of its work with other IOs.

Another IGO that is fully part of the UN, and that has interests relating to refugees specifically, is UNICEF, which was founded in 1946 as the United Nations International Children's Emergency Fund. Like several other IOs, it was set up with

SPOTLIGHT 7

OVERLAPPING INTERESTS

Although this book has different chapters for the different areas of interest addressed by international organizations, the divisions among their interests are not clear-cut. This is particularly true when it comes to migration, refugee concerns, humanitarian challenges, human rights and international health. Multiple IOs – particularly non-governmental – have been created with a focused interest in mind, and have subsequently seen those interests blend with others, compelling a wider approach to a connected set of challenges. Consider these examples:

- The International Committee of the Red Cross (Chapter 4) was founded with the interests of wounded soldiers in mind, since when it has been involved with the needs of refugees and the victims of epidemics.

- Oxfam was founded as a famine relief organization, but its interests later spilled over into development more broadly, and into gender justice, women's rights and even climate change (see Chapter 5).

- Save the Children and UNICEF were both created to help children and their mothers, but have regularly found themselves involved in helping refugees and providing health care in global trouble spots, while the interests of Save the Children overlap with human rights.

- The original purpose of Doctors Without Borders (Chapter 10) was to provide medical assistance to the victims of conflict and natural disasters, but inevitably its mission has had to address questions related to refugees, human rights and development.

The same phenomenon is at work with intergovernmental organizations. This is reflected, for example, in how the International Labour Organization needs to be understood from the perspective both of migration and human rights, and in how the World Food Programme (included in Chapter 9 on food and hunger) is a humanitarian organization. It is also reflected in the number of initiatives set up to coordinate the work of UN agencies and programmes: examples include the UN Office for the Coordination of Humanitarian Affairs, the UN Network on Migration and the Joint UN Programme on HIV and AIDS (now UNAIDS, see Chapter 10). On the single issue of humanitarian aid, IGOs and non-state actors are involved from the chapters in this book dealing with security, development, migration, human rights, agriculture, health and the environment.

a specific post-war mission – relief for children and mothers impacted by World War II – and then had its mission extended and expanded. Its formal name was changed in 1953 to the United Nations Children's Fund, although it still goes by the acronym UNICEF. Its mission is primarily humanitarian, its main goal being to provide community-level services in the interests of the health and wellbeing of children, but its work often overlaps with addressing the needs of refugees in the wake of natural disasters or political unrest; see *Spotlight 7*. It has another split personality in the sense that while it is a full agency of the UN, it relies not just on voluntary contributions from governments, but also on charitable contributions from individuals and corporations, prompted by the support of celebrities. From its headquarters in New York, it works with 36 national committees that are NGOs responsible for fundraising and promoting the goals of UNICEF. It was awarded the Nobel Peace Prize in 1965.

NON-STATE MIGRATION AND REFUGEE ACTORS

INGOs play a smaller political role in the global migration regime than is the case with many other regimes, for the simple reason – as noted earlier – that migration is a controversial issue in many countries and governments typically want to reserve their authority over migration policy. National and international NGOs might challenge the policies of states (or the lack of such policies) from a human rights or humanitarian perspective, but otherwise there are few that are active solely or directly on migration issues.

One of the few INGOs with a policy interest in migration, as opposed to refugees, is the Migration Policy Institute (MPI). This is a think-tank with offices in the US and the EU, and a mission to undertake and disseminate research aimed at improving immigration and integration policies. Its first office was founded in Washington DC in 2001, with a sister organization – MPI Europe – opened in Brussels in 2011. It is funded mainly through research grants from foundations, as well as funding from government agencies, corporations and individuals, and IGOs such as the International Organization for Migration, the World Bank and the World Health Organization. A related and older organization is Refugees International, a Washington DC-based body that advocates on behalf of stateless and displaced people. Although founded in the US, its interests are global, and its target audiences ae policymakers and aid agencies.

Beyond rare examples such as these, the interests of INGOs overlap with migration and refugees mainly in the area of humanitarian issues, or human welfare broadly defined. Such organizations are also often described as relief agencies, and have even occasionally been assessed as an extension of the official development assistance programmes of governments. Help for refugees – including emergency aid and assimilation – has prompted the creation and work of multiple INGOs (see Table 7.4 for the prime examples), as well as many more NGOs that are nationally funded and based but have international interests and operations; the latter include Refugee Action (UK), the Norwegian Refugee Council, Alight (formerly the American

Table 7.4: Refugee INGOs: Examples

Name	Founded	Headquarters	Interests
International Committee of the Red Cross	1863	Geneva, Switzerland	Emergency relief, economic migrants, missing persons and divided families. (See Chapter 3.)
Save the Children	1919	London, UK	Humanitarian activities aimed at children.
International Rescue Committee (IRC)	1931	New York, USA	Responds to crises with education, health care, clean water, sanitation, legal assistance and resettling.
International Catholic Migration Commission (ICMC)	1951	Geneva	Helps migrants, refugees and IDPs.
Refugees International	1979	Washington DC, USA	Political advocacy on behalf of refugees.
Jesuit Refugee Service (JRS)	1980	Rome, Italy	Helps migrants, refugees and IDPs.

Refugee Committee), World Relief (US), PRO ASYL (Germany), and multiple faith-based NGOs such as World Vision, Church World Service and Lutheran Immigration and Refugee Service (all US).

Humanitarian INGOs have become so ubiquitous, argues Dromi (2020), that 'few today can imagine a global order without them, and their legitimacy is often taken for granted'. Although they routinely offer valuable assistance in the wake of conflict or natural disasters, however, numerous questions have been asked about their efficacy. In her study of how they make decisions and determine priorities, for example, Krause (2014) concludes that they are often driven by a need to 'produce projects'. In other words, they sell projects to key institutional donors, as a result of which both the beneficiaries of aid and the projects run by NGOs become commodities; in order to guarantee success, those that are easiest to help are helped, while those in the hardest situations might receive no assistance at all.

When it comes specifically to the welfare of refugees, few INGOs are better known than the International Committee of the Red Cross, discussed in Chapter 3. Although it was founded to help soldiers wounded on the battlefield, it has since adopted a wider range of interests that mean that it could be discussed in several chapters in this book, including those on security, development, agriculture, human rights and migration. The Red Cross has recently been involved in helping those displaced by wars in Syria, Libya and Ukraine, but – notes Forsythe (2018) – it no longer tries to restrict itself to emergency relief. It has instead moved gradually into addressing the needs of economic migrants, those displaced by urban violence, environmental refugees, missing persons and divided families.

Another humanitarian INGO whose mission has evolved to include refugee assistance is Save the Children. Founded in London in 1919 by two sisters named Eglantyne Jebb and Dorothy Buxton, it now has nearly 30 national member bodies. Its perspective was international from the beginning, as it set out to help alleviate the starvation of children in multiple European countries in the wake of World War I. Initially designed as a temporary response, it became a permanent organization after the Russian famine of 1921, helping refugee children in Russia and Turkey. Its activities continued after World War II, focusing on crises ranging from the Korean War to the Vietnam War and the secession of Biafra from Nigeria in 1967. Baughan (2021) notes that Save the Children has always gone beyond relief, and has always sought to 'rehabilitate' and change the communities in which it has been active, sometimes causing pushback from the recipients of its assistance. At a wider scale, Save the Children was also active – along with other humanitarian INGOs – in developing what would eventually become the UN Declaration of the Rights of the Child (adopted in 1959) and the UN Convention on the Rights of the Child, adopted in 1989.

In 1931, the International Rescue Committee was founded in New York as the US branch of the International Relief Association, founded in Germany at the suggestion of Albert Einstein to help refugees fleeing Nazi Germany. It later combined with the Emergency Rescue Committee – helping refugees from Vichy France – to form the new organization. It focused on Europe immediately after World War II, expanding its activities to the Americas and Africa in the 1960s, and now has offices in more than 40 countries, a staff of 20,000, a budget of $800 million, and provides responses to crises with education, health care, clean water, sanitation, legal assistance and resettlement.

Another INGO with a focus on refugees is the International Catholic Migration Commission, a Geneva-based body that helps migrants, refugees, and internally displaced people. Founded in 1951 in the wake of the post-war European refugee crisis, it was championed by the Catholic Church, and was formally established by a papal letter from Pope Pius XII. It was active in helping address the refugee crises arising from the Vietnam war, the genocide in Cambodia, the war in Yugoslavia, the war in Afghanistan and political instability in the Middle East. It has programmes and staff in more than 40 countries, and a global network of 132 member organizations. In 1980, it was joined by the Jesuit Refugee Service, another Catholic organization with the goal of aiding refugees and IDPs. Inspired by the problem of the so-called boat people escaping from Vietnam in the wake of the war, it is based in Rome and currently has programmes in about 50 countries.

THINKING POINTS

− What are the main barriers to the development of a global migration regime?

− Why have so many states failed to develop workable policies on migration?

− Should (or could) there be a World Migration Organization?

− Is migration better addressed by regional organizations or international organizations?

− Why is it that so much of the responsibility for helping refugees still lies with non-state actors?

IOs RELATED TO THIS CHAPTER

Global Forum on Migration and Development (GFMD)

International Catholic Migration Commission (ICMC)

International Organization for Migration (IOM)

International Rescue Committee (IRC)

Jesuit Refugee Service (JRS)

Migration Policy Institute (MPI)

Refugees International

Save the Children

UN High Commissioner for Refugees (UNHCR)

UN Relief and Works Agency (UNRWA)

United Nations Children's Fund (UNICEF)

FURTHER READING

Bradley, Megan (2020) *The International Organization for Migration: Challenges, Commitments, Complexities* (Routledge), and Antoine Pécoud and Martin Geiger (2020) (eds) *The International Organization for Migration: The New 'UN Migration Agency' in Critical Perspective* (Springer). Two surveys of the work of the IOM, including chapters on its history, structure and culture.

Chetail, Vincent (2019) *International Migration Law* (Oxford University Press). A review of international migration law that includes detailed analyses of the structure and work of the main IOs involved in migration governance.

Geddes, Andrew, Leila Hadj Abdou, Leiza Brumat, and Marcia Vera Espinoza (eds) (2019) *The Dynamics of Regional Migration Governance* (Edward Elgar). An edited collection of studies of regional and sub-regional migration governance in Africa, Asia-Pacific and Central Asia, Europe, the Middle East, and North and South America.

International Organization for Migration (various years) *World Migration Reports* (IOM). Annual reports produced by the key UN migration IO, discussing developments in global governance and keeping records of changes in the global migration picture.

HUMAN RIGHTS

PREVIEW

The focus of this chapter is on international organizations that work to promote human rights, as outlined in the Universal Declaration of Human Rights. It opens with a definition of those rights and the threats they face, before reviewing the troubled and controversial efforts made to build a human rights regime after 1945. The struggles of the Commission on Human Rights are discussed, followed by an outline of the major pieces of international human rights law. The chapter then moves on to the current UN human rights regime, revolving around the UN Human Rights Council (HRC) and the Office of the High Commissioner for Human Rights (OHCHR). The structure and goals of both organizations is discussed, along with the challenges they face. The work of other IGOs is then discussed, with a focus on the International Criminal Court (ICC) and on regional human rights courts. Prime among the latter is the European Court of Human Rights (ECHR), whose growing reach and workload contrasts with the difficulties faced by the ICC. The chapter concludes with a review of the non-state actors active on human rights, focusing on the achievements of two international non-governmental organizations: Amnesty International (AI) and Human Rights Watch (HRW).

CONTENTS

- The context
- Building a global human rights regime
- The UN human rights regime
- The International Criminal Court
- Regional human rights courts
- Non-state human rights actors

THE CONTEXT

One of the more effective defenders of human rights in the world is the European Court of Human Rights (ECHR), headquartered in the north-eastern French city of Strasbourg. Associated with the Council of Europe, a 46-member IGO founded to promote European unity, the task of the court is to review and issue judgements on disputes involving parties to the European Convention on Human Rights which include almost all the states of Europe. One of them was Russia, which was the target of numerous ECHR judgements for violations of terms of the convention. When the court ruled against Russia in 2015 for violating the privacy rights of its citizens, the Russian parliament passed a law allowing Russia to overrule judgements from the court. Then, following the February 2022 Russian invasion of Ukraine, the Council of Europe expelled Russia, giving notice that it would cease to be a party to the convention six months later. Unwilling to wait, the Putin government unilaterally removed Russia from the jurisdiction of the ECHR in June 2022.

Incidents such as this say much about the growing intensity of the debate over human rights. Although the debate has a heritage dating back centuries, it has only been since 1945 that it has moved to the forefront of the global governance agenda. The definition of human rights has been tightened, deepened and broadened, democratic states have taken more action to protect and promote rights, more attention has been paid to the abuse of rights in authoritarian states, new international organizations have been active in the field, and multiple treaties have been agreed to protect and promote human rights.

The dimensions of human rights are captured in this definition offered by the Office of the High Commissioner for Human Rights (2023):

> Human rights are rights inherent to all human beings, whatever our nationality, place of residence, sex, national or ethnic origin, colour, religion, language, or any other status. We are all equally entitled to our human rights without discrimination. These rights are all interrelated, interdependent, and indivisible.

This may seem clear enough, but human rights are often threatened and limited, even in democracies. Measuring and comparing the state of human rights around the world is not easy, however, in part because of different perceptions about performance. Every UN member state undergoes a review of its human rights record every five years by the Human Rights Council, but the results can vary according to which countries are doing the reviewing (Lam and DeSilver, 2019). When the US was recently reviewed, for example, Asian and African states raised concerns about its record on racial discrimination, Latin American states emphasized concerns about migrants' rights and Western European states criticized the US for its use of the death penalty.

Much of what we know about the state of human rights comes in annual reports published by the NGOs Amnesty International and Human Rights Watch, from which few countries have emerged unscathed in recent years. We can also see the state of human rights reflected in the multiple ranking systems for the state of democracy, including the *Freedom in the World* reports produced by the research group Freedom House, and the Democracy Index produced by the Economist Intelligence Unit. The results of these reviews are mainly similar: all countries have human rights problems to a greater or lesser degree, there are positive trends in some and negative trends in others, while older and more stable states tend to have a stronger record than newer and more unstable states.

Overall, though, there has been a worrying recent decline in the global state of democracy and the health of human rights, as reflected in Figure 8.1. This shows the results of recent reports from Freedom House, which rates all the countries of the

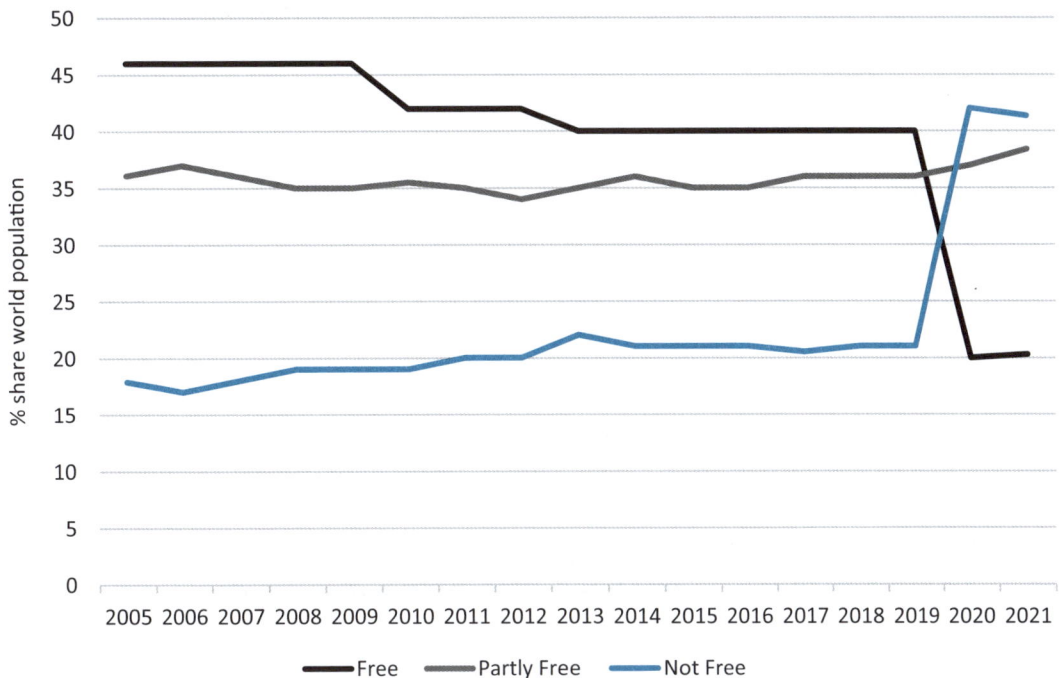

Figure 8.1: Global democratic trends.
Source: Based on data in Freedom House (2022).

world as either Free, Partly Free or Not Free. Its research, based on using multiple measures of political rights and the functioning of government, shows a sharp recent drop in the number of people living in democracies, and a rise in the number living in authoritarian states. Even democracies, argues Freedom House, have seen a decline in pluralism, equality and accountability: there have been attacks on media freedom, an undermining of the rule of law, baseless charges against the results of elections, and increased discrimination and mistreatment of migrants. In short, human rights face numerous threats.

BUILDING A GLOBAL HUMAN RIGHTS REGIME

Unlike the other chapters in this book, where the story of the development of most regimes can be broadly divided into two eras (pre-1945 and post-1945), most of the discussion about human rights at the international level, along with the formation of human rights IOs and the passage of international laws, has taken place since 1945. That discussion was given new and urgent meaning by the discovery of the extent of the horrors of the Holocaust. This prompted the introduction of the term *genocide* in the closing years of the war by the Polish-born lawyer Raphael Lemkin (1944), who described 'an old practice in its modern development': the systematic destruction of a nation or an ethnic group. Meanwhile, the concept of crimes against humanity was introduced during the Nuremberg and Tokyo war crimes trials in 1945–49 at which Nazi and Japanese leaders were held accountable for their actions.

Human rights were headlined in the Preamble to the 1945 Charter of the United Nations, which noted its determination 'to reaffirm faith in fundamental human rights … [and] in the equal rights of men and women', and also declared that the purposes of the new UN included 'promoting and encouraging respect for human rights'. One of the first actions taken by the UN in 1946 was to form a Commission on Human Rights (CHR) that was charged with drawing up a complete listing of human rights, and then with overseeing their promotion. The commission had 18 members, with Eleanor Roosevelt serving as chair, and the drafting of what was to become the Universal Declaration of Human Rights (UDHR) was led by John Peters Humphrey, a Canadian legal scholar. The finished declaration – whose opening article stated that 'All human beings are born free and equal in dignity and rights' – was unanimously adopted by the UN General Assembly on 10 December 1948, Roosevelt dubbing it 'the international Magna Carta of all humankind'. A selection of the 30 articles in the UDHR is listed in Table 8.1; for a detailed analysis of its content, see Morsink (2022).

Table 8.1: The Universal Declaration of Human Rights: Selected rights

Life, liberty and security of person.	Freedom of opinion and expression.
Not to be a slave.	Freedom of peaceful assembly and association.
Not to be subjected to torture or to cruel, inhuman or degrading treatment.	To take part in government.
Equal protection before the law.	To work, with just and favourable work conditions.
No arbitrary arrest, detention or exile.	Equal pay for equal work.
To be presumed innocent until proved guilty.	Just and favourable remuneration ensuring an existence worthy of human dignity.
Freedom of movement and residence within borders of a state.	Rest and leisure, including periodic time off with pay.
To seek and enjoy asylum from persecution.	A standard of living adequate for health and wellbeing., including food, clothing, housing and medical care.
To a nationality.	Security in the event of unemployment, sickness, disability or old age.
To marry by consent and found a family.	To education.
To own property alone or with others.	To freely participate in the cultural life of the community.
Freedom of thought, conscience and religion.	

The Commission on Human Rights was to be the key IGO in the field for 60 years, but its work was restricted by the tensions of the Cold War; during debates in the Commission, notes Seiderman (2019), states could not even be mentioned by name, and an effort by CHR Director Theo van Boven in the 1970s and early 1980s to be more assertive led to a conflict with offended states and a termination of his contract. As a result of the restrictions, the Commission opted to promote rights and to report on violations rather than to investigate or condemn transgressions (see Pace, 2020). It was able to oversee the initiation and development of key human rights treaties, including those aimed at eliminating all forms of racial discrimination (1966) and all forms of discrimination against women (1979). Overall progress remained slow, though, a problem that sparked the creation of several NGOs, including Amnesty International in 1961 and Human Rights Watch in 1978.

Political turning points came with the convening of the International Conference on Human Rights in Tehran in 1968 and the World Conference on Human Rights in Vienna in 1993. Concerned about the increasing difficulties of managing an accumulating body of covenants and treaties, human rights NGOs at Vienna – led by Amnesty International – endorsed the idea of a high commissioner with the capacity to act quickly in the face of violations, and to ensure the coordination of human rights activities within the UN. The idea dated back to the drafting of the UDHR, when a suggestion had been made for an 'attorney general' for human rights who could help aggrieved individuals with petitions to the Commission on Human Rights. The move, noted Clapham (1994), would give the UN an official who could 'take up human rights concerns with governments without waiting for a mandate from a political body'. The resolution was accepted in December 1993, the Office of the High Commissioner for Human Rights (OHCHR) was created, and the first commissioner took office in April 1994.

The OHCHR initially worked with the Commission on Human Rights, but the latter was losing credibility against a background of its structural weaknesses, and of concerns that its membership often included states that were human rights violators. The Commission had no permanent members, its seats instead being apportioned by region, with about one third coming up for re-election every year, and appointments lasting three years. The number of seats had also grown, making it harder to reach decisions. States that violated human rights were able to use procedural methods in the Commission to avoid or water down condemnations, and critics charged that member states spent more time and energy trying to avoid criticism than they did defending rights (Ghanea, 2006). A final straw came in 2003 when Libya – a country with a weak human rights record – was elected as chair of the Commission.

The Commission met for the last time in 2006, when it was replaced by the UN Human Rights Council (HRC). The US had wanted the new HRC to be a smaller body, with members elected using a two-thirds majority and chosen mainly because of their commitment to human rights, with a ban on countries subject to UN sanctions because of their rights violations. In the event, the HRC had a similar structure to the Commission, but it is supervised by the High Commissioner and is empowered to carry out reviews of the human rights situation in all UN member states, and to receive complaints from states as well as from individuals and organizations. It is still, though, subject to the politicization of its work.

International human rights law

Along with the passage of the UDHR, and the activities of human rights IOs, work has also progressed on the development of a body of international law. This began in December 1948 when the UN General Assembly unanimously adopted the Convention on the Prevention and Punishment of the Crime of Genocide. However, a plan to convert the UDHR into a binding legal instrument was resisted on the basis that not all rights were interconnected: civil and political rights, it was argued, could be monitored by independent experts, and required simply that states did not interfere with the rights of individuals, while economic and social rights needed legal action to ensure implementation (De Schutter, 2019). In the end, two separate covenants were adopted in 1966: the International Covenant on Civil and Political Rights (favoured by the US), and the International Covenant on Economic, Social and Cultural Rights (favoured by the Soviet Union). Both eventually came into force in 1976, and the combination of the Declaration of Human Rights and the two covenants has since been often described as the 'International Bill of Rights' and the ultimate exposition of those rights.

Meanwhile, more focused international treaties were agreed, including those on torture (1984), the rights of the child (1989) and migrant workers (1990). As this happened, committees of independent experts were formed under UN auspices to monitor the implementation of the treaties and to publish periodic reports. The coexistence of committees, commissions and councils reached such a level of complexity that, note Alston and Mégret (2020), it was not always immediately obvious which were the most important and why. To add further complications, human rights are not only an interest of the UN itself, but also of multiple UN agencies and programmes, notably the International Labour Organization (see later in this chapter) and UNESCO (see Chapter 12). At first the UN had been primarily concerned with matters of peace and security, but its goals had been repackaged into the three pillars of security, development and human rights.

Of the more than 100 international agreements that now address human rights topics, Donnelly and Whelan (2020) point to seven that are usually understood to provide the core of international human rights law; these are listed in Table 8.2, along with two others. Although the body of law would seem to be substantial, the data on signatories paint a picture of a world in which many countries – particularly the authoritarian ones – are reluctant to provide support. For example, Malaysia, Myanmar, Saudi Arabia and Yemen have not signed the International Covenant on Civil and Political Rights, while China has signed but not ratified. Meanwhile, as noted in Chapter 7, the majority of countries have also shied away from the Migrant Workers Convention, which has been signed by of the major migrant-receiving countries of the world.

Table 8.2: Major human rights agreements

Opened for signature	Where signed	Subject
Core agreements		
1965	New York	Elimination of All Forms of Racial Discrimination
1966	New York	International Covenant on Civil and Political Rights
1966	New York	International Covenant on Economic, Social and Cultural Rights*
1979	New York	Elimination of All Forms of Discrimination Against Women*
1984	New York	UN Convention Against Torture
1989	New York	Rights of the Child*
2006	New York	Rights of Persons with Disabilities*
Others		
1990	New York	Protection of the Rights of all Migrant Workers and Members of their Families**
2007	Paris	Protection of All Persons from Enforced Disappearance**

* US signed but not ratified

** US not signed

THE UN HUMAN RIGHTS REGIME

In her 2022 annual report to the UN Human Rights Council, Anaïs Marin – a Polish political scientist appointed in 2018 as Special Rapporteur on the human rights situation in Belarus – painted a bleak picture of life in the country. Under the iron rule of President Aleksandr Lukashenko since 1994, Belarus has become one of the most authoritarian states in the world, with a weak record on human rights. The newest HRC report on Belarus made clear that the situation was worsening: a February 2022 constitutional referendum was neither free nor fair, capital punishment was being used not just for serious crimes but for the planning of what the state defined as terrorist acts, independent NGOs and media had undergone a 'virtual annihilation', and systematic human rights violations had 'engulfed Belarus in a climate of arbitrariness and fear'.

This single national report was just one example of the work of UN bodies charged with monitoring and drawing attention to violations of human rights around the world, a never-ending and increasingly demanding task given recent downward trends in the health of democracy. More than is the case with most other regimes addressed in this book, the international regime on human rights is centred on UN activities and on two main kinds of IGOs: charter bodies (established under the terms of the UN Charter) that are responsible for monitoring the compliance of states with the goals of the UDHR, and treaty bodies with a more targeted interest in the main pieces of international human rights law.

The UN Human Rights Council

The primary charter body is the UN Human Rights Council (HRC), founded in 2006 to replace the Commission on Human Rights. Its structure is as follows:

- *Secretariat and executive head.* From its headquarters in Geneva, the HRC is overseen by a president elected for a term of one year, working with a Bureau of five vice-presidents. In 2022, the president was from Argentina, and the vice-presidents were from Armenia, Gambia, Germany, Libya and Uzbekistan. Secretariat functions are provided by the Office of the High Commissioner for Human Rights.

- *Assembly.* The HRC meets at least three times per year for a total of at least ten weeks, with additional crisis meetings convened as needed. It has 47 national members elected by the UN General Assembly in a secret ballot for three-year terms (no more than two consecutively), with a regional quota: 13 African states, 13 Asian-Pacific states, 8 Latin American and Caribbean states, 7 Western European and other states, and 6 Eastern European states. (The defunct Commission had not been too different: 53 members elected for three-year terms by ECOSOC, with a similar geographical quota.)

- *Other elements.* The HRC has a Bureau consisting of the president and four vice-presidents, serving one-year terms. It also has an Advisory Committee made up of 18 independent experts nominated to three-year terms by governments and confirmed by the Council, that meets biannually to provide input into the work of the Council.

- Reviews of the HRC are carried out every five years by the UN General Assembly, and any member state found to have engaged in systematic violations of rights can be suspended. Libya was suspended in 2011, and Russia in 2022 in the wake of charges of its attacks on civilians during its invasion of Ukraine.

- *Budget.* The HRC and the Office of the High Commissioner for Human Rights are both financed in part through the regular UN budget, but almost two-thirds of their budgets in 2022 was covered by voluntary contributions from a combination mainly of states and other IOs, with some from corporations and NGOs. Less than 40 states made contributions, though, and most of those that did were European: Sweden topped the list with a contribution of nearly $24 million, while the European Union provided funding of nearly $23 million. No funding came from China, France, India or the US, four of the sixth biggest economies in the world (Office of the High Commissioner for Human Rights, 2023).

Much like its predecessor, the HRC is expected to promote and protect human rights globally, to point out violations of right, and to make recommendations on responses. It does this through four main channels:

- Under the *Universal Periodic Review* (UPR), the HRC reviews the human rights situation in every UN member state. The reviews are completed in four-year cycles, with 42–48 countries reviewed each year, based on information provided by each of the states being reviewed, and information from independent Special Procedures (see below), as well as human rights treaty bodies and other UN bodies.

- Under the *Complaint Procedure*, individuals, groups, and NGOs that have been victims of human rights violations, or have direct and reliable knowledge of such violations, can lodge a formal complaint with the HRC. Recent examples have included complaints about the general human rights situation in multiple countries, as well as concerns about the place of trade unions and religious minorities in Iraq.

- Under the *Special Procedure*, groups of experts, rapporteurs and special representatives work together to examine and advise on thematic issues (such as the human rights implications of climate change, or the problem of systemic racism in law enforcement) or on the human rights situation in specific countries. Recent examples of the latter have included Afghanistan, Belarus, Ethiopia and Sudan.

- The HRC organizes commissions of inquiry and fact-finding missions targeted at particularly egregious violations of human rights. These can last from a few weeks to multiple years, depending on the depth of the problem; recent subjects have included Ethiopia, Nicaragua, Ukraine and the Israeli-occupied Palestinian territories.

Despite the differences between the HRC and the old Commission on Human Rights, the challenges faced by the HRC are not dissimilar. The key division it faces, argues Lakatos (2022), continues to be one between states that prioritize the global promotion of human rights, and states that want to weaken their domestic human rights without serious international consequences. China is a case in point, having emerged in recent years – argues Piccone (2018) – as a 'pivotal player' in the international human rights system, shifting from a more defensive posture to a more activist role, particularly in the HRC. This stems, Piccone believes, from a long game based on blocking international criticism of its repressive regime, and promoting the idea of national sovereignty and non-interference in the internal affairs of states. Richardson (2020) concurs, arguing that China's engagement with human rights is based on trying to rewrite norms and procedures in order to minimize scrutiny of the conduct not just of its own government, but also that of all governments.

It is not only authoritarian regimes that complain about the HRC, though. The Trump administration, for example, withdrew the US from the Council in June 2018, claiming a lack of necessary reforms and a bias against Israel. In announcing the withdrawal, Nikki Haley – then the US ambassador to the UN – described the HRC as a 'cesspool of political bias'. Meanwhile, US Vice-President Mike Pence charged that it had 'engaged in ever more virulent anti-American and anti-Israeli invective' (Koran, 2018). It was an unusually blunt attack, from an administration with a questionable rights

SPOTLIGHT 8

THE UNUSUAL CASE OF THE UNITED STATES

Throughout this book there are examples of the leading role played by the US in promoting and encouraging international cooperation. It was, for example, the key actor in the creation of the UN and in the design of the Bretton Woods system, and has been a leader in the activities of the North Atlantic Treaty Organization and of the major international financial IGOs, as well as using its power and influence to encourage many of the most important pieces of international law. It is also the major source of funds for multiple IGOs, ranging from the IMF and the World Bank to the World Trade Organization and the Food and Agriculture Organization of the UN.

All of which makes it so surprising that the US can sometimes be one of the outliers on international cooperation. In other chapters, we see it opposing the creation of the International Trade Organization, often dragging its feet on international efforts to address climate change, and opting not to sign several key agreements on migration and refugees. In the field of human rights, meanwhile, the US often claims to be a beacon of democracy, and yet it led the opposition to the creation of the International Criminal Court (see later in this chapter) and has only ratified three of the seven major human rights treaties: those on racial discrimination, civil and political rights, and against torture.

Much of the explanation lies with the requirement that the US can only ratify a treaty with the support of the US Senate, where there is conservative opposition to the more progressive ideas associated with human rights treaties. The Convention on Discrimination against Women, for example, includes the advocacy of reproductive rights and the enforcement of gender-neutral work rules that American conservatives mainly oppose. At the same time, religious conservatives in the US oppose some of the moral implications of the Convention on the Rights of the Child, which they worry will limit parental authority. This is not to say, though, that the US is not a global champion of human rights, and its record of reticence can be contrasted with the record of multiple countries with weak human rights records – including China, North Korea, Saudi Arabia and Syria – that have ratified most of the major human rights treaties, but clearly have not met their goals.

record of its own, but it was not the first time that the US had resisted efforts on human rights; see *Spotlight 8*. The withdrawal by the Trump administration was reversed by the Biden administration, and the US was elected back onto the Council in October 2021.

The Office of the High Commissioner for Human Rights

The second UN charter body is the Office of the High Commissioner for Human Rights (OHCHR), which was one of the concrete outcomes of the 1993 Vienna Conference on Human Rights. Based in the Palais Wilson in Geneva, the former home of the League of Nations, the High Commissioner is the primary human rights official of the UN system, the office also acting as the secretariat of the Human Rights

Council. The High Commissioner is appointed by the Secretary General of the UN – with the approval of the General Assembly, and with an informal geographical rotation – for a maximum of two four-year terms. There have been eight office-holders to date, with one each from Austria, Brazil, Canada, Chile, Ecuador, Ireland, Jordan and South Africa. The fate of the High Commissioner from Brazil – Sérgio Vieira de Mello – captured news headlines in August 2003 when he was killed in a suicide truck bombing in Baghdad, Iraq.

With a staff of about 850, including officers serving in UN field missions, the OHCHR provides support for the HRC's special procedures, provides research and secretariat support for human rights treaty bodies, works to make sure that human rights are prioritized in the work of the UN, and supports the activities of national human rights institutions. The latter includes support for the Global Alliance of National Human Rights Institutions, which brings together independent national bodies. These include advisory bodies, institutes and commissions such as the National Human Rights Commissions of Canada, India, Nigeria and South Korea. NGOs are not members of the alliance.

Although it might be considered logical to blend the Human Rights Council and the Office of the High Commissioner into a single UN human rights body, the purpose of having a separate High Commissioner was to create a position unencumbered by the political divisions that are so often found in the HRC. The job of the office is summarized, in part, by some of the wording of the General Assembly resolution containing its mandate: 'To play an active role in removing the current obstacles and in meeting the challenges to the full realization of all human rights and in preventing the continuation of human rights violations throughout the world' (United Nations General Assembly, 1993).

The value of the independence of the OHCHR was illustrated in the late 1990s and early 2000s when High Commissioners Mary Robinson and Louis Arbour criticized efforts by states – even democratic ones – to respond to terrorism with security initiatives that threatened human rights (Seiderman, 2019). The frustrations of the job, though, were reflected in the final speech made by High Commissioner Zeid Ra'ad al Hussein of Jordan in 2018 when he announced that he would not be seeking a second four-year term because the position had become untenable (Al Hussein, 2018). The UDHR and the whole body of subsequent human rights law was under attack not only from violent extremists, he warned, 'but also from authoritarian leaders, populists, demagogues, cultural relativists, some Western academics, and even some UN officials'. He went on to note that there was 'a dangerous remove and superficiality' to many UN discussions about human rights, and worried about the rise of 'chauvinistic nationalism' and the challenges it posed to peace.

Other human rights IGOs

In addition to these two charter bodies, the UN human rights regime consists of treaty bodies or committees of independent experts charged with monitoring and publishing reports on the implementation of UN human rights treaties. There are now ten of them (see Table 8.3), with members nominated and elected for fixed and

Table 8.3: UN human rights treaty bodies

Committee against Torture

Subcommittee on Prevention of Torture

Committee on Economic, Social and Cultural Rights

Committee on Enforced Disappearances

Committee on the Elimination of Discrimination Against Women

Committee on the Elimination of Racial Discrimination

Committee on Migrant Workers

Committee on the Rights of Persons with Disabilities

Committee on the Rights of the Child

Human Rights Committee

renewable terms of four years by the state parties to the treaties. They receive periodic reports from those parties, carry out their own enquiries, and review complaints received about states from individual citizens, human rights NGOs or other UN bodies. A study by Carraro (2019) concludes that the committees have a surprisingly high level of independence given the political nature of the process by which they are elected. However, Oette (2018), while recognizing the value of their work, points to the challenges they face in terms of the growing number of reports and cases from state parties to the treaties, and the tribulations of being caught between the demands of those parties and of NGOs, and of worsening challenges to human rights.

Another actor in the UN human rights regime is the International Labour Organization (ILO), which describes its mission as one of promoting social justice as well as human and labour rights (see also Chapter 7). Headquartered in Geneva, it has a uniquely tripartite structure, acting as a meeting place for governments, employers and workers, and posing interesting questions for theories of institutional development and performance; see *IOs in Theory 8*. Although it won the 1969 Nobel Peace Prize for its work, it has had to struggle against a difference of political opinion about the content and nature of workers' rights. It has also made little use of the tools it has available: it can launch a commission of inquiry to investigate complaints made by one member state against another, but has done so only 12 times in its history, and it has only once invoked its power to impose economic sanctions against a country that violates ILO rules (against Myanmar in 2000). Its modest record is part of the reason why it is the least known of the UN human rights bodies, and prompted Digiacomo (2019) in his analysis of the ILO to ask whether it was a champion of workers' rights or a 90-pound weakling.

IOs IN THEORY 8

INSTITUTIONALISM AND NEW INSTITUTIONALISM

The study of governing institutions has long been a central interest of political science. In fact, institutions were long regarded as the core subject matter of political science, and much of the early research was dominated by institutionalism. This is a theoretical approach that focuses on the structure and dynamics of governing institutions: how they work, where their strengths and weaknesses lie, and what can be done to make them more efficient. Although institutional approaches briefly fell out of favour in the 1960s with the new popularity of behaviouralism (emphasizing the actions of people over those of institutions), it was revived in the 1980s as new institutionalism. This looked not just at the formal rules of government but also at how institutions shaped political decisions, at the interaction of institutions and society, and at the informal patterns of behaviour within formal institutions.

Although these theories were founded in studies of national and comparative politics, they also lent themselves to international relations as researchers tried to better understand how international organizations evolved in response to changing needs and circumstances. Institutionalism shares realist ideas about the anarchic nature of the international system, but is interested in how cooperation via IGOs can be a way for states to establish common interests and achieve joint gains. It can be used to understand the motives behind the creation of IGOs, to understand how the structures and rules of IGOs are worked out, and to follow the patterns of cooperation (or lack of cooperation) between states.

Human rights IGOs might not seem to be the best example of the possibilities of the application of institutionalism, given their political difficulties. On the other hand, institutionalism can be used to help us better understand why they have had more difficulties than is the case with the work of IGOs in fields such as security, finance, and trade. For international relations institutionalists, argues Scholte (2021), 'global governance is about explicit rules and concrete regulatory organizations with a planetary span – and about the ways that agents engage with these apparatuses, both cooperatively and competitively, to pursue their ideas and interests'.

THE INTERNATIONAL CRIMINAL COURT

Outside the UN, the most prominent IGO focused on human rights issues, and also one of the more controversial IGOs of any type, is the International Criminal Court (ICC). Founded in 2002, its job is to step in as a last resort should states be unable or unwilling to try perpetrators of the four most serious violations of human rights: genocide, crimes against humanity, war crimes and aggression. It traces its origins back to the post-war Nuremburg and Tokyo war crimes trials, which were convened on an ad hoc basis. The UN General Assembly discussed the idea of a permanent criminal court in 1948, but Cold War tensions scotched the prospect and it was not until the end of the Cold War that the idea was revisited. The need for the court was emphasized with the cumbersome work of the tribunals set up to investigate crimes against humanity in Rwanda and the former Yugoslavia in 1992–95. Negotiations led to the convening of a 1998 conference in Rome, at which a combination of pro-ICC states, legal experts, activists and NGOs pressed for the court, and 120 states supported the signing of its founding Statute (see Koomen, 2019).

Despite its name, the court does not have jurisdiction over violations of international treaties, which means that it is not active in cases of cross-border drug trafficking or human trafficking, for example, or of environmental destruction by multinational enterprises. The Court issued its first arrest warrants in 2005, aimed at Ugandan warlords, and indicted its first head of state in 2009 when Omar al-Bashir of Sudan was charged with supporting a programme of rape and murder by paramilitary groups in the western region of Darfur. It held its first trial in 2009 when Thomas Lubanga – a militia leader from the Democratic Republic of Congo – was charged and convicted of the war crime of conscripting children. By almost every report, the Court's earliest cases were poorly organized, and it struggled to efficiently work through its new procedures (Koomen, 2019).

Organizationally, the court has the following components:

- Within its headquarters in the Hague, the court has 18 *judges* elected for non-renewable terms of nine years by the Assembly of States Parties of the court (the ASP), which meets at least once annually in the UN or at the seat of the ICC. The election uses a complex process that ensures a 'fair' representation of male and female judges, and that factors in where they come from and their home legal systems. The judges do not meet as a whole, but instead work in three chambers: groups of three pre-trial judges will decide if there is enough evidence to go to trial, separate groups of three trial judges will conduct the trials and groups of five judges will handle any appeals filed by parties.

- The Court is headed by a *President* and two Vice-Presidents, elected by the judges from among their ranks on a majority basis for renewable three-year terms. The Presidency assigns cases to chambers and oversees the administration of the ICC.

- The *Registry* is responsible for the safekeeping of evidence, the protection of witnesses and victims, and providing translation, interpretation and other support services.

- The *Office of the Prosecutor* is an independent part of the Court that is responsible – with the support of a large staff of investigators and lawyers – for investigating cases where crimes appear to have been committed and deciding which cases to prosecute. The Prosecutor and Deputy Prosecutor are elected by the ASP for non-renewable nine-year terms.

- Each defendant is given a *defence* team recruited from outside the ICC.

- *Budget.* The Court is funded by mandatory contributions from its member states, calculated on the same capacity to pay formula used by the UN. Its biggest contributors are Japan, Germany, France, the UK and Canada, while multiple states – notably Brazil, Argentina and Nigeria – have fallen behind in their contributions.

The court has not been universally welcomed, facing opposition and doubts even before it was founded, and being the target of criticism since then for its sometimes-flawed investigations and its choice of cases. It was opposed not just by states that might have been the target of its work, such as Israel and Russia, but also by the US. Complaining that its soldiers might be subject to politically motivated or frivolous prosecutions, the US worked with China during the early negotiations to have the Court subordinated to the UN Security Council, where the US has the power of veto (see Elsea, 2002). When it failed, President George W. Bush threatened to withdraw US personnel from peacekeeping operations unless they were given immunity from prosecution, and negotiated bilateral immunity agreements with individual governments under which they agreed not to surrender US nationals to the Court.

Criticism of the Court's selectivity has come particularly from African states that accuse it of focusing too much on African targets (Clarke, 2019). Between 2002 and 2016, for example, it pursued 22 cases in eight African countries – the Central African Republic, the Democratic Republic of the Congo, Ivory Coast, Kenya, Libya, Mali, Sudan and Uganda – but failed to investigate similar cases in Colombia, Palestine, Venezuela or the actions of British troops in Iraq. Ba (2020) responds to this criticism by pointing out that African states were particularly eager to see the creation of the ICC, and by looking at where the ICC's cases come from: they can be triggered by self-referral from states, by a referral from the UN Security Council or by the Office of the Prosecutor. As of the end of 2019, he found that of the 12 cases then under investigation, ten were from African states, but six of those were self-referred, leading Ba to conclude that some states have outsourced the problem of prosecuting serious crime to the ICC.

The doubts about the Court have led to a patchy pattern of membership, made possible because it is a treaty-based organization:

- As of 2022, a total of 123 countries were full members of the Court; these included almost all of Europe, almost all of Latin America (with the exceptions of Cuba and Nicaragua), most African countries, and Australia, Canada, Japan, New Zealand and South Korea; see Map 8.1.

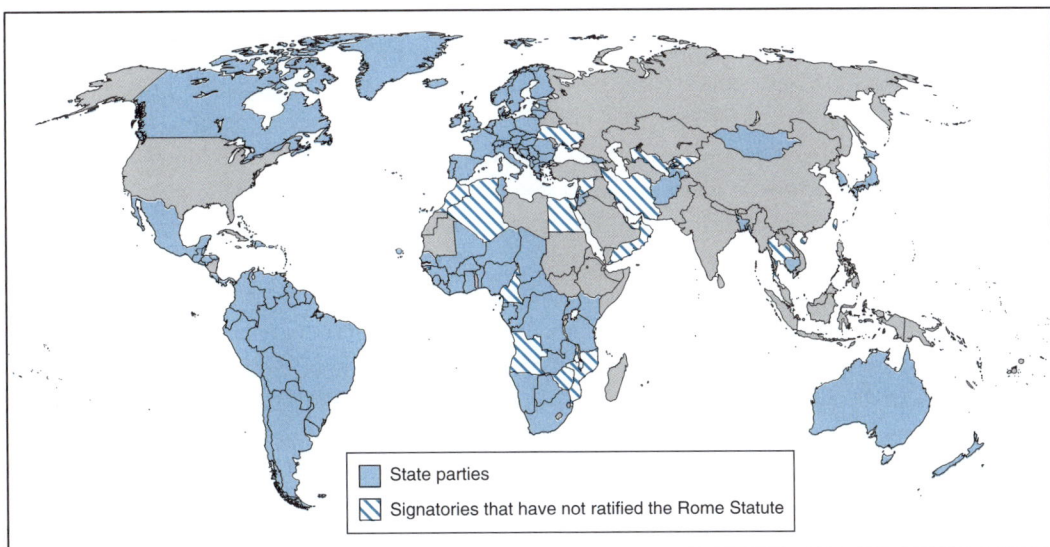

Map 8.1: International Criminal Court.

- The US signed the Rome Statute during the Clinton administration, but the Bush administration revoked the US signature, while the Trump administration imposed targeted sanctions on Court officials and threatened to support its dissolution.

- Israel and Russia also revoked their signatures, the former over concerns about how the ICC was approaching the Israeli occupation of Palestinian territory, and the latter after the Court described the Russian presence in Crimea (part of Ukraine) as an on-going state of occupation.

- The Philippines was a full state party but withdrew in 2019 after the Court launched an investigation into possible crimes committed by the administration of President Rodrigo Duterte in its war on drugs.

- About 30 mainly African and Middle Eastern countries have signed but not ratified the Statute, while another 41 countries – including China, India, Indonesia, Pakistan, Saudi Arabia and Turkey – have neither signed nor acceded to the Statute.

Much like the difficulties of reaching agreement on the structure of UN agencies dealing with human rights, it has been hard to agree the best way to prosecute individuals or groups accused of the most serious violations of human rights. The temporary arrangements set up in Nuremburg and Tokyo after World War II addressed an immediate problem in a climate of a strong desire to hold war criminals to account. However, the world – and our understanding of human rights – has changed a great deal since then, making it hard to imagine how the structure the ICC could be changed so as to make it more politically palatable.

REGIONAL HUMAN RIGHTS COURTS

Periodically, the UN Human Rights Council (HRC) will appoint an independent expert to report or advise on a theme in human rights, or the situation in a given country. One of them was Maina Kiai, a Kenyan lawyer and human rights activist who served as the UN Special Rapporteur on the Rights to Freedom of Peaceful Assembly and Association between 2011 and 2017. In his 2014 report, he reached a deeply critical conclusion: 'The UN system is notoriously impotent when it comes to enforcing the human rights it espouses; it simply does not have the tools, and its Member States are not going to make them available anytime soon'. He went on to argue that national and regional courts or human rights commissions were often in a better position to protect human rights (Kiai, 2015).

Some of the evidence for this can be found in the work of three courts working at the regional level and all associated with a regional IGO (see summary in Table 8.4). The model is provided by the European Court of Human Rights (ECHR), which was an outgrowth of the Council of Europe, founded in 1949 to champion the idea of European unity. One of the first products of the Council was the signature in 1950 of the European Convention on Human Rights, which was followed in January 1959 by the founding of the ECHR. If a state that is a party to the convention – or a citizen of one of those states – feels that their human rights have been violated, they can apply to the Court, whose job (if it accepts the application) is to review the case and to issue a judgement.

Table 8.4: Regional human rights courts

Name	Founded	Headquarters	Associated IO
European Court of Human Rights	1959	Strasbourg, France	Council of Europe
Inter-American Court of Human Rights	1979	San José, Costa Rica	Organization of American States
African Court on Human and People's Rights	1987	Banjul, The Gambia	African Union

The ECHR was a temporary body until 1998 when it became a permanent institution to which direct access was available to citizens of the member states of the Council of Europe. This new permanence, combined with expanded membership of the Council, greater media interest in the work of the Court and simplified procedures, led to a new burst of activity: in its first 40 years the Court issued just under 840 judgements, since when it has delivered about as many every year, peaking with more than 1,600 judgements in 2009 (European Court of Human Rights, 2023). Turkey, Russia (before its 2022 expulsion) and Italy have routinely topped the list of countries against which judgements have been issued; nearly one-third of the judgements for Turkey relate to the right to a fair trial, and more than half of those for Italy relate to the excessive length of proceedings.

The ECHR consists of 46 judges, one for each of the member states of the Council of Europe, but when they hear cases, they do so as individuals, not as representatives of their home states. Judges are elected by the Parliamentary Assembly of the Council of Europe from lists of candidates proposed by each state, and serve a single nine-year term (with an age limit of 70), and they in turn elect a President and two Vice-Presidents. The Court is divided into five Sections, each with its own President and each balanced by geography, gender and the different legal systems of the member states; the membership of each Section is changed every three years. Judges review cases either working as individuals, or as three-person committees, or in seven-member chambers, or – with the more important cases – as a 17-member Grand Chamber. The latter includes the President, the Vice-Presidents, all five Section Presidents and the balance of judges selected by the drawing of lots.

The Inter-American Court of Human Rights (IACHR) follows a similar model, having been formed out of the 1969 American Convention on Human Rights, which was championed by the Organization of American States (see Chapter 4). The Court has seven judges appointed to renewable six-year terms by the General Assembly of the OAS. Even though the OAS has 35 members, however, only 24 have been active in the IACHR, the absentees citing a variety of concerns: Canada objects to the implied provisions against abortion in the convention, for example, while Venezuela has charged the IACHR with interfering in its domestic affairs. Neither Belize, Canada, Cuba, Guyana, the US nor most Caribbean states have signed the treaty or joined the court. Partly as a result, the budget of the court is small and its workload is insubstantial, with less than 20 cases on its docket in an average year.

For its part, the African Court on Human and Peoples' Rights (ACHPR) is the judicial arm of the African Union, and is associated with the African Charter on Human and Peoples' Rights, which came into force in 1986. Illustrating the kind of impact that NGOs can have on inter-state agreements, the idea of the court was championed as early as 1961 by the International Commission of Jurists. This is a Geneva-based body founded in 1952, consisting of 60 senior judges, attorneys and academics working to promote international human rights standards. The idea was subsequently kept alive, note Huneeus and Madsen (2019), by the UN Commission on Human Rights, NGOs and individual states. When the Charter came, though, it was not supported by a strong institutional arrangement, and the ACHPR has suffered from a lack of political interest: only 33 of the member states of the African Union have ratified the 1998 Protocol that established the court, of which only eight have accepted the legal competence of the court.

The regional courts, the ICC and UN human rights bodies all have at least one feature in common: a resistance to their work that has led to a backlash – which might also be termed bad behaviour, pushback or resistance – against what Hillebrecht (2021) describes as the international justice regime (combining criminal and human rights). Multiple states have threatened to leave the ICC (although only two have: Burundi and the Philippines, in 2017 and 2019), the US withdrew from the Human Rights Council in 2018, political leaders in the UK have threatened to leave the European Court of Human Rights, which Russia finally left in 2022 after years of threats. Meanwhile, Contese (2019) has found increased evidence of pushback against the Inter-American court, typically stemming from a member state objecting to a ruling from, or threatened action by, the court.

NON-STATE HUMAN RIGHTS ACTORS

Human rights are a topic that excites the interest of many people, whether in states where the protection of rights is strong and there is a movement to see similar protections elsewhere, or in states where those rights are threatened or under attack. It is not hard for many to argue that the work of states and IGOs is moving too slowly, and to form or to support campaigning organizations. As a result, multiple human rights NGOs and INGOs have been formed over the decades; see Table 8.5 for examples. Some have developed such a strong reputation, argue Alston and Mégret (2020), that they 'clearly punch above their weight in terms of influence, especially compared to some of the less influential UN bodies'. In fact, they note, most people outside the field of international human rights are more likely to have heard of bodies such as Amnesty International than of the UN Human Rights Council.

McGaughey (2021) argues that NGOs were once almost extraneous to the UN human rights system, but have become increasingly important over time. Even if states are the primary actors in the development of international law, she continues, NGOs have played multiple key roles:

– Promoting public awareness of the implications of international law.

– Drawing attention to human rights abuses.

Table 8.5: Human rights INGOs: Examples

Name	Founded	Headquarters	Interests
Anti-Slavery International	1839	London, UK	Child labour, human trafficking, forced labour and other modern forms of slavery.
Save the Children	1919	London	Health, education and gender equality for children. (See Chapter 7.)
International Federation for Human Rights	1922	Paris, France	Encourages and reinforces work of national, regional and international human rights organizations.
Amnesty International	1961	London	Mass membership body that investigates and reports on human rights abuses. Multiple national offices.
Survival International	1969	London	Rights of indigenous or tribal peoples.
Human Rights Watch	1978	New York, USA	Investigates and reports on human rights abuses. Multiple national offices.
Medica Mondiale	1993	Cologne, Germany	Advocates for the rights of girls and women affected by sexual violence in war zones.

- Making constructive use of the Universal Periodic Review process offered by the UN Human Rights Council.

- Lobbying for people's rights.

- Lobbying for new treaties.

- Contributing to the drafting of treaties.

- Launching cases on behalf of people and communities whose rights have been breached.

The world's oldest human rights organization – and one of the oldest of all NGOs – is Anti-Slavery International (ASI), founded in London in 1839 as the British and Foreign Anti-Slavery Society in the wake of the abolition of slavery in the British Empire. It worked to abolish slavery in other parts of the world, became ASI in 1995, and now campaigns against child labour, human trafficking, forced labour and other modern forms of slavery. Although it has an office only in the UK, its runs projects in multiple parts of the world, with a focus on Africa, Central Asia and South Asia. For Craig et al. (2019), one of the challenges faced by bodies such as ASI has been to convince people that slavery is not something found only in history, or in another part of the world. Even now, they argue, many people do not believe that the more severe forms of human exploitation do not happen in their own countries, sometimes in plain sight. The rising problem of slavery has led to the creation of multiple new NGOs in different parts of the world with this problem as their chief concern.

Globally, non-governmental action on human rights is dominated by two organizations. The first of these is Amnesty International, founded in the UK in 1961. It works to draw attention to human rights abuses, with a focus on prisoners of conscience, ending torture, the abolition of the death penalty, sexual and reproductive rights, and the rights of women, children, minorities, refugees and migrants. Amnesty, as it is often known, was founded by a British lawyer named Peter Benenson (1921–2005). While commuting to work one day in London, he was shocked to read in a newspaper about two Portuguese students who had been sentenced to long terms in prison for giving a toast 'to liberty' against the authoritarian regime of Prime Minister Antonio Salazar. Berenson wrote an article titled 'The Forgotten Prisoners' that was published in the British weekly newspaper *The Observer*, asking for readers to write letters in support of the students. In the wake of the response, and to coordinate further letter-writing campaigns, he founded Amnesty International in July 1961. The

IOs IN ACTION 8

AMNESTY INTERNATIONAL AND THE FIFA WORLD CUP

The quadrennial football World Cup is one of the premier international sporting events, with a following that runs into the billions. Inevitably, the country that hosts the event attracts international attention, although not all of it is positive. The 2022 event was held – somewhat controversially – in Qatar, a country known for its hot temperatures, for a willingness to spend enormous amounts to build the infrastructure needed to host the World Cup, and – thanks in part to the work of Amnesty International – for its poor human rights record.

Years before the event, Amnesty and other human rights organizations had criticized Qatar for the flaws in its labour system, allowing it to employ thousands of migrant workers from countries such as Bangladesh and India to build World Cup infrastructure, to offer low wages for long working hours (up to 18 hours per day in often extreme heat without weekly days off), to provide poor living conditions and to sometimes use forced labour with few workplace protections. The government of Qatar made changes, including the introduction of a minimum wage, enhanced rights for workers and improved working conditions (Brannagan and Reiche, 2022). Despite this, research by the *Guardian* (2021) suggested that as many as 6,750 migrant workers had died in Qatar since it had been given the right to host the World Cup.

Amnesty International continued the pressure, urging FIFA (*Fédération Internationale de Football Association*, the international governing body of football), to earmark at least $440 million to compensate workers. Even in the weeks leading up to the competition, Amnesty was calling on national football associations to support worker compensation, and was warning of the persistence of human rights abuses on a significant scale, describing the event as the 'Qatar World Cup of Shame'. These and multiple other appeals and reports were indicative of the capacity of Amnesty International to draw attention to human rights abuses, their efforts often standing in contrast to those of governments that did much less to publicize the problem.

organization went on to win the 1977 Nobel Peace Prize, and to become the biggest human rights INGO in the world, with more than seven million members, seven regional offices and sections in more than 70 countries; see *IOs in Action 8*.

Across the Atlantic, the second global NGO – Human Rights Watch – was founded in the US in 1978. Like ASI, it is headquartered in one country but has projects in multiple parts of the world. In 1997 it shared the Nobel Peace Prize as a founding member of the International Campaign to Ban Landmines (see Chapter 4), and it went on to play a leading role in the 2008 treaty banning cluster munitions. As well as publishing an annual report that has become an authoritative source on the state of human rights around the world, Human Rights Watch – together with Amnesty – also plays a key role in pointing out human rights abuses and supporting the work of activists. Its efforts have expanded on the back of the information revolution, as a result of which campaigns to promote and protect human rights have spread to almost every part of the world, with the notable exceptions of the most authoritarian regimes, such as North Korea and Saudi Arabia. The driving force behind these changes, argues Neier (2020), has been the non-governmental human rights movement. At the same time, as we have seen in other chapters, the work of humanitarian NGOs such as Doctors Without Borders, the Red Cross and Save the Children should not be overlooked.

THINKING POINTS

- Are the recent declines in pluralism, equality and accountability around the world reversible?

- Given the controversial nature of human rights, is the structure of the UN Human Rights Council the best we can hope for?

- What would be the costs and benefits of blending the UN Human Rights Council and the Office of the High Commissioner into a single UN human rights body?

- Is the International Criminal Court a good idea?

- Are human rights better addressed by intergovernmental organizations or international non-governmental organizations?

IOs RELATED TO THIS CHAPTER

African Court on Human and Peoples' Rights (ACHPR)

Amnesty International (AI)

Anti-Slavery International (ASI)

European Court of Human Rights (ECHR)

Human Rights Watch (HRW)

Inter-American Court of Human Rights (IACHR)

International Criminal Court (ICC)

International Labour Organization (ILO)

Office of the High Commissioner for Human Rights (OHCHR)

UN Human Rights Council (UNHRC)

FURTHER READING

DiGiacomo, Gordon, and Susan L. King (eds) (2019) *The Institutions of Human Rights: Developments and Practices* (University of Toronto Press). An edited collection on the human rights regime, with chapters on each of the key international organizations.

McGaughey, Fiona (2021) *Non-governmental Organisations and the United Nations Human Rights System* (Routledge). A review of the place of NGOs in the UN human rights system, and the ways in which NGOs influence that system.

Mégret, Frédéric, and Philip Alston (eds) (2020) *The United Nations and Human Rights: A Critical Appraisal*, 2nd edn (Oxford University Press). An edited collection of studies of the work of the UN on human rights, including chapters on the structure and activities of all its major organs and commissions.

Schabas, William A. (2020) *An Introduction to the International Criminal Court*, 6th edn (Cambridge University Press). A survey of the origins, structure, jurisdiction, procedures and work of the ICC.

Tistounet, Eric (2020) *The UN Human Rights Council: A Practical Anatomy* (Edward Elgar). A survey of the goals and structure of the HRC, including chapters on its major stakeholders, activities and voting procedures.

FOOD AND AGRICULTURE

PREVIEW

This chapter addresses the international regime that has evolved around food and agriculture, and more specifically around the so far unmet challenge of ensuring global food security. It opens with a review of the causes of food insecurity and of the dimensions of the problem, asking whether access to food should be considered a human right. It then looks at the evolution of the post-war global food regime, noting that agriculture was barely addressed internationally until after World War II, being given a boost by the first world food crisis in the 1970s (followed by a second in 2007–08). The chapter then discusses the goals and structures of the major agricultural IGOs: the Food and Agriculture Organization of the UN (FAO), the World Food Programme (WFP), the International Fund for Agricultural Development (IFAD) and the Consultative Group on International Agricultural Research (CGIAR). It goes on to review the place in the regime of international commodity bodies such as those concerned with coffee and with tropical timber. The chapter closes with an assessment of the influence of agribusiness multinationals and the implications of having large elements of global agriculture and food supply being controlled by a small number of large corporations.

CONTENTS

- The context
- Building a global food regime
- The UN food security regime
- Other agricultural IGOs
- Non-state food and agricultural actors

THE CONTEXT

In 2020, the Nobel Peace Prize was awarded to the World Food Programme (WFP), another arm of the UN (UN). Since its foundation in 1961, the Rome-based programme has become the world's largest humanitarian organization, with a focus on tackling hunger and building food security. It relies on voluntary donations to keep it active, providing emergency food relief in parts of the world afflicted by natural and human-made disasters, and helping poorer countries build their capacity to feed themselves. Although it is debatable whether or not food security helps or even replaces peacebuilding, the Nobel committee recognized the WFP for 'its efforts to combat hunger, for its contribution to bettering conditions for peace in conflict-affected areas and for acting as a driving force to prevent the use of hunger as a weapon of war and conflict'.

The work of the WFP is just one reminder of the many dimensions of one of the oldest and most fundamental global questions: how long will the world be able to feed itself? There have been worried analyses about the mismatch between population and food production dating back to the arguments made by the British cleric and scholar Thomas Malthus, whose 1798 *An Essay on the Principle of Population* became a bestseller. In it, he argued that an increase in food production led to an increase in population, leading to new levels of demand for food, in a fashion that would inevitably lead to famine or war, leading to poverty and depopulation. However, he did not foresee the improvements in agricultural techniques at the heart of the green revolution of the 1950s, which led to remarkable increases in crop yields, ensuring that supplies mainly kept up with demand.

Even today, with the global population now standing at eight billion, the world produces enough food to feed everyone. The problem is less one of quantity than of distribution, meaning that we have failed to ensure food security: making sure that people have access at all times to a predictable supply of sufficient, safe and nutritious food. Although we have made much progress towards achieving this goal, about 800 million people still experience hunger, while about 930 million people are food insecure (Food and Agriculture Organization of the UN, 2022a). Worst affected are marginalized groups such as small-scale farmers, landless workers and the urban poor, who suffer either because they are too poor to buy what they need, or because food supplies are disrupted by war or natural disasters.

The threats to food supply are multiple and often persistent (see Table 9.1), offering an example of the complexity of the global challenges we face, and of the difficulties involved in formulating responses. The importance of food and agriculture to us all is reflected in the fact that most of the 17 Sustainable Development Goals (SDGs) address them in some fashion, whether in the form of ending hunger and achieving food security (SDG 2), providing clean water for all (SDG 6), ensuring sustainable patterns of consumption and production (SDG 12), conserving marine resources (SDG 14), or reversing land degradation (SDG 15).

The global food system is also made more complex by the different levels and patterns of food production and consumption found in different states, and the different degrees to which they are exporters and importers. Comparing agricultural productivity is not easy, because states with more agricultural land almost inevitably produce more, the wealthier states consume more, and patterns of demand vary according to different diets. Cereals, though, lie at the heart of demand in most parts of the world, so using data on their production gives us some insight in the extent of the differences. Figure 9.1 shows the ten major producers, who among them account for about 80 per cent of global production.

We must also consider the question of access to food as a human right. Curiously, the word *food* appears only once in the Universal Declaration of Human Rights (UDHR), towards the end of the list of rights (Article 25 out of 30), and as part of a list of qualities necessary for a standard of living 'adequate' for the health of individuals

Table 9.1: The challenges faced by food and agriculture

Problem	Features
Food waste	About one-third of all food produced globally for human consumption is lost or wasted each year.
Declining investment	Underinvestment in research and development is a persistent problem in most countries.
Climate change	More extreme weather events and changing climate patterns are impacting crop yields and the location of food production.
Poverty and inequality	Most of the world's poorest people live in rural areas and work in low-scale agriculture.
Nutrition transition	Demographic transitions have reduced the diversity of diet and altered patterns of physical activity.
Volatile food prices	A combination of economic pressures, conflict and speculative investment has caused fluctuations in food prices.
Population change	Rising demand, coupled with more demand for processed foods from urban dwellers, is changing agricultural markets.
Environmental pressures	These include land scarcity, water degradation, the use of chemicals in farming, intensive farming and pressures on biodiversity.
Corporate concentration	A few large multinationals dominate the processing, distribution and retail of food, influencing prices and policymaking.
Food safety	Food poisoning and the contamination of soil and water are widespread problems.

Source: Based on Johnson (2018).

and their families. The sheer complexity of the list of these qualities – including food, clothing, housing and medical care – has meant that numerous international organizations are involved in promoting and protecting these rights (Peterson, 2018). However, while the right to 'an adequate standard of living, including adequate food' and the 'right to be free from hunger' were recognized by the 1966 International Covenant on Economic, Social and Cultural Rights (see Chapter 8), only 106 countries have acted through law to protect the right to food. Meanwhile, the UDHR does not mention the right to water, despite its critical role not just in human health but also in agriculture. It was only in July 2010 that the UN General Assembly adopted a resolution recognizing the human right to water and sanitation.

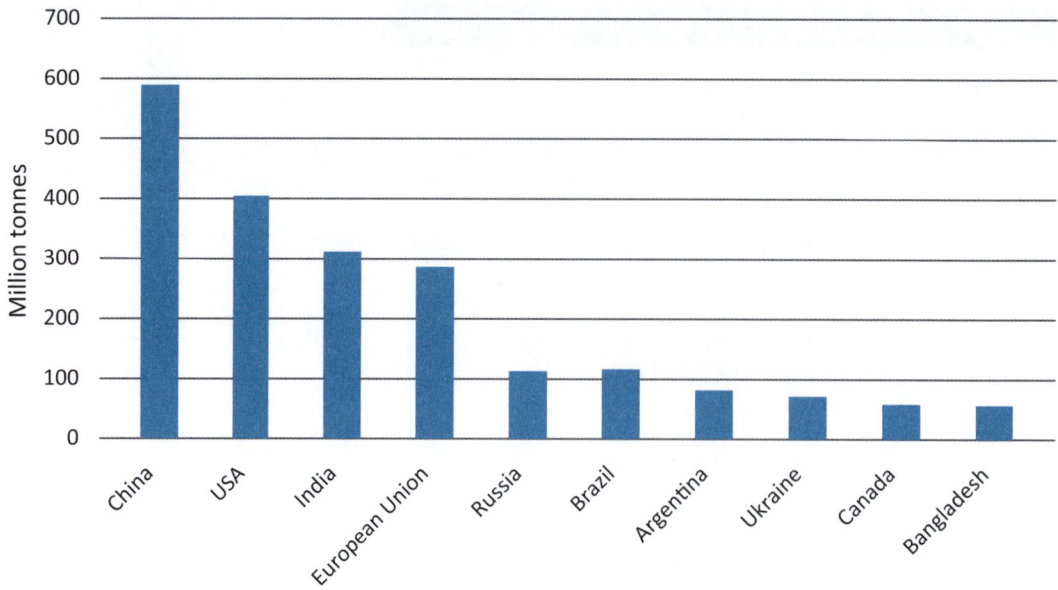

Figure 9.1: The world's ten biggest cereal producers.
Source: Based on data in Food and Agriculture Organization of the UN (2022b). Data are for 2020. Cereals include maize, wheat, rice, barley, rye and millet.

Even though there are many challenges to food security, there are also multiple potential solutions, including changes in consumer behaviour, addressing climate change, intervening along food supply chains to lower the cost of nutritious food and tackling inequality. Achieving such goals, though, is easier said than done, and faces numerous hurdles. Not least among them is the need to bring together the wide variety of actors involved in the global governance of food, agriculture, fisheries and forestry. These include states, corporate food producers and retailers, large and small farmers, traders and the international organizations that sometimes struggle to make the connections among the parts.

At the heart of these efforts is a cluster of IOs described by Lele at al. (2021) as the Big Five:

- The Food and Agriculture Organization of the UN

- The World Food Programme

- The International Fund for Agricultural Development

- The research bodies working under the auspices of the Consultative Group on International Agricultural Research

- The World Bank

This chapter discusses the first four (the World Bank was discussed in Chapter 5), while also looking at the input of autonomous IOs that influence the dynamics of the markets for commodities such as cocoa, coffee, cotton, grains and sugar, and the influential role of large multinationals involved in the production and retailing of food.

BUILDING A GLOBAL FOOD REGIME

Food insecurity and malnutrition have been features of human existence for centuries, stemming from causes that range from drought to disease and war. The struggle over land and access to food has often been a cause of conflict, while food insecurity and starvation have often been either a cause, a tactic or a result of war. As an example of a cause, the French Revolution of 1789 was sparked in part by population growth outpacing food supply, with crop failures leading to bread shortages, high prices, famine and starvation. As an example of a tactic, the Union side during the US civil war was guided in part by the Lieber Code, which allowed Union soldiers to starve 'hostile belligerents' if needed. As an example of a result, the sixth edition of the *Global Report on Food Crises* reported that about 140 million people in 24 countries were facing food crises in 2021 where the primary driver of the problem was conflict or insecurity (Global Network Against Food Crises, 2022).

Historically, the causes and the effects of food insecurity – as well as responses in the form of new and improved agricultural techniques – have mainly been localized, and while developments in farming technology travelled across borders, agriculture was rarely the subject of international cooperation. In 1905, the International Institute of Agriculture was founded in Rome as a clearinghouse for agricultural statistics, but its impact was limited (although its resources were transferred to the new FAO in 1946, which was later relocated from Washington DC to Rome as a result of the link). For the League of Nations, the priorities were peace and security and, although forerunners were created to today's major IGOs dealing with health, refugees and labour, there was no organizational response to agriculture (or human rights, or the environment, for that matter). This was despite a precipitous decline in world crop prices in 1929, prompting a report by the Economic Committee of the League of Nations (1931) on the causes and effects of the crisis: a combination of trade restrictions and skewed market forces, prompting a recommendation only of 'further study'.

Developments since 1945

As we have seen, the era of accelerated international cooperation that began after World War II was motivated mainly by the question of how to promote human welfare by encouraging peace and security. The elevation of food security to that process was emphasized by the creation of a new intergovernmental organization, the Food and Agriculture Organization of the UN (FAO), whose constitution was enacted on 16 October 1945. It had four key objectives:

- Raising levels of nutrition and the standards of living of the peoples under the jurisdictions of its member states.

- Securing improvements in the efficiency of the production and distribution of all food and agricultural products.

- Improving the condition of rural populations.

- Contributing towards an expanding world economy and ensuring humanity's freedom from hunger.

The priority was to fight hunger by exploiting the potential for improvements in food and agricultural science. The FAO, notes Margulis (2013), set out to address the food problem by trying to coordinate the production and trade of grain, and by steering surpluses from the producing countries to those facing shortages. The major grain producers balked at this, though, and instead emphasized efforts to improve food production within developing countries. Meanwhile, there was worried speculation about the effects of the post-war growth in global population, up from about 2.5 billion in 1950 to about three billion in 1960. (Neo-Malthusian concerns about over-population were later given further fuel by the publication in 1968 of the bestselling book *The Population Bomb*, by American biologist Paul Ehrlich.)

In 1961, the World Food Programme was created under the auspices of the FAO to provide food aid to developing countries. In 1967, the first of a series of Food Aid Conventions was signed by 17 mainly wealthy countries, establishing the rules on food aid, and emphasizing the growing importance of food in national official development aid programmes. At about the same time, the green revolution was well under way: led by the work of agricultural sciences, it resulted in dramatic increases in food production as a result of the use of new high-yield crop varieties, chemical fertilizers and pesticides, and improved water supply. As part of the revolution, new specialized international research centres were created with a focus on specific regions or crops. Among them were the following:

- The International Rice Research Institute (IRRI, founded in 1960 in the Philippines), whose work addressed a staple food of a part of the world that had suffered multiple famines, and which has since developed new rice varieties and encouraged the sustainability of rice farming.

- The International Wheat and Maize Improvement Centre (CIMMYT, founded in 1966 near Mexico City) has done much the same for wheat and maize as IRRI has done for rice.

- The Consultative Group on International Agricultural Research (CGIAR, founded in 1971 in Paris) is a coordinating body for the specialized research centres; see later in this chapter.

Although food security had been at the heart of many of these developments, the term did not begin to enter the policy debate until the breaking in the early 1970s of what later came to be recognized as the first world food crisis (Headey and Fan, 2010). Food prices increased because of a combination of bad weather in growing regions, a spike in oil prices (leading to a separate but related global energy crisis) and bulk buying by the Soviet Union. The prices of staples such as wheat and corn tripled between 1971 and 1975, food stocks fell, and the mismatch between supply and demand pushed prices up even further. The crisis, notes Clapp (2018), illustrated the fragility of the global food system and its susceptibility to disruptions that could worsen levels of hunger.

In November 1974, the FAO hosted the World Food Conference, designed to discuss the causes and effects of the crisis, and to agree reforms to the food supply system. It resulted in the creation of several new IGOs with more focused interests; see

Table 9.2: Agricultural IOs created out of the 1970s food crisis

Name	Founded	Purpose
Committee on World Food Security	1974	Forum for discussions about food security policy.
World Food Council	1974	Coordinating body for national agricultural ministers on matters of hunger and malnutrition. Closed down in 1994 and its work absorbed into the FAO and the World Food Programme.
International Food Policy Research Institute	1975	Promoting policy research on agricultural development.
International Fund for Agricultural Development	1977	Channelling investments into developing countries to promote agricultural production and improve livelihoods for rural populations.
UN Standing Committee on Nutrition	1977	Monitoring and improving nutritional programmes among UN members.

Table 9.2. Responding to problems in global governance by creating new organizations might help, but it offers no guarantees, and the drawbacks and shortfalls in the work of IGOs saw the increasing input into food security matters during the 1980s and 1990s of NGOs and INGOs. Many of these – including Oxfam, CARE International and World Vision – had been active for decades in helping address famine and hunger (see Chapter 5), and now found their services needed more than ever. International news headlines were captured in 1983–85 by a famine in Ethiopia that sparked public and private fundraising in Britain with the release of the multi-artist single *Do They Know it's Christmas?*, the holding of the Live Aid concerts in London and Philadelphia, and the release in the US of the single *We Are The World*.

The persistence of hunger led to renewals of the Food Aid Convention and the convening in 1996 of a World Food Summit that agreed a pledge to achieve 'food security for all'. Meanwhile, the creation of the World Trade Organization in 1995 had begun to take the debate about food security in new directions, which Margulis (2013) describes as the replacement of an international food security regime with a regime complex for food security: the proliferation of IOs resulted in an overlap of authority among regimes dealing with food security, international trade and human rights. This was reflected in the agreement and adoption of new international treaties that came into force with the creation of the WTO, dealing with agricultural trading rules and food safety rules (see later in this chapter for more details).

There were additional World Food Summits in 1996 and 2002, but the lack of progress was confirmed by the breaking of yet another global food crisis in 2007–08. This came on the back of another increase in food prices, this time intertwined with the global financial crisis, but drawing much less attention than the latter. The causes of the food crisis, note Lele et al. (2021), were complex. They began with the declining share of official development assistance directed during the 1990s at agriculture, forestry and fisheries. This was followed by growing demand for biofuel (a fuel source made from crops such as maize and sugar cane), supported by large subsidies to biofuel production in the US and Europe. This was accompanied by poor harvests in several producer countries, export bans in others, and new demand from China and India, leading to higher food prices. New attention was drawn to the fragility of the global food regime, and to how much work still needed to be done to bring states together on agricultural policy, issues that were addressed in further world food summits in 2009 and 2022.

Illustrating the changing nature of the debate about food security, FAO published a report in 2011 on women in agriculture (Food and Agriculture Organization of the UN, 2011), sending a clear message: agriculture was underperforming in large part because half of the farmers in the world were women, who lacked equal access to the resources and opportunities they needed to be more productive. This was hardly news, because an FAO report in 1983 had made similar arguments, and the point had been repeated by the work of the UN Development Fund for Women, and by the umbrella organization UN Women. The place of women in agriculture had since become more important, as migration to cities and a move away from agriculture by many rural households had led to women playing a greater role in farming (Sachs et al., 2021). The case illustrates the importance of applying feminist theory to understanding international organizations; see *IOs in Theory 9*.

Despite all the efforts of international organizations to improve the global agricultural system, many of the problems that cause food insecurity persist. Yet another renegotiation of the Food Aid Convention (by now redubbed the Food Assistance Convention) was agreed in 2012, and yet another food conference (the Global Food Security Summit, the fifth of its kind) was convened in New York in 2022, against a background of multiple threats to food security: regional conflicts, economic shocks, the fallout from Covid-19, rising fertilizer prices, climate extremes and the war in Ukraine. These had combined to undermine the production of critical cereals such as wheat and rice, and to increase prices once again, placing food out of reach for millions. Despite decades of international action, questions remained about just how much had been achieved.

International agricultural law

Although there are multiple international laws and treaties on food and agriculture, they fall short of a structured approach to the topic; instead, they have been developed for disparate focused reasons, with agriculture often being only a supporting concern. An example of this dynamic at work is the International Plant Protection Convention (IPPC) of 1952, the focus of which is plant health. Championed and overseen by FAO, the treaty aims to protect wild and cultivated plants by preventing and controlling the introduction and spread of pests. This obviously has important implications for agriculture, but the IPPC is not an agricultural agreement as such. The treaty currently

IOs IN THEORY 9

FEMINISM

Feminist approaches to understanding international organizations are based on the idea that many of the agendas and policy choices of global governance are dominated by the perspectives of men. Although feminist ideas about government and politics have a long history, and long focused on achieving gender equality, feminism has more recently drawn attention to the problems inherent in the gendering of political institutions and processes: the phenomenon by which the formal rules and informal conventions of domestic and international organizations intentionally or unintentionally advantage men over women. Feminism seeks to end the subordination of women and provides for a more inclusive understanding and operation of politics, economics and society.

Although there are multiple approaches to feminism, ranging from its liberal, radical and Marxist forms to libertarian, postmodernist and Western variations, they all include efforts to understand the place of gender in government and governance, building a feminist perspective into other theoretical approaches, and pursuing gender equality. In her review of feminist political theory, Bryson (2016) argues that 'western political theory has been almost entirely written by men', and that feminist political theorists ask 'why it is that in virtually all known societies men appear to have more power and privilege than women, and how this can be changed'. In other words, she concludes, feminist political theory 'seeks to understand society in order to challenge and change it'.

A new development in thinking along these lines is *governance feminism*, so dubbed by Halley et al. (2018) as a way of describing 'every form in which feminists and feminist ideas exert a governing will within human affairs'. Feminism, they argue, has found its way into the institutions of governance, and has been successful in changing laws, institutions and practices at the domestic level. As this happens, so feminist views are reflected in the work of international organizations, and feminist interpretations are applied to the problems that IOs address. There are IOs dedicated specifically to women's issues – such as UN Women, the UN Development Fund for Women and Women for Women International – but it is also important to note how few women have been appointed to the highest levels of leadership in most IGOs. For an analysis of how women in leadership roles have helped develop gender equality in the UN, for example, see Haack (2022).

has 183 parties, has sparked the creation of ten regional plant protection organizations, and is overseen by a Rome-based Commission on Phytosanitary Measures that meets annually to debate progress and promote cooperation among parties.

A related and later treaty, linked more directly to agriculture, is the International Treaty on Plant Genetic Resources for Food and Agriculture (the ITPGRFA, otherwise known more simply as the Plant Treaty or the Seed Treaty). Another product of FAO initiatives, the treaty came into force in 2004, aimed at encouraging food security through the sustainable use of plant genetic resources: the genetic variability in plants – including modern cultivars as well as their wild relatives – that have economic or social value to humans. The treaty is also designed to encourage the equitable sharing of the benefits of the exploitation of these resources and recognition of the rights of farmers.

The more specific goal of managing food aid has been the subject of a set of related treaties aimed at improving the capacity of the international community to respond to emergency food situations. The first was the 1967 Food Aid Convention, which committed its 12 signatories (mainly developed countries) to providing minimum specified quantities of food aid. It was succeeded with new agreements signed in 1971, 1980, 1986, 1991 and 1999, leading to the sixth and current agreement – the Food Assistance Convention – in 2012. This has 16 parties: Australia, Canada, Japan, Russia, South Korea, the US, the European Union and nine European states. Rather than simply providing food to vulnerable communities, notes Adams (2021), the agreement was designed to address the underlying causes of food insecurity by helping those communities meet their own needs.

More agreements on agriculture came out of the transition from the General Agreement on Tariffs and Trade (GATT) to the World Trade Organization. GATT negotiations had included agricultural trade, but their results were limited by exemptions and exceptions, so, as part of the design of the WTO, an Agreement on Agriculture (AA) was reached that defined the trading rules as they applied to agriculture, including food subsidies, export bans and the use of food reserves (all of which might otherwise have gone against international trade rules). At the same time, it was designed to encourage the liberalization of agricultural trade and to discourage the kind of overproduction in the Global North that caused agricultural crises in parts of the Global South.

Two other agriculturally related agreements were signed at the same time:

- The Agreement on the Application of Sanitary and Phytosanitary Measures (SPS) was negotiated under the auspices of the General Agreement on Tariffs and Trade (see Chapter 6), came into force with the establishment of the WTO, and sets out the basic rules for food safety and animal and plant health standards.

- The Agreement on Trade Related Aspects of Intellectual Property Rights (TRIPS) sets requirements in several areas of agriculture and food, including geographical indications (the names given to products with a specific geographical origin, such as Champagne, tequila or Florida oranges), the use of hormones and new plant varieties.

International agriculture is also impacted by a wide range of regional and bilateral trade agreements, including those dealing with trade in live animals and animal products between the US and the EU, agreements on agriculture and forestry brokered by the Association of Southeast Asian Nations (ASEAN) and the substantial body of international law governing agriculture within the European Union – see later in this chapter. Finally, there are other treaties with a different focus but agricultural implications, including the UN Watercourses Convention (covering the non-navigational uses of international watercourses), and the UN Convention on Biological Diversity and the UN Convention to Combat Desertification (see Chapter 11).

THE UN FOOD SECURITY REGIME

In 2014, the Houthis – a rebel movement supported by Iran – overthrew the government of Yemen, sparking a military intervention by Saudi Arabia and the United Arab Emirates that left the Yemeni economy and infrastructure in ruins. One of the effects was to greatly increase food prices and shortages. Within four years, with as many as 20 million Yemenis (two-thirds of the population) facing food insecurity, the World Food Programme (2018) was describing the situation in Yemen as 'the world's worst humanitarian crisis'. With funding support from the European Union and from other UN agencies, the FAO launched programmes with titles such as Emergency Livelihoods Response Plan, and Smallholder Agricultural Production Restoration and Enhancement Project. The emphasis was on making investments in local communities, providing emergency support and improving access to water. A UN-mediated ceasefire brought some respite in 2022, but fell apart within months. A vicious combination of political, religious and cultural differences, topped by foreign interventions, created barriers that agricultural IOs found impossible to cross, leaving millions short of access to food, clean water and sanitation.

The Yemeni crisis is just one example of human-induced food insecurity problems, illustrating how the problem with food supply is less one of quantity than of distribution. This was emphasized by two global food crises and a host of regional and local crises, and the challenges have since been deepened by a problem – climate change – that was barely imagined in 1945 when the foundations of today's system of global agricultural governance were laid. Global changes, note Lele et al. (2021), 'have put considerable stress on the old modes of conducting business at all levels', requiring 'the big organizations [to] search for new ways to operate and cooperate with the growing number of players on the global scene'. For some, the Big Five agricultural IGOs have become less relevant, and should now be seen as part of new alliances that include philanthropists, development banks and emerging states. Having said that, we need first to understand how four of those organizations work. (The fifth, the World Bank, is addressed in Chapter 5.)

The Food and Agriculture Organization of the UN

As noted earlier, the focus of the Food and Agriculture Organization of the UN (FAO) is on food security, improved nutrition and bettering the condition of rural populations. It works to achieve these goals by collecting, interpreting and disseminating information on food and agriculture, including fisheries, marine products and forest products. Its priorities include the sustainable management of natural resources, the improvement of food processing and distribution, policies on agricultural credit and policies on agricultural commodities. Helping national governments achieve these goals is a key part of its work, but Johnson (2018) notes that it is not in the business of critiquing the actors involved in the international food system, or recommending structural reforms to that system.

The FAO is a specialized agency of the UN with the following key components:

– *Secretariat and executive head.* From its headquarters in Rome, the FAO is headed by a Director General who is elected by the FAO Conference. Much of the direction of FAO was set by its first Director General, the Scottish teacher and medical doctor John Boyd Orr (who won the 1949 Nobel Peace Prize for his efforts to end hunger). There have since been nine holders of the office, all of them men, including citizens of India, the Netherlands, Lebanon, Senegal, Brazil and China. Two of those – Edouard Souma and Jacques Diouf – between them headed FAO for 36 years (1976–2011), at which point the Conference decided to limit the office to two four-year terms.

– *Assembly.* The governing assembly of the FAO is the Conference, bringing together the full membership at meetings normally held biennially to set broad policy goals. FAO has 194 state members with equal votes, and – unusually – an organizational member in the form of the European Union.

– *Executive council.* The Council of the FAO is the executive body that manages FAO business between meetings of the Conference, normally meeting five times within a two-year period. It is headed by a Chairperson appointed by the Conference for renewable two-year terms, and consists of representatives from 49 member states elected for staggered three-year terms. The membership is apportioned geographically, with 12 for Africa, 10 for Europe, 9 for Asia, 9 for Latin America and the Caribbean, 6 for the Near East, 1 for the Southwest Pacific, and 1 each for the US and Canada.

– *Other elements.* The FAO has an extensive array of specialist committees and commissions dealing with focused concerns that range from fisheries research to plant protection and forestry.

– Since 1961, the FAO has maintained the Codex Alimentarius (Latin for *Food Code*), a reference guide for international standards, codes of practice and other measures as they relate to food, food production, food labelling and food safety. It is maintained by its own IGO, the Codex Alimentarius Commission, which has 189 state members and nearly 240 mainly non-governmental observers. It has become the global standard-setting body for food safety, used by consumers, producers and in disputes brought before the World Trade Organization.

– Like most major UN agencies, the FAO is a fount of statistics, and publishes the annual *State of the World* report on a variety of agricultural topics, including food and agriculture, food security, forests, genetic resources and fisheries. It also maintains the Globally Important Agricultural Heritage Systems (GIAHS) initiative, designed to identify and protect parts of the world that are important for their biodiversity, landscapes, knowledge systems and cultures.

– *Budget.* The FAO is funded through a combination of mandatory and voluntary contributions. The total budget in 2022–23 was $3.25 billion, of which 31 per cent came from mandatory contributions, headed by the US (22 per cent of the total), China, Japan, Germany and the UK, with the 15 biggest contributors accounting for nearly 80 per cent of total contributions.

The FAO structure includes the Committee on World Food Security (CFS), which was set up in 1974 to serve as a forum for discussions about food security policies. It mainly failed in this objective, leading to reforms in the wake of the 2007–08 global food crisis that included bringing more non-governmental and expert input into its work (Clapp, 2018). With a small secretariat based within the offices of the FAO, the committee meets annually in plenary session in Rome, bringing together the representatives of its 137 member states, as well as representatives of other IGOs interested in food security, NGOs, agricultural research groups and the private sector. Membership is free, the work of the Committee being funded by the FAO, IFAD and voluntary contributions. Decisions are made by the Plenary and execution is overseen by a Bureau made up of the Chairperson and 12 national representatives. Experts meet in a High-Level Panel of Experts on Food Security and Nutrition, whose recommendations are the basis for Plenary discussions.

The World Food Programme

The World Food Programme (WFP) is the UN's food aid organization, helping threatened communities prepare for natural and human-made emergencies, and providing food aid and cash assistance in the wake of such emergencies. Founded in 1961 on the initiative of the Kennedy administration in the US to make better use of surplus US food aid (Lele et al., 2021), the WFP has since grown to the point where it delivers about 75 per cent of all the world's food aid. Once again, though, most of its funding (88 per cent of the total) comes from just 15 countries, whose donations are voluntary.

From its headquarters in Rome, the WFP is headed by an executive director who is appointed by the UN secretary general in agreement with the director general of the FAO. With time, the WFP has broadened its view of food assistance, moving beyond short-term food transfers and technical help to focus more on working to combat the root causes of hunger, such as conflict, climate change and gender inequality (Lele et al., 2021). Despite a growth in its revenues, from about $2.2 billion in 2009 to a record $14 billion in 2022, and despite having more than 22,000 staff (most of them working in the field), the WFP was able to help only 140 million people in 120 countries in 2022. This may sound a lot until we appreciate that it was just 17 per cent of the 800 million people estimated to be hungry at the time. Its job is made more difficult not only by the sheer size of the problem of hunger, but also by the number of operations in which it is active at any given time, and by the complexities involved in responding internationally to large emergencies, such as the 2023 Turkish earthquake; see *IOs in Action 9*.

The International Fund for Agricultural Development

In contrast to the FAO, with its emphasis on coordinating research as a basis for policy, the International Fund for Agricultural Development (IFAD) is a financial institution, related to the multilateral development banks (MDBs) assessed in Chapter 5. Although much smaller than any of the latter, it helps by providing loans

IOs IN ACTION 9

THE WORLD FOOD PROGRAMME IN TURKEY AND SYRIA

In early February 2023, a major earthquake shook eastern Turkey and Northern Syria, killing an estimated 50,000 people, and leaving many more homeless. This is a region that is prone to earthquakes, because of a confluence of tectonic plates that has for millions of years been slowly pushing Arabia north and forcing the Turkish peninsula west towards Greece. An earthquake that struck in 1999 killed more than 17,000 people, and more earthquakes will inevitably blight the region in the future. The situation was made worse in 2023 by the large number of Syrian refugees living in Turkey, having been forced out of their homes by the Syrian civil war, and living in poorly built refugee accommodations.

Soon after the earthquake, news headlines in different parts of the world declared – as they often do after natural disasters - that the World Food Programme 'stood ready' to help. Why, some might have asked, was it standing ready and not moving immediately? Although it claims to be able to move into a disaster zone within 72 hours of an event, the story is not that simple (see World Food Programme, 2023). To begin with, the WFP needs a legal basis to act, which means that it must be formally invited to begin operations by the government of the affected country, an invitation that must be relayed through the Secretary General of the UN. (Only in exceptional circumstances, where national authorities have lost control over their territory, can the WFP arrive without an invitation.)

At the same time, an emergency response plan must be developed, which the WFP tries to achieve within 24 hours of an emergency. It outlines who will be helped, how they will be helped and how long it is anticipated the help will be needed. The WFP then organizes the food or cash distributions needed, activates communications support through the Emergency Telecommunications Cluster (operated by 29 private and government humanitarian organizations), releases funds from its Immediate Response Account (sustained by voluntary and non-earmarked donations from governments) and activates flights through the UN Humanitarian Air Service (using passenger and light cargo transport). It must also plan to work with the national government involved, with local humanitarian programmes in the country, with the private sector and with other humanitarian IOs. If all goes well, then it must eventually decide when and how to bring an end to its emergency operations. This usually happens when local access to food is restored to pre-emergency levels.

and debt-relief grants, and by setting up co-financing schemes with MDBs. One of the major outcomes of the 1974 World Food Conference, its main job is to provide support for projects aimed at improving income and food security among the rural poor. Its formation was privately opposed by the US, which saw it as challenging the role of the World Bank in agriculture (Bazbauers and Engel, 2021), but the US changed its position when it became clear that much of the funding for IFAD would come from the Organization of Petroleum Exporting Countries (OPEC). In fact, OPEC has gone on to remain a key presence in the work of IFAD, with several of its presidents and about 12 per cent of its funding coming from OPEC member states.

Founded in 1977, IFAD is headquartered in Rome, membership is open to all members of the UN (although only 177 have joined), and it is led by a President elected to the post by the member states for four-year terms, renewable once. Decisions are made by a Governing Council, consisting of representatives from all member states, and meeting annually. Between meetings, operations are overseen by an Executive Board whose 18 members are elected by the Governing Council to three-year terms, and whose sessions are chaired by the President.

Much like the World Bank and the IMF, votes in IFAD are determined by contributions to the budget, with the US having a 6.76 per cent share of the total, while Canada, France, Germany, Italy, Japan, the Netherlands, Saudi Arabia, Sweden and the UK have shares ranging between 2.9 and 4.2, and China has a two per cent share. Lele and Baldwin (2021) note that IFAD is focused on people living at the bottom of the food pyramid, including rural people, marginalized communities and those living in remote areas. It has a reputation for being small, agile and effective, but now has to ask itself whether it plans to help only poor people in poor countries, or whether it will continue also helping the poor in middle-income countries.

The Consultative Group on International Agricultural Research

The last and the most specialized of the Big Five agricultural IOs, the Consultative Group on International Agricultural Research (CGIAR) brings together the world's 15 major agricultural research centres, its goal being to encourage investment in those centres and to make their findings widely available. From an initial focus on cereals, it has expanded to include research on fisheries, forestry, livestock and water. Founded in 1971, it has a complex system of governance ranging from system-wide to inter-centre and intra-centre (see Table 9.3), and has often suffered from a shortage of funding that undermines its longer-term planning. Unlike the World Food Programme, whose mission of providing emergency food aid is relatively immediate and direct, Lele et al. (2021) note that while CGIAR research might be valuable, years can pass between the launch of a research programme and demonstrated results on the ground.

With a headquarters in Montpelier, France, CGIAR has an Executive Managing Director, an eight-person System Board responsible for governance of the group and for appointing and overseeing the management team, and a System Council consisting of 15 representatives from the group's main funders and five representatives from developing countries. All funding to CGIAR is voluntary, and most comes from the official development assistance agencies of countries such as Canada, Ireland, Japan, Sweden and the US, as well as the African Development Bank, the World Bank, and the Bill and Melinda Gates Foundation.

OTHER AGRICULTURAL IGOs

Agriculture is so closely related to so many other areas of international cooperation that there are few IGOs that have not added it to their institutional agenda. For example, grants and loans provided by the World Bank and the multilateral development banks

Table 9.3: Members of the Consultative Group on International Agricultural Research

Office	Name
Abidjan, Côte d'Ivoire	Africa Rice Centre
Bogor, Indonesia	Centre for International Forestry Research
Beirut, Lebanon	International Centre for Agricultural research in the Dry Areas
Patancheru, India	International Crops Research Institute for the Semi-Arid Tropics
Washington DC	International Food Policy Research Institute
Ibadan, Nigeria	International Institute of Tropical Agriculture
Kenya and Ethiopia	International Livestock Research Institute
Texcoco, Mexico	International Maize and Wheat Improvement Centre
Lima, Peru	International Potato Centre
Los Baños, Philippines	International Rice Research Institute
Colombo, Sri Lanka	International Water Management Institute
Rome, Italy	The Alliance of Biodiversity International and the International Centre for Tropical Agriculture
Nairobi, Kenya	World Agroforestry
Penang, Malaysia	WorldFish

have often been directed at agriculture. Meanwhile, negotiations under the auspices of the World Trade Organization frequently include agricultural trade (and disputes over the terms of that trade), natural and human-made disruptions to farming and food supplies (as well as the need for seasonal agricultural workers) have been a key motive behind migration and the creation of refugees, the World Health Organization works on nutritional and food safety standards, and there is an intimate relationship between the welfare of agriculture and the environment.

One of the products of the 2007–08 global financial and food crises was the Global Agriculture and Food Security Programme (GAFSP). A multilateral financial body launched by the G20 group of countries, the programme is funded by donors in wealthy states and targets sustainable agriculture in the poorest states. Hosted in Washington DC by the World Bank Group, it is collectively administered by governments, farmers, producers and the private sector (all of which participate in the work of the programme's steering committee), it provides grants, loans and technical advice. The inaugural donors were the Bill and Melinda Gates Foundation, Canada, South Korea, Spain and the US, which have since been joined (as voting members) by Australia, Germany, Ireland, Japan, the Netherlands, Norway and the UK.

Agricultural policy has also long been an expensive and contentious part of the work of the European Union, impacting not just the EU itself but all those parts of the world that trade with the EU or receive European food aid. Its role dates back to the creation of the European Economic Community in 1958, which included agreement of a Common Agricultural Policy (CAP) by which guarantees were made to EEC farmers that anything they produced and could not sell on the open market would be bought from them using CAP funds. With production growing and the market unable to absorb it all, the costs of the CAP grew to the point where it accounted for as much as 70 per cent of EEC spending. It also skewed global agricultural markets and caused resentment among the Community's trade partners (see McCormick, 2020). It was only after many years of troubled internal negotiations that the CAP was reformed to the point where it became manageable. Along the way, European farmers became some of the most productive in the world, making the EU self-sufficient in almost all the agricultural commodities it could produce in the European climate.

International commodity bodies

Often overlooked in the work of this community of organizations is the work of a group of more focused IGOs: international commodity bodies (ICBs). A commodity is a raw material or primary agricultural product that can be bought and sold, and then turned into something else. Examples include metals (such as gold, copper and iron ore) and sources of energy (such as oil and coal), while agricultural commodities include cotton that is made into textiles, the wheat that is made into bread, the olives that are made into olive oil, and the coffee, grains, meat, cocoa and other commodities that are in demand all over the world. ICBs are autonomous organizations that are mainly interested in promoting the interests of producer countries.

The UN Conference on Trade and Development (UNCTAD) has recognized 24 ICBs representing more than 30 commodities (see Table 9.4 for examples) and serves as an observer member of them all. Some of these ICBs are related to international commodity agreements (such as those on olive oil, cocoa and tropical timber), others take the form of international study groups charged with gathering and sharing information on markets, and organizing meetings between producers and consumers, and yet others are intergovernmental groups within the FAO. The latter usually meet every two years, or on an as-needed basis, and provide a forum in which interested member states of FAO can debate and discuss the economic and technical aspects of the production, marketing, trade and consumption of their target commodity.

Martin (2022) notes that many of ICBs date back to the era of the Great Depression, and were established to control the global production and exchange of their target commodities. They were encouraged by the League of Nations as tools of economic stabilization, their goal – Martin suggests – being to replace 'competition with collusion in order raise the price of a particular good, usually by reducing its

Table 9.4: International commodity bodies: Examples

Commodity bodies	FAO bodies
International Cocoa Organization	Intergovernmental Group on Bananas and Tropical Fruits
International Coffee Organization	Intergovernmental Group on Citrus Fruit
International Cotton Advisory Committee	Intergovernmental Group on Grains
International Grains Council	Intergovernmental Group on Meat
International Olive Council	Intergovernmental Group on Oilseeds, Oils and Fats
International Sugar Organization	Intergovernmental Group on Rice
International Tropical Timber Organization	Intergovernmental Group on Tea

supply'. They were reinvigorated and expanded after World War II, being joined in 1960 by what he describes as 'the most powerful intergovernmental commodity institution ever created': the Organization of Petroleum Exporting Countries (see Chapter 6). Because they have always been government bodies, they have tended to more powerful and durable than agreements reached among private firms.

One of these ICBs, whose activities impact a large proportion of the world's population, is the International Coffee Organization (ICO). This is a London-based intergovernmental organization that was created in 1963 in the wake of the signature of the first International Coffee Agreement, which has been renewed or extended periodically ever since. The ICO – once described by Bates (1997) as a 'government of coffee' – brings together 43 exporting member states and six importing member states, and works to promote the production and consumption of coffee to the approximately 30–40 per cent of humans who consume it. It has most of the structural elements of a typical IGO, including an executive director, a secretariat, a council that meets biannually and a conference that meets every 4–5 years. The popularity of coffee continues to grow, as does the specialty coffee market (higher-grade coffee) and demand for coffee pods. The ICO works to monitor the effects of fluctuating prices, the sustainability of production, the adulteration of coffee and questions about the health effects of high consumption.

Another example of an ICB is the International Tropical Timber Organization (ITTO), established a year after the signature of the 1994 International Tropical Timber Agreement. Headquartered in Yokohama, Japan, the ITTO was at first focused on trade in tropical timber, later adding the sustainable use of tropical forests to its agenda. It has 36 producing member states and 38 consuming member states, but its work has been undermined by the conflict between maximizing trade and profits while imposing environmental safeguards that might restrict trade. Questions were early raised about the potential effects of this conflict (Colchester, 1990), and subsequent analyses of the work of the ITTO have been mainly negative. Nagtzam (2014), for example, concluded that the international tropical forestry regime was failing for the simple reason that the economic interests of both producer and consumer states 'are best served by allowing the harvesting of tropical timbers to continue virtually unabated at the expense of good environmental outcomes'.

Related to the international commodity bodies is the Common Fund for Commodities (CFC), an intergovernmental financial organization. Headquartered in Amsterdam, the CFC was founded in 1989 and invests voluntary contributions from 28 mainly European states (along with China, India and Nigeria) in helping producers in the Global South to strengthen and diversify their production and trade of commodities. It has 101 member states – notable non-members including Australia, Canada, New Zealand, Saudi Arabia, South Africa and the US – and nine institutional members (including the African Union and the European Union). Its five biggest contributors in 2022 were OPEC, Japan, Germany, Norway and France. One of the CFC's priorities has been to help smallholder farmers in the face of the problems caused by climate change, which poses a critical challenge to agriculture more generally; see *Spotlight 9*.

NON-STATE FOOD AND AGRICULTURAL ACTORS

There are two kinds of non-state actors that play key roles in the global food and agriculture regime: the multinationals engaged in agribusiness and the NGOs that are active in the fight against hunger. The former play a profit-driven role in shaping food production and supply, while the latter – large in number – can be seen as either complementing the work of the Big Five organizations, or taking up the slack for the failures of governments to eliminate hunger and famine.

The dominance of multinationals in the global food system is clear and incontrovertible (see Wise, 2019), despite the constant changes in market share in the wake of acquisitions and mergers as companies expand their scale, purchase new technologies and exploit growing markets. Consider these examples:

- The global commercial market for seeds has been dominated in recent years by four companies: Bayer and BASF of Germany, Corteva Agriscience of the US and Syngenta of Switzerland.

- Somewhere between 75 and 90 per cent of global grain trade is controlled by the US companies Archer Daniel Midlands, Bunge and Cargill, and by Louis Dreyfus of France (the so-called ABCD companies). Exactly how much they control is uncertain because Cargill and Dreyfus are privately owned and do not provide data.

- In the world of agrochemicals, which includes pesticides, the global market is dominated by MNEs such as Syngenta, Bayer, BASF, Corteva, UPL of India and FMC of the US.

- The biggest fertilizer companies – dominating a market in which most of the product is synthetic and inorganic – include Nutrien of Canada, Wesfarmers of Australia, the Saudi Arabian Fertilizer Company and the Mosaic Company of the US.

SPOTLIGHT 9

AGRICULTURE AND THE ENVIRONMENT

It is impossible to divorce the interests of agriculture and the environment, the state of one having an intimate connection to the state of the other. The green revolution may have produced astonishing results, but this was in part because it was based on the use of chemical pesticides, fungicides, herbicides and fertilizers, with their negative environmental effects. These continue to be a concern today, as does the chemical pollution caused by run-off from agriculture into rivers and groundwater. Concerns about genetic modification were also raised by the reliance of the green revolution on new strains of wheat, corn, rice and other basic foods that were engineered to yield bigger and more predictable levels of production. Modern farming techniques are also often inefficient in terms of the balance between energy expended in production and transportation, on the one hand, and calories produced in food, on the other.

Environmental challenges have grown as agriculture both contributes to and feels the harmful effects of climate change. Its contribution stems from the reliance of modern farming (in the Global North, at least) on chemicals and mass production, which have resulted in a growth in emissions of two key greenhouse gases: carbon dioxide is a by-product of the use of fertilizers, and of the storage and transport of agricultural products, while methane is produced by rice paddies and by flatulent livestock. Recent estimates suggest that more than ten per cent of global greenhouse gas emissions come from agriculture (World Resources Institute, 2021).

As to the effects of climate change, temperature rises are leading to changes in crop-growing patterns, as well as subjecting farmers to more serious droughts and flooding, and they might have to change the crops they grow in order to adapt. Warnings were made about this decades ago – see Parry (1990), for example – and climate change was the focus of the 2016 edition of *The State of Food and Agriculture* published by the FAO (Food and Agriculture Organization of the UN, 2016). It warned that smallholders were likely to feel the effects most seriously, leaving food production hardest hit in countries that already have the lowest levels of food security. Food prices might rise, warned the FAO, yields might fall, efforts to reduce hunger and poverty might be undermined, and the lives of millions of rural people who depend on agriculture for their livelihoods might be impacted, potentially creating greater numbers of environmental migrants and refugees. The need to address climate change lay at the heart of FAO's Strategic Framework 2022–31.

– Most of the world's most popular food and beverage brands are owned by just ten companies, including Nestlé of Switzerland, Mondelez and General Mills of the US, Unilever and Associated British Foods of the UK and Danone of France.

– At the retail end of the equation, the hold of the world's biggest supermarket chains has grown, including among their number Walmart and Costco of the US, Lidl and Aldi of Germany, Tesco and Sainsbury's of the UK, Carrefour of France and Aeon of Japan.

Lawrence and Friel (2020) argue that the concentration of power has increased at all stages in the food chain, as a result of the industrialization of food production and processing, and of globalization. Where once it was the big commodity traders such as the ABCD companies dominating international trade, particularly in cereals, the concentration has come also to the input end of the chain (the agrochemical industry) and the output end in the form of the major retailers. The big supermarkets prefer – for convenience and profit – to source from large suppliers, allowing them – argue Willoughby and Gore (2018) – to 'squeeze value from vast supply chains that span the globe, while at the bottom the bargaining power of small-scale farmers and workers has been steadily eroded in many of the countries from which they source'. In order to achieve sustainability and equality, they conclude, governments need to work with food companies, small-scale farmers, and consumers to rebalance power in food supply chains and to ensure they more fairly reward those producing our food.

As for those NGOs that have the fight against hunger as at least one of their core goals, establishing their number is hard. There are probably thousands working at the national level in multiple countries, and perhaps hundreds working at the international level. Some of the latter operate in a single country but provide aid to multiple other countries, while others are more truly international in both their scope and their interests. There are also many – with a broad set of humanitarian interests that includes food security – that have been reviewed in other chapters, including CARE International and Oxfam in Chapter 5, and Save the Children and UNICEF in Chapter 7. Finally, it is hard to establish a list of the most important food security INGOs because of questions about what criteria to use: should we rank them by funds raised, people helped, the number of countries in which they are active or other criteria? Despite this, they include among their number such bodies as Bread for the World, The Hunger Project, Rise Against Hunger, Action Against Hunger and Project Concern International.

THINKING POINTS

- Should access to food be more clearly defined as a basic human right?

- What does the evolution of the global food regime suggest about its likely future direction?

- What does the record of the World Food Programme tell us about the best way to design intergovernmental humanitarian and relief organizations?

- Is there a case to be made for the better integration of food aid, research and commodity organizations in the response to food security challenges?

- What can be done to offset the concentrated power of the major agribusiness corporations?

IOs RELATED TO THIS CHAPTER

Codex Alimentarius Commission

Committee on World Food Security (CFS)

Common Fund for Commodities (CFC)

Consultative Group on International Agricultural Research (CGIAR)

Food and Agriculture Organization of the UN (FAO)

Global Agriculture and Food Security Programme (GAFSP)

International Coffee Organization (ICO)

International Fund for Agricultural Development (IFAD)

International Tropical Timber Organization (ITTO)

World Food Programme (WFP)

FURTHER READING

Adams, Francis (2021) *The Right to Food: The Global Campaign to End Hunger and Malnutrition* (Palgrave Macmillan). A survey of the causes of food insecurity, the UN-led responses, and chapters on Latin America, Africa, the Middle East and Asia.

Lele, Uma, Manmohan Agarwal, Brian C. Baldwin, and Sambuddha Goswami (2021) *Food for All: International Organizations and the Transformation of Agriculture* (Oxford University Press). One of the very few general surveys of agricultural IOs, with chapters on their context and work.

Oehl, Maximilian Eduard (2022) *Sustainable Commodity Use: Its Governance, Legal Framework, and Future Regulatory Instruments* (Springer). An overview of the way in which international commodity bodies and the laws that drive them function.

Wise, Timothy A. (2019) *Eating Tomorrow: Agribusiness, Family Farmers, and the Battle for the Future of Food* (New Press). A critique of the impact of agribusiness and big corporations on the small-scale farmers who grow most of the food eaten in developing countries.

Zhou, Zhang-Yue (2020) *Global Food Security: What Matters?* (Routledge). A survey of the causes of food insecurity, including cases studies on the responses being pursued, and an assessment of the work of IGOs such as the FAO and the World Food Programme.

HEALTH

PREVIEW

Cooperation on health, and particularly on controlling the spread of infectious disease, is the focus of the organizations assessed in this chapter. It opens with a review of the challenges posed by such disease and draws attention to the inequalities found in health care around the world. It then outlines the most important steps in the development of the global health regime, underlining the transformations that have come in recent decades. The focus of the chapter is on the World Health Organization (WHO), whose structure is outlined and whose goals are explained before the work of the organization is critically reviewed. Other IGOs involved in health matters are then discussed, notably the UNAIDS joint programme, UNICEF, the World Bank and the UN Population Fund (UNFPA). The chapter then reviews the place of public–private partnerships such as the Global Fund to Fight AIDS, Tuberculosis and Malaria, and the Gavi Alliance that works to promote access to immunization in poorer countries. The chapter assesses the work of non-state actors involved in health, notably the Bill and Melinda Gates Foundation (BMGF) and Doctors Without Borders (MSF), and concludes with a reminder of the key roles played by faith-based organizations and by pharmaceutical companies.

CONTENTS

- The context
- Building a global health regime
- The World Health Organization
- Other health IGOs
- Non-state health actors

THE CONTEXT

When the first reports of a novel coronavirus began to emerge in December 2019 from the northern Chinese city of Wuhan, few could have anticipated the consequences. The virus would not only impact human health, but would also have long-term political, economic and social effects that we are still working to understand today. Based on reports from Chinese health authorities, the World Health Organization (WHO) issued a global alert about the virus on 2 January 2020, which it upgraded four weeks later to a 'public health emergency of international concern'.

The new virus was given a name (Covid-19) on 11 February, by when there were few countries in the world that had not reported cases. On 11 March, as the number of confirmed cases reached 100,000, the WHO declared a Covid-19 pandemic. By the end of 2022, after more than 34 months of lockdowns and disruptions, the development of several vaccines, and the identification of several subvariants of the virus, the global death toll had reached 6.7 million and the number of people who were estimated to have contracted Covid-19 had reached nearly 745 million (World Health Organization, 2023a).

The advent of Covid-19 emphasized once again not only the global connections that bind us, but also the importance of taking a global view of health care. It was a lesson that we might have learned from history, because Covid-19 was far from the first pandemic (defined as an outbreak of an infectious disease over a large region, spilling over borders). There had been, for example, at least three great plague pandemics: the Justinian Plague of 541, the Black Death of 1347–52 (from which an estimated 25 million Europeans died), and the pandemic of 1894 (from which an estimated 12 million Indians died over a period of 20 years) (Glatter and Finkelman, 2021). Along the way, Europeans had taken diseases such as smallpox, influenza and measles with them to the Americas, resulting in the deaths of millions who lacked immunity. Then came the 'Spanish' flu of 1918–20, so-called because Spanish media were the only ones allowed to report news of the pandemic. An estimated 25–50 million people died from the flu in the space of just two years.

The story does not end there:

- In 2003 there was an outbreak in China of what came to be known as severe acute respiratory syndrome, or SARS. It was the first experience for health care IOs with the transmission of an unknown disease, and although it took almost 1,000 lives it had been contained within six months.

- In 2009, the H1N1 strain of influenza behind the Spanish flu pandemic returned, taking an estimated 284,000 lives.

- In 2014 there was an outbreak of Ebola disease in Guinea, Liberia and Sierre Leone, contracted by an estimated 28,000 people, with about 11,000 mortalities.

It is not just infectious disease that is a matter of international concern, but also the broader state of health care, the unequal access to that health care, the fact that many people continue to die from preventable diseases or conditions, and the different threats that continue to be faced by people in different circumstances. In wealthy communities and societies, for example, heart disease, dementia, obesity and diabetes tend to dominate, while in poorer societies the most serious threats are posed by limited access to health care, contaminated water and inadequate sanitation. Medical science has made enormous strides, and humans as a whole are mainly living longer and better lives, but inequalities persist, distinguishing the rich from the poor, and the urban from the rural; see Figure 10.1 for just one indicator of the differences.

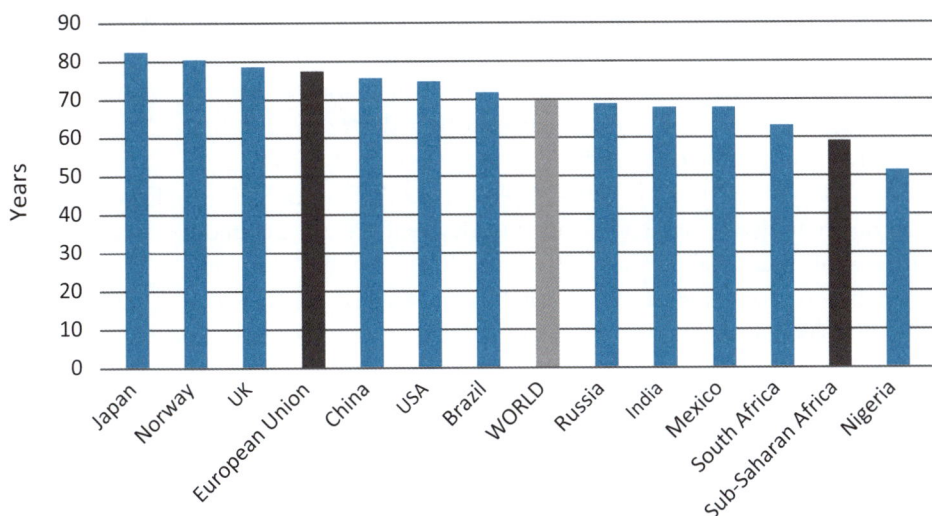

Figure 10.1: Life expectancy in selected parts of the world.
Source: Based on data in United Nations Population Division (2022).

These inequalities help draw attention to a debate about the extent to which health care can be regarded as a human right. Article 25 of the Universal Declaration of Human Rights seems clear on this:

> Everyone has the right to a standard of living adequate for the health and well-being of himself and of his family, including food, clothing, housing and medical care and necessary social services, and the right to security in the event of unemployment, sickness, disability, widowhood, old age or other lack of livelihood in circumstances beyond his control.

Health care as a human right was mentioned again in the 1966 International Covenant on Economic, Social and Cultural Rights (see Chapter 8). Despite this, Meier and Gostin (2018) note that scholars long shunned the study of health as a human right. Although globalization and the end of the Cold War changed perceptions, it has only been recently that human rights have come to be understood to be central to global health, and that global governance institutions have developed policies, programmes and practices aimed at blending the two.

In order to implement and protect health rights, there needs to be a rational and effective system of global health governance, but it is questionable how much has been achieved in this regard. The main actors in health care are still national governments and their ministries or departments of health, particularly in those countries with universal health care systems paid for out of taxes. There is no question that numerous IGOs and INGOs are active in health care at the global level, but the health regime is perhaps the most disjointed and even possibly incoherent of the different regimes assessed in this book. It may seem to be dominated by the World Health Organization, but it involves multiple UN funds and agencies, ranging from the World Bank to the UN Population Fund. It also involves other IGOs such as the World Trade Organization (WTO), as well as regional integration bodies such as the European Union (EU). Finally, it brings in a wide range of non-state actors, including everything from the pharmaceutical industry to faith-based NGOs with a long presence in some of the world's poorer states.

For Burci and Cassels (2016), 'global health is populated by diverse entities with different legal status and structures, different governance models, and complex patterns of accountability and interaction'. Meanwhile, Harman (2016) describes global health governance as 'an ever-expanding field of governance … [that] involves specialized public–private partnerships, multilateral and bilateral institutions, epistemic communities, private companies, celebrities, ex-politicians and a variety of civil society organizations, and is underpinned by questions of equality, rights, and the efficacy of development assistance'. The sheer complexity of the global health regime was exemplified by two events in 2007.

The first was the formation of an informal and somewhat secretive group known as the Health 8 (or the H8), bringing together the eight biggest health IOs (including the WHO, UNICEF, the World Bank, Gavi and the Bill and Melinda Gates Foundation). The second was the formation of the International Health Partnership with the goal of improving health care in the spirit of helping meet the Millennium Development Goals (see Chapter 5). Now known as UHC2030, it works to advance progress towards universal health coverage (UHC), bringing together just over 80 states, 17 international organizations, four philanthropic organizations and nearly 55 NGOs.

BUILDING A GLOBAL HEALTH REGIME

The effect of health emergencies such as Ebola and Covid-19 has been not just to remind us once again of global interconnectedness, but also of the shortfalls in our response to human health needs from an international perspective. It makes practical sense that the delivery of health care is treated mainly as a local and national responsibility, but it also makes sense that governments should work together in sharing knowledge, methods and responses. They have mainly done so only slowly, though, with the result that millions of people continue to die from infectious diseases or from health problems that can be resolved with the appropriate care, and that health care is one of the regimes that still relies heavily on the work of non-state actors. The evolution of that regime has been summarized by Youde (2018) as involving seven key 'moments or processes', which are summarized in Table 10.1.

The first step (actually, 14 separate steps under a common label) was taken between 1851 and 1938 with a series of International Sanitary Conferences held in Paris and several other cities, including Istanbul, Vienna, Rome and Washington DC. Their work was prompted by what Harman (2018) describes as the 'golden age' of biomedical discovery, including the breakthroughs on germ theory that transformed scientists such as Louis Pasteur into celebrities. The goal behind the conferences – the

Table 10.1: Key steps in the development of the global health regime

Step	Date	Event	Effect
1	1851–1938	Convening of 14 International Sanitary Conferences.	Standardizing quarantine measures against spread of cholera, plague and yellow fever.
2	1923	Foundation of Health Organization of the League of Nations.	Epidemic control, quarantine measures and drug standardization.
3	1948	Foundation of World Health Organization.	To encourage international cooperation on improving health conditions.
4	1969	Adoption of International Health Regulations by the World Health Assembly of the WHO.	Providing legally binding obligations on WHO member states to prevent, control and respond to international spread of disease.
5	1977	Adoption of Global Strategy for Health for All by UN General Assembly.	Everyone should have a level of health by 2000 that would permit them to lead socially and economically productive lives.
6	2000	Launch of Bill and Melinda Gates Foundation.	Improving health care and reducing poverty.
7	2002	Foundation of Global Fund to Fight AIDS, Tuberculosis (TB) and Malaria.	Attracting and leveraging investments in the fight against AIDS, TB and malaria.

first of which was organized by the government of France – was to standardize rules on quarantining against the spread of cholera, plague and yellow fever. Among the results was the adoption of the 1892 International Sanitary Convention, which had the goal of establishing quarantine regulations for ships travelling through the Suez Canal, which had officially opened 30 years earlier.

The conferences (specifically the eleventh, held in Paris in 1903) also resulted in the creation in 1907 of the International Office of Public Hygiene (or OIHP, an acronym based on its French name *Office International d'hygiène Publique*), based in Paris. With just 13 member states (all European except for Brazil, Egypt, Russia and the US), its focus was on overseeing quarantine rules to prevent the spread of plague and cholera, and coordinating efforts to address epidemics. It was clearly found lacking in the response to the 1918 Spanish flu pandemic, although it is debatable whether the fault lay with the structure of OIHP or the secrecy with which most governments responded to the pandemic. The OIHP was joined in 1923 by the Health Organization of the League of Nations, charged with encouraging the steps needed to prevent and control the spread of disease. It has been argued (see Cueto et al., 2019, and Hollings, 2022) that the goal of these early organizations was less to improve global health than to protect their member states (mainly European powers) from diseases imported from other parts of the world.

Developments since 1945

The change in attitudes towards international cooperation after World War II was reflected in the third of the seven steps: the foundation in 1948 of the World Health Organization (WHO). Sometimes described as *the* global health institution (see Harman, 2018), the WHO built on the foundations provided by the OIHP and the League of Nations to create a body focused on promoting health by monitoring threats and providing advice and guidelines. Like all new post-war IGOs, the WHO started modestly as it worked to give substance to its mission against a background of an understanding of global health problems that was still evolving. For many years it was almost alone in the field, although health was also on the agenda of the World Bank and of the UN Children's Fund (UNICEF, founded 1946). They were later joined by the UN Development Programme (UNDP, founded 1965, with interests in the right to health and eventually in HIV/AIDS) and by the UN Population Fund (UNFPA, founded 1969, with interests in reproductive health).

In the minds of the earliest WHO leaders and staff, notes Beigbeder (2018), the organization was to keep its distance from the politics of the UN and its member states, and to focus on its own health mandate. This view was reflected in the adoption in 1969 by the World Health Assembly of a set of International Health Regulations (IHRs). With origins dating back to the International Sanitary Conferences, these new regulations took a broader approach to the spread of disease by requiring that all WHO members 'prevent, protect against, control, and provide a public health response to the international spread of disease'. Meanwhile, the Security Council and the General Assembly of the UN joined the fray by agreeing health-related initiatives, such as the adoption in 1977 of the Global Strategy for Health for All.

Further change came in the wake of the June 1981 publication of a report from the Centers for Disease Control and Prevention in the US about a disease that had led to the deaths of many young gay men who were previously healthy. It would be named Acquired Immune Deficiency Syndrome (AIDS), and in 1983 the causative agent was identified and named the human immunodeficiency virus (HIV). The number of illnesses and deaths grew, particularly in low-income and middle-income countries, and the political response was undermined by prejudice and even outright denial from governments hostile to the interests of the two groups at first most often associated with HIV/AIDS: intravenous drug users and the gay community. The pandemic went much further, though, affecting people who had had blood transfusions, and being passed from mothers to their babies, and initially giving those affected a life expectancy of about 1–2 years. Antiretroviral drugs would eventually become available in 1987, greatly changing the face of HIV/AIDS, but access was limited, and by 2018 it was estimated that more than 70 million people had been infected and that 35 million had died.

The WHO response to HIV/AIDS – and indeed the response of many national governments and the international community generally – was found wanting. According to Merson and Inrig (2017), the WHO initially claimed leadership, saying that it would pursue the pandemic as vigorously as it had pursued smallpox; see *IOs in Action 10* later in this chapter. It created a Global Programme on AIDS in 1987, but was unable to encourage most governments to contribute, and it also made the mistake of approaching AIDS as a rich country problem. The WHO then became caught up in a struggle among UN agencies (including the UN Development Programme and UNICEF) to provide leadership, and some of its administrators worked to undermine the new joint UN Programme on HIV/AIDS (UNAIDS) created in 1994. In the end, it was – argue Kavanagh and Gostin (2018) – the work of social movements, activists and generic drug companies that brought the greatest changes in policy on HIV/AIDS.

In retrospect, it can be seen that attitudes towards global cooperation on health had begun to undergo an important transformation. In the 1980s, notes Youde (2018), health was still a marginal issue on the international political agenda, barely even figuring into the official development assistance programmes of donor states. Within a generation, he argues, health had developed a 'robust set of governance structures' that were driving significant global political action, incorporating a wide range of actors, and receiving increasing levels of funding. Rather than health being left to states to handle on their own, he continues, the international community had embraced a sense that it had a moral obligation and responsibility to respond to health issues, particularly in poorer states. The change was reflected in new approaches to humanitarian intervention, environmental protection and food security, as well as health.

While these changes might have been welcome, a spate of pandemics – ranging from SARS in 2003 to Covid-19 in 2020–22 – still found global health governance wanting. For Ginsbach et al. (2021), the weaknesses lay in a combination of the failure of countries to comply with the terms of the International Health Regulations, weak management on the part of the WHO, inadequate support for lower-income countries, and a lack of transparency that led to confusion and mistrust. The WHO, they argued, could help by encouraging better preparedness in its member states, establishing better warning systems, improving transparency, expanding funding for lower-income countries, and by using the IHRs to synchronize and synergize responses to emergencies from all corners of society.

International health law

The long-standing tradition of regarding public health as a domestic issue rather than a matter for international cooperation is reflected in the field of global health law. There have been efforts to agree international treaties on focused topics such as occupational safety and health, the control of narcotics and the use of tobacco (see Table 10.2), and

Table 10.2: International health treaties: Examples

Opened for signature	Where signed	Subject
1892	Venice, Italy	International Sanitary Convention
1961	New York, USA	Single Convention on Narcotic Drugs
1969	Geneva, Switzerland	International Health Regulations
1971	Vienna, Austria	Convention on Psychotropic Substances
1981	Geneva	Occupational Safety and Health Convention
1988	Vienna	UN Convention Against Illicit Traffic in Narcotic Drugs and Psychotropic Substances
2003	Geneva	WHO Framework Convention on Tobacco Control
2005	Geneva	International Health Regulations (revised)
2006	New York	Convention on the Rights of Persons with Disabilities
2011	Geneva	Pandemic Influenza Preparedness Framework

the WHO adopted its IHRs in 1969, but otherwise it has only been since the late 1990s that the body of global health law has begun to grow. It has addressed everything from organ transplantation to infectious disease, access to medicines, the control of toxic pollutants, radiation protection, and some of the links between trade and health. Even so, argues Taylor (2017), law has played only a limited role in the field of international cooperation on health.

The first binding agreement on health – the 1892 International Sanitary Convention (focused on the control of cholera) – may have been reached long ago and may have been followed by several replacements and revisions, ending in 1944. However, it was not until the WHO was created and then given the unusual authority to adopt international regulations on health that more progress was made. Despite this, it was not until 1969 that the International Health Regulations (IHR) were adopted, becoming – in the words of Taylor (2017) – 'the sole international legal instrument designed to provide a framework for multilateral efforts to combat infectious diseases'. They established the radical requirement that certain public health incidents could be designated as public health emergencies of international concern. Examples of such emergencies were later to include the SARS, swine flu, Ebola and Covid-19 pandemics. The IHRs were revised in 2005 to break away from a disease-specific model and to adopt an 'all-hazards' strategy to addressing the international spread of disease (Gostin and Katz, 2016). Even so, the record in responding to emergencies has only been as good as the ability or willingness of governments to comply, and pressures continued to revise the IHRs again, even before the Covid-19 pandemic shook the world.

Tobacco use has been the focus of one of the rare, targeted health care treaties (see *Spotlight 10*), while occupational safety and health have been a focus of the agreement of a long line of international treaties dating back to 1921. The first was the white lead convention (prohibiting the use of white lead in paint), later joined by agreements on the protection of dockers from accidents (1932), radiation protection (1960), occupational cancer protection (1974), and occupational safety and health (1981). There have also been multiple environmental treaties agreed that have important health implications, including the protection of the ozone layer (1985), climate change (1992), industrial accidents (1992), hazardous chemicals and pesticides in international trade (1998), and persistent organic pollutants (2001).

SPOTLIGHT 10

HEALTH AND TOBACCO

The WHO Framework Convention on Tobacco Control was adopted in 2003, came into force in 2005, and was expanded with the 2012 Protocol to Eliminate Illicit Trade in Tobacco Products. It was not only the first treaty to be negotiated under the auspices of the WHO, whose constitution (Article 19) gives it the authority to adopt conventions on any matter within its competence, but it was also the first multilateral and binding agreement on a chronic and non-infectious disease. The WHO, in fact, describes tobacco use as an epidemic, and recorded that while the number of people who used tobacco was expected to fall from about half of the human population to about one-third between 2000 and 2023, eight million people still died from tobacco-related diseases in 2017 (World Health Organization, 2019).

The health effects of tobacco use had long been a topic of concern at meetings of the membership of the WHO, taking a new turn in the 1990s as new controls imposed in the North encouraged tobacco companies to turn new attention to the South. While North Americans and Europeans turned away from tobacco in growing numbers (although many of them still smoke, even today), consumption has grown in countries such as China, Indonesia, Russia and parts of Southeast Asia and the Middle East. The 2003 treaty places controls on interaction between the tobacco industry and lawmakers, encourages the use of taxes to reduce demand for tobacco products, places a comprehensive ban on tobacco advertising, includes obligations on protection from passive smoking and requires health warnings on packaging.

Every state has signed and become a party to the convention with the exception of six: Argentina, Cuba, Haiti, Morocco, Switzerland and the US. American opposition is based on the domestic opposition of the big US tobacco companies, such as Philip Morris International (the biggest tobacco company in the world by sales), which have worked to undermine the goals of the treaty. Despite efforts to limit and control the use of tobacco around the world, smoking even now remains the second leading risk factor for early death, after high blood pressure.

THE WORLD HEALTH ORGANIZATION

One of the effects of the spate of pandemics in recent decades has been to make national governments realize how poorly prepared they are to prevent, prepare and respond to future emergencies. With that in mind, and noting the 'catastrophic failure of the international community in showing solidarity and equity' in its response to Covid-19, the World Health Assembly of the World Health Organization (WHO) convened a special meeting in late 2021 to draft a new global accord on pandemics. The experience with Covid-19, said the WHO Director General at the time, had shone a light 'on the many flaws in the global system to protect people from pandemics'. Negotiations finally opened in March 2023, with the hope that a final version of the agreement would be ready for adoption in 2024.

Driving the negotiation of agreements of this kind is one of the standard tasks of intergovernmental organizations, and the focus on pandemics is one that has kept the WHO busy for many years. Founded in 1948, the WHO spent decades as almost the sole representative of the idea that health could and should be seen in global terms. Its tasks include coordinating approaches to health care within the UN system, providing advice to the UN's member states, setting standards, encouraging research, monitoring health trends, issuing alerts about health emergencies and coordinating disease eradication programmes. It is not a funding agency, and it does not have enough staff to deliver health care, but it instead works as a facilitator, a processor of information, and a body that can call attention to problems and bring governments and other stakeholders together to design and implement a response to these problems. It also promotes 7 April – the date of its founding – as World Health Day.

The WHO has the following structural elements:

- *Secretariat and executive head.* From its headquarters in Geneva, the WHO is headed by a Director General nominated by the Executive Board and elected in a secret ballot by the World Health Assembly for five-year terms, renewable once. The director general during the Covid-19 pandemic was Dr Tedros Adhanom Ghebreyesus, a former Minister of Health from Ethiopia, and the first African to hold the post. Previous directors general have come from Canada, Brazil, Denmark, Japan, Norway, South Korea and China.

- *Assembly.* The main decision-making body is the World Health Assembly, which consists of delegates from each WHO member state, who meet once annually to set policy and make strategic decisions, such as reviewing and approving the budget.

- *Executive council.* A 34-member Executive Board meets at least biannually to oversee implementation of decisions taken by the Assembly. Its members must be qualified in the field of health, are designated by the member states and are elected to three-year terms by the Assembly. A quota ensures a geographical distribution of seats to cover Africa, the Americas, Southeast Asia, Europe, the Eastern Mediterranean and the Western Pacific.

- *Other elements.* The WHO has regional health organizations for Africa, the Americas, the Eastern Mediterranean, Europe, Southeast Asia and the Western Pacific. Each has its own budget and leadership, giving the WHO an unusually decentralized personality, criticized by Legge (2012) for undermining the coherence of the WHO programme and for weakening accountability.

Uniquely, the WHO regional office for the Americas is also the Pan American Health Organization (PAHO), which was founded in 1902 as the International Sanitary Bureau, has 35 member states, and is headquartered in Washington DC. Plans for PAHO to be merged into the new WHO in 1948 did not work out, since when it has fulfilled double duty. PAHO has its own director, assembly, council and executive committee.

– *Budget*. The WHO is in the disadvantaged position of having to rely for its funding on a combination of assessed membership dues and of voluntary contributions from other sources. The dues are based on the size of the economies of states, but they account for less than one-fifth of the total budget, so the balance comes from voluntary contributions. These are sometimes provided by member states, but a loss of control over the regular public budget has meant – notes Velásquez (2018) – a progressive privatization of the WHO, with sources such as the Bill and Melinda Gates Foundation and Rotary International playing a key role; see Figure 10.2. In 2020–21, the total income of the WHO was just under $4.9 billion, a modest amount when compared to the World Bank, for example, which provided more than $98 billion in loans in the 2021 fiscal year.

As with most intergovernmental organizations, the performance of the WHO has met with mixed reviews (Beigbeder, 2018). It was criticized for its slow response to the HIV/AIDS, Ebola and Covid-19 pandemics, for moving *too quickly* in declaring an H1N1 pandemic in 2009, and has attracted the common charges of inadequate

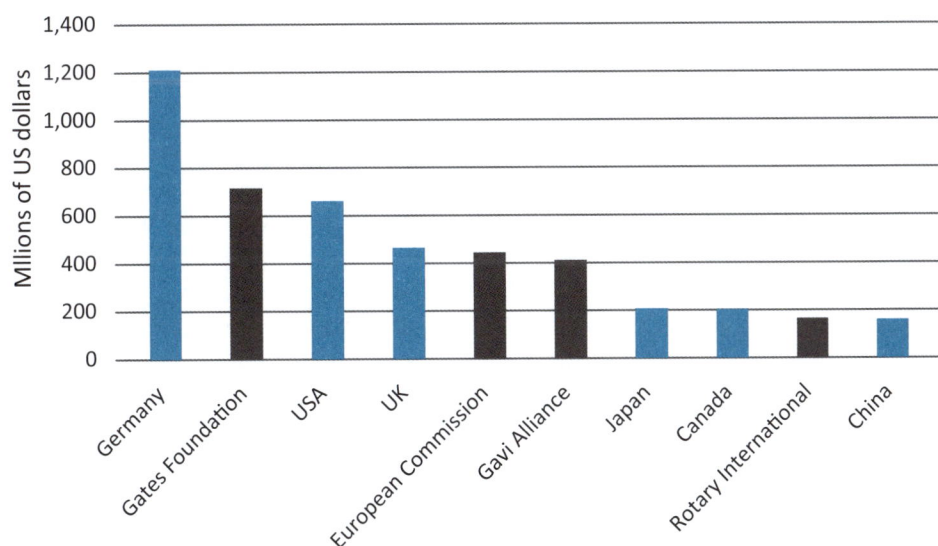

Figure 10.2: Ten biggest sources of funding for the World Health Organization.
Source: Based on data in World Health Organization (2023b). Figures are for 2020–21.

leadership and slow bureaucracy. It has responded by pointing out that its job is often misunderstood: it is not expected to lead so much as to issue alerts on health emergencies, to give advice, and to encourage coordination among governments and non-state actors. It also argues that its funding has never been adequate to the size of its task, leading, for example, to a financial crisis in 2010–11 when the WHO had a $300 million deficit thanks to a fall in voluntary contributions caused in part by a weakening of the US dollar (Beigbeder, 2018).

To further complicate matters, parts of the WHO's mandate are either addressed by other IOs with bigger budgets (such as the World Bank) or have been distracted by the creation of newer IOs such as UNAIDS and the Gavi Alliance – see later in this chapter. The WHO must also work beside a large community of non-state actors that play a significant role in funding health initiatives, sometimes complementing

IOs IN ACTION 10

THE WORLD HEALTH ORGANIZATION, VACCINES AND DISEASE

Among many other initiatives, the WHO has launched multiple programmes over the years aimed at the eradication of infectious diseases such as tuberculosis, malaria, smallpox, leprosy and polio. Its most successful programme focused on smallpox, a devastating disease that had blighted humans for centuries, producing ulcers, skin rash and blisters, and having a 30 per cent mortality rate. It was the target of the world's first vaccine, developed by Edward Jenner in Britain in 1796, but the disease – whose origins were unknown – continued to take millions of lives. When the WHO smallpox programme was launched in 1959, two million people were still dying annually from the affliction. The key to eradication was the reporting of outbreaks and the distribution of vaccines, both of which were coordinated by the WHO. Thanks in part to these efforts, the last known case of smallpox was recorded in 1977, and on 8 May 1980 the WHO declared that smallpox had become the first disease in history to be eradicated by human effort.

Although only one more disease has since been eradicated (rinderpest, a disease afflicting cattle, buffalo and related animals), the case of smallpox is an indication of what is possible with the right degree and efficiency of cooperation. This has been lacking in the WHO response to malaria, a disease carried by mosquitoes that has been eliminated (but not eradicated) from Europe, North America and Australia, but is still widespread in many rural parts of sub-Saharan Africa. The WHO launched an eradication programme in 1955, but it attracted little support and was suspended in 1969. Torn between trying to control, eliminate or eradicate the disease, the WHO by the late 1990s had moved to a malaria 'rollback' programme, but found itself struggling not only against its budgetary restraints, and the challenge of coordinating the work of public and private agencies, but also against growing resistance to anti-malarial drugs and to the insecticides used to kill mosquitoes (Beigbeder, 2018). While the global mortality rate from malaria was halved between 2000 and 2020 – from 30 to 15 deaths per 100,000 population – the disease still claimed 627,000 lives in 2020, while 241 million cases were reported in the same year. Africa accounted for 95 per cent of all cases and 96 per cent of deaths (World Health Organization, 2022).

the work of the WHO but often pursuing their own interests. Through a 2016 agreement, for example, the WHO engages with more than 700 non-state actors, including more than 200 NGOs that have an official relationship with the WHO (including non-voting participation in the work of its governing bodies). The days in which the WHO was almost alone in the global health field have long gone, to be replaced by a crowded field in which there is often duplication of effort and too little effective coordination.

Clinton and Sridhar (2017) are critical of the problems contained in the governing structure of the WHO, and its inability to engage effectively within this crowded field. They also criticize it for being insufficiently transparent in its work, and for failing to put forward a consistent message about that work. Finally, they note the problems inherent in the heavy dependence of the WHO on voluntary contributions, which leaves the organization subject to the whims of its donors. The point remains, though, that intergovernmental organizations such as the WHO can only do as much as their member states allow them to do, and the problems it faces are at least as much a result of the limits placed on its functions and its budget as on management problems within the organization. We should also not forget that the glass is at least half full, and that the WHO – despite its problems – has achieved a great deal; see *IOs in Action 10*.

OTHER HEALTH IGOS

Despite the prominence of the WHO within the global health regime, it does not have the same distinction, for example, as the UN in global trade, or the World Bank in global development. Instead, it works in a crowded and overlapping field of IGOs that have often evolved independently, some of them founded in an effort to avoid concerns about the bureaucracy that can slow down the work of the WHO (Beigbeder, 2018). This is illustrated by the experience of the global response to AIDS, where the WHO had been running its own Global Programme for AIDS since 1986, but was joined in 1994 by UNAIDS and in 2002 by the Global Fund to Fight AIDS, Tuberculosis and Malaria.

UNAIDS (formally the Joint United Nations Programme on HIV and AIDS) was founded to coordinate the UN's response to AIDS, becoming the first (and so far only) cosponsored joint programme in the UN system. It brings together the efforts of no less than 11 UN bodies – including the WHO, the World Bank, UNICEF and UN Women – with the goal of working to provide strategic direction to the UN response, gathering data on the HIV pandemic, and connecting interested governments and IOs. In particular, it declared the 90-90-90 targets on HIV in 2013: by 2020, 90 per cent of all people living with HIV were to have been diagnosed, 90 per cent of those diagnosed were to have been on antiretroviral therapy, and 90 per cent of those on therapy were to have achieved viral suppression. UNAIDS research suggested that the actual figures reached were 84-87-90 (UNAIDS, 2021), at which point the target was amended and tightened to 95-95-95 by 2030.

UNAIDS has the following structure:

- *Secretariat and executive head.* From its headquarters in Geneva, where it shares offices with the WHO, UNAIDS has an Executive Director appointed by the UN Secretary General on the advice of the Board of UNAIDS. The third officeholder, appointed in 2019, was Winnie Byanyima of Uganda, who came to the job having been Executive Director of Oxfam International, prior to which she had been a member of the Ugandan parliament.

- *Executive council.* The work of UNAIDS is guided by a Programme Coordinating Board made up of representatives from 22 member states (with an arranged geographical distribution), cosponsoring UN bodies, five NGOs and people living with HIV. The Board meets biannually for two days to establish policies, and to review the UNAIDS plan of action and budget. UNAIDS also has a Committee of Co-sponsoring Organizations that brings together the 11 participating UN agencies, offering them a channel into the work of the organization.

- *Budget.* The costs of UNAIDS are met through contributions from its participating organizations.

In addition to the WHO, other UN specialized agencies also have a key role in setting and implementing global health policy. Among them is UNICEF (see Chapter 7), whose founding mandate included the provision of emergency assistance and health services to children in states torn by conflict. It has since expanded its goals to provide long-term help to children, including the promotion of their health and human rights. Its earliest programme was to work with the WHO in the 1950s to cure children of yaws, a chronic skin infection that is disfiguring but rarely fatal. The disease is today endemic to just 15 countries, and can be cured by a single oral dose of an inexpensive antibiotic.

Meanwhile, the World Bank (see Chapter 5) has become one of the largest sources of funding for health programmes in developing countries (Park, 2018). This included being the single largest funder of the global response to Covid-19, with about $14 billion committed to more than 100 countries by mid-2022. There is a notable irony in the fact that the Bank is a champion of the idea of universal health care, despite being situated in, dominated by and typically led by a president from the US, notable for being the only advanced free market democracy without universal health care. The web site of the World Bank (2023) makes much of the interest of the World Bank Group in supporting national efforts to 'provide quality, affordable health services to everyone – regardless of their ability to pay – by strengthening primary health care systems and reducing the financial risks associated with ill health and increasing equity'. However, its own research indicated that even before the outbreak of Covid-19, more than half a billion people had been pushed further into poverty because they had to pay for health services out of their own pockets.

Another UN programme active in health care is the UN Population Fund (UNFPA), whose interests focus on improving reproductive and maternal health. This includes increasing access to birth control, and campaigning against child marriage, intimate partner violence and female genital mutilation. Founded in 1969 as the UN Fund for Population Activities (whose acronym it still uses), it was placed under the authority of the UN General Assembly in 1971. It is the world's largest multilateral source of funding for reproductive health, working with voluntary contributions from governments, foundations and other UN agencies. It has an Executive Director appointed by the Secretary General of the UN, and shares a 36-member executive board (and a secretariat in New York) with the UN Development Programme (UNDP).

Because it addresses issues that are not always popular with conservative politicians and governments, the UNFPA has been the target of efforts to undermine or limit its work. The US has been a leading actor in this regard, being behind the Mexico City Policy (otherwise known as the Global Gag Rule) that was announced by the Reagan administration at the 1984 World Population Conference. Under the rule, NGOs outside the US are blocked from receiving American family planning assistance if they use funding from any source to perform abortions in cases other than rape, incest or a threat to the life of the mother. They cannot even provide counselling or referrals for abortions. The rule was rescinded by the Clinton administration, reinstated by the George W. Bush administration, rescinded again by Barack Obama, and then reinstated and expanded by Donald Trump, who also defunded the UNFPA (see McGovern et al., 2020).

Another part of the global health field is occupied by public-private partnerships (PPPs) that combine non-profit and for-profit enterprises to address specific challenges. A primary driver for the emergence of these organizations, note Clinton and Sridhar (2017), has been a belief that they will address health problems and fund shared efforts more effectively than other approaches. Prominent among them is the Global Fund to Fight AIDS, Tuberculosis and Malaria (known more usually as the Global Fund), which was set up in 2002 as a hybrid organization bringing together governments, NGOs and the private sector but working separately from the WHO. Encouraged by then-UN Secretary General Kofi Annan, it was endorsed by the leaders of the G7 and has subsequently been funded mainly by the G7 states.

The Global Fund separated from the WHO in 2009, becoming an autonomous body with a role similar to UN agencies. It is governed by a combination of donor states, NGOs and private foundations, but while its 28-member ruling Board includes the WHO, the latter does not have voting rights. This is a hard reality that – for Beigbeder (2018) – reflects the lack of donor confidence in the capacity of the WHO to manage the tasks entrusted to the Fund. This is ironic given that the Fund had to undergo a reorganization in 2011 following revelations about the fraudulent use of some of its funding by grant recipients. It has a small secretariat based in Geneva that oversees and monitors the distribution of grants to in-country partners such as domestic ministries of health. As of 2023, it was reporting that it was investing about $4 billion per year and claimed to have saved 50 million lives and to have made antiretroviral therapy available to more than 23 million people.

Another public-private gathering of UN agencies, states, foundations and the vaccine industry is the Gavi Alliance. Founded in 2000 as the Global Alliance for Vaccines and Immunization, and now known simply by its acronym, Gavi's goal is to promote access to immunization in poorer states. Run in five-year funding cycles, most of its funding comes from Western Europe and North America, with donations also from the Bill and Melinda Gates Foundation and other philanthropic sources. With a joint secretariat in Geneva and Washington DC, it is led by a Chief Executive Officer appointed by a 28-member Board on which permanent seats are held by UNICEF, the WHO, the World Bank and the BMGF. Nine of the seats are reserved for private individuals chosen to bring independent input to board decisions, including from investment and fundraising perspectives, while others are occupied by NGOs and vaccine companies.

Gavi claimed to have helped vaccinate nearly 900 million children in 77 countries between 2000 and 2020, saving nine million lives. Evidence from a study of the effect of the Gavi Alliance on rates of immunization for DPT (diphtheria, pertussis and tetanus) and measles suggest that the work of the Alliance has indeed been effective (Jaupart et al., 2019). The study found that immunization rates for DPT had grown by 12 per cent between 1995 and 2016, and those for measles by nearly nine per cent. Extrapolating from these results, the study suggested that there was an average reduction of six per cent in infant mortality rates over the same period, and of 12 per cent in under-five child deaths. The result backed up many of Gavi's own claims, leading the authors of the study to conclude that vaccines were a global public good for which the kind of coordination provided by Gavi was invaluable.

NON-STATE HEALTH ACTORS

As with many other global regimes, health care is impacted by the activities of an array of non-state actors. It is surprising, then, that so little attention has been paid to theoretical approaches to international relations that incorporate the influence of non-state actors; see *IOs in Theory 10*. In particular, there is much to be learned from the work of philanthropic foundations that have placed health care high up their agendas, and that have funded much of the work undertaken at the global level. In the US, for example, the Rockefeller Foundation was behind the development of a vaccine for yellow fever in 1935, while the Ford Foundation helped draw attention during the 1950s and 1960s to the potential problems of overpopulation, and Rotary International is today one of the major funders of the WHO, contributing more than either China, Saudi Arabia or France.

No private foundation has played so prominent a role in global health as the Bill and Melinda Gates Foundation (BMGF), which was not only the second biggest donor to the WHO in 2020–21 (after Germany and ahead of the US), but also has its own programmes on HIV, malaria, vaccines and maternal health. With an endowment in 2020 of nearly $50 billion, it was the wealthiest philanthropic organization in the world, with a global health budget that is bigger than that of the WHO. Created in 1994 by Bill Gates, the co-founder of Microsoft, as the William H. Gates Foundation, it adopted its current name in 2000. Although headquartered in the US, it has a clearly international reach, notably in the fields of health and development. Many of its grants in recent years have gone to the control of infectious disease, malaria, sexually transmitted disease and tuberculosis, as well as to the promotion of reproductive

IOs IN THEORY 10

BRINGING IN NON-STATE ACTORS

As a quick review of much of the scholarship on international organizations reveals, more attention is usually paid to IGOs such as the United Nations (UN), the World Trade Organization (WTO) and the European Union (EU) than to non-state actors such as international non-governmental organizations. This imbalance is reflected in international relations theory, where the importance of non-state actors is routinely marginalized. The effect of this, as noted by DeMars and Dijkzeul (2015), is to leave the significance and impact of NGOs on world politics unclear. More than any other set of actors in world politics, they continue, NGOs have an unparalleled ability to connect with political and social actors of many kinds, networking with everything from informal neighbourhood groups to warlords, governing elites, business, UN agencies and ethnic or religious communities. As a result, they conclude, a refinement of mainstream theories such as realism (Chapter 1), liberalism (Chapter 4) and constructivism (Chapter 7) is needed in order to consider the impact and role of non-state actors.

Willetts (2011) makes the point that NGOs are key players in global politics, and there are many more NGOs exercising influence within the UN – and over the shaping of international law – than just the few more famous examples. He also argues in favour of the need to integrate their work into mainstream international relations theory, along with the work of governments, multinational enterprises and – in fact – all types of international organizations. Using constructivism (see *IOs in Theory 7*) to analyse mobilization of support for values and norms, he argues, 'is essential to explaining how NGOs that lack the ability to coerce others and lack access to substantial economic resources can nevertheless change policy-making outcomes'.

For their part, Carayannis and Weiss (2021) build on an earlier suggestion by Claude (1996) that there is a 'First UN' (the member states) and a 'Second UN' (the staff members of UN secretariats) to identify a 'Third UN' of non-state actors; specifically, intellectuals, scholars, consultants, think-tanks, NGOs, for-profit organizations and the media. This Third UN, they argue, interacts with the intergovernmental machinery of the First and Second UNs to influence and refine ideas and policies, and to help the UN 'think'. Going outside an organization can help inject new ideas and perspectives, they continue, changing the way that issues are perceived, setting agendas for action, mobilizing coalitions to press for action and becoming imbedded in the organizations. Going outside the mainstream theories, then, can also provide us with new insights.

health care and family planning. It is also one of the biggest contributors to the budget of the Gavi Alliance and the Global Fund to Fight AIDS, Tuberculosis and Malaria.

Despite the considerable funding often provided by the biggest philanthropic organizations, opinion on their value and role is divided. Barkan (2013) argues that the emergence of 'big philanthropy' in the US in the opening decades of the twentieth century was sometimes seen by its detractors as resulting in the creation of centres of plutocratic power that threaten democratic governance. A century later, Barkan continued, little had changed: big philanthropy still aims to solve the world's problems, but the trustees of these big foundations often define these problems and how to address them while being subject to few democratic controls. In other words, they have the resources to shape public policy, but they have no accountability to the public or to the people directly affected by their programmes.

Looking specifically at the BMGF, Harman (2016) argues that the sheer degree of its authority in the field of global health politics illustrates the 'legitimacy problem' with global philanthropy. Questions have arisen about how and where its funds are spent, the nature of its partnerships, and the 'Bill Chill' effect of the foundation on global health institutions. The latter refers to the problem of Bill Gates having so much influence over public health decisions that there is a reluctance on the part of those who disagree with him to criticize him or his priorities for fear of losing the support of his foundation (Twohey and Kulish, 2020). The problem is amplified, notes Gostin (2021), by the way in which much of the BMGF funding to the WHO is tied to the specific agendas of the foundation, restricting the ability of the WHO to set global health priorities. The answer to this problem, he continues, lies in a major increase in mandatory (and non-earmarked) state contributions to the WHO, and more non-earmarked support from foundations. Neither, though, is likely to happen any time soon.

On the INGO front, meanwhile, there are multiple organizations that focus on the quality of health care, and others that focus on advocacy and improved access to health care; see Table 10.3 for examples. Among the best-known of those involved

Table 10.3: Health care and medical non-state actors: Examples

Name	Founded	Headquarters	Goals
World Medical Association	1947	Near Geneva, Switzerland	Promote standards and independence of physicians.
Doctors Without Borders (MSF)	1971	Geneva	Medical assistance to victims of conflict and natural disasters.
Global Health Council	1972	Alexandria, VA, USA	Promote improved global health. Membership of NGOs, corporations, foundations and academic bodies.
Health Action International	1981	Amsterdam, the Netherlands	Expand access to essential medicines.
International AIDS Society	1988	Geneva	Membership of AIDS professionals. Advocacy, research and hosting conferences.
Health Right International	1990	New York, USA	Access to health care for marginalized communities.
Bill and Melinda Gates Foundation (BMGF)	1994	Seattle, USA	Philanthropic foundation that prioritizes health care.

in providing health care is *Médecins Sans Frontières* (MSF or Doctors Without Borders), which was founded in France in 1971 to help victims of conflict and natural disasters. The small group of doctors and journalists that launched the organization was prompted by the humanitarian disaster in the wake of the civil war of 1967–70 in the breakaway Nigerian state of Biafra. Focusing on mobilizing doctors, nurses and engineers, who volunteer their services in places and times of need, MSF has since been active in more than 70 countries (mainly in Africa, the Middle East and Latin America). It also engages with human rights and wider humanitarian issues and has been an advocate for addressing the problem of unequal access to medical care and to pharmaceuticals.

Headquartered in Geneva, MSF has 25 national associations that each function independently in their home states (about half are in Europe and the rest distributed around the world), and cooperate through six operational centres that manage the work of MSF in the field. MSF International hosts an International General Assembly that meets annually to make decisions, safeguard the organization's mission, monitor the work of the governing International Board (two-thirds of whose 12 members must have a medical background), and both appoint and monitor the President. MSF has chosen to rely almost entirely on private funding (much of it coming in small amounts from individual donors) so that it can remain politically independent. It was awarded the Nobel Peace Prize in 1999 and if imitation is the sincerest form of flattery, then Doctors Without Borders can consider itself flattered: INGOs with the phrase 'without borders' in their names have been formed for engineers, lawyers, libraries, musicians, reporters and translators, among others.

Many other INGOs discussed in other chapters of this book also have interests and operations that overlap with health care: prime among them are the Red Cross (Chapter 4), BRAC (Chapter 5) and Save the Children (Chapter 7). Beigbeder (2018) also notes the importance in the health field of faith-based organizations (FBOs), many of whose activities date back to the colonial era, and many of which stayed on after the independence of the mainly African states in which they were based. These organizations have been an important part of the provision of health care in many countries, often providing services where governments have not been able to meet the needs of their citizens. There are numerous Christian organizations, for example, such as the Salvation Army, the Catholic Church and the Adventist Church, that run hospitals and clinics in multiple countries. Many are members of INGOs such as the Geneva-based World Council of Churches or the US-based Christian Connections for International Health. However, Olivier et al. (2015) point out that while FBOs clearly play an important role in providing health care in Africa in particular, little research has been undertaken into their role. Questions must also be asked about the extent to which the health services they provide are linked to efforts to convert patients to their religious beliefs.

At another and quite different point on the scale, pharmaceutical companies play a critical role in determining the quality of health care, and access to that care, thereby influencing the dynamics of the global health regime. A handful of large and mainly Western-based pharmaceutical multinationals such as Pfizer and Novartis (see

Table 10.4: Ten major multinational pharmaceutical companies

Name	Home country	Known for
Pfizer	USA	First successful Covid-19 vaccine
AbbVie	USA	Arthritis drug Humira
Johnson and Johnson	USA	Drug treatments in multiple areas
Novartis	Switzerland	Drug treatments in multiple areas
Roche	Switzerland	Oncology, immunology and infectious diseases
Bristol Myers Squibb	USA	Oncology, haematology and immunology
Merck	USA	Oncology, diabetes and animal health
AstraZeneca	UK	Drug treatments in multiple areas
Sanofi	France	Drug treatments in multiple areas
GlaxoSmithKline	UK	Drug treatments in multiple areas

Table 10.4) not only drive the creation of new medicaments, but also shape their production and access through the decisions they make about pricing. The unfortunate reality is that many of these companies continue to make large profits, while many of the drugs they make are too expensive – or hard to access – for many people.

For most of the world, argues Hassoun (2020), critical medications that would treat diseases such as tuberculosis, AIDS and malaria are 'scarce, costly, and growing obsolete, as access to first-line drugs remains out of reach and resistance rates rise'. Rather than focusing their research on affordable medicines that could treat diseases of this kind, she continues, pharmaceutical companies instead invest in commercially lucrative products for more affluent customers. In their assessment of the global pharmaceutical industry, Hoffman and Bowditch (2021) argue that the prices now charged for prescription drugs by what is often pejoratively known as 'Big Pharma' have escalated at a rate that is four to five times the rate of increases in the cost of living in wealthy countries. Governments have sometimes found it necessary to take legal action against the biggest pharmaceutical companies, but broader change is needed – conclude Hoffman and Bowditch – if the pharmaceutical industry is to equitably advance the health of the world's population and regain public esteem.

THINKING POINTS

- Disjointed and incoherent; is this a fair assessment of the global health regime?

- How far beyond their emphasis on limiting the spread of infectious disease should the work of health IGOs extend?

- Has the creation of newer IOs such as UNAIDS and the Gavi Alliance been a distraction or a complement to the work of WHO?

- How much does the model of UNAIDS as a cosponsored joint programme have to offer the UN approach to other international needs?

- To what extent does the influence of private organizations such as the Bill and Melinda Gates Foundation threaten democratic governance over health care?

IOs RELATED TO THIS CHAPTER

Bill and Melinda Gates Foundation (BMFG)

Gavi Alliance

Global Fund (Global Fund to Fight AIDS, Tuberculosis and Malaria)

International Health Partnership (UHC2030)

Médecins Sans Frontières (MSF or Doctors Without Borders)

Pan American Health Organization (PAHO)

UNAIDS (UN Programme on HIV/AIDS)

UN Population Fund (UNFPA)

World Health Organization (WHO)

FURTHER READING

Beigbeder, Yves (2018) *The World Health Organization: Achievements and Failures* (Routledge). A pre-Covid assessment of the work of the WHO, critically reviewing its response to pandemics and its work with other global health care actors.

Clinton, Chelsea, and Devi Sridhar (2017) *Governing Global Health: Who Runs the World and Why?* (Oxford University Press). A survey of the global health regime, with a focus on the key intergovernmental organizations involved, and the rising influence of public-private partnerships.

McInnes, Colin, Kelley Lee, and Jeremy Youde (eds) (2020) *The Oxford Handbook of Global Health Politics* (Oxford University Press). An edited collection of chapters on the global health landscape, the dimensions of global health and the key international organizations involved.

Merson, Michael, and Stephen Inrig (2017) *The AIDS Pandemic: Searching for a Global Response* (Springer). A case study of the response to the HIV/AIDS pandemic, showing how and why the WHO was unable to take the leadership that was hoped and expected of the organization.

Youde, Jeremy (2018) *Global Health Governance in International Society* (Oxford University Press). An assessment of the reasons behind the rise in the importance of global approaches to health, including chapters on the key governance actors involved.

ENVIRONMENT AND NATURAL RESOURCES 11

PREVIEW

In this chapter, international organizations are focused on the management of the environment and natural resources, a challenge that has deepened in the wake of climate change and threats to biodiversity. National responses to these problems vary in quality and in quantity, reflected in the slowness with which the foundations of a global environmental regime were built; it was not until after the 1972 Stockholm conference that the UN Environment Programme (UNEP) was founded, and while there was progress on addressing acid pollution and threats to the ozone layer, the story on other problems was less positive. After reviewing achievements in agreeing environmental law, the chapter focuses on the structure and goals of UNEP, noting the failure of efforts to create a World Environment Organization. It then discusses the work of the Global Environment Facility (GEF), and the varied results in building regimes around forests and energy. On the latter, the work of IOs such as the International Energy Agency (IEA) is reviewed. The chapter ends with an assessment of the work of non-state actors, arguing that environmental INGOs have been a source of pressure on governments and IGOs, and noting the impact of changes in the policies of multinational enterprises.

CONTENTS

- The context
- Building a global environmental regime
- The United Nations Environment Programme
- Other environmental and natural resource IOs
- Non-state environmental actors

THE CONTEXT

In July 2022, delegates to a meeting of the UN General Assembly adopted a resolution declaring that a clean, healthy and sustainable environment should be considered a human right. 'These resolutions may seem abstract,' noted UN Special Rapporteur for Human Rights and the Environment David Boyd before the vote, 'but they are a catalyst for action, and they empower ordinary people to hold their governments accountable in a way that is very powerful.' Perhaps the only surprising quality about the resolution was that it had taken so long to agree: more than 70 years after the adoption of the Universal Declaration of Human Rights, more than 50 years after an international conference in Stockholm had pushed the environment to the forefront of global governance concerns, and decades into the deepening crises of climate change and biodiversity loss.

Of the many issues that have been addressed at the international level, few are more clearly international or global in scope than the state of the environment. Defined simply as the physical surroundings in which all life on earth exists, the environment has been reshaped by human activity for thousands of years, a process that has accelerated since the industrial revolution, creating problems such as air pollution, water pollution, waste and habitat destruction. None of these problems respect national borders and, while they can be addressed to a degree by domestic action on the part of states, there is no prospect of a full or universal resolution without international cooperation. That cooperation, where it happens, must address multiple challenges:

- A growing human population (crossing the eight billion mark in 2022), with all the increased pressure on natural resources that this involves.

- A heavy reliance in most parts of the world on pollutive fossil fuels: coal, oil and natural gas.

- Rises in the levels of airborne chemicals, posing threats to human health.

- The continued production and careless disposal of waste, including its toxic, hazardous and radioactive forms.

- Human pressure on biodiversity, leading to countless numbers of species extinctions and pushing other species to the brink of extinction.

Environmental policy is not just concerned with qualitative matters such as clean air and water, but also with quantitative matters, prime among them being the management of natural resources. These are materials or commodities found naturally on earth that have value to humans, including land, water, plants, animals, soil, minerals, fossil fuels, forests, fisheries and the open ocean. They can be consumed directly, as in the case of food and drinking water, or indirectly, as in the case of forests that provide timber and fuelwood. Most are local, meaning that they are geographically restricted, with different parts of the world being relatively well or badly endowed, and states usually treating them as a national issue subject to national control. Other resources – including forests and fisheries – have global significance, and are more logically managed through international cooperation. However, resistance by countries such as Brazil to international management of its tropical rain forests, for example, and the problems the international community has had in agreeing shared management of the world's oceans, show the difficulties faced by efforts to manage shared resources.

Above all, human activity has generated the ultimate existential problem of climate change (see Hulme, 2022). At its heart is the greenhouse effect, a natural phenomenon which makes life on earth possible because water vapour, carbon dioxide and methane trap enough solar radiation to keep global temperatures stable. Our use of fossil fuels, coupled with intensive farming and the removal of the forests that are natural sinks for many pollutants (notably carbon dioxide or CO_2), has resulted in an enhanced greenhouse effect. Higher CO_2 concentrations have trapped more solar radiation in the atmosphere, with a host of negative effects: warming temperatures, changing weather patterns, more extreme weather events, melting icecaps and glaciers, rising sea levels and changing crop-growing patterns. The science of the problem has been understood since the late nineteenth century, the first evidence of rising CO_2 concentrations was gathered in the 1950s, and political warnings were issued in the late 1980s, but an international treaty on climate change was not agreed until 1992, and even today there are many states that still equivocate on taking action.

The extent to which states are prepared to work together in addressing environmental problems depends on a variety of factors, ranging from the degree to which each of them experiences a problem to levels of public awareness, levels of political interest and the influence of domestic industries, notably energy and automobile companies. The states with the strongest records of factoring environmental concerns into politics and economics have been variously described as environmental states, ecological states or green states. Duit et al. (2016) define environmental states as those which possess 'a significant set of institutions and practices dedicated to the management of the environment and societal–environmental interactions'. The opposite, meanwhile, are those states that possess fewer of these features and are less supportive of global governance on the environment.

One of the effects of the differences has been the creation of a leader-laggard dynamic by which leader states pull others behind them to more ambitious standards and goals, while laggard states either follow along later or force compromises that result in more modest goals (Knill et al., 2011). Leader states such as Germany, the UK, the US, and the Nordic countries have long played the most influential role in driving the definition and implementation of environmental policy at the international level, while laggard states – most of them in sub-Saharan Africa and Asia – have been slower to change. The balance has changed in recent decades with the rise of new economic powers, such as China and India, exerting new levels of influence. These changes have combined to complicate the building of a global environmental regime, with states bringing different perspectives to the debate: where many of the environmental problems of the leader states are associated with the long-term effects of industrialization and consumption, many of the laggards are driven by a more complex combination of shorter-term economic change and poverty.

The challenges involved are reflected in the results of the Environmental Performance Index, maintained by Yale and Columbia universities. This ranks countries out of 100 according to several performance criteria, such as environmental health, levels of air and water pollution, habitat protection and land use. What it finds is that the countries to which industrialization came first (Western Europe and North America) do best, with scores in the range of 55–80, while the newer industrializing countries (such as the BRICS) and the poorest countries in the world

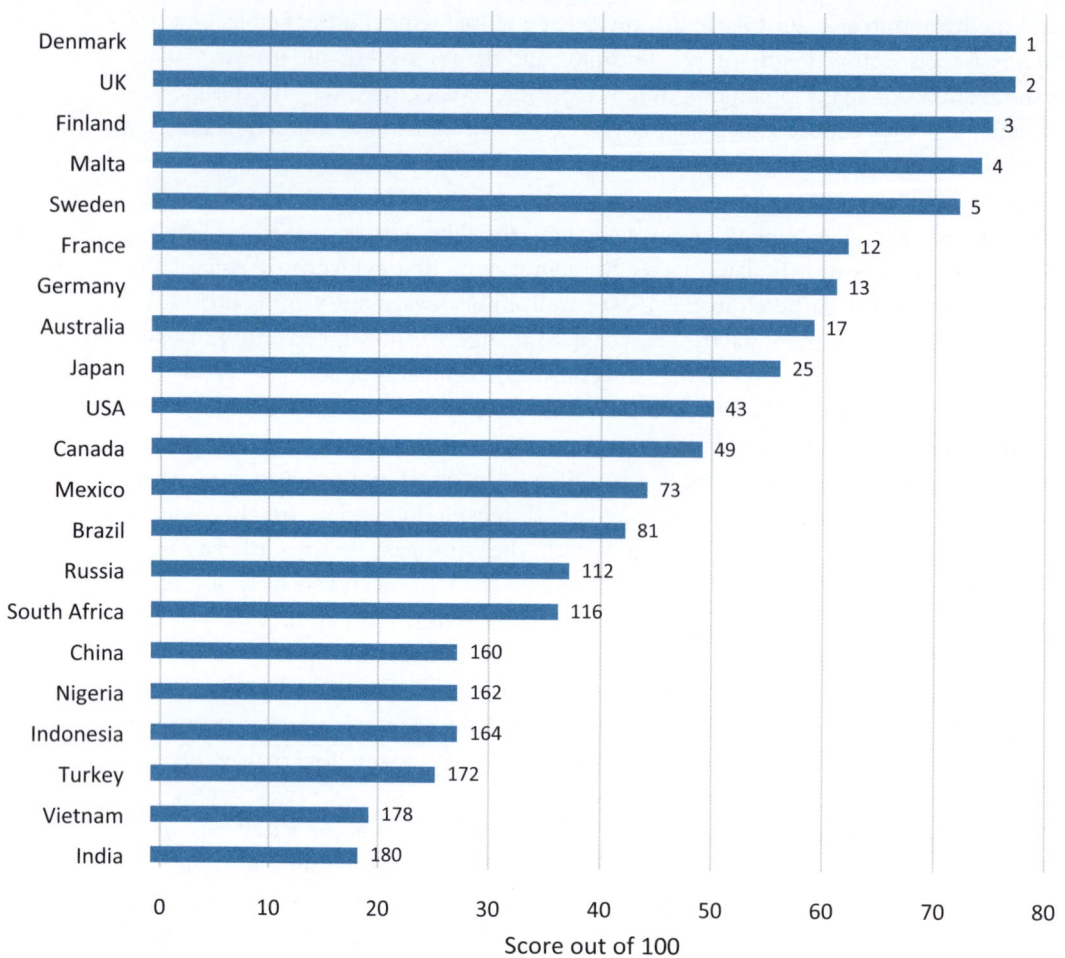

Figure 11.1: The Environmental Performance Index.
Source: Based on data in Environmental Performance Index (2023). Numbers at the end of columns indicate ranking.

(mostly in Asia and sub-Saharan Africa) languish in the range of 20–50 (see Figure 11.1). While the leaders show what can be done, and work to encourage improved environmental policies in other parts of the world, the emerging and poorer countries often see environmental regulation as a brake on their economic development that the industrialized countries did not have to face.

As if these challenges were not enough, finding agreement on international environmental policy is made harder by the difficulty of separating the environment from many other issues, including the economy, energy, agriculture, transport, health, land use and urban development. This is a reality that states have faced domestically as they have tried to divide responsibility for different areas of policy to different government departments. It has also been a reality at the international level, where multiple international organizations have been active in areas with an environmental dimension, and there have sometimes been difficulties in deciding the divisions of interest and responsibility.

BUILDING A GLOBAL ENVIRONMENTAL REGIME

Like many other topics in international affairs, the environment has been a relatively recent addition to the agenda of global governance. The states that were earliest to industrialize were the first to experience the most serious effects of air and water pollution, and of habitat destruction. Governments did little to respond, though, giving little thought to the environmental effects of economic policy. As a topic, the environment was on the margins of the agenda of the United Nations, which at first addressed it only so far as it related to food production and the elimination of hunger. When the Food and Agriculture Organization of the UN (FAO) was founded in 1945 to address long-term food supply needs, attention was paid to the protection and extension of forest cover to check soil erosion, protect watersheds, control floods, act as windbreaks and shelter wildlife. Its leaders later realized that resource mismanagement and population growth were standing in the way of a solution to the post-war global food crisis, and it was only then that FAO began to develop an interest in environmental management. (For background on the early years of environmentalism, see McCormick, 1995.)

At about the same time, the new UN Educational, Scientific and Cultural Organization (UNESCO) was interested in the protection of nature, but lacked either the necessary staff or the resources to act. Instead, it helped support the creation in 1947 of a new hybrid body named the International Union for the Protection of Nature, whose members included representatives from governments and from NGOs. It changed its name in 1956 to the International Union for Conservation of Nature (IUCN), signifying the new idea that nature should not be protected in isolation, but should be planned to be used sustainably. The term *conservation* (wise use) had been used since the early twentieth century, and was later to evolve into the idea of sustainable development discussed in Chapter 5. Unlike many of the other regimes assessed in this book, science lies at the heart of the environmental regime, changing the dynamic both of how decisions are taken and of the voices that must be heard as those decisions are shaped. The environment has not only been part of the interests of a cluster of IOs with more limited agendas, such as the International Union of Biological Sciences (founded 1919) and the International Council of Scientific Unions (founded 1931), but it has also spawned epistemic communities of experts whose work feeds into that of IOs; see *Spotlight 11*.

It was not until the 1960s that public opinion in the Global North began to pay more attention to the deteriorating state of the environment, and to demand political responses. Science was offering new and alarming evidence of the problem, and there was a change in political and public attitudes with the rise of what Inglehart (1971) described as post-materialism: in distinction to the materialist interest in economic growth and security, there was a new focus on quality-of-life issues such as environmental protection, nuclear disarmament and gender equality. His thesis was that Westerners born after World War II had grown up during a time of unprecedented prosperity and relative international peace, freed from many of the concerns about security and survival that had influenced earlier generations. This combination of affluence, peace and security had led to a 'silent revolution' in Western political cultures, in which the

SPOTLIGHT 11

EPISTEMIC COMMUNITIES AND THE ENVIRONMENT

As we saw in Chapter 1, an epistemic community is a group of experts with recognized skills and knowledge in a particular area who have been drawn together to share and pass on their knowledge. They often play a key role in the work of international organizations, as we will see in Chapter 12 with their contributions to bodies with a scientific or technical focus. Because science is so central to our understanding of environmental problems, these communities have also been a part of international cooperation on a range of such problems. One of the most effective was the community that evolved around the problem of ozone depletion in the 1980s; see later in this chapter. It began with a network of mainly American scientists, then expanded – via UNEP – to include European scientists. They built on the 1985 Vienna Convention to undertake research on ozone depletion, to publish reports and to organize conferences, and to lobby governments for policy change, playing a key role in the adoption of the Montreal Protocol in 1987 (Morin et al., 2020).

The most important epistemic community working on environmental issues today is undoubtedly the network of more than 1,300 scientists and other experts from almost every country in the world that contribute to the work of the Intergovernmental Panel on Climate Change (IPCC). This was created in 1988 by UNEP and the World Meteorological Organization (WMO) to synthesize knowledge and understanding about climate change and to publish periodic reports that could be used to help guide policy. The IPCC – headquartered within the WMO offices in Geneva – does not produce its own research so much as it pulls together the research of others. The first of its reports was published in 1990 and the sixth in 2022. Among them they offer a road map through the changing scientific understanding of climate change, work that earned the IPCC the 2007 Nobel Peace Prize (shared with former US vice president Al Gore).

priority given to economic achievement had given way to an increased emphasis on the quality of life: 'the disciplined, self-denying and achievement-oriented norms of industrial society are giving way to the choices over lifestyle which characterize post-industrial economies' (Inglehart, 1997).

Developments since 1972

A turning point in the story of global environmental governance came in 1972 with the convening in Stockholm, Sweden, of the UN Conference on the Human Environment, usually known simply as the Stockholm conference. This was the first conference at which national governments (113 in all) met to discuss the state of the environment from a global perspective, along with the potential political responses. While the environment until then had meant mainly an interest in the state of nature, and environmental problems had been discussed mainly as a localized matter in industrialized states, the definition of the environment now widened, the perspective of emerging states was added to the debate and there was a new emphasis on looking at these problems internationally. Stockholm encouraged the creation of new national environmental protection departments in multiple countries and led to the founding in 1973 of the United Nations Environment Programme (UNEP). (For background, see Morin et al., 2020.)

Citizen initiatives also played a key role at Stockholm, with the work of national environmental interest groups being reinforced by the work of newer INGOs, including the World Wildlife Fund (founded 1961), Friends of the Earth (1969) and Greenpeace (1971). The first of these initially had the older and narrower interest in nature, but both Friends of the Earth and Greenpeace took a broader view that included concerns about pollution, deforestation, commercial whaling, the overuse of natural resources, climate change, and even the links between environmental damage and human rights; see later in this chapter for more details.

The environment was proving to be a distinctive issue of international cooperation not only because it had spawned a global social movement, but also because it began to spark the creation of political parties based on environmental concerns. Green parties were formed in multiple parts of the Global North, and went on to be members of coalition governments in several countries, including Austria, Belgium, Estonia, Finland, Germany, Ireland and New Zealand. At first considered to be radical outsiders, the greens later entered mainstream politics, evolving from single-issue environmentalists into more broadly,based political parties (McBride, 2022). As such, they changed the perspectives of domestic politics, their influence spilling over into the way governments have approached environmental issues at the international level and offering a new set of theoretical approaches to understanding international organizations; see *IOs in Theory 11*.

The importance of the revised post-Stockholm approach to the environment – and specifically its new emphasis on international cooperation – was illustrated by the responses to two major environmental problems. The first was the worsening in North America and Europe of acid pollution, created when emissions of sulphur dioxide (SO_2) and nitrogen oxides from power plants and road vehicles react with atmospheric water vapour to increase the acidity of rain, snow and fog. This, in turn, caused dieback in forests, undermined the ecosystems of rivers and lakes, eroded buildings and monuments, and harmed human health.

Under the auspices of the UN Economic Commission for Europe, which included members from Eastern and Western Europe, the Convention on Long-Range Transboundary Air Pollution was signed in 1979, committing signatories to work to limit air pollution. Later, the European Community (forerunner to today's European Union (EU)) agreed a 1988 directive on emissions from large combustion plants (such as power stations). As a result of the two agreements, emissions of SO_2 – after growing steadily since 1900 and peaking in 1970 – fell in Europe between 1990 and 2015 by 74 per cent and in North America by 61 per cent; see Figure 11.2. The 1979 convention, however, applied only to Europe and North America; while the air in these two regions is much cleaner, in two other parts of the world the story is not so hopeful: emissions of SO_2 in East Asia (mainly China) grew by 66 per cent before tailing off and in India they grew by 300 per cent.

IOs IN THEORY 11

ENVIRONMENTALISM AND GREEN THEORY

Environmentalism is a term that is used interchangeably to describe a theory, a philosophy or an ideology that promotes deeper understanding of the threats posed to the environment by human activity, and of the means to developing improved management and protection (Peterson del Mar, 2012). It supports a view of the world shaped by the argument that humans are ethically responsible for Earth's ecological integrity, and that efforts are needed to rebalance the relationship between humans and their environment. These efforts include changes in individual behaviour, but environmentalism is also an example of a social movement: one emerging from society and aimed at pursuing broad goals, by orthodox and/or unorthodox means, usually driven by traditional outsiders challenging existing elites, and seeking to change public policy without becoming part of government. In this sense, environmentalism is usually – if not entirely accurately – equated with activism.

As a social movement, environmentalism seeks political and economic change, but there are competing views about how this can be achieved, ranging from change within the existing capitalist system to an entire rejection of that system. It has become usual, for example, to distinguish between reformist and radical environmentalism. The former supports human-centred change within existing political, economic and social structures, while the latter argues that we face urgent dangers that cannot be resolved within existing structures, and that we need fundamental change and entirely new approaches to both economic growth and environmental protection.

The recent and related rise of green theory ties into the growing popularity of green politics in many countries, based on a desire to build sustainable societies rooted in ecological wisdom, social justice, non-violence, diversity and grassroots democracy, overlapping with the views of feminists and peace activists. Green theory is used to look at the role of international organizations in either promoting or hindering efforts to address environmental problems, and also spills over into studies of the greening of IGOs dealing with trade, finance and development.

The second problem concerned damage caused to the Earth's ozone layer by synthetic chlorofluorocarbons (CFCs) used in refrigerants and aerosol accelerants. Stratospheric ozone helps screen out ultraviolet radiation from the sun, elevated levels of which can cause increased incidence of skin cancer and eye disorders, kill micro-organisms and cells in animals and plants, damage seed quality and reduce crop yields. Research in the 1970s revealed that CFCs were thinning the ozone layer, particularly over the polar icecaps. In 1977, the World Meteorological Organization (see Chapter 12) took the lead in publishing a plan of action. In the face of opposition from industry, the US took action to limit the release of CFCs, and the European Community followed suit. In 1985, the Vienna Convention for the Protection of the Ozone Layer was signed, and given more teeth and tighter targets in 1987 with the signature of the Montreal Protocol to the convention. By 1998, these actions had

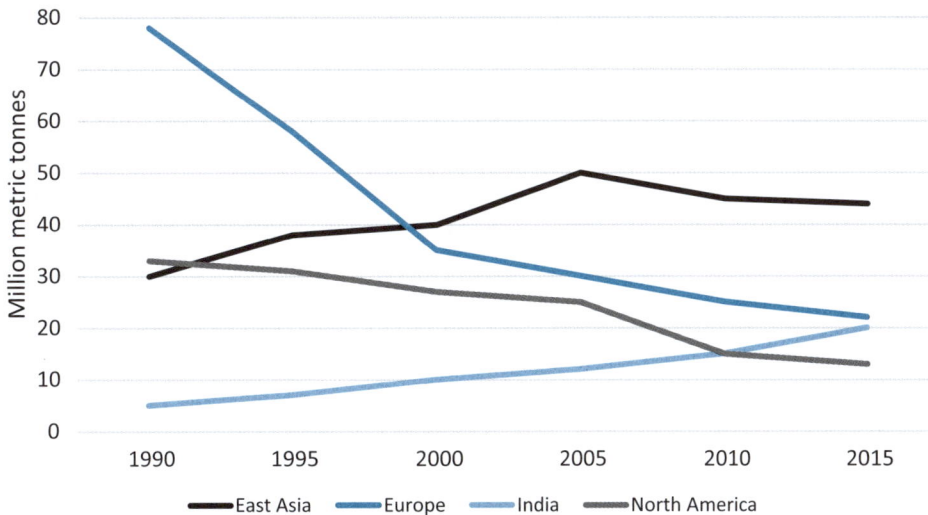

Figure 11.2: Sulphur dioxide emissions.
Source: Based on data in Aas et al. (2019).

helped cut the global annual production of ozone-depleting substances by as much as 80–90 per cent.

Although these two examples showed that it was possible to identify a problem, and for IOs to help develop – and implement – a response, numerous challenges remain. The debate was given new focus by the convening of the 1992 UN Conference on Environment and Development, held in Rio de Janeiro, and usually known as the Rio Earth Summit. The goal was to give new momentum to the changes begun 20 years before at Stockholm, but while the conference resulted in the signature of new treaties on climate change and biological diversity, not much else was achieved. Two later conferences – the 2002 Johannesburg Earth Summit (otherwise known as Rio+10) and the 2012 Rio Earth Summit (Rio+20) – were even more disappointing. By the time that delegates to the 2022 UN General Assembly meeting adopted their resolution on a clean, healthy and sustainable environment being a human right, it was evident that the global environmental picture was mixed at best, with new threats posed by climate change, the loss of tropical rain forests and the degradation of reefs.

International environmental law

If the achievements of global governance on the environment could be measured by the sheer size of the body of international law, then the results are impressive. According to one database (Mitchell, 2022), there are about 3,750 treaties dealing with environmental topics: more than 2,200 bilateral agreements, about 1,300 multilateral agreements and nearly 250 other types of agreements, including protocols. They range in scope from the targeted (including the protection of whales, mangrove management and limits on fishing for Atlantic tuna) to the universal (including climate change and protection of biological diversity). The database maintained by Mitchell lists numerous

IOs involved in managing these treaties, including the African Union, the European Forest Institute, the Indian Ocean Fishery Commission, the International Maritime Organization, the Mekong River Commission and the International Seabed Authority.

Quantity, though, is not enough, and the achievements of global governance must be measured by the quality of the achievements, which are variable. The treaties listed in Table 11.1 are those that have attracted the most political attention and have been highest up the agenda of global governance, but in almost every case – from marine pollution to biological diversity and climate change – much still remains to be done. Most notably, a division has developed in the approaches of Northern and Southern states. The latter often argue that the North developed its wealth on the back of all but uncontrolled industrialization and exploitation of natural resources, and that the South should not be handicapped by regulation, or that it should be compensated for the costs of regulation. This argument was at the heart of discussions in 2022 about climate change, resulting in an agreement at the meeting of parties to the climate change convention to provide 'loss and damage' funding to compensate the states most vulnerable to the effects of climate change.

Table 11.1: Major environmental treaties

Opened for signature	Where signed	Subject
1946	Washington DC, USA	Regulation of Whaling
1971	Ramsar, Iran	Wetlands of International Importance, Especially as Waterfowl Habitat
1972	London, UK	Prevention of Marine Pollution by Dumping Wastes and Other Matter
1973	Washington DC	International Trade in Endangered Species of Wild Flora and Fauna
1979	Geneva, Switzerland	Long-Range Transboundary Air Pollution
1979	Bonn, Germany	Conservation of Migratory Species of Wild Animals
1980	Canberra, Australia	Conservation of Antarctic Marine Living Resources
1985	Vienna, Austria	Protection of the Ozone Layer
1989	Basel, Switzerland	Control of Transboundary Movements of Hazardous Wastes and their Disposal
1992	Rio de Janeiro, Brazil	Biological Diversity
1992	Rio de Janeiro	Climate Change

THE UNITED NATIONS ENVIRONMENT PROGRAMME

Plastics have long been a ubiquitous part of human life; we use them in packaging, building, textiles, consumer products, transport and electronics. While their utility is unquestioned, though, the extent to which we use them and then dispose of them without much care or thought has created a massive global waste problem. Noting that about 400 million tonnes of plastics are produced annually around the world, and that about seven billion tonnes of the plastics produced between 1950 and 2017 had become waste, the United Nations Environment Programme (UNEP) in 2018 launched a New Plastics Economy Global Commitment aimed at encouraging governments and industries to agree a life-cycle approach to plastics. This would involve more careful design and manufacture of plastics, and more active recycling and reuse of plastic waste. UNEP estimated that a shift to this new circular approach could cut the volume of plastics dumped into the world's oceans by more than 80 per cent, reduce greenhouse gas emissions by 25 per cent and create 700,000 new jobs.

It is initiatives such as this that mark out the work of UNEP (pronounced *You-nep*), the primary IGO with a focus on the environment. Created in 1973 as a result of the Stockholm conference, UNEP has a charge to 'provide leadership and encourage partnership in caring for the environment by inspiring, informing, and enabling nations and peoples to improve their quality of life without compromising that of future generations' (United Nations Environment Programme, 2023a). It does this primarily through monitoring environmental trends, encouraging and supporting research, developing and sometimes managing international treaties, hosting environmental conferences, and promoting education and public information. It has a particular interest in climate change, environmental disasters, ecosystem management and improving environmental governance.

Despite the size and challenge of international and global approaches to the environment, UNEP is constitutionally weak. It is not a specialized agency of the UN in the same mould as the Food and Agriculture Organization or the World Health Organization, but is instead a programme that has few powers, a huge constituency (the entire world), and limited finances. As a programme, it lacks the status or independence of older and larger UN agencies, and is instead subsidiary to the UN General Assembly. It has had to involve itself in many different activities, and has often had to take action based more on opportunity than on any carefully considered long-term plans. It also has no power to involve itself directly in the domestic affairs of states, and has had limited opportunities for encouraging national governments to agree domestic or regional environmental policies.

Its structure is as follows:

– *Secretariat and executive head*. Headquartered in Nairobi, the capital of Kenya, UNEP is headed by an Executive Office that includes the Executive Director, who is nominated by the UN Secretary General and elected to four-year renewable terms by the General Assembly of the UN. Underlining the connections between UNEP and environmental INGOs, two of the eight executive directors to date – Achim Steiner of Brazil and Inger Andersen of Denmark – served as directors general of IUCN (see later in this chapter) before moving to UNEP.

– *Assembly.* UNEP initially had a Governing Council consisting of 58 member states, but this was replaced in 2012 with an *Environment Assembly* designed to engage all 193 UN member states more directly in UNEP decision-making. The Assembly is the governing body of UNEP, and meets every two years to review progress and set priorities.

– *Executive council.* Between meetings of the Assembly, UNEP is overseen by a 118-member Committee of Permanent Representatives, which meets quarterly to develop advice and the agenda for the Assembly. Meanwhile, the UNEP Secretariat of Governing Bodies supports the work of its governing bodies, and includes a Civil Society Unit designed to manage links between UNEP and NGOs.

– *Other elements.* UNEP has seven divisions addressing topics such as communication, law and science, six regional offices, 14 sub-regional or country offices, and divides its interests into topics ranging from biosafety to energy, forests and regional seas; see *IOs in Action 11*. UNEP is also home to the secretariats of 15 international treaties, including the Convention on Biological Diversity, the Migratory Species Convention and the Ozone Layer Convention.

– *Budget.* Like many UN bodies, UNEP must rely on voluntary contributions rather than regular and mandatory contributions from UN member states. It must do its work with a staff of about 950 people and an annual income in 2022 of just over $500 million (United Nations Environment Programme, 2023b).

Writing in 2010, Ivanova concluded that there was no consensus on UNEP's performance over its first four decades, with views ranging from praise for its having achieved a great deal with few resources to criticism for its having been weak and ineffective. Twelve years later, in UNEP's fiftieth anniversary year, Ivanova (2021) concluded that UNEP still remained unknown to many, was often misunderstood, and was often unfairly thought of as a 'lifeless bureaucracy'. She described it instead as an 'anchor institution' for the global environment, in the sense that it played an integral role in global environmental governance, functioning as a hub that provided expertise, leadership, capacity and connectivity. It was never intended, she continued, to be a service organization that would conduct specific environmental activities on its own, but was instead intended to be an advocate that would create reactions in other organizations, notably the family of UN agencies.

UNEP's difficulties once sparked suggestions – spearheaded by France, Germany and the EU – (see Biermann, 2000, and Biermann and Bauer, 2005) that it should be transformed into a specialized agency of the UN: a World Environment Organization with more autonomy, an international legal personality, a stronger voice in UN environmental affairs and a budget based on mandatory contributions from its members rather than voluntary contributions. Ivanova (2012) was not convinced of this logic, arguing that UNEP's shortcomings were related less to its institutional form than to the barriers that UNEP faced in fulfilling its mission. Rather than wholesale structural change, she concluded, it would be 'bolder and more effective, and also more feasible, to focus instead on empowering UNEP to properly fulfil its original, visionary mandate'.

IOs IN ACTION 11

THE UN ENVIRONMENT PROGRAMME AND REGIONAL SEAS

One of UNEP's major successes has been its Regional Seas Programme (RSP), which identifies key regional seas around the world and then brings together neighbouring countries to cooperate in their management. As we saw in Chapter 3, the advantage of regional approaches is that they include smaller numbers of countries, each of which has a more direct and immediate vested interest in resolving a problem. The first RSP was launched in 1975 to focus on the Mediterranean, which was heavily polluted at the time, and it was followed by programmes that included those focused on the Caribbean, the Black Sea, the Red Sea and the Baltic. So successful was the initial Mediterranean Action Plan that there are now 18 regional seas plans and conventions, involving 146 countries (Mead, 2021). UNEP administers seven of them, while the rest are independently administered, with or without input from UNEP.

The plans have multiple targets, including the control of pollution, the control of litter and waste, the creation of protected marine areas and the protection of coral reefs. One assessment of the programme (Mead, 2021) describes the agreements involved as the 'crown jewels of environmental diplomacy', arguing the advantages of the regional approach, but also noting the differences in the degree of political will, the amount of funding available and the strength of enforcement mechanisms. Even though the Mediterranean programme is the oldest, and hailed as one of the most effective, the sea is still blighted by pollution from microplastics (plastic waste broken down by water, wind and sunlight into pellets and granules). With about 150 million people living on its often densely populated shores, a popular tourist industry, intensive navigation and variable waste water treatment facilities, waste and litter remain critical problems in the Mediterranean. One study (Cincinelli et al., 2019) estimates that about 100,000 tons of plastics still find their way into the sea every year.

UNEP also faces the unusual challenge of being a UN body that is not headquartered either in Europe or North America. A deliberate decision was taken during the debates about its creation in 1972 to base it outside the usual centres of power, part of the hope being that this would help encourage support for its work by developing countries doubtful about the benefits of environmental planning. Several wealthier countries argued that, given its coordinating role, it should be sited closer to existing UN agencies, but Nairobi was ultimately chosen. Only one other UN body – the Human Settlements Programme UN-HABITAT – is based outside Europe and North America, and happens also to be in Nairobi.

At first, siting UNEP in Nairobi did not lead to the degree of input into environmental governance once envisaged, while travel to Kenya from other developing countries proved difficult and expensive, and the instability and corruption suffered by Kenya has not made it an attractive duty station for potential employees (Ivanova, 2021). Changes in technology, though, have made its distance from the centres of power less problematic: video conferencing has made travel to its headquarters less necessary, and the internet has meant instant communication of the kind that was only dreamed of in the 1970s and 1980s. There is still little sign, though, that the siting of UNEP in Nairobi has led to any broader effort for the headquarters of IGOs to be located anywhere other than in their usual locations in Europe and North America.

OTHER ENVIRONMENTAL AND NATURAL RESOURCE IOs

There are three IOs with an environmental/natural resource focus that provide different insights into the way that governments have approached these topics. The first of these, which is also the newest, is the Global Environment Facility (GEF), which was founded in 1991, just before the first Rio Earth Summit. The GEF is an independent IO that is best described as a trust fund to help developing countries meet their commitments to several international environmental agreements (including those on climate change, desertification and biological diversity) (Martinez-Diaz and Thwaites, 2018). Based in Washington DC, its members include states, IGOs, NGOs, development banks and corporations. It has an Assembly that brings national government ministers together every three to four years to review policies, refill the trust fund, and negotiate packages of policy measures. It has a 32-member Council with a mix of members from developed and developing countries that meets twice annually, and a Chief Executive Officer appointed by the Council for a maximum of two four-year terms. Although the GEF has 184 member states, most of the funding – nearly $25 billion as of 2022 – has so far come from about 40 national donors, including most of Europe, along with Japan, Mexico, the US and the four BRICs (Brazil, Russia, India, China).

There was early concern (Streck, 2001) that the GEF did not have enough private sector investment, and that it suffered the problem of power asymmetries common to many IOs, but it was also predicted that it was flexible enough to adapt to changing needs, and had the advantage of the strong participatory element that came from close cooperation with NGOs. The questions about private sector investment continued to be asked several years later, along with questions about whether the GEF had worked out a sensible division of labour with its peer institutions (Martinez-Diaz and Thwaites, 2018). For Morin et al. (2020), the work of the GEF has been a compromise between the wishes of developed countries to have a structure such as the World Bank (favouring efficiency and decisions driven by how much each country contributes), and the wishes of developing countries, NGOs and UN agencies (favouring UN values such as transparency, democracy and universality).

Meanwhile, another effective regional approach to environmental governance has been pursued by the EU. Although its original priorities – as we saw in Chapter 3 – were economic, including the building of a single market, its leaders soon found that in order to achieve this, multiple unexpected barriers to trade had to be removed. Among these barriers were different environmental standards and regulations that made it harder to sell goods and services across borders. By the late 1970s, the European Community (precursor to the EU) had begun agreeing and adopting new environmental laws, and developing Environmental Action Programmes that contained an expanding and increasingly ambitious set of goals. The EU has since adopted a wide range of laws on waste, air and water quality, chemicals, biodiversity, climate change, pesticides, genetically modified organisms and even noise pollution.

Such was the strength of the logic behind developing these shared approaches that domestic environmental policy in the member states of the EU has long been driven more by requirements set jointly at the EU level than individually at the level of member states. (For more details, see Jordan and Gravey, 2021.) This has been particularly important for those poorer and newer Eastern European member states that lacked much in the way of environmental laws or policies before joining the EU. The consequences also reach outside the EU: as the world's wealthiest marketplace, with a population of about 450 million people, the EU has come to have what Bradford (2020) describes as 'the Brussels effect' (a reference to the city that is the home of the major EU institutions). She describes this as the EU's 'unilateral power to regulate global markets', which it does not coercively or through IGOs, but instead through market forces as EU corporations extend the impact of EU policy globally. The EU policy on chemicals, for example, is the most stringent such scheme in the world, imposing obligations not just on EU member states but also on states wishing to trade with the EU (including the US). The EU has also been a global leader in responses to climate change, the protection of biodiversity and sustainable development (Eritja, 2021).

A third IO with an environmental focus, and which is an unusual blend of governmental and non-governmental members, is the Swiss-based International Union for Conservation of Nature (IUCN). Founded in 1948, IUCN has more than 1,400 members, including government agencies and NGOs, as well as being one of a select group of IOs that has permanent observer status at the UN General Assembly. From its headquarters in Gland, Switzerland, it works to influence governments through the collection and analysis of information, supports field research and education, and has played a key role in developing several international treaties, including those on wetlands, biological diversity and trade in endangered species of wildlife. It also maintains the world's most authoritative source on the status of endangered species, the Red List of Threatened Species.

A key role in global environmental governance is played by treaty secretariats (see Table 11.2, and *IOs in Action 1*), although opinion is divided on how well they are performing. In her assessment of their influence, Jinnah (2014) concludes that they have had the most impact when the states involved do not have strong preferences on the issue at hand, or when there are no international organizations that can better manage a particular treaty. In the case of the Convention on Biological Diversity (CBD), for example, she argues that state preferences were weak to begin with, that no other organization could better manage the treaty than the CBD secretariat, and hence the secretariat has enjoyed a high degree of independence. By contrast, agreements dealing with fisheries have come up against states with strong preferences about how commercially important fish stocks should be managed, while the secretariat for the Convention on International Trade in Endangered Species has faced strong organizational competition from the Food and Agriculture Organization of the UN.

Table 11.2: Environmental treaty secretariats: Examples

Treaty	Secretariat location
Convention on Biological Diversity	Montreal, Canada
UN Framework Convention on Climate Change	Bonn, Germany
Convention for the Protection of the Ozone Layer	UNEP, Nairobi, Kenya
Convention on International Trade in Endangered Species	UNEP, Geneva, Switzerland
Convention on the Control of Transboundary Movements of Hazardous Wastes	Châtelaine, Switzerland
Convention on the Prevention of Marine Pollution by Dumping of Wastes and Other Matter	International Maritime Organization, London, UK

Natural resource regimes

Forests offer not only an example of a natural resource with a more targeted global governance regime, but also one that has had limited success. The value of forests is clear: they not only serve essential ecological functions as natural habitat, carbon sinks, producers of oxygen, managers of water supply, and generators of clouds and rain, but they are a renewable source of timber for construction and fuelwood (see Nikolakis and Innes, 2020). Despite this, mismanagement and overuse have combined to reduce the proportion of the world's land surface that is covered by forest from about 45 per cent in the pre-industrial era to just over 30 per cent today.

Efforts to draft a global convention on forests in time for the 1992 Rio Earth Summit ended when it became obvious that governments were far from reaching a consensus on its potential content and goals, with a clear North–South split (Bass and Guéneau, 2005): most Northern states wanted forests to be considered a global resource, and thus subject to the protection of a convention, but the US was opposed, prompted by the influence of its domestic timber industry. Meanwhile, most Southern countries – notably big forest states such as Brazil, India and Malaysia – argued that forests were a national resource and were concerned about the potential effect of an agreement on their sovereignty (Humphreys, 2005). As a result, plans for a convention failed, and the status of forests varies from one part of the world to another: while the EU has built a successful reforestation programme that has expanded the area under forest, tropical forests in most of sub-Saharan Africa face the quadruple threats of growing population, the unregulated removal of trees for fuel, logging to meet growing demand from China, and new demands for access from mining, oil and gas companies.

Given the critical role of energy in global affairs, and the unequal distribution of sources of energy, it might be expected that there would be a global energy regime, but there is not. This is for the simple reason that the major producers of energy – such as China, the US, Russia, Saudi Arabia, Canada and India – prefer as far as possible to control their own energy resources and to make their own decisions on energy policy (many of which are actually shaped by energy industries and corporations rather than governments). There is clearly an international trade dynamic at work when it comes to importing states working with their suppliers, and the case of OPEC (Chapter 6) is the clearest illustration of that dynamic. Trade in energy is also high on the agenda of the World Trade Organization. Beyond that, though, energy is the subject of a complex array of interests, involving governments, state-owned energy companies (notably in China), private corporations, producers, consumers, market forces, the different dynamics of different fossil fuels and renewable sources of energy, and debates that are often deeply politically charged. States come to the conversations with quite different priorities, resources and policies, and the work of energy IOs is often focused less on making policy than on providing the knowledge needed to help inform that policy.

The oldest IO dealing with energy issues is the World Energy Council. It was founded in London in 1924 as the World Power Conference, a gathering of experts brought together to discuss trends in energy use. Its name was changed to the World Energy Council in 1989, and as a UN-accredited body it brings together more than 3,000 member organizations from nearly 90 countries. Representatives from governments, multinationals, academia and NGOs meet every three years in the World Energy Congress to share ideas and information on energy, and the Council publishes regular reports on energy security.

The International Energy Agency (IEA) is an autonomous IGO whose origins date back to the energy crisis of the early 1970s. Set up under the framework of the OECD (see Chapter 6), it has 31 mainly European and North American member states, and its task is to accumulate and manage data on global energy as a basis for making recommendations on energy policy. It also coordinates the use of the oil reserves held by its members, as well as encouraging the use of renewable sources of energy and promoting efforts to address climate change. Based in Paris, it is headed by an Executive Director appointed for renewable four-year terms, its main decision-making body is a 31-member Governing Board that meets at least three times annually, and it also convenes biennial conferences of the energy ministers of its member states, and has multiple standing groups and committees with interests in focused parts of the energy debate. It publishes an annual *World Energy Outlook* that is the authoritative source on global energy use and projections for future developments, and also publishes a wide range of more focused studies of the markets in different sources of energy. In 2021 it published *Net Zero by 2050*, which outlined the changes that needed to be made globally to achieve net zero emissions by 2050.

The International Energy Forum (IEF) is an IGO with 72 member states that describes itself as 'the global home of energy dialogue'. Much as the International Energy Agency was a product of the 1970s energy crisis, the IEF was a product of the oil supply disruptions that came in the wake of the 1991 Gulf War. Designed as a forum in which energy ministers from producing and consuming states can meet (along with executives from the energy industry), it has a mandate to review energy in the broadest definition of the term. Headquartered in Riyadh, Saudi Arabia, it has a Secretary General and a 30-member Executive Board with 22 permanent members and eight rotating members, and a permanent secretariat.

NON-STATE ENVIRONMENTAL ACTORS

The slowness of states to take the initiative on environmental or resource management issues, or to create international organizations whose primary focus was the environment, is reflected in the long history of non-state action in this area. National NGOs have a history dating back to the nineteenth century, and the creation of, for example, the Royal Society for the Protection of Birds (UK, founded 1889), Naturschutzbund Deutschland (Germany, 1899), the Sierra Club (US, 1892) and the Norwegian Society for the Conservation of Nature (1914). A similar dynamic can be found at the international level: several INGOs pre-dated the creation of IGOs, including the International Committee for Bird Protection (founded in London in 1922), the International Union for the Protection of Nature (created in 1948) and the World Wildlife Fund (created 1961).

Exactly how many environmental INGOs are now in existence is hard to say, for the same reasons that explain the difficulties in counting INGOs generally: the lack of comprehensive data and of an agreed definition of what constitutes an INGO. The best guess is that the numbers probably run into the hundreds because of the long history of non-governmental action on the environment; some examples of INGOs are listed in Table 11.3. They include bodies founded in one country that have opened office in others, coordinating bodies made up of delegations from participating national and local NGOs, and bodies that might be situated in a single country but that have global interests and activities. There are also federations that act as conduits for contacts between NGOs and an IGO. One example of the latter is the Environment Liaison Centre International, an NGO network based in Nairobi. Set up in 1974, it acts as a conduit between the UNEP Environment Assembly and its NGO members. NGOs are also part of the decision-making structure of the Global Environment Facility, with ten seats on the 32-member GEF Council.

The work of environmental INGOs has been less deeply studied and noticed than that of IGOs, but there have been two roles in which they have been particularly effective: as information brokers and as whistle-blowers. For example, discussions leading to many international environmental treaties have been heavily influenced by research generated by INGOs, and by INGO influence over media coverage of treaty negotiations. Only national governments can actually take decisions on treaties, and INGOs usually have only observer status at meetings, but they can – with care – alter the direction of the negotiations through the perspectives they provide, which can change both the negotiating process and the results (Corell and Betsill, 2008). In their study of the influence of indigenous peoples and local community delegates on negotiations at the 10th Conference of Parties of the Convention on Biological Diversity in 2010, Witter et al. (2015) concluded that non-state delegates achieved 'moments of influence' by 'sounding an alarm, for shaming, and aligning with state

Table 11.3: Environmental INGOs: Examples

Name	Founded	Headquarters	Interests
Birdlife International	1922	Cambridge, UK	Protection of birds and their natural habitats. National 'partner' organizations in nearly 120 countries or territories.
World Wide Fund for Nature	1961	Switzerland	Protection of endangered species and habitats. International office coordinates work of national offices in nearly 70 countries.
Friends of the Earth	1969	Amsterdam, the Netherlands	Focus on climate change, economic justice, 'food sovereignty', forests and diversity. International office and 75 national groups.
Greenpeace	1971	Amsterdam	Direct action to stop environmental degradation. International office and 30 national/regional groups.
World Resources Institute	1982	Washington DC, USA	Climate, energy, food, forests, water, and cities and transport. Think-tank with offices in Brazil, China, EU, India, Indonesia and US.
Green Cross International	1993	Geneva, Switzerland	Poverty, security and the environment. Founded by former Soviet leader Mikhail Gorbachev. International office and 27 national offices.
African Biodiversity Network	1996	Thika, Kenya	Seeking African solutions to Africa's environmental problems. 36 partners in 12 countries.

actors'. As whistle-blowers, meanwhile, INGOs have used their media contacts and membership lists to draw attention to failures on the part of states to live up to their obligations, and to help treaty secretariats keep track of implementation.

There are no environmental INGOs that have had the same clear influence over environmental governance as, for example, Amnesty International and Human Rights Watch have had on human rights issues, but two offer useful cases of the problems and possibilities of environmental INGOs. The first, which is also one of the oldest, is the World Wide Fund for Nature (WWF), founded in 1961. Originally called the World Wildlife Fund, it changed its name in 1985 (except in the US and Canada) (while keeping the same acronym) in order to recast itself as a body interested in the whole natural environment, rather than simply wildlife. Its main goal has been to raise funds to spend on nature protection, research, the management of protected areas and encouraging sustainable practices by corporations. Its international office is in Gland, near Geneva, and it has national offices in about 50 countries, and claims a membership of 1.2 million people (World Wide Fund for Nature, 2023).

Greenpeace offers a contrast, opting for what it describes on its web site as 'non-violent creative action' to draw public attention to environmental problems more broadly. Founded in Canada in 1971, it has a looser structure than most INGOs: it has an international office in Amsterdam, through which the work of 26 independent regional offices is coordinated. In order to maintain its independence, it does not accept government or corporate funding, instead relying on its more than three million members, foundation grants and several thousand volunteers for support. It is opposed to nuclear power, has called out corporations that it accuses of being complicit in deforestation, has a long history of campaigning against commercial whaling, is critical of genetically modified organisms (a position that attracted criticism from scientists), has drawn attention to the problems of toxic waste and deep-sea mining, and has been visible in campaigning on climate change.

When it comes to forest policy, NGOs have been on the margins of decision-making, given the attitude of those governments more interested in the utilitarian value of wood and wood products than in the environmental value of forests. Even so, several INGOs have been active on forest science and management, including the following:

- The International Union of Forest Research Organizations (based in Vienna) was founded in 1892 and networks scientists from several hundred member organizations.

- The Global Forest Coalition (headquartered in Asunción, Paraguay) brings together interest groups and indigenous people's organizations working on behalf of people dependent on forests.

- The Forest Stewardship Council (based in Bonn, Germany) runs a certification and labelling scheme for forest products.

- The Rainforest Action Network (based in San Francisco) focuses on changing the policies of corporations and consumers through direct action, including consumer boycotts.

Although the science of forests is well understood, as is their ecological value, they remain under threat in most parts of the world. This is one problem – as we saw earlier in the chapter – where international cooperation has made minimal headway.

Multinationals and the environment

For their part, multinational enterprises (MNEs) play a core role in shaping environmental and natural resource policy at both the national and the international level. Not only can they influence the content of international treaties and help determine the degree of support given to those treaties by their home governments, but also they lead the way in exploiting natural resources such as oil and timber, and are the inventors of new products and technology that have key implications for environmental policy. The development of batteries for electric and hybrid vehicles, for example, has come more from MNEs than from governments. The fact that so many of the biggest MNEs are based in Europe, North America and China also has a role in explaining their priorities and thinking, leaving most emerging states at a relative disadvantage in global governance.

At first glance, the environmental role of MNEs is controversial at best, and negative at worst. The conventional view is that they place profits above environmental concerns, and exploit differences in national environmental standards by closing down operations in countries with tighter regulations and moving them to those with looser restrictions, as well as lower wages. They are also often deeply implicated in tendencies in poorer countries to exploit natural resources unsustainably, as in the case of multinational oil companies such as Shell and their environmentally harmful extraction of oil in Nigeria (Hennchen, 2022).

On the other hand, there is evidence that MNEs have not been unaffected by consumer demand that they adopt more sustainable policies, and many have self-regulated by adopting environmental policies and performance standards that exceed those of national governments. An example is offered by the work of the Business Council for Sustainable Development, founded in 1991 to represent business at the Rio Earth Summit. Its leader Stephan Schmidheiny recruited 48 chief executive officers from around the world, and promoted the idea of corporate social responsibility (CSR) by arguing that companies should meet their ethical, social and environmental responsibilities towards society (Wickert and Risi, 2019). (The name was changed in 1995 to the World Business Council for Sustainable Development, and it now has more than 200 corporate members, and a headquarters in Geneva.)

As an idea, CSR dates back to the 1950s (see Bowen, 1953), and is not restricted to environmental matters (it also includes attitudes towards working conditions, gender and racial equity, and human rights, for example), but Schmidheiny brought it into the environmental realm by speaking of 'eco-efficiency'. This implies that companies can cut costs through reducing energy inputs and waste, for example, while building greener records that could help attract customers and create new markets (Schmidheiny, 1992). Many businesses have since made significant efforts to change their practices and to capitalize on claims of their new environmental sensitivity, often using it as a positive marketing tool. Critics, though, are less convinced of such claims, and point to numerous examples of MNEs being linked to visible and substantial environmental degradation, whether in the form of pollution or the over-use of resources. Nonetheless, consumers, shareholders and local communities have increasingly expected assurances that goods and services meet minimum standards of environmental responsibility, and many corporations and business sectors have accordingly created codes of conduct, certification schemes and other means of promoting voluntary environmental practices. Among them is the ISO 14001 standard created in 1996 by the International Organization for Standardization (founded in 1947, and based in Geneva), which sets standards aimed at improving environmental management, environmental auditing and environmental labelling.

THINKING POINTS

- What do the results of international cooperation on acid pollution and the ozone layer tell us about the prospects for such cooperation on climate change?

- How far can the model of epistemic communities such as the Intergovernmental Panel on Climate Change be applied to addressing other international challenges?

- Should UNEP be converted into a World Environment Organization, or at least into a full agency of the UN?

- Are the barriers to the development of natural resource regimes insurmountable?

- Is corporate social responsibility a convincing and practical way forward on environmental needs?

IOs RELATED TO THIS CHAPTER

Environment Liaison Centre International (ELCI)

Global Environment Facility (GEF)

Greenpeace

Intergovernmental Panel on Climate Change (IPCC)

International Energy Agency (IEA)

International Energy Forum (IEF)

International Union for Conservation of Nature (IUCN)

United Nations Environment Programme (UNEP)

World Business Council for Sustainable Development (WBCSD)

World Energy Council (WED)

World Wide Fund for Nature (WWF)

FURTHER READING

Axelrod, Regina S., and Stacy D. Vandeveer (eds) (2020) *The Global Environment: Institutions, Law, and Policy*, 5th edn (SAGE). An edited textbook collection of chapters on the major international environmental actors and institutions, including cases of different areas of policy.

Harris, Paul G. (ed.) (2022) *Routledge Handbook of Global Environmental Politics*, 2nd edn (Routledge). An edited collection of chapters on the study of global environmental politics, and the key institutions, actors, ideas and themes involved.

Ivanova, Maria (2021) *The Untold Story of the World's Leading Environmental Institution: UNEP at Fifty* (MIT Press). A thorough survey of UNEP, including its origins, its structure, its priorities, its leadership and the challenges it continues to face.

Morin, Jean-Frédéric, Amandine Orsini, and Sikina Jinnah (2020) *Global Environmental Politics* (Oxford University Press). A review of the nature of global environmental politics, including chapters on the key issues involved, the role of states, the major international organizations and the key non-state actors.

Rasche, Andreas, Mette Morsing, and Jeremy Moon (2017) *Corporate Social Responsibility* (Cambridge University Press). An edited collection on this contested idea, looking at its origins, applications and implications.

SCIENCE AND TECHNOLOGY

This final chapter focuses on a wide range of international organizations engaged in activities with an emphasis on science and technology. It opens with an explanation of the parameters of these two areas, noting that while neither has a broad regime, or a dominating IGO, both have still been the target of important international collaboration. The breadth and depth of this collaboration has grown and changed with advances in scientific knowledge and technological applications. The chapter looks at the work of the UN Educational, Scientific and Cultural Organization (UNESCO) before reviewing the more focused interests of the International Atomic Energy Agency (IAEA), the World Meteorological Organization (WMO) and the European Organization for Nuclear Research (CERN), as well as several scientific INGOs. It then assesses the work of IOs engaged in shipping, aviation and space, including the International Maritime Organization (IMO) and the International Civil Aviation Organization (ICAO). International standards organizations are then reviewed, with a focus on the International Organization for Standardization (ISO), and the chapter ends with a discussion of the complex regime surrounding governance of the internet. Opinion is divided on how best to understand the latter given the prominence of self-regulating and private sector organizations.

THE CONTEXT

In late 2022, videos began to appear on Facebook and Twitter that purportedly showed anchors for an outlet called Wolf News, narrating clips on topics such as gun violence in the US and the outcomes of international conferences. Something, however, was not quite right about the videos: the voices of the anchors were stilted, their faces had a video-game quality, the movement of their mouths did not synchronize with what they were saying and the captions contained grammatical errors. It turned out that the anchors were not real people at all, but computer-generated avatars created by artificial intelligence software, or a new 'deepfake' technology that was the latest example of digital media manipulation. In this case, they were being used to promote disinformation with a pro-Chinese and anti-American slant. Earlier in the year, a similar fake video had circulated on social media that falsely showed President Volodymyr Zelensky of Ukraine announcing a surrender. (For details, see Satariano and Mozur, 2023.)

The development of artificial intelligence has critical implications for governance and communications at every level, from the local to the international. 'What would global politics and globalization be', ask Eriksson and Newlove-Eriksson (2021), 'if the rapid development and diffusion of global information and communications technologies (ICTs) were not taken into account?' It is all the more surprising, then, how selective has been the attention paid to the implications of technology for global governance. While there has been progress in the fields of internet governance, cybersecurity and digital diplomacy, much less attention has been paid to studies of IR and global governance as they relate to artificial intelligence, autonomous weapons systems, robotics, the internet of things and genetic engineering. Most of the major theories of IR, contend Eriksson and Newlove-Eriksson, still tend to treat technology as external to politics. And yet, argues Mueller (2017), technology can alter the scope and scale of social relations, reshuffling the distribution of power among actors and creating the need for new kinds of cooperation or coordination.

Similar arguments can be made about science and global governance. International scientific cooperation has a long history, and we have seen how the work of scientists lies at the heart of food security, human health and environmental quality, while technology lies at the heart of military security, communications and trade. Despite this, the interdisciplinary field of science and technology studies (STS) – which emerged in the 1960s and 1970s and is interested in the confluence of science, technology, politics, economics, ethics and society – has made fewer inroads into international studies than into domestic studies. We know much about the political and economic interests of international organizations, but much less about the work of those with scientific or technological interests.

Most of the initiatives have come without the creation of intergovernmental organizations of the kinds that we have seen in previous chapters. There is, for example, no World Technology Organization, no UN Scientific Programme and no International Internet Council. Instead, international collaboration on science and technology has been driven mainly by self-generated collaborations among researchers from different countries working in joint research programmes or scientific exchanges. Archibugi and Filippetti (2015) point to the example of the Swiss-based European Organization for Nuclear Research (CERN) (see details later in this chapter) as one of the best-known cases of 'a genuine global laboratory'.

Just as there are no scientific or technological IGOs, so there are no discernible scientific or technological regimes; instead, there are multiple sets of organizations and epistemic communities with specialized interests that are either scientific or technological in nature, and that all share the goal of a search for knowledge, and of collaboration in that search. In order to provide a sense of the variety of the work of international organizations active in these fields, this chapter will focus on four examples:

- Scientific research broadly defined.

- The work of shipping, aviation and space organizations.

- International standards organizations.

- The governance of the internet.

IOs IN THEORY 12

SYSTEMS THEORY

In most of the other *IOs in Theory* features in this book, the focus is on the theories most often used by scholars of international relations (IR) to understand global governance and international organizations. In this final feature, the focus is on a set of theories that is less often used in IR, and yet has the potential to offer important insights. Systems theory – which has its origins in the natural sciences – is focused on studying the way in which the parts of a system relate to the whole, which would seem to lend itself well to a study of how different states work within an IO, or how different IOs work within a regime, or how different policy needs are addressed by networks of IOs.

We saw in Chapter 2 how efforts to apply systems theory to understanding governance date back to the work of David Easton, whose book *The Political System* (1953) looked at government as a system of demands (inputs) and actions (outputs). Despite its apparent value to political science generally, and to international relations in particular, systems theory began to fall out of favour in the 1970s when it was accused of having too little predictive power in most political studies.

Interest was revived in systems theory by Kenneth Waltz in his book *Theory of International Politics* (1979), which sparked new debate on how to apply systems theory to international relations. Waltz argued that system-level processes, with states both working together and competing, encouraged states to behave in similar ways. Individual theories have proved difficult to build or support, though, and there is little agreement on the question of how best to understand and define the international system. Fundamental questions are raised about key concepts such as the balance of power, the relative roles of great powers and middle powers, and how power is distributed. Schneider et al. (2017) point out that while there has been much research on how organizations in general respond to the complexity of systems by expanding their internal structures and processes, much less research has been undertaken into how they respond externally, for example through establishing alliances or developing common standards.

It is interesting to speculate why different theories are used (or not) in the study of government and politics. The problem lies in a combination of the sheer number of theories available to scholars of international relations, the faddishness to which theory often falls victim, the uncertainties that are often involved in studying the social sciences and the dominance of Western thinking in political theory. To this list we could add the challenge of how little we often still understand about the dynamics of many of the different elements of global governance. Given all these circumstances, it is worth keeping an open mind on the potential of different theoretical approaches, which continues to change as our understanding changes.

Each area has its own needs, challenges, motivations and approaches, often bringing together a combination of intergovernmental organizations and non-state actors. Overall, there is still plenty of room for new research on their work, the possibilities illustrated by the unmet potential of explanations for their work coming out of systems theory; see *IOs in Theory 12*.

BUILDING GLOBAL SCIENCE AND TECHNOLOGY REGIMES

Efforts to push forward the boundaries of science and technology are not limited by state borders. Scientists and inventors share ideas, build on the work of others, and are ultimately interested in discoveries of the kind that are of broad interests and value to all humans, regardless of who they are or where they live. For these reasons, science and technology are both inherently international (or, perhaps, non-national) in character, and have a long history of cooperation. The creation of the League of Nations in 1920 is often cited as the major landmark in the growth of international cooperation, and yet advanced international scientific and technological cooperation had begun decades before.

It had been given a boost by the sheer speed with which the boundaries of knowledge were expanded in the nineteenth and early twentieth centuries. During that time, we saw the invention or the discovery of the internal combustion engine, the electric telegraph, telephones, the radio, anaesthesia, the table of elements, many of the laws of physics and thermodynamics, automobiles, electric lights, photography, radar, motion pictures and aeroplanes, to name just a few. Most of these developments stemmed from the work of individuals working in laboratories (or even in their own homes, or – in the case of Albert Einstein – as a part-time interest), but ideas were shared, leading to the creation of some of the earliest international cooperative bodies.

Consider these examples:

- The International Meteorological Organization (IMO) was founded in 1879 to standardize observations of weather and to facilitate the exchange of information on weather and climate (Cerveny, 2023). Plans to invite government representatives to its meetings and to draw up a World Meteorological Convention were disrupted by World War II, when the IMO moved to Switzerland from the Netherlands. In 1950 the IMO evolved into the World Meteorological Organization, a specialized agency of the UN.

- The International Association of Academies was founded in 1899 and the International Research Council in 1919, both to encourage international cooperation. They were blended in 1931 into the International Council of Scientific Unions (ICSU), which later supported the International Geophysical Year (1957–58) and the International Biological Programme (1964–74). In 1998, ICSU was renamed the International Council for Science, which in 2018 merged with the International Social Science Council to become the International Science Council.

- When the Wright brothers first successfully flew an aircraft in December 1903, the spark was provided for the rapid development of aeronautical technology, and the need for governance of the field. The International Air Navigation Conference was held in Paris in 1910 to begin discussions about an international air regime, and the Convention Relating to the Regulation of Aerial Navigation was signed in October 1919, just four months after the first non-stop transatlantic flight by John Alcock and Arthur Whitten-Brown. Eventually, in 1944, the Convention on International Civil Aviation (otherwise known as the Chicago Convention) was signed, creating the International Civil Aviation Organization.

Most of the earliest international cooperation was based in Europe and North America, where most of the leading-edge scientific and technological breakthroughs were taking place. It was only after World War II that this cooperation would begin to develop a more global character.

Developments since 1945

The birth of the post-war era of international cooperation is best represented by the creation of the United Nations and of its multiple specialized agencies. Their emphasis, though, was on peace and security, and on resolving the problems created by war, and although both science and technology could be seen as key elements of peace (and war), neither was mentioned in the UN Charter. Nor were they mentioned in the lengthy list of interests for the UN Economic and Social Council: 'international economic, social, cultural, educational, health, and related matters'. While many of the new UN agencies had an agenda that included scientific elements – the needs of agriculture and health, for example – the closest the UN came to addressing science directly was with the creation in November 1945 of the UN Educational, Scientific and Cultural Organization (UNESCO).

Despite its title, science was mentioned only in passing in UNESCO's founding constitution. Since 'wars begin in the minds of men,' the document said, 'it is in the minds of men that the defences of peace must be constructed'. With that in mind, the job of UNESCO would be to address ignorance, suspicion and mistrust, and to 'collaborate in the work of advancing the mutual knowledge and understanding of peoples, through all means of mass communication'. This was to be done by 'encouraging cooperation among the nations in *all* branches of intellectual activity' (emphasis added), but UNESCO has mainly been a facilitator of scientific collaboration rather than a leader (one exception being its Man and the Biosphere programme; see later in this chapter). Among the initiatives it has supported, the following stand out:

- The International Centre for Theoretical Physics (ICTP), founded in Italy in 1964 at the suggestion of Pakistani physicist Abdus Salam (later a Nobel laureate) to provide training for scientists from the Global South.

- The collaboration that produced *The Soil Map of the World*, providing a global view of the soil resources of the planet.

- The International Centre for Synchrotron Light for Experimental Science and Applications in the Middle East (SESAME), created in 2017 in Jordan as a means of encouraging collaborative research in the region.

- The European Organization for Nuclear Research (CERN) and its work on high-energy physics research.

The continued expansion of the boundaries of scientific and technological knowledge since 1945 have provided an ongoing impetus for international collaboration. Consider just a few of the breakthroughs of the last 80 years: the birth of the nuclear era, invention of the transistor, understanding of the helical structure of DNA, advances in cloning, advances in organ transplants, the birth and expansion of the era of space exploration and satellites, the proliferation of television, breakthroughs in pharmaceutical and medical technology, the green revolution in agriculture, the switch to container transport, the development of supersonic and stealth aviation technology, the invention of personal computers, the development of the internet, the invention and proliferation of cellular phones, and the development of electric vehicles, again to name just a few.

Ideas have spread, scientists have talked to one another, and governance structures have continued to be formed or revised in the wake of these developments. Although it is questionable exactly how science makes its way into policy, or how far policymakers listen to scientists or understand the scientific advice they are given, Ruffini (2017) and Gui et al. (2017) make several important points about recent changes in the international landscape of science:

- Science – and scientific research – is increasingly global and globalized. Science, technology and innovation are no longer dominated as they once were by North America and Europe, and the centre of gravity of the global production of knowledge is shifting to Asia.

- The role of research and development in the global economy is growing.

- Investments in 'big science' are growing, as reflected in the examples of the International Space Station and the Human Genome Project that has provided advances in human genetics.

- Many of the challenges faced at the international level – including human health, food security and environmental quality – are science-related and technology-driven.

Archibugi and Filippetti (2015) point to the history since World War II of multinational enterprises creating research laboratories and technical centres in the countries in which their subsidiaries are based, and setting up research and development alliances. The growing influence of China is confirmed by Appelbaum et al. (2018), who write about the large investments its government is making in science parks, the surge in its large multinationals, and the increase in the number of its scientific publications and patents; see Figure 12.1. The influence of the US over internet governance, though, is illustrated by its resistance to the formation of a global regulatory regime, leaving behind a complex mix of public and private administration; see later in this chapter.

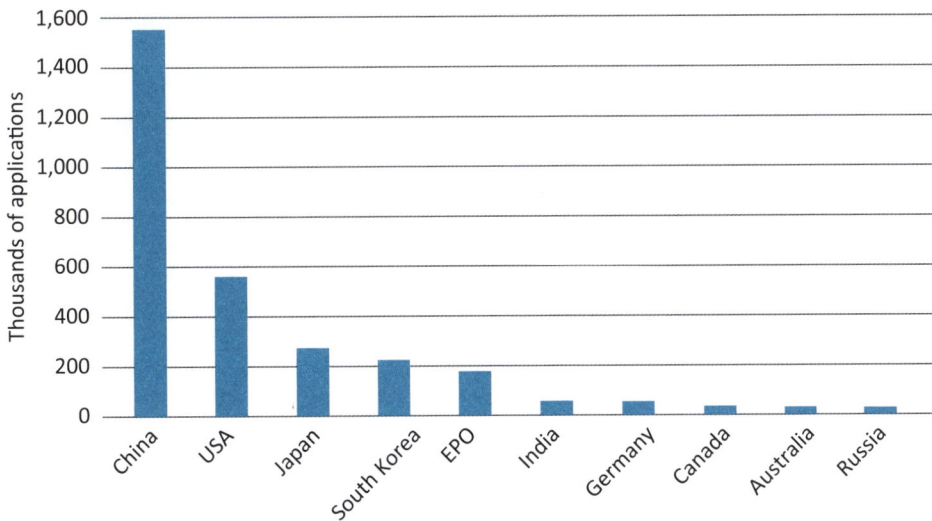

Figure 12.1: The ten biggest sources of patent applications.
Source: Based on data in World Intellectual Property Organization (2023). Data are for 2022. EPO is European Patent Office.

Under the circumstances, there may be cause for concern about the absence of clear intergovernmental initiatives in monitoring advances in science and technology. The American astronomer Carl Sagan (1996) once argued that global civilization had been arranged in such a way that 'most crucial elements profoundly depend on science and technology … [while] almost no one understands science and technology. This is a prescription for disaster. We might get away with it for a while, but sooner or later this combustible mixture of ignorance and power is going to blow up in our faces.'

INTERNATIONAL SCIENTIFIC ORGANIZATIONS

The community of international scientific and technological organizations is large, varied and complex. In the earlier chapters of this book, a distinction has been made between the work of IGOs and INGOs, but in the field of science and technology that work is more blended, the IGOs usually taking something of a back seat to the work of non-state actors. In the absence of distinctive regimes for science or technology, and of UN bodies that clearly dominate in either field, the relevant UN agencies take their places alongside large communities of national and international organizations with interests in topics as varied as chemistry, geography, geology, horticulture, hydrology, meteorology, mineralogy, physics and seismology.

Despite the complexity of the field, and the extent of the work done by the members of these organizations, it is questionable how much of that work is heard by policymakers or finds its way into policy. Kasperson (2011) argues that the findings of scientific research are often overlooked because they have been framed to meet the needs of science rather than the needs of policy. He concludes that there needs to be more of a two-way interaction between science and policy so that each learns from – and meets the needs of – the other. In his study of the interface between environmental science and policy, Haas (2017) argues that states need 'usable knowledge', and that panels of scientists are often the primary source of the kind of expert knowledge that can help states meet their obligations to international agreements. While these panels aspire to play the role of experts, however, few have succeeded: because decision-makers rarely directly access scientific knowledge, they do not automatically recognize the insights made available.

Haas could have gone further by pointing out some of the tensions that exist between science and policy:

– While decision-makers seek a high degree of certainty before making policy, our understanding of natural processes is incomplete and scientific understanding is always evolving.

– While elected officials are driven by the limits of their terms in office, and will be looking to make progress before the next election, scientific research takes time to conduct, and often demands the kind of financial investment that may not be readily available thanks to stretched government budgets or multiple demands on private philanthropy.

– While scientists are interested in facts and experimentation, and thus tend to be cautious, politicians are motivated more by subjective issues such as the political feasibility of pursuing a particular course of action, or whether or not a law or policy will be popular, credible, effective or constitutional.

To the extent that there is a major IGO with an interest in science, it is the UN Educational, Scientific and Cultural Organization (UNESCO), another specialized agency of the UN. Headquartered in Paris, its underlying goal is to promote peace and security through cooperation in education, the social and natural sciences, culture and communication, a charge that has not always been easily met. It might be best known as a champion and monitor of the 1972 World Heritage Convention under which World Heritage sites (of which there are now nearly 1,160) are declared because of their natural or cultural importance. UNESCO is also a champion and monitor of the 2003 Convention for Intangible Cultural Heritage and the 2005 Convention on the Protection and Promotion of the Diversity of Cultural Expressions. (Intangible heritage includes practices, expressions, knowledge and skills that are recognized by communities as part of their cultural heritage.)

Although the *S* in the acronym *UNESCO* is less evident in the work of the organization, one exception is its Man and the Biosphere Programme (MAB). Launched in 1971, it has resulted in the creation of Biosphere Reserves committed to research into the coexistence of humans and nature. There are now nearly 740 such reserves in 134 countries, including the Serengeti–Ngorongoro reserve in Tanzania, the Sunderban mangrove forest in India, the Camargue wetlands in France, the Yellowstone–Grand Teton national parks in the US and the Galapagos Islands of Ecuador. Biosphere reserves may be designed to draw attention to the ecological value of outstanding natural areas, and to encourage research and education, but Reed and Price (2020) note that there has been 'no effort by sustainability scientists to establish a global network of research platforms from which lessons can be learned', and the programme remains relatively unknown and even misunderstood.

UNESCO has also been a champion of open science, which it defines as efforts to make scientific knowledge openly available, accessible and reusable for all. It published a recommendation in November 2021 emphasizing the urgency of addressing complex and interconnected environmental, social and economic challenges, and the vital role of science, technology and innovation in responding to these challenges. On that basis, it encouraged the use of open access online publishing, the sharing of open research data, the public availability of open-source software, and collaboration between scientists and other actors outside the scientific community (UNESCO, 2022). A recommendation is, of course, different from a practical action, and the publication of the recommendation was an indication of how much still needs to be done to achieve open science.

Outside the work of UNESCO, most IOs active in the fields of science and technology have more focused objectives; see Table 12.1. Science combines with

Table 12.1: International scientific organizations

Name	Founded	Headquarters	Purpose
UN Educational Scientific and Cultural Organization (UNESCO)	1945	Paris, France	IGO that is a specialized agency of the UN, promoting cooperation in intellectual activity.
World Meteorological Organization (WMO)	1950	Geneva, Switzerland	IGO that encourages cooperation among national meteorological and hydrological services.
European Organization for Nuclear Research (CERN)	1954	Near Geneva	IGO focused on high-energy physics research.
International Atomic Energy Agency (IAEA)	1957	Vienna, Austria	IGO that promotes the peaceful use of nuclear energy.
Antarctic Treaty secretariat	1957	Buenos Aires, Argentina	IGO promoting peaceful scientific use of Antarctica.
World Academy of Sciences (TWAS)	1983	Trieste, Italy	INGO promoting South–South and North–South scientific cooperation.
Arctic Council	1996	Tromsø, Norway	IGO with a combination of scientific, environmental, geopolitical and cultural goals.
InterAcademy Partnership (IAP)	2016	Trieste	INGO acting as a network for national academies.
International Science Council (ISC)	2018	Paris	INGO promoting science as a public good.

intergovernmental cooperation, for example, in the work of the International Atomic Energy Agency (IAEA). Based in Vienna, its mission is to promote the peaceful use of nuclear energy and to discourage its use for military purposes, including the development of nuclear weapons. Its origins lie in the UN Atomic Energy Commission, founded in 1946 as a result of the first resolution passed by the UN General Assembly. In 1953, US President Dwight D. Eisenhower made a landmark 'Atoms for Peace' address in which he called for the peaceful use of the new technology, and four years later the IAEA was founded.

Working as an autonomous organization within the UN, it reports to both the UN Security Council and the UN General Assembly. As well as conducting research into nuclear science, promoting civilian nuclear applications in fields that range from food preservation to cancer research, and monitoring the development of nuclear energy and the disposal of radioactive waste, it has also – since the ratification of the 1968 Treaty on the Non-Proliferation of Nuclear Weapons – had the authority to monitor nuclear programmes and to inspect nuclear facilities. It has been active, for example, in supporting the goals of the 2015 Joint Comprehensive Plan of Action on the Iranian nuclear programme (signed by Iran, Germany and the five permanent members of the UN Security Council). Although the staff of the agency are described by Roehrlich (2022) as 'inspectors for peace', she also notes the paradoxical mission of the IAEA in sharing nuclear knowledge and technology while working to deter nuclear weapons programmes. Spreading nuclear technology, notes one expert quoted by Roehrlich, spreads the ability to make nuclear weapons.

The IAEA has a General Conference made up of representatives from its 175 member states (each with one vote), which meets annually to make and approve decisions on policy and the agency's budget. It also has a Board of Governors elected by the Conference, consisting of 22 members elected using a formula to ensure geographical variety, and which is the main policy-making body of the IAEA. Finally, it has a secretariat headed by a Director General who is chosen by the Board of Governors and approved by the General Conference. Any member state of the UN qualifies also as a member state of the IAEA provided its application to join is approved by the Board and the Conference, which it normally is. Several countries have joined and then left, most notably North Korea, which was a member from 1974 to 1994, but then withdrew after being declared to be in non-compliance with IAEA standards on the peaceful use of nuclear energy.

Another specialized agency of the UN with a predominantly scientific brief is the World Meteorological Organization (WMO). Headquartered in Geneva, with the same 193 member states as the UN, its mandate is to encourage cooperation among national meteorological and hydrological services, to be a clearinghouse for information, and to improve our understanding of the state of the Earth's atmosphere and its interactions with oceans. It runs an Integrated Global Observing System as an umbrella for a network of thousands of manned or automatic surface and upper-air weather stations and radars, using ships and aircraft to augment its works. It also has a Space Programme that coordinates data generated by a network of national weather satellites. The WMO has a governing World Meteorological Congress that meets every four years to make decisions, which are implemented by a 37-member Executive

Council (made up mainly of national meteorological service directors elected to the Council by Congress), and a Secretariat headed by a Secretary General.

The charge of the WMO notably overlaps with that of environmental IOs (such as the UN Environment Programme) with which it works on topics such as climate change, the improved management of water, and early warning systems for natural disasters such as hurricanes, tornadoes, droughts and forest fires. In 1988, UNEP and the WMO cooperated in setting up the Intergovernmental Panel on Climate Change (see Chapter 11), whose secretariat is hosted by the WMO. The organization has also become increasingly active in cooperation on the science of the polar icecaps because of what their welfare tells us about the evolution of climate change; see *Spotlight 12*.

A prominent international scientific organization with a regional base (but a global reputation) is the European Organization for Nuclear Research, known more widely as CERN (the *Conseil Européen pour la Recherche Nucléaire*). Founded in 1954 (with the support of UNESCO), and based near Geneva, it is the largest particle physics laboratory in the world, run as an IGO with 23 European member states. It is governed by a Council consisting of representatives from all member states,

SPOTLIGHT 12

INTERNATIONAL SCIENTIFIC COOPERATION IN THE POLAR REGIONS

Two prominent examples of regionally focused scientific cooperation, including governments and non-governmental scientific bodies, can be found in the polar regions. The oldest is the Antarctic Treaty, signed by 12 states in 1957 with the goal of ensuring that the continent was used only for peaceful purposes, with freedom of scientific investigation and free availability of the results of that investigation. One study of the treaty (Elzinga, 1993) described Antarctica as a continent built 'by and for science'. There are now 29 full parties to the treaty and 27 non-voting observers, full membership coming only with proof of substantial research activity in the continent, usually confirmed by the building of a research station by the signatory. The treaty and a 1991 Protocol on Environmental Protection are monitored by a secretariat based in Buenos Aires, Argentina, whose tasks include supporting an annual Antarctic Treaty Consultative Meeting. Antarctic research is also monitored and supported by the UK-based Scientific Committee for Antarctic Research, an INGO whose members include scientific bodies from 46 countries.

The newer example is the Arctic Council, created by eight Arctic states in 1996 with a combination of scientific, environmental, geopolitical and cultural goals. Seen mainly as a channel for addressing any tensions that might arise in the region as a result of post-Cold War tensions, its work has taken on a new significance with the effects of climate change, the melting of Arctic ice making navigation through the region easier. Headquartered in Tromsø, Norway, the Council is open only to Arctic states, is overseen by a biennial meeting of ministers of the member states, and gives observer status to participants representing environmental groups, indigenous people's organizations and scientific bodies. The polar regions were at the heart of the response in the 1980s and 1990s to the thinning of the world's ozone layer (it was thinner over the poles than elsewhere; see Chapter 11) and are at the heart today of concerns about climate change.

responsible for making decisions, approving programmes, adopting the budget and appointing the director general. Each state has a single vote, and decisions are made by a simple majority, with a preference for achieving a consensus.

Created in part to help stop the brain drain of scientific talent that was leaving for the US after World War II, CERN does not engage in military research. Instead, it is best known for its Large Hadron Collider, used in research into particle physics and the laws governing the subatomic world. It was built at a cost of nearly $5 billion and involved a collaboration among thousands of scientists in more than 100 countries. CERN is also known for its role in the invention of the World Wide Web, which was developed by the British scientist Tim Berners-Lee while working at CERN in 1989. Originally intended to be a means by which scientists at multiple institutions around the world could communicate with one another, the Web was placed into the public domain in 1993.

Moving to examples of INGOs, the most prominent is the International Science Council (ISC), headquartered in Paris. With origins dating back to 1899, the ISC was founded in 2018 through the merger of the International Council for Science and the International Social Science Council. It has more than 220 member organizations active in the natural and social sciences and in the humanities, and describes its goal as the promotion of science as a global public good. It has a General Assembly that brings its member bodies together every three years to set the general direction and polices of the ISC, a 16-member Governing Board elected by the Assembly for three-year terms, and a Chief Executive Officer appointed by the Assembly. Among its numerous members are organizations focused on astronomy, biophysics, economics, food science, geography, pharmacology, political science, sociology and soil sciences.

The InterAcademy Partnership (IAP) is a network of more than 140 mainly national academies active in the social sciences, humanities, technology and engineering. Academies – the oldest of which date back to the 1600s in Europe – bring together scholars, scientists and artists at the national level – and are today found in almost every country in the world. The IAP was launched in South Africa in 2016, but it brought together three pre-existing INGOs whose origins date back as far as 1993. With offices in Trieste, Italy and in Washington DC, and affiliations with regional academies for Africa, the Americas, Asia and Europe, it claims to bring together more than 30,000 scientists with the goals of advancing new policies, improving public health and promoting science education.

The IAP shares its offices in Trieste with the World Academy of Sciences, the focus of which is on linking science and policy in emerging states. Founded in 1983 as the Third World Academy of Sciences, changing its name in 2004 to the Academy of Sciences for the Developing World (TWAS) and then adopting its new name – but keeping its old acronym – in 2012. Although based in Italy, most of its members come from the Global South, it works to promote South–South and North–South cooperation, it provides research grants and fellowships, and it works with regional partners in Brazil, China, Egypt, India and South Africa. It also works with the Organization for Women in Science for the Developing World (OWSD), which was founded in 1989 and works to strengthen the role of women scientists and technologists in the development process.

SHIPPING, AVIATION AND SPACE ORGANIZATIONS

The relationship between science, technology and policy is at play in the work of several organizations involved in the related fields of transport and space exploration. In the case of the London-based International Maritime Organization (IMO), for example, the initial interest was in technology-driven questions about safety at sea, but then science-driven environmental questions became more important in the wake of a growing number of large marine oil spills. Despite this, Campe (2009) argued just after the IMO's fiftieth anniversary that while it had been influential in providing technical expertise on ship design and construction, it had been less influential on environmental policy. Much like the International Tropical Timber Organization (see Chapter 9), its interests have been divided between demands for efficient and low-cost shipping (from ship owners, traders and oil companies) and for clean seas (from environmental, tourism and fishing interests).

There has been little sign of a change at IMO in the wake of pressures to address climate change, and to reduce pollutive emissions from ships. Van Leeuwen and Monios (2022) note that the IMO, as principal regulator of maritime transport, is the obvious venue for devising policies on greenhouse gases and shipping, and yet emissions from ships continue to climb and are not expected to fall much before 2050. The problem, they conclude, is that the IMO has a habit of using existing technologies rather than pushing its members to use new ones, and that it lacks initiative, leaving action on climate change and shipping to regional organizations, ports and private actors.

While the focus of the International Civil Aviation Organization (ICAO) is also on transport, its more particular interest is in monitoring and promoting the terms of the 1944 Convention on International Civil Aviation, otherwise known as the Chicago Convention. This established the core principles of international air transport in the wake of the rapid technological advances made in aircraft during World War II. Although air travel was available only to a privileged few in the years after the war, and international freight was mainly carried by sea, the landscape was changing, and standards and procedures were needed for an anticipated increase in air traffic. The ICAO was created to help states achieve uniformity in civil aviation regulations, becoming a specialized agency of the new UN in 1947 when enough ratifications of the Chicago Convention had been achieved. It has since gone on to oversee the agreement of more than 12,000 standards and recommended practices (SARPs), including those on rules of the air, airworthiness of aircraft, communication systems, accident investigations, aircraft noise and the design of airports.

It should be emphasized that ICAO is not a regulator, and that all these SARPs are enforced by states. The organization goes to some trouble on its web site to point out the inaccuracies about its work contained in 'many dramatic and media portrayals of UN agencies', and to point that that 'critiques of the UN are often rooted in allegations founded on fantastical capabilities and authorities which sovereign states would never assign to a multilateral organization'. Just as INTERPOL is not an international police force, it argues, so ICAO is not an international aviation regulator: 'We cannot

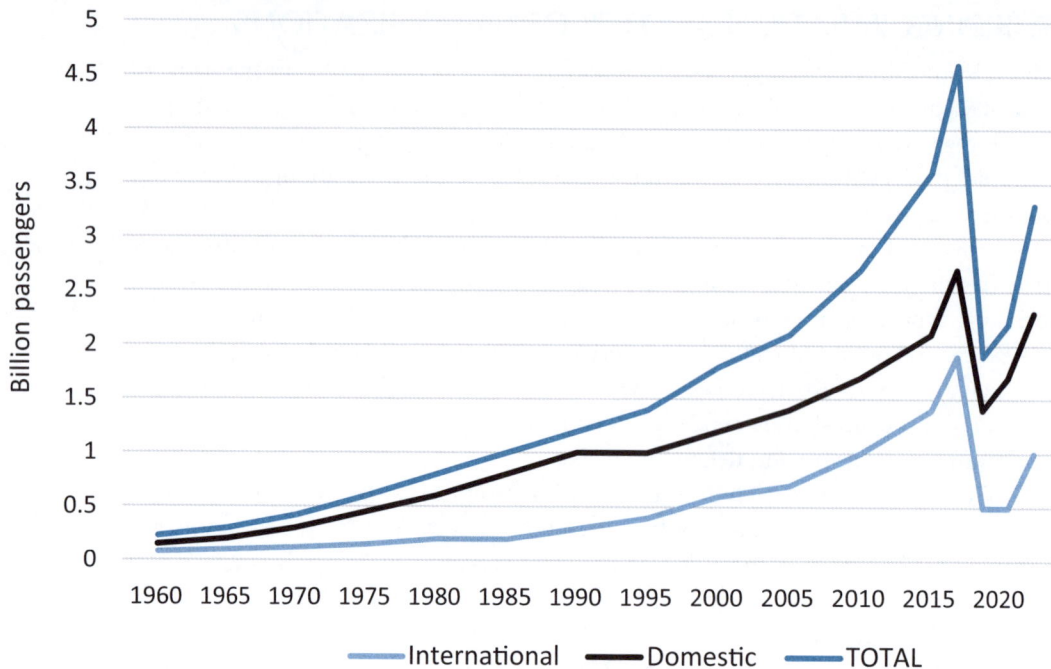

Figure 12.2: Air passenger traffic trends.
Source: Based on data in International Civil Aviation Organization (2023b).

arbitrarily close or restrict a country's airspace, shut down routes, or condemn airports or airlines for poor safety performance or customer service' (International Civil Aviation Organization, 2023a).

The global aviation landscape has changed out of all recognition since ICAO was created, with an almost 2,000 per cent increase in the number of air passengers travelling annually between 1960 and the pre-Covid peak in 2019; see Figure 12.2. The volume of freight carried by air increased at a similar rate, except that air freight is usually limited to goods that are perishable or needed urgently, and still faces more significant competition from rail, road and marine transportation. ICAO also works in conjunction with other IGOs representing specific constituencies, such as the Geneva-based International Air Traffic Association (IATA) (founded in 1945) that represents the interests of the more than 300 airlines that make up its membership.

Given the degree of international cooperation on maritime and air transport, it might be logical to assume that there would also be cooperation on space exploration, particularly given its expense. In fact, most endeavours in this regard have been based in the work of individual states, notably the US, the USSR (now Russia) and – in more recent decades – China. There has been cooperation, though, in the building and operation of the International Space Station (ISS), the first components of which were launched in 1998, the first long-term residents arriving in 2000. The ISS is a joint venture involving the national space agencies of the US, Russia, Japan and Canada, along with the only example of an international space organization: the European Space Agency (ESA).

The latter traces its roots back to the 1950s, when a combination of the early ventures in space exploration and the same 'brain drain' of European scientists to the US that was behind the creation of CERN prompted a group of western European scientists to explore coordination and cooperation among their peers. Two bodies – the European Launch Development Organization and the European Space Research Organization – were founded in 1964, and made their first modest contributions with research satellites launched on American rockets. In 1975 the two organizations were merged to form the ESA, which that same year launched its first major mission, gathering information on gamma-ray emissions in the universe. The European Astronaut Corps was later formed, and by 2022 had sent more than 60 astronauts into space, aboard either US space shuttles or Russian *Soyuz* missions to the International Space Station.

Headquartered in Paris, ESA has 22 member states: all western European EU member states, along with Canada, the Czech Republic, Estonia, Hungary, Norway, Poland, Romania, Switzerland and the UK. It has a staff of nearly 2,200, and in 2023 had a budget of nearly €4.9 billion ($5.3 billion). It also operates a launch facility at Korou in French Guiana, and an astronaut training facility in Cologne, Germany. ESA focuses on space exploration and research, working mainly with the French commercial satellite company Arianespace (founded in 1980) and on human space flight through its participation in the ISS. There has been speculation about the possibilities for a regional space agency for Latin America, based on the ESA model, but this has not progressed far (Froelich and Soria, 2021).

INTERNATIONAL STANDARDS ORGANIZATIONS

The strength and consistency of the economic, trading and communication links among states depends to a large degree on the setting of common standards: comparing professional standards for the training of doctors and engineers, for example, or ensuring the interoperability of cross-border communication systems, or assuring consumers of the safety and quality of the food they buy (assisted by the Codex Alimentarius Commission reviewed in Chapter 9), or reducing accidents in the workplace, or simply working to agree on units of weights and measures. Whatever the goal, having common standards is a key part of a functioning international system, and one of the most important ways in which global governance shapes everyday life. The economic implications are particularly clear: common technical standards make it possible for products to be made by different manufacturers and sold in different countries, as well as contributing to the expansion of consumer choices, the promotion of technological innovation, the promotion of environmental quality and the removal of barriers to trade.

States have long had their own sets of national standards, and most have their own national standards organizations that are members of international networks. The increased pace of innovations in technology, combined with the increased importance of protecting intellectual property and new competition from emerging markets, has increased the pace and the competitiveness of the work of standards organizations (Schneiderman, 2015). The result has been the growth of what Gustafsson (2020) describes – somewhat darkly – as a 'global control regime' that has become nested in the private and public sectors, and that has evolved in silence and without debate despite impacting companies, governments and consumers on a daily basis.

While standardization has been a predictable consequence of globalization, Gustafsson continues, it is also a matter of concern because it 'leaves us with a faceless bureaucratic system with no name and no one in charge. This has severe consequences for responsibility: if no one is in charge, then no one is to be held accountable for how standards rule the world'. To say that these organizations 'rule the world' is an overstatement, though, particularly as international standards are typically used voluntarily. Also, the degree to which these bodies are accountable or unaccountable varies from one to another, and between those that are intergovernmental and those that are non-governmental. Meanwhile, supporters of the process of standardization argue that standards are the 'lubricant for international trade' (Heires, 2008), and that one of their values lies in promoting openness based on addressing global challenges with scientific and technical solutions rather than political solutions (Murphy and Yates, 2009).

The oldest standards body is the International Telecommunication Union (ITU), whose origins date back to the creation in 1865 of the International Telegraph Union. Headquartered in Geneva, its original focus was on the then-new technology of telegraph communication (which was just as revolutionary then as the internet has been more recently) and on setting up a system that allowed messages to be broadcast seamlessly across national borders. Its current name was adopted in 1934, reflecting the rapid changes in communications technology then taking place. In 1947, the ITU became a specialized agency of the United Nations, and it has gone on to develop international standards for almost all forms of information and communications technology. As well as being at the heart of the expansion of phone use around the world, it also coordinates the use of the global radio and television spectrum, the orbits of communication satellites, the availability of GPS navigation, access to the internet (most internet connections are subject to ITU standards) and the development of new technology. All 193 member states of the UN are members of the ITU, along with nearly 750 private sector members and academic institutions.

The biggest and most far-reaching standards body is the International Organization for Standardization (known as ISO, which is a name – pronounced *eye-soh* – and not an acronym). An independent INGO, it was founded in 1947, is based in Geneva and has a membership of national standards organizations from 167 countries. ISO had drawn up and adopted nearly 25,000 standards by 2023 in a variety of sectors of the market, including electronics, energy, food supply, road vehicles, health care and environmental management; see *IOs in Action 12*. It has most of the usual organizational elements of an IO, including a president, a General Assembly that meets annually, a 20-member Council that meets three times annually, a network of technical committees and a secretariat. Standards are drawn up by committees staffed by all interested member bodies, going through a six-stage process aimed at achieving a consensus, when the agreed new standards are published. About one-fifth of its funding comes from subscriptions paid by its members, the balance coming from member bodies and businesses that pay for their experts to participate in the work of the ISO.

IOs IN ACTION 12

ISO AND THE ENVIRONMENT

International standards impact our lives on a daily basis, and yet remarkably little is known about them, about how they are made, about who makes them, about how they are implemented, and about the impact they have. Understanding them is made more difficult both by the technical qualities that many of them contain, and by the relative anonymity of the key international standards bodies, such as ISO; these are not organizations that capture news headlines. In order to shed some light on the process, we could do worse than focus on just one among the thousands of sets of international standards that have been agreed: the ISO 14000 series that helps organizations reduce the adverse effects of their activities on the environment (including land, air and water), by using resources more efficiently, reducing waste and being less pollutive.

The ISO 14000 series was born in 1996, growing out of the adoption in 1992 by the British Standards Institution of BS 7750, the world's first environmental management systems standard. As with all ISO standards, the ISO 14000 series is based on voluntary principles, designed to give organizations a reference point for the development of their own targets and performance measures. The standards are reviewed periodically by ISO to make sure that they keep up with understandings about environmental quality, some of the later additions to the series, for example, focusing on how to measure and reduce greenhouse gas emissions (ISO 14064) and how to adapt to climate change (ISO 14090).

In principle, explains Heires (2008), ISO's international standards 'are technical specifications for the design, dimensions, interoperability or performance of products and processes – they specify how something should operate or interact'. For Woellner (2020), national environmental regulations – if well thought through – can be productive and helpful, but they can also be ineffective because they are nationally focused and often spark the opposition of industry and national politicians. Standards, by contrast, address environmental concerns on a global basis, and they engage corporations in the process. Pollution prevention is more effective than pollution control because it focuses on eliminating the problem before it begins, and the ISO 14000 series of standards has helped corporations manage risk and minimize the creation of environmental problems.

One of the products of the work of the ISO can be found on the copyright page of this book in the form of its assigned ISBN number. Copied by ISO off a numbering system developed in Britain, and published in 1970 as ISO 2108, the International Standard Book Number gives every commercially published book a unique numeric identifier that promotes an efficient book supply chain, and is used by publishers, booksellers and libraries to ensure the accuracy of ordering and stock control. The numbers are assigned and monitored by the London-based International ISBN Agency, appointed to the job by ISO, and working in conjunction with national ISBN agencies. Meanwhile, the ISSN (International Standard Serial Number) is used for journals, magazines, newspapers and other serials, and is overseen by the Paris-based ISSN International Centre, founded in 1976.

In addition to international standards organizations, the European Union (EU) has its own regional bodies:

- The European Telecommunications Standards Institute (ETSI) is headquartered south-west of Nice in France, and is an independent non-profit organization with more than 700 national member organizations from 62 countries. Despite its name, it produces global standards for information and communications technology, including fixed, mobile, broadcast, internet and aeronautical communications.

- The European Committee for Standardization (CEN) and the European Committee for Electrotechnology Standardization (CENELEC) both work within the EU, their members being the relevant national bodies of EU member states, along with Iceland, Norway, Switzerland, Turkey and the UK. CEN focuses on removing trade barriers among EU states, while CENELEC focuses on standards in electrotechnical engineering.

The most basic of all standards are weights and measures: how much (exactly) does a kilogram weigh, how long (exactly) is a metre and what (exactly) is the time, and how can we be sure that everyone around the world is on the same time (allowing, of course, for different time zones) and using the same measures? Many of these questions are addressed by the work of the International Bureau of Weights and Measures, known by its acronym BIPM from its name in French (*Bureau international des poids et mesures*). Based in the suburbs of Paris, BIPM was founded in 1875 in the wake of the signature of the Metre Convention, an agreement on units of mass and length. Under the International System of Units, agreements have since been reached on units of time, temperature, electric current and luminosity. BIPM maintains the system and is also home to the Coordinated Universal Time that is the global common time standard. Only 64 countries are member states, each of which pays a subscription to support the work of the Bureau.

GOVERNING THE INTERNET

In almost every other example discussed in this book, global governance has evolved through a mainly logical series of steps that have built upon one another and produced an identifiable set of IOs with mainly clear (albeit often overlapping) functions. By contrast, governance of the internet has followed an entirely different path. For Biersteker (2019), internet governance is 'an ongoing, complex, contested, and unfinished project … [that has] evolved into a composite arrangement of public and private actors interacting in different multi-stakeholder initiatives … with no clear hierarchy among them'.

Although the record of research into internet governance dates back several decades, it has only been in the last few years – argues DeNardis (2018) – that the topic has entered the public consciousness, with troubled questions about who controls the internet, and the implications of that control on freedom of information and the right to privacy. Revelations about election hacking, facial recognition technology and government surveillance have – argue DeNardis et al. (2020) – made the design and governance of the internet 'one of the most pressing geopolitical issues of our era', with the stability of economies, democracy and the public sphere wholly dependent on its security and stability. Despite this, our understanding of internet governance is still being formed; the research on the topic comes from all over the world, covers numerous disciplines, and is often both technical and compartmentalized.

The internet emerged from the work of a small number of researchers working mainly in the US and supported by funding mainly from the US Department of Defence and the National Science Foundation. Its forerunner, known as Arpanet, was developed in an informal manner, driven by finding practical solutions to problems using what was later described by Castells (2001) as 'ad hoc governance'. It was only in the late 1990s that the US government transferred operational control over the internet to the private sector, giving oversight to the US Department of Commerce (Santaniello, 2021). With the number of users growing, and more web sites being created, there was an opportunity to set up a new IO to manage domain names. This was bypassed, though, when the US in 1998 founded the Internet Corporation for Assigned Names and Numbers (ICANN), effectively creating an internet self-governance regime at the domestic and international levels. As a result, private corporations and non-state actors came to play a central role in making policy and setting standards for the internet (DeNardis, 2014; Radu, 2019).

Opposition to trends of this kind was led by China and the EU, with calls for the creation of an internet IGO and for an internationalization of internet governance, a philosophy resisted by the US. At the prompting of members of the International Telecommunication Union (ITU), a two-part World Summit on the Information Society was convened in 2003 and 2005 to discuss developments. One of the outcomes was the creation of the Internet Governance Forum (IGF), which met for the first time in Athens in 2006, and has convened annually ever since.

Efforts to formalize internet governance made little progress, though, with an initiative to agree a new set of International Telecommunications Regulations supported by China and Russia but resisted by the US and the EU. The first set had been agreed in 1988 with a merging of long-standing telephone and telegraph regulations. A heated debate was now held on integrating traditional telecommunications and the internet. When the new treaty was opened for signature in 2012 it avoided including specific provisions on the internet, and was more a set of principles than of regulations. Fewer than half the member states of the UN have since become parties.

Opinion is divided on where the focus of the governance of the internet now lies, assuming that there is such a focus. It is clear that most of it takes place less in conventional IGOs than in self-regulating organizations whose growing numbers have created a bewildering alphabet soup (or spaghetti bowl) of organizations. Prominent among these are technically focused organizations that develop standards and set policy for naming and numbering resources created by those standards (Mueller, 2017). These include the following:

- The US-based Internet Engineering Task Force (IETF) is made up of volunteers who create voluntary standards for internet operating protocols such as TCP/IP (Transmission Control Protocol/Internet Protocol), which is the basic communication language for the internet. Founded in 1986, it operates under the auspices of the Internet Society (ISOC), a US NGO with chapters all over the world, to develop internet-related standards, education and policy.

- Meanwhile, IP addresses (assigned to every computer in the world) are coordinated by five Regional Internet Registries (private sector non-profit organizations), while domain name assignment is coordinated globally by the Internet Corporation for Assigned Names and Numbers (ICANN). With the explosion in the availability and applicability of the internet in the early 1990s, and the launch of the World Wide Web, an organization was needed to manage domain names, and ICANN was launched in 1999 as an entirely new kind of IO: a private corporation with global governance responsibilities (Mueller, 2017).

- The World Wide Web Consortium (W3C) was founded in 1994, and is the main international standards body for the Web. Based in the US, and describing itself as an 'international community', it has more than 450 member organizations.

- The Global Knowledge Partnership (GKP) was founded in 1997, and works to promote innovation to help bride the digital divide between those who have access to the internet and those who do not. Headquartered in Kuala Lumpur, Malaysia, it has members in more than 50 countries.

- The Wi-Fi Alliance is another US-based NGO, founded in 1999 with member companies from multiple countries, that owns the Wi-Fi trademark and encourages the security, development and interoperability of Wi-Fi (which is a brand name, not an acronym).

- The Organization for the Advancement of Structured Information Standards (OASIS) is an international NGO that researches and supports the adoption of open standards in information computing. Founded in 1993, it is again based in the US.

In addition to these, Mueller (2017) also notes the role of so-called multi-stakeholder entities that bridge the gap between private sector-led organizations and mechanisms, on the one hand, and conventional IGOs on the other. The latter include IOs for which the internet is only part of their particular interests, and include the World Trade Organization, the International Telecommunication Union and the World Intellectual Property Organization. An example of a multi-stakeholder entity is the Internet Governance Forum (IGF). This is less an organization than a neutral forum within which the stakeholders in the management of the internet (governments, NGOs, the private sector and technical experts) meet to discuss shared interests and concerns. It has a small secretariat based in Geneva, and a Multistakeholder Advisory Group that meets three times annually to prepare for IGF annual meetings. All it can do is to make recommendations, and it has no decision-making authority.

The internet regime is both convoluted and complex, consists of a unique combination of governmental, corporate and technical elements, and can be hard to grasp. Weiss (2009) some time ago made the point that *governance* and *the internet* were two terms that did not always sit comfortably together. The roots of the internet lay in the efforts of the US military to develop a new system of communication in the context of the Cold War, and yet the internet came to be celebrated as a mainly unregulated vehicle for freedom of expression and commercial exploitation. This tension is still reflected today in the dynamics of internet governance. It is part of the reason why the US was resistant to intergovernmental regulation of the internet, a philosophy that directed efforts away from the creation of a new World Internet Organization, or the adoption of new responsibilities for IGOs such as the ITU, instead creating the complex system of internet governance that exists today.

THINKING POINTS

- Should there be a specialized UN agency with responsibility for coordinating scientific collaboration and disseminating the findings of science?
- How far is the degree of the interaction between state and non-state actors in science and technology transferable to other regimes?
- Is there a case to be made for a global space agency?
- Is the limited accountability and transparency of international standards organizations a matter of concern?
- Should there be more intergovernmental management of the internet?

IOs RELATED TO THIS CHAPTER

Arctic Council

Antarctic Treaty

European Organization for Nuclear Research (CERN)

European Space Agency (ESA)

InterAcademy Partnership (IAP)

International Atomic Energy Agency (IAEA)

International Bureau of Weights and Measures (BIPM)

International Civil Aviation Organization (ICAO)

International Maritime Organization (IMO)

International Organization for Standardization (ISO)

International Science Council (ISC)

International Telecommunication Union (ITU)

Internet Corporation for Assigned Names and Numbers (ICANN)

Internet Engineering Task Force (IETF)

Internet Governance Forum (IGF)

UN Educational, Scientific and Cultural Organization (UNESCO)

World Academy of Sciences (TWAS)

World Meteorological Organization (WMO)

FURTHER READING

DeNardis, Laura, Derrick L. Cogburn, Nanette S. Levinson, and Francesca Musiani (eds) (2020) *Researching Internet Governance: Methods, Frameworks, Futures* (MIT Press). An edited collection of chapters on origins and development of internet governance, and the challenges it currently faces.

Gustafsson, Ingrid (2020) *How Standards Rule the World: The Construction of a Global Control Regime* (Edward Elgar). One of the (surprisingly few) studies of the international standards regime, looking at many of the standards IOs and the context within which they work.

Haggart, Blayne, Kathryn Henne, and Natasha Tusikov (eds) (2020) *Information, Technology and Control in a Changing World: Understanding Power Structures in the 21st Century* (Springer). An edited collection of studies of the ways in which the control of knowledge has move to the core of global governance.

Moro, Niccolò, Francesco, Giampiero Giacomello, and Marco Valigi (eds) (2021) *Technology and International Relations: The New Frontier in Global Power* (Edward Elgar). One of the rare assessments of the interface between technology and international relations, with chapters on military technology artificial intelligence and cyberspace.

Radu, Roxana (2019) *Negotiating Internet Governance* (Oxford University Press). A survey of the origins, evolution and structure of international governance of the internet.

BIBLIOGRAPHY

Aas, Wenche., Augustin Mortier, Van Bowersox, et al. (2019) 'Global and regional trends of atmospheric sulfur', in *Scientific Reports* 9: 953.

Adams, Francis (2021) *The Right to Food: The Global Campaign to End Hunger and Malnutrition* (Cham, Switzerland: Palgrave Macmillan).

Akdag, Yavuz (2018) 'The likelihood of cyberwar between the United States and China: A neorealism and power transition theory perspective', in *Journal of Chinese Political Science* 24:2, June, pp. 225–47.

Al Hussein, Zeid Ra'ad (2018) 'Opening statement and global update of human rights concerns by UN High Commissioner for Human Rights Zeid Ra'ad Al Hussein at the 38th Session of the Human Rights Council', 18 June, at https://www.ohchr.org.

Alhammadi, Abdullah (2022) 'The neorealism and neoliberalism behind international relations during Covid-19', in *World Affairs* 185:1, pp. 147–75.

Allende, Héctor Hugo Juárez (2022) *The World Customs Organization: Past, Present and Future* (Cham, Switzerland: Springer).

Alston, Philip, and Frédéric Mégret (2020) 'Introduction: Appraising the United Nations Human Rights regime', in Frédéric Mégret and Philip Alston (eds) *The United Nations and Human Rights: A Critical Appraisal*, 2nd edn (Oxford: Oxford University Press).

Alter, Karen J. (2014) *The New Terrain of International Law: Courts, Politics, Rights* (Princeton, NJ: Princeton University Press).

Alter, Karen J. (2019) 'Critical junctures and the future of international courts in a post-liberal world order', in Avidan Kent, Nikos Skoutaris, and Jamie Trinidad (eds) *The Future of International Courts: Regional, Institutional and Procedural Challenges* (Abingdon: Routledge).

Appelbaum, Richard P., Cong Cao, Xueying Han, Rachel Parker, and Denis Simon (2018) *Innovation in China: Challenging the Global Science and Technology System* (Cambridge: Polity).

Arana, Arantza Gomez (2017) *The European Union's Policy Towards Mercosur: Responsive Not Strategic* (Manchester: Manchester University Press).

Archibugi, Daniele, and Andrea Filippetti (eds) (2015) *The Handbook of Global Science, Technology, and Innovation* (Chichester: John Wiley & Sons).

Ashiagbor, Diamond, Nicola Countouris, and Ioannis Lianos (eds) (2012) *The European Union After the Treaty of Lisbon* (Cambridge: Cambridge University Press).

Ba, Oumar (2020) *States of Justice: The Politics of the International Criminal Court* (Cambridge: Cambridge University Press).

Babb, Sarah (2009) *Behind the Development Banks: Washington Politics, World Poverty, and the Wealth of Nations* (Chicago: University of Chicago Press).

Baiden, Max, Melanie Book, Susan Leedham, Gareth Owen, and Andrew Thompson (2022) *INGOs and the Long Humanitarian Century*. Nuffield College, University of Oxford.

Balogun, Emmanuel (2022) *Region-Building in West Africa: Convergence and Agency in ECOWAS* (Abingdon: Routledge).

Baluarte, David (2019) 'The arrival of "statelessness studies"?', in *Statelessness and Citizenship Review* 156, pp. 156–60.

Barkan, Joanne (2013) 'Plutocrats at work: How big philanthropy undermines democracy', in *Social Research* 80:2, Summer, pp. 635–52.

Barnett, Michael, and Martha Finnemore (2005) 'The power of liberal international organizations', in Michael Barnett and Raymond Duvall (eds) *Power in Global Governance* (New York: Cambridge University Press).

Barnett, Michael N., Jon C. W. Pevehouse, and Kal Raustiala (eds) (2021) 'Introduction', in *Global Governance in a World of Change* (Cambridge: Cambridge University Press).

Bass, Steven, and Stéphane Guéneau (2005) 'Global forest governance: Effectiveness, fairness and legitimacy of market-driven approaches', in Sophie Thoyer and Benoît Martimort-Asso (eds) *Participation for Sustainability in Trade* (Aldershot: Ashgate).

Bates, Robert H. (1997) *Open-Economy Politics: The Political Economy of the World Coffee Trade* (Princeton, NJ: Princeton University Press).

Baughan, Emily (2021) *Saving the Children: Humanitarianism, Internationalism, and Empire* (Oakland, CA: University of California Press).

Bazbauers, Adrian Robert, and Susan Engel (2021) *The Global Architecture of Multilateral Development Banks: A System of Debt or Development?* (Abingdon: Routledge).

Beigbeder, Yves (2018) *The World Health Organization: Achievements and Failures* (Abingdon: Routledge).

Benjamin-Britton, Taylor, Matthew Bray Bolton, and Sarah Njeri (2019) 'The humanitarian disarmament movement: An assessment and review', in Matthew Bray Bolton, Sarah Njeri, and Taylor Benjamin-Britton (eds) *Global Activism and Humanitarian Disarmament* (Cham, Switzerland: Springer).

Bennett, Elizabeth A. (2020) 'The global fair trade movement: For whom, by whom, how, and what next?', in Michael Bell, Michael Carolan, Julie Keller, and Katharine Legun (eds) *The Cambridge Handbook of Environmental Sociology* (Cambridge: Cambridge University Press).

Bhagwati, Jagdish (1992) 'A champion for migrating peoples', in *The Christian Science Monitor*, 28 February.

Bhagwati, Jagdish N., Pravin Krishna, and Arvind Panagariya (2016) 'The World Trade system today', in Jagdish N. Bhagwati, Pravin Krishna, and Arvind Panagariya (eds) *The World Trade System: Trends and Challenges* (Cambridge, MA: MIT Press).

Biermann, Frank (2000) 'The case for a World Environment Organization', in *Environment* 42:9, pp. 22-31.

Biermann, Frank, and Steffen Bauer (eds) (2005) *A World Environment Organization: Solution or Threat for Effective International Environmental Governance?* (Aldershot: Ashgate).

Biersteker, Thomas (2019) 'Foreword', in Roxana Radu (2019) *Negotiating Internet Governance* (Oxford: Oxford University Press).

Bird, Graham, and Dane Rowlands (2016) *The International Monetary Fund: Distinguishing Reality from Rhetoric* (Cheltenham: Edward Elgar).

Bishwarkama, Jham Kumar, and Zongshan Hu (2022) 'Problems and prospects for the South Asian Association for Regional Cooperation', in *Politics & Policy* 50:1, February, pp. 154–79.

Borzyskowski, Inken von, and Felicity Vabulas (2019) 'Credible commitments? Explaining IGO suspensions to sanction political backsliding', in *International Studies Quarterly* 63:1, March, pp. 139–52.

Bowen, Howard R. (1953) *Social Responsibilities of the Businessman* (New York: Harper and Row).

Bower, Adam (2017) *Norms Without the Great Powers: International Law and Changing Social Standards in World Politics* (Oxford: Oxford University Press).

BRAC (2023) Web site at http://www.brac.net/vision-mission-values. Retrieved May 2023.

Bradford, Anu (2020) *The Brussels Effect: How the European Union Rules the World* (Oxford: Oxford University Press).

Bradley, Megan (2020) *The International Organization for Migration: Challenges, Commitments, Complexities* (Abingdon: Routledge).

Brandt Commission (1980) *North–South: A Programme for Survival. The Report of the Independent Commission on International Development Issues* (London: Pan Books).

Brandt Commission (1983) *Common Crisis: North–South Cooperation for World Recovery* (London: Pan Books).

Brannagan, Paul Michael, and Danyel Reiche (2022) *Qatar and the 2022 FIFA World Cup: Politics, Controversy, Change* (Cham, Switzerland: Palgrave Macmillan).

Brundtland Commission (1987) *Our Common Future: The World Commission on Environment and Development* (Oxford: Oxford University Press).

Bryson, Valerie (2106) *Feminist Political Theory*, 3rd edn (London: Palgrave).

Burchill, Scott (2022) 'Liberalism', in Richard Devetak and Jacqui True (eds) *Theories of International Relations*, 6th edn (London: Bloomsbury).

Burci, Gian Luca, and Andrew Cassels (2016) 'Health', in Jacob Katz Cogan, Ian Hurd, and Ian Johnstone (eds) *The Oxford Handbook of International Organizations* (Oxford: Oxford University Press).

Burges, Sean (2018) 'UNASUR's dangerous decline: The risks of a growing left–right split in South America', in *Americas Quarterly*, 3 May.

Campe, Sabine (2009) 'The Secretariat of the International Maritime Organization: A tanker for tankers', in Frank Biermann and Bernd Siebenhüner (eds) *Managers of Global Change: The Influence of International Environmental Bureaucracies* (Cambridge, MA: MIT Press).

Carayannis, Tatiana, and Thomas G. Weiss (2021) *The 'Third' United Nations: How a Knowledge Ecology Helps the UN Think* (Oxford: Oxford University Press).

CARE International (2022) '75 years of CARE', on CARE web site at https://www.care-international.org/who-we-are/75-years-care. Retrieved May 2023.

Carraro, Valenina (2019) 'Electing the experts: Expertise and independence in the UN human rights treaty bodies', in *European Journal of International Relations* 25:3, September, pp. 826–51.

Castells, Manuel (2001) *The Internet Galaxy: Reflections on the Internet, Business, and Society* (Oxford: Oxford University Press).

Catino, Maurizio (2019) *Mafia Organizations: The Visible Hand of Criminal Enterprise* (Cambridge: Cambridge University Press).

Cerveny, Randy (2023) 'The history of the World Meteorological Organization', in *Weatherwise* 76:2, pp. 34–40.

Chatin, Mathilde, and Giulio M. Gallarotti (eds) (2018) *Emerging Powers in International Politics: The BRICS and Soft Power* (Abingdon: Routledge).

Chesterman, Simon (2016) 'Executive heads', in Jacob Katz Cogan, Ian Hurd, and Ian Johnstone (eds) *The Oxford Handbook of International Organizations* (Oxford: Oxford University Press).

Chetail, Vincent (2019) *International Migration Law* (Oxford: Oxford University Press).

Chimni, B S (2018) 'Global Compact on Refugees: One step forward, two steps back', in *International Journal of Refugee Law* 30:4, December, pp. 630–4.

Cincinelli, Alessandra, Tania Martellini, Cristiana Guerranti, Costanza Scopetani, David Chelazzi, and Tommaso Giarrizzo (2019) 'A potpourri of microplastics in the sea surface and water column of the Mediterranean Sea', in *TrAC Trends in Analytical Chemistry* 110, January, pp. 321–6.

Clapham, Andrew (1994) 'Creating the High Commissioner for Human Rights: The outside story', in *European Journal of International Law* 5:4, pp. 556–68.

Clapp, Jennifer (2018) 'Food and hunger', in Thomas G. Wiess and Rorden Wilkinson (eds) *International Organization and Global Governance*, 2nd edn (Abingdon: Routledge).

Clark, Richard, and Lindsay R. Dolan (2021) 'Pleasing the principal: US influence in World Bank policymaking', in *American Journal of Political Science* 65:1, January, pp. 36–51.

Clarke, Kamari Maxine (2019) *Affective Justice: The International Criminal Court and the Pan-Africanist Pushback* (Durham, NC: Duke University Press).

Claude, Inis L. (1996) 'Peace and security: Prospective roles for the two United Nations', in *Global Governance* 2:3, September–December, pp. 289–98.

Clinton, Chelsea, and Devi Sridhar (2017) *Governing Global Health: Who Runs the World and Why?* (New York: Oxford University Press).

Cogan, Jacob Katz (2016) 'Financing and budgets', in Jacob Katz Cogan, Ian Hurd, and Ian Johnstone (eds) *The Oxford Handbook of International Organizations* (Oxford: Oxford University Press).

Colchester, Marcus (1990) 'The International Tropical Timber Organization: Kill or cure for the rainforests?' in *The Ecologist* 20:5, September/October, pp. 166–73.

Colgan, Jeff D. (2021) *Partial Hegemony: Oil Politics and International Order* (New York: Oxford University Press).

Collins, Alan, Adam Cox, and Gianpiero Torrisi (2022) 'A picture of regret: An empirical investigation of post-Brexit referendum survey data', in *Rationality and Society* 34:1, pp. 56–71.

Columbia Center on Sustainable Investment (2021) *Development Banking in the Global Economy: State of Play and Future Direction* (New York: Columbia Center on Sustainable Investment).

Contese, Jorge (2019) 'Resisting the inter-American human rights system', in *Yale Journal of International Law* 44:2, Summer, pp. 179–237.

Conway, Ed (2014) *The Summit: Bretton Woods, 1944 – J. M. Keynes and the Reshaping of the Global Economy* (New York: Pegasus).

Cooper, Andrew, and Thomas Legler (2006) *Intervention Without Intervening? The OAS Defense and Promotion of Democracy in the Americas* (New York: Palgrave Macmillan).

Copelovitch, Mark S. (2010) 'Master or servant? Common agency and the political economy of IMF lending', in *International Studies Quarterly* 54:1, March, pp. 49–77.

Corell, Elisabeth, and Michele M. Betsill (2008) 'Analytical framework: Assessing the influence of NGO diplomats', in Michele M. Betsill and Elisabeth Corell (eds) *NGO Diplomacy: The Influence of Nongovernmental Organizations in International Environmental Negotiations* (Cambridge, MA: MIT Press).

Cox, Robert W. (1983) 'Gramsci, hegemony and international relations: An essay in method', in *Millenium: Journal of International Studies* 12:2, pp. 162–75.

Craig, Gary, Alex Balch, Hannah Lewis, and Louise Waite (eds) (2019) *The Modern Slavery Agenda: Policy, Politics and Practice in the UK* (Bristol: Policy Press).

Crips, Jeff (2020) 'UNHCR at 70: An uncertain future for the international refugee regime', in *Global Governance: A Review of Multilateralism and International Organizations* 26:3, pp. 359–68.

Cross, Mai'a K. Davis (2013) 'Rethinking epistemic communities twenty years later', in *Review of International Studies* 39:1, January, pp. 137–60.

Crump, Laurien (2015) *The Warsaw Pact Reconsidered: International Relations in Eastern Europe 1955–69* (Abingdon: Routledge).

Cueto, Marcos, Theodore M. Brown, and Elizabeth Fee (2019) *The World Health Organization: A History* (Cambridge: Cambridge University Press).

Davies, Michael D. V. (2002) *The Administration of International Organizations: Top Down and Bottom Up* (Abingdon: Routledge).

De Schutter, Olivier (2019) *International Human Rights Law: Cases, Materials, Commentary*, 3rd edn (Cambridge: Cambridge University Press).

Delikanli, Ihsan Ugur, Todor Dimitrov, and Roena Agolli (2018) *Multilateral Development Banks: Governance and Finance* (Cham, Switzerland: Springer).

DeMars, William E., and Dennis Dijkzeul (eds) (2015) *The NGO Challenge for International Relations Theory* (Abingdon: Routledge).

Dembele, Demba Moussa (2007) 'The International Monetary Fund and World Bank in Africa: A "disastrous" record', in Vicente Navarro (ed) *Neoliberalism, Globalization and Inequalities: Consequence for Health and Quality of Life* (Abingdon: Routledge).

DeNardis, Laura (2014) *The Global War for Internet Governance* (New Haven, CT: Yale University Press).

DeNardis, Laura (ed.) (2018) *Global Internet Governance* (Abingdon: Routledge).

DeNardis, Laura, Derrick L. Cogburn, Nanette S. Levinson, and Francesca Musiani (eds) (2020) *Researching Internet Governance: Methods, Frameworks, Futures* (Cambridge, MA: MIT Press).

Digiacomo, Gordon (2019) 'The International Labour Organization: Champion of worker rights or 90-pound weakling?' in Gordon DiGiacomo and Susan L. King (eds) *The Institutions of Human Rights: Developments and Practices* (Toronto: University of Toronto Press).

Dollar, David (2015) 'China's rise as a regional and global power: The AIIB and the "one belt, one road"', in *Horizons* 4, Summer.

Donnelly, Jack (2022) 'Realism', in Richard Devetak and Jacqui True (eds) *Theories of International Relations*, 6th edn (London: Bloomsbury).

Donnelly, Jack, and Daniel J. Whelan (2020) *International Human Rights*, 6th edn (New York: Routledge).

Dromi, Shai M. (2020) *Above the Fray: The Red Cross + the Making of the Humanitarian NGO Sector* (Chicago: University of Chicago Press).

Duit, Andreas, Peter H. Feindt, and James Meadowcroft (2016) 'Greening Leviathan: The rise of the environmental state?', in *Environmental Politics* 25:1, pp. 1–23.

Easton, David (1953) *The Political System: An Inquiry into the State of Political Science* (New York: Knopf).

Economist, The (2019) 'Mausoleum of broken institutions', 22 March.

Economist, The (2022) 'What is the point of the Commonwealth Games?', 29 July.

Ehrlich, Paul (1968) *The Population Bomb* (New York: Ballantine Books).

Eichengreen, Barry, and Douglas A. Irwin (2010) 'The slide to protectionism in the Great Depression: Who succumbed and why?', in *The Journal of Economic History* 70:4, December, pp. 871–97.

Eilstrup-Sangiovanni, Mette (2020) 'Death of international organizations: The organizational ecology of intergovernmental organizations, 1815–2015', in *The Review of International Organizations* 15, pp. 339–70.

Elsea, Jennifer (2002) 'US Policy regarding the International Criminal Court', Congressional Research Service/US Library of Congress, 3 September.

Elsig, Manfred, Michael Hahn, and Gabriele Sprilker (eds) (2019) 'Introduction', in *The Shifting Landscape of Global Trade Governance: World Trade Forum* (Cambridge: Cambridge University Press).

Elzinga, Aant (1993) 'Antarctica: The construction of a continent by and for science', in Elisabeth Crawford, Terry Shinn, and Sverkler Sörlin (eds) *Denationalizing Science: The Contexts of International Scientific Practice* (Dordrecht: Springer).

Environmental Performance Index (2023) About the EPI, at https://epi.yale.edu. Retrieved May 2023.

Eriksson, Johan, and Lindy M. Newlove-Eriksson (2021) 'Theorizing technology and international relations: Prevailing perspective and new horizons', in Francesco Niccolò Moro, Giampiero Giacomello, and Marco Valigi (eds) *Technology and International Relations: The New Frontier in Global Power* (Cheltenham: Edward Elgar).

Eritja, Mar Campins (2021) *The European Union and Global Environmental Protection* (Abingdon: Routledge).

European Court of Human Rights (2023) Web site at https://www.echr.coe.int. Retrieved May 2023.

European Union Agency for Asylum (2023) Web site at https://euaa.europa.eu. Retrieved May 2023.

Eurostat (2023) 'Migration and migrant population statistics', at https://ec.europa.eu. Retrieved May 2023.

Ezrow, Natasha (2017) *Global Politics and Violent Non-State Actors* (London: SAGE).

Finkelstein, Lawrence S. (1995) 'What is global governance?', in *Global Governance* 3, September–December, pp. 367–72.

Foley, C. Fritz, James R. Hines, and David Wessel (eds) (2021) *Global Goliaths: Multinational Corporations in the 21st Century Economy* (Washington DC: Brookings Institution).

Food and Agriculture Organization of the UN (2011) *The State of Food and Agriculture, 2010–11, Women in Agriculture: Closing the Gender Gap for Development* (Rome: FAO).

Food and Agriculture Organization of the UN (2016) *The State of Food and Agriculture 2016: Climate Change, Agriculture and Food Security* (Rome: FAO).

Food and Agriculture Organization of the UN (2022a) *The State of Food Security and Nutrition in the World 2021* (Rome: FAO).

Food and Agriculture Organization of the UN (2022b) *The State of Food and Agriculture 2022* (Rome: FAO).

Forsch, Sebastian (2018) 'Moving to the Global South: An analysis of the relocation of international NGO secretariats', in *St Antony's International Review* 13:2, February, pp. 159–86.

Forsythe, David P. (2018) 'A new International Committee of the Red Cross?', in *Journal of Human Rights* 17:5, pp. 533–49.

Fortune (2023) Global 500, at https://fortune.com/global500. Retrieved May 2023.

Frank, Matthew, and Jessica Reinisch (eds) (2017) *Refugees in Europe, 1919–1959: A Forty Years' Crisis?* (London: Bloomsbury).

Freedom House (2022) *Freedom in the World 2022* (Washington DC: Freedom House).

Freire, Maria Raquel (2018) 'The Shanghai Cooperation Organization', in Andrei P. Tsygankov (ed.) *Routledge Handbook of Russian Foreign Policy* (Abingdon: Routledge).

Froehlich, Annette, and Diego Alonso Amante Soria (2021) *A Regional Space Agency for Latin America: Legal and Political Perspectives* (Cham, Switzerland: Springer).

Fund for Peace (2023) Fragile States Index, at https://fragilestatesindex.org. Retrieved May 2023.

Fung, Courtney J., and Shing-Hon Lam (2020) 'China already leads 4 of the 15 UN specialized agencies – and is aiming for a 5th', in *The Washington Post*, 3 March.

Galbreath, David J. (2019) 'The Organization for Security and Cooperation in Europe', in David J. Galbreath, Jocelyn Mawdsley, and Laura Chappell (eds) *Contemporary European Security* (Abingdon: Routledge).

Gallagher, Kevin P., and Franco Maldonado Carlin (2020) 'The role of IMF in the fight against COVID-19: The IMF COVID REPONSE INDEX', in *Covid Economics* 42, 19 August, pp. 112–24.

Garavini, Giuliano (2019) *The Rise and Fall of OPEC in the Twentieth Century* (Oxford: Oxford University Press).

Garsten, Christina, and Adrienne Sörbom (2018) *Discreet Power: How the World Economic Forum Shapes Market Agendas* (Stanford, CA: Stanford University Press).

Geddes, Andrew, Leila Hadj Abdou, Leiza Brumat, and Marcia Vera Espinoza (eds) (2019) *The Dynamics of Regional Migration Governance* (Cheltenham: Edward Elgar).

Geiger, Martin, and Martin Koch (2018) 'World organization in migration politics: The International Organization for Migration', in *Journal of International Organizations Studies* 9:1, pp. 25–44.

Gelles, David, and Alan Rappeport (2022) 'World Bank leader, accused of climate denial, offers a new response', in *New York Times*, 22 September.

Ghanea, Nazila (2006) 'From UN Commission on Human Rights to UN Human Rights Council: One step forwards or two steps sideways?', in *International and Comparative Law Quarterly* 55:3, pp. 695–705.

Ginsbach, Katherine F., John T. Monahan, and Katie Gottschalk (2021) 'Beyond COVID-19: Reimagining the role of International Health Regulations in the global health law landscape', *Health Affairs* blog, 1 November.

Giorgetti, Chiari (2016) 'International adjudicative bodies', in Jacob Katz Cogan, Ian Hurd, and Ian Johnstone (eds) *The Oxford Handbook of International Organizations* (Oxford: Oxford University Press).

Glas, Aarie (2018) 'African Union security culture in practice: African problems and African solutions', in *International Affairs* 94:5, September, pp. 1121–38.

Glatter, Kathryn A., and Paul Finkelman (2021) 'History of the plague: An ancient pandemic for the age of Covid-19', in *American Journal of Medicine* 134:2, February, pp. 176–81.

Global Commission on International Migration (2005) *Migration in an Interconnected World: New Directions for Action* (Geneva: GCIM).

Global Network Against Food Crises (2022) *Global Report on Food Crises* (Rome: World Food Programme).

Gondwe, Grace (2021) 'Regional integration and trade: The case of the COMESA Free Trade Area', in *Journal of African Trade* 8:1, December, pp. 1–2.

Gostin, Lawrence O. (2021), quoted in Julia Crawford, 'Does Bill Gates have too much influence in the WHO?', in *International Geneva*, at https://www.swissinfo.ch.

Gostin, Lawrence O., and Rebecca Katz (2016) 'The International Health Regulations: The governing framework for global health security', in *The Milbank Quarterly* 94:2, June, pp. 264–313.

Götz, Norbert (2019) 'The emergence of NGOOs as actors on the world stage', in Thomas Davies (ed.) *Routledge Handbook of NGOs and International Relations* (Abingdon: Routledge).

Graham, Erin R. (2017) 'Follow the money: How trends in financing are changing governance at international organizations', in *Global Policy* 8:S5, August, pp. 15–25.

Grant, Wyn (2018) *Lobbying: The Dark Side of Politics* (Manchester: Manchester University Press).

Gray, Julia (2018) 'Life, death, or zombie? The vitality of international organizations', in *International Studies Quarterly* 62:1, March, pp. 1–13.

Guardian (2021) 'Revealed: 6,500 migrant workers have died in Qatar since World Cup awarded', 23 February.

Gui, Qinchang, Chengliang Liu, and Debin Du (2017) 'Globalization of science and international scientific collaboration: A network perspective', in *Geoforum* 105, October, pp. 1–12.

Gustafsson, Ingrid (2020) *How Standards Rule the World: The Construction of a Global Control Regime* (Cheltenham: Edward Elgar).

Haack, Kirsten (2022) *Women's Access, Representation and Leadership in the United Nations* (Cham, Switzerland: Palgrave Macmillan).

Haas, Ernst B. (1958) *The Uniting of Europe: Political, Social, and Economic Forces, 1950–1957* (Stanford, CA: Stanford University Press).

Haas, Peter M. (1992) 'Introduction: Epistemic communities and international policy coordination', in *International Organization* 46:1, Winter, pp. 1–35.

Haas, Peter M. (2017) 'Coupling science to governance: Straddling the science-policy interface', in Annabelle Littoz-Monnet (ed.) *The Politics of Expertise in International Organizations: How International Bureaucracies Produce and Mobilize Knowledge* (Abingdon: Routledge).

Halley, Janet, Prabha Kotiswaran, Rachel Rebouché, and Hila Shamir (2018) *Governance Feminism: An Introduction* (Minneapolis, MN: University of Minnesota Press).

Harman, Sophie (2016) 'The Bill and Melinda Gates Foundation and legitimacy in global health governance', in *Global Governance* 22:3, July–September, pp. 349–68.

Harman, Sophie (2018) 'Global health governance', in Thomas G. Weiss and Rorden Wilkinson (eds) *International Organization and Global Governance* (Abingdon: Routledge).

Harrington, Alexandra R. (2018) *International Organizations and the Law* (Abingdon: Routledge).

Hassoun, Nicole (2020) *Global Health Impact: Extending Access to Essential Medicines* (New York: Oxford University Press).

Headey, Derek, and Shenggen Fan (2010) *Reflections on the Global Food Crisis: How Did it Happen? How Has it Hurt? And How Can We Prevent the Next One?* (Washington DC: International Food Policy Research Institute).

Heater, Derek (1992) *The Idea of European Unity* (New York: St Martin's Press).

Heinzel, Mirko, Jonas Richter, Per-Olof Busch, Hauke Feil, Jana Herold, and Andrea Liese (2020) 'Birds of a feather? The determinants of impartiality perceptions of the IMF and the World Bank', in *Review of International Political Economy* 28:5, pp. 1249–73.

Heires, Marcel (2008) 'The International Organization for Standardization', in *New Political Economy* 13:3, September, pp. 357–67.

Hennchen, Esther (2022) 'Mind the gap: Shell's political CSR agenda and challenges in Nigeria', in Thomas Maak, Nicola M. Pless, Marc Orlitzky, and Sukhbir Sandhu (eds) *The Routledge Companion to Corporate Social Responsibility* (Abingdon: Routledge).

Herren, Madeleine (2016) 'International Organization, 1865–1945', in Jacob Katz Cogan, Ian Hurd, and Ian Johnstone (eds) *The Oxford Handbook of International Organizations* (Oxford: Oxford University Press).

Hickmann, Thomas, Oscar Widerberg, Markus Lederer, and Philipp Pattberg (2021) 'The United Nations Framework Convention on Climate Change Secretariat as an orchestrator in global climate policymaking', in *International Review of Administrative Sciences* 87:1, March, pp. 21–38.

Hillebrecht, Courtney (2021) *Saving the International Justice Regime: Beyond Backlash Against International Courts* (New York: Cambridge University Press).

Hoffman, Daniel, and Alan Bowditch (2021) *The Global Pharmaceutical Industry: The Demise and the Path to Recovery* (New York: Routledge).

Hollings, Stephanie (2022) 'Guiding philosophies and conflicting interests of the WHO', in *Educational Philosophy and Theory* 54:6, pp. 707–16.

Hönnige, Christoph, and Diana Panke (2016) 'Is anybody listening? The Committee of the Regions and the European Economic and Social Committee and their quest for awareness', in *Journal of European Public Policy* 23:4, pp. 624–42.

Hooghe, Liesbet, and Gary Marks (2009) 'A postfunctionalist theory of European Integration: From permissive consensus to constraining dissensus', in *British Journal of Political Science* 39:1, January, pp. 1–29.

Hough, Peter (2018) *Understanding Global Security*, 4th edn (Abingdon: Routledge).

Hulme, Mike (2022) *Climate Change* (Abingdon: Routledge).

Humphreys, David (2005) 'The elusive quest for a global forests convention', in *Review of European Community and International Environmental Law* 14:1, April, pp. 1–10.

Huneeus, Alexandra, and Mikael Rask Madsen (2019) 'Between universalism and regional law and politics: A comparative history of the American, European, and African human rights systems', in *International Journal of Constitutional Law* 16:1, January, pp. 136–60.

Ikenberry, G. John (2011) 'The Future of the liberal world order', in *Foreign Affairs*, May/June, pp. 56–68.

Inboden, Will (2012) 'Two parties, two approaches to multilateralism', in *Foreign Policy*, 31 May.

Inglehart, Ronald (1971) 'The silent revolution in Europe: Intergenerational change in post-industrial societies', in *American Political Science Review* 65:4, December, pp. 991–1017.

Inglehart, Ronald (1997) *Modernization and Postmodernization: Cultural, Economic and Social Change in 43 Societies* (Princeton, NJ: Princeton University Press).

International Civil Aviation Organization (2023) 'About ICAO', on ICAO Web site at https://www.icao.int/about-icao/Pages/default.aspx. Retrieved May 2023.

International Civil Aviation Organization (2023b) *Air Transport Monthly Monitor* (Geneva: ICAO).

International Monetary Fund (2023) Web site at https://www.imf.org. Retrieved May 2023.

International Organization for Migration (2018) *World Migration Report 2018* (Geneva: IOM).

International Organization for Migration (2021) Programme and Budget for 2022, at https://governingbodies.iom.int.

International Organization for Migration (2023a) 'Missing Migrants Project', at https://missingmigrants.iom.int . Retrieved May 2023.

International Organization for Migration (2023b) 'About migration', at https://www.iom.int/about-migration. Retrieved May 2023.

International Tribunal for the Law of the Sea (2023) Web site at https://www.itlos.org. Retrieved May 2023.

Irrera, Daniela, and Mairanna Charountaki (eds) (2022) *Mapping Non-State Actors in International Relations* (Cham, Switzerland: Springer).

Irwin, Douglas A. (2018) *Peddling Protectionism: Smoot-Hawley and the Great Depression* (Princeton, NJ: Princeton University Press).

Ivanova, Maria (2010) 'UNEP in global environmental governance: Design, leadership, location', in *Global Environmental Politics* 10:1, February, pp. 30–59.

Ivanova, Maria (2012) 'Institutional design and UNEP reform: Historical insights on form, function and financing', in *International Affairs* 88:3, May, pp. 565–84.

Ivanova, Maria (2021) *The Untold Story of the World's Leading Environmental Institution: UNEP at Fifty* (Cambridge, MA: MIT Press).

Jaubart, Pascal, Lizzie Dipple, and Stefan Dercon (2019) 'Has Gavi lived up to its promise? Quasi-experimental evidence on country immunisation rates and child mortality', in *BMJ Global Health* 4:6, November, pp. 1–11.

Jayawickrama, Sherine (2011*) Developing Managers and Leaders: Experiences and Lessons from International NGOs* (Cambridge, MA: The Hauser Center for Nonprofit Organizations and the Harvard Humanitarian Initiative, Harvard University).

Jessop, Bob (2016) *The State: Past, Present, Future* (Cambridge: Polity Press).

Jinnah, Sikina (2014) *Post-Treaty Politics: Secretariat Influence in Global Environmental Governance* (Cambridge, MA: MIT Press).

Johnson, Hope (2018) *International Agricultural Law and Policy: A Rights-Based Approach to Food Security* (Cheltenham: Edward Elgar).

Jordan, Andrew, and Viviana Gravey (eds) (2021) *Environmental Policy in the EU: Actors, Institutions and Processes*, 4th edn (Abingdon: Routledge).

Kaloudis, George (2021) *Non-Governmental Organizations in the Global System* (Lanham, MD: Lexington Books).

Kant, Immanuel ([1795] 2009) *Perpetual Peace: A Philosophical Essay* (London: Penguin).

Karns, Margaret P. (2016) 'General assemblies and assemblies of states parties', in Jacob Katz Cogan, Ian Hurd, and Ian Johnstone (eds) *The Oxford Handbook of International Organizations* (Oxford: Oxford University Press).

Kasperson, Roger E. (2011) 'Characterizing the science/practice gap', in Roger E. Kasperson and Mimi Berberian (eds) *Integrating Science and Policy* (London: Earthscan).

Kaunert, Christian, Sarah Léonard, and John D. Occhipinti (eds) (2015) *Justice and Home Affairs Agencies in the European Union* (Abingdon: Routledge).

Kavanagh, Matthew M., and Lawrence O. Gostin (2018) 'The World Health Organization's momentous struggle to respond to the AIDS pandemic', in *American Journal of Public Health* 108:10, October, pp. 1272–3.

Keck, Margaret E., and Kathryn Sikkink (1998) *Activists Beyond Borders: Advocacy Networks in International Politics* (Ithaca, NJ: Cornell University Press).

Khanna, Parag (2016) 'These 25 companies are more powerful than many countries' in *Foreign Policy*, 15 May.

Kiai, Maina (2015) 'Reclaiming civic space through UN-supported litigation', in *International Journal of Human Rights*, December.

Kilroy, Richard J. (2022) 'Challenging the "Colossus of the North": Mexico, CELAC, and the implications of replacing the Organization of American States with a new regional security organization'. Rice University Baker Institute for Public Policy, May.

Knill, Christoph, Daniel Arndt, and Stephan Heichel (2011) 'Really a front-runner, really a straggler? Of environmental leaders and laggards in the European Union and beyond – a quantitative policy perspective'. Paper given at 6th ECPR General Conference, Reykjavik, Iceland, 25–27 August.

Knill, Christoph, and Yves Steinebach (eds) (2023) *International Public Administrations in Global Public Policy: Sources and Effects of Bureaucratic Influence* (Abingdon: Routledge).

Knutsen, Torbjorn L. (2016) *A History of International Relations Theory*, 3rd edn (Manchester: Manchester University Press).

Koomen, Jonneke (2019) 'The International Criminal Court', in Gordon DiGiacomo and Susan L. King (eds) *The Institutions of Human Rights: Developments and Practices* (Toronto: University of Toronto Press).

Koops, Joachim, Norrie MacQueen, Thierry Tardy, and Paul D. Williams (eds) (2015) *The Oxford Handbook of United Nations Peacekeeping Operations* (Oxford: Oxford University Press).

Koran, Laura (2018) 'US leaving UN Human Rights Council: A "cesspool of political bias"', on CNN at https://www.cnn.com, 20 June.

Krasner, Stephen D. (ed.) (1983) *International Regimes* (Ithaca, NY: Cornell University Press).

Krause, Monika (2014) *The Good Project: Humanitarian Relief NGOs and the Fragmentation of Reason* (Chicago: University of Chicago Press).

Kubicek, Paul (2009) 'The Commonwealth of Independent States: An example of failed regionalism?', in *Review of International Studies* 35:1, pp. 237–56.

Lakatos, István (2022) *Comparative Human Rights Diplomacy* (Cham, Switzerland: Palgrave Macmillan).

Lall, Ranjit (2017) 'Beyond institutional design: Explaining the performance of international organization', in *International Organization* 71:2, Spring, pp. 245–80.

Lam, Onyi, and Drew DeSilver (2019) 'Countries have different priorities when they review each other's human rights records'. Pew Research Center at https://www.pewresearch.org, 20 March.

Lang, Sabine (2013) *NGOs, Civil Society, and the Public Sphere* (Cambridge: Cambridge University Press).

Lawrence, Mark, and Sharon Friel (eds) (2020) *Healthy and Sustainable Food Systems* (Abingdon: Routledge).

League of Nations Economic Committee (1931) *The Agricultural Crisis* (Geneva: Publications Department of the League of Nations).

Legge, David (2012) 'Future of WHO hangs in the balance', in *BMJ* 345, October, pp. 23–25.

Lele, Uma, Manmohan Agarwal, Brian C. Baldwin, and Sambuddha Goswami (2021) *Food for All: International Organizations and the Transformation of Agriculture* (Oxford: Oxford University Press).

Lele, Uma, and Brian C. Baldwin (2021) 'The International Fund for Agricultural Development', in Uma Lele, Manmohan Agarwal, Brian C. Baldwin, and Sambuddha Goswami *Food for All: International Organizations and the Transformation of Agriculture* (Oxford: Oxford University Press).

Lemkin, Raphael (1944) *Axis Rule in Occupied Europe* (Washington DC: Carnegie Endowment for International Peace).

Lewis, David, Nazneen Kanji, and Nuno S. Themudo (2021) *Non-governmental Organizations and Development*, 2nd edn (Abingdon: Routledge).

Libman, Alexander, and Anastassia V. Obydenkova (2018) 'Understanding authoritarian regionalism', in *Journal of Democracy* 29:4, October, pp. 151–65.

Littoz-Monnet, Annabelle (ed.) (2017) *The Politics of Expertise in International Organizations: How International Bureaucracies Produce and Mobilize Knowledge* (Abingdon: Routledge).

MacHaffie, James (2021) 'Mutual trust without a strong collective identity? Examining the Shanghai Cooperation Organization as a nascent security community', in *Asian Security* 17:3, March, pp. 349–65.

Malthus, Thomas (1798) *An Essay on the Principle of Population* (London: J. Johnson).

Margulis, Matias E. (2013) 'The regime complex for food security: Implications for the global hunger challenge', in *Global Governance* 19:1, pp. 53–67.

Martin, Jaimie (2022) *The Meddlers: Sovereignty, Empire, and the Birth of Global Economic Governance* (Cambridge, MA: Harvard University Press).

Martinez-Diaz, Leonardo, and Joe Thwaites (2018) 'A key week for the future of the Global Environment Facility as countries re-up its funding'. World Resources Institute, 24 April, at https://www.wri.org.

Masters, Jonathan, Andrew Chatzky, and Anshu Siripurapu (2021) 'The IMF: The world's controversial financial firefighter'. Council of Foreign Relations Backgrounder at https://www.cfr.org, 8 September.

Mattli, Walter (1999) *The Logic of Regional Integration: Europe and Beyond* (Cambridge: Cambridge University Press).

McBride, James (2022) 'How green party success is reshaping global politics'. Council of Foreign Relations backgrounder at https://www.cfr.org/backgrounder/how-green-party-success-reshaping-global-politics.

McCormick, John (1995) *The Global Environmental Movement* (Chichester: John Wiley).

McCormick, John (2020) *European Union Politics*, 3rd edn (London: Red Globe Press).

McCormick, John (2021) *Understanding the European Union*, 8th edn (Red Globe Press).

McGaughey, Fiona (2021) *Non-governmental Organisations and the United Nations Human Rights System* (Abingdon: Routledge).

McGovern, Terry, Marta Schaaf, Emily Battistini, Emily Maistrellis, Kathryn Gibb, and Sara E. Casey (2020) 'From bad to worse: Global governance of abortion and the Global Gag Rule', in *Sexual and Reproductive Health Matters* 28:3, pp. 54–63.

Mead, Leila (2021) 'The "crown jewels" of environmental diplomacy: Assessing the UNEP Regional Seas Programme'. International Institute for Sustainable Development, Briefing 137, April.

Meier, Benjamin Mason, and Lawrence O. Gostin (2018) 'Introduction', in Meier and Gostin (eds) *Human Rights in Global Health: Rights-Based Governance for a Globalizing World* (New York: Oxford University Press).

Merke, Federico, and Gino Pauselli (2015) 'In the shadow of the state: Think tanks and foreign policy in Latin America', in *International Journal* 70:4, December, pp. 613–28.

Merke, Federico, Oliver Stuenkel, and Andreas E. Feldmann (2021) 'Reimagining regional governance in Latin America', in Working Paper, June, Carnegie Endowment for International Peace.

Merson, Michael, and Stephen Inrig (2017) *The AIDS Pandemic: Searching for a Global Response* (Cham, Switzerland: Springer).

Mertens, Daniel, and Matthias Thiemann (2019) 'Building a hidden investment state? The European Investment Bank, national development banks and European economic governance', in *Journal of European Public Policy* 26:1, pp. 23–43.

Migration Policy Institute (2023) 'Profile of the unauthorized population: United States', at https://www.migrationpolicy.org/data/unauthorized-immigrant-population/state/US . Retrieved May 2023.

Miller, Rory, and Sarah Cardaun (2020) 'Multinational security coalitions and the limits of middle power activism in the Middle East: The Saudi Case', in *International Affairs* 96:6, November, pp. 1509–25.

Mingst, Karen A., Margaret P. Karns, and Alynna J. Lyon (2022) *The United Nations in the 21st Century*, 6th edn (New York: Routledge).

Mitchell, Ronald B. (2022) International Environmental Agreements Database Project, at https://iea.uoregon.edu.

Mitrany, David (1966) *A Working Peace System* (Chicago: Quadrangle).

Monnet, Jean (1978) *Memoirs* (Paris: Fayard).

Morin, Jean-Frédéric, Amandine Orsini, and Sikina Jinnah (2020) *Global Environmental Politics* (Oxford: Oxford University Press).

Morrow, Dwight (1919) *The Society of Free States* (New York: Harper and Brothers).

Morsink, Johannes (2022) *Article by Article: The Universal Declaration of Human Rights for a New Generation* (Philadelphia, PA: University of Pennsylvania Press).

Moschella, Manuela (2016) 'International finance', in Jacob Katz Cogan, Ian Hurd, and Ian Johnstone (eds) *The Oxford Handbook of International Organizations* (Oxford: Oxford University Press).

Mowell, B. D. (2021) 'Barriers to UN–civil society collaborations: An exploratory study of CSOs within the UN–ECOSOC Consultative Status Programme', in *International Studies* 58:4, October, pp. 466–90.

Mueller, Milton (2017) 'Communications and the internet', in Jacob Katz Cogan, Ian Hurd, and Ian Johnstone (eds) *The Oxford Handbook of International Organizations* (Oxford: Oxford University Press).

Müller, Joachim (2021) *Reforming the United Nations: Fit for Purpose at 75?* (Leiden: Brill Nijhoff).

Muntschick, Johannes (2018) *The Southern African Development Community and the European Union: Regionalism and External Influence* (Cham, Switzerland: Springer).

Murphy, Craig N., and JoAnne Yates (2009) *The International Organization for Standardization (ISO): Global Governance Through Voluntary Consensus* (Abingdon: Routledge).

Nagtzaam, Gerry (2014) 'Into the woods: Analyzing normative evolution and the International Tropical Timber Organization', in *Arts and Social Sciences Journal* 5:2, open access.

Nathan, Otto, and Heinz Norden (eds) (1960) *Einstein on Peace* (New York: Simon & Schuster).

Neier, Aryeh (2020) *The International Human Rights Movement: A History* (Princeton, NJ: Princeton University Press).

Nikolakis, William and John L. Innes (eds) (2020) *The Wicked Problem of Forest Policy: A Multidisciplinary Approach to Sustainability in Forest Landscapes* (Cambridge: Cambridge University Press).

Nye, Joseph S. (1970) 'Comparing common markets: A revised neofunctionalist model', *International Organization* 24:4, pp. 796–835.

Nye, Joseph S. (2020) 'Introduction', in Enekin Tikk and Mika Kerttunen (eds) *Routledge Handbook of International Cybersecurity* (Abingdon: Routledge).

O'Connell, Mary Ellen (ed.) (2012) *What is War? An Investigation in the Wake of 9/11* (Leiden: Martinus Nijhoff Publishers).

Oette, Lutz (2018) 'The UN human rights treaty bodies: Impact and future', in Gerd Oberleitner (ed.) *International Human Rights Institutions, Tribunals and Courts* (Singapore: Springer).

Office of the High Commissioner for Human Rights (2023) Web site at https://www.ohchr.org. Retrieved May 2023.

Olivier, Jill, Clarence Tsimpo, Regina Gemignani, Mari Shojo, Harold Coulombe, Frank Dimmock, Minh Cong Nguyen, Harrison Hines, Edward J. Mills, Joseph L Dieleman, Annie Haakenstad, and Quentin Wodon (2015) 'Understanding the roles of faith-based health-care providers in Africa: Review of the evidence with a focus on magnitude, reach, cost, and satisfaction', in *The Lancet* 386:10005, 31 October–9 November, pp. 1765–75.

O'Neill, Jim, and Allesio Terzi (2018) 'The G7 is dead, long live the G7'. Blog post on web site of Bruegel, 13 June, at https://www.bruegel.org/blog-post/g7-dead-long-live-g7.

Organization of Petroleum Exporting Countries (2023) Web site at https://www.opec.org. Retrieved May 2023.

Orsini, Amandine, Jean-Frédéric Morin, and Oran Young (2013) 'Regime complexes: A buzz, a boom, or a boost for global governance?', in *Global Governance* 19:1, January–March, pp. 27–39.

Oumazzane, Tarik (2021) *Regional Integration in the Middle East and North Africa: The Agadir Agreement and the Political Economy of Trade and Peace* (Singapore: Springer).

Overy, Richard (2017) *The Origins of the Second World War*, 4th edn (Abingdon: Routledge).

Pabst, Adrian (2019) *Liberal World Order and Its Critics: Civilisational States and Cultural Commonwealths* (Abingdon: Routledge).

Pace, John P. (2020) *The United Nations Commission on Human Rights* (Oxford: Oxford University Press).

Palmeter, David, Petros C. Mavroidis, and Niall Meagher (eds) (2022) *Dispute Settlement in the World Trade Organization: Practice and Procedure*, 3rd edn (Cambridge: Cambridge University Press).

Panke, Diana (2020) 'Regional cooperation through the lenses of states: Why do states nurture regional integration?', in *The Review of International Organizations* 15:2, April, pp. 475–504.

Parent, Joseph M. (2011) *Uniting States: Voluntary Union in World Politics* (New York: Cambridge University Press).

Park, Susan (2018) *International Organizations and Global Problems: Theories and Explanations* (Cambridge: Cambridge University Press).

Parry, Martin L. (1990) *Climate Change and World Agriculture* (Abingdon: Routledge).

Pedersen, Susan (2015) *The Guardians: The League of Nations and the Crisis of Empire* (Oxford: Oxford University Press).

Peet, Richard (2009) *Unholy Trinity: The IMF, World Bank and WTO*, 2nd edn (London: Zed Books).

Peterson, Trudy Huskamp (2018) 'The Universal Declaration of Human Rights: An archival commentary'. International Council on Archives at https://www.ica.org.

Peterson del Mar, David (2012) *Environmentalism* (Abingdon: Routledge).

Piccone, Ted (2018) 'China's long game on human rights at the United Nations'. Brookings Institution, Washington DC, September.

Piper, Nicola, and Laura Foley (2021) 'Global partnerships in governing labour migration: The uneasy relationship between the ILO and IOM in the promotion of decent work for migrants', in *Global Policy and Governance* 1, pp. 256–78.

Radu, Roxana (2019) *Negotiating Internet Governance* (Oxford: Oxford University Press).

Ray, Rebecca, and Rohini Kamal (2019) 'Can South–South Cooperation Compete? The Development Bank of Latin America and the Islamic Development Bank', in *Development and Change* 50:1, January, pp. 191–220.

Reed, Maureen G., and Martin F. Price (eds) (2020) *UNESCO Biosphere Reserves: Supporting Biocultural Diversity, Sustainability and Society* (Abingdon: Routledge).

Reinsberg, Bernhard, Thomas Stubbs, and Alexander Kentikelenis (2021) 'Unimplementable by design? Understanding (non-)compliance with International Monetary Fund policy conditionality', in *Governance* 35:3, July, pp. 689–715.

Reinsch, William A. (2018) 'Whither, or wither, WTO?'. Commentary, on the Web site of the Center for Strategic and International Studies at https://www.csis.org, 6 August.

Reuters (2022) 'Key takeaways from the G20 summit in Bali', 16 November, at   https://www.reuters.com.

Richardson, Sophie (2020) 'China's influence on the global human rights system'. Brookings Institution, Washington DC, September.

Rittberger, Volker, Bernhard Zangl, Andreas Kruck, and Hylke Dijkstra (2019) *International Organization*, 3rd edn (London: Red Globe Press).

Robertson, Roland (1992) *Globalization: Social Theory and Global Culture* (London: Sage).

Roehrlich, Elisabeth (2022) *Inspectors for Peace: A History of the International Atomic Energy Agency* (Baltimore, MD: Johns Hopkins University Press).

Ruffini, Pierre-Bruno (2017) *Science and Diplomacy: A New Dimension of International Relations* (Cham, Switzerland: Springer).

Russell, Martin (2021) 'The Organization for Security and Cooperation in Europe (OSCE): A pillar of the European security order', 2 September, European Parliamentary Research Service.

Rutherford, Kenneth R. (2011) *Disarming States: The International Movement to Ban Landmines* (Santa Barbara, CA: Praeger).

Sachs, Carolyn E., Leif Jensen, Paige Castellanos, and Kathleen Sexsmith (eds) (2021) *Routledge Handbook of Gender and Agriculture* (Abingdon: Routledge).

Sachs, Jeffrey D. (2016) *The Age of Sustainable Development* (New York: Columbia University Press).

Sagan, Carl (1996) *The Demon-Haunted World: Science as a Candle in the Dark* (New York: Ballantine Books).

Santaniello, Mauro (2021) 'From governance denial to state regulation: A controversy-based typology of internet governance models', in Blayne Haggart, Natasha Tusikov, and Jan Aart Scholte (eds) *Power and Authority in Internet Governance* (Abingdon: Routledge).

Satariano, Adam, and Paul Mozur (2023) 'The people onscreen are fake. The disinformation is real', in *New York Times*, 7 February.

Sayle, Timothy Andrews (2019) *Enduring Alliance: A History of NATO and the Postwar Global Order* (Ithaca, NJ: Cornell University Press).

Schmelzer, Matthias, and Matthieu Leimgruber (eds) (2017) *The OECD and the International Political Economy Since 1948* (Cham, Switzerland: Palgrave Macmillan).

Schmidheiny, Stephan (1992) *Changing Course: A Global Business Perspective on Development and the Environment* (Cambridge, MA: MIT Press).

Schmidt, Julia (2020) *The European Union and the Use of Force* (Leiden: Koninklijke Brill).

Schnable, Allison (2021) *Amateurs Without Borders: The Aspirations and Limits of Global Compassion* (Oakland, CA: University of California Press).

Schneider, Anselm, Christopher Wickert, and Emilio Marti (2017) 'Reducing complexity by creating complexity: A systems theory perspective on how organizations respond to their environments', in *Journal of Management Studies* 54:2, March, pp. 182–208.

Schneiderman, Ron (2015) *Modern Standardization: Case Studies at the Crossroads of Technology, Economics, and Politics* (Chichester: John Wiley & Sons).

Scholte, Jan Aart (2021) 'Beyond institutionalism: Toward a transformed global governance theory', in *International Theory* 13:1, March, pp. 179–91.

Schütze, Robert (ed.) (2015) *EU Treaties and Legislation* (Cambridge: Cambridge University Press).

Seiderman, Ian (2019) 'The UN High Commissioner for Human Rights in the age of global backlash', in *Netherlands Quarterly of Human Rights* 31:1, pp. 5–13.

Selin, Henrik (2014) 'Global environmental law and treaty-making on hazardous substances: The Minamata Convention and mercury abatement', in *Global Environmental Politics* 14:1, February, pp. 1–19.

Servent, Ariadna Ripoll (2018) *The European Parliament* (London: Red Globe Press).

Shaffer, Gregory (2021) *Emerging Powers and the World Trading System* (Cambridge: Cambridge University Press).

Shah, Dhruti (2022) 'The shops that connect people with their home countries'. BBC News at https://www.bbc.com/news, 10 November.

Shamshad, Rizwana (2017) *Bangladeshi Migrants in India: Foreigners, Refugees, or Infiltrators?* (New Delhi: Oxford University Press).

Shanghai Cooperation Organization (2023) Web site at http://eng.sectsco.org. Retrieved May 2023.

Shaw, Malcolm N. (2021) *International Law*, 9th edn (Cambridge: Cambridge University Press).

Shaw, Timothy M. (2007) *Commonwealth: Inter- and Non-state Contributions to Global Governance* (Abingdon: Routledge).

Siebenhüner, Bernd (2015) 'Secretariats', in Jean-Frédéric Morin, and Amandine Orsini (eds) *Essential Concepts of Global Environmental Governance* (Abingdon: Routledge).

Simma, Bruno, Daniel-Erasmus Khan, Georg Nolte, and Andreas Paulus (eds) (2012) *The Charter of the United Nations: A Commentary*, 3rd edn (Oxford: Oxford University Press).

Smith, Adam (1776) *The Wealth of Nations* (W. Strahan).

Streck, Charlotte (2001) 'The Global Environment Facility: A role model for international governance?', in *Global Environmental Politics* 1:2, May, pp. 71–94.

Stubbs, Richard (2019) 'ASEAN sceptics versus ASEAN proponents: Evaluating regional institutions', in *The Pacific Review* 32:6, pp. 923–50.

Taylor, Allyn L. (2017) 'Global health law: International law and public health policy' in Stella R. Quah (ed.) *International Encyclopedia of Public Health*, 2nd edn (Kidlington: Elsevier).

Telò, Mario (2023) *Multilateralism Past, Present and Future: A European Perspective* (Abingdon: Routledge).

Tieku, Thomas Kwasi (2021) 'Punching above weight: How the African Union Commission exercises agency in politics', in *Africa Spectrum* 56:3, December, pp. 254–73.

Trachtman, Joel P. (2009) *The International Law of Economic Migration: Toward a Fourth Freedom* (Kalamazoo, MI: WE Upjohn Institute Press).

Trouille, Jean-Marc (2021) 'Introduction: A journey towards regional integration', in Jean-Marc Trouille, Helen Trouille, and Penine Uwimbabazi (eds) *The East African Community: Intraregional Integration and Relations with the EU* (Abingdon: Routledge).

Twohey, Megan, and Nicholas Kulish (2020) 'Bill Gates, the virus, and the quest to vaccinate the world', in *New York Times*, 23 November.

UN Climate Change (2023) Web site of the secretariat for the UN Framework Convention on Climate Change, at https://unfccc.int/about-us/about-the-secretariat. Retrieved May 2023.

UNAIDS (2021) 'Confronting inequalities: Lessons for pandemic responses from 40 years of AIDS'. Global AIDS Update 2021 (Geneva: UNAIDS).

UNESCO (2022) 'Recommendation on open science', adopted on 3 November. UNESCO, web site at https://unesdoc.unesco.org.

Union of International Associations (2023) *Yearbook of International Organizations*, UIA web site at https://www.uia.org. Retrieved May 2023.

United Nations (1945) United Nations Charter, at https://www.un.org/en/about-us/un-charter.

United Nations (2015) *The Millennium Development Goals Report* (New York: United Nations).

United Nations Conference on Trade and Development (2020) *World Investment Report 2020* (Geneva: UNCTAD).

United Nations Conference on Trade and Development (2022) 'Digital MNEs are growing at breakneck speed', in *Global Investment Trends Monitor* 41, January.

United Nations Department of Economic and Social Affairs (2021) International Migrant Stock 2020, at https://www.un.org/development/desa.

United Nations Department of Economic and Social Affairs (2023) The 17 Goals, at https://sdgs.un.org. Retrieved May 2023.

United Nations Development Programme (1994) *Human Development Report 1994* (Oxford: Oxford University Press).

United Nations Development Programme (2022) *Human Development Report 2021/2022* (New York: UNDP).

United Nations Environment Programme (2023a) About the United Nations Environment Programme, at https://www.unep.org/about-un-environment. Retrieved May 2023.

United Nations Environment Programme (2023b) Budget, at https://www.unep.org/about-un-environment/funding-and-partnerships/funding-facts. Retrieved May 2023.

United Nations General Assembly (1993) 'High Commissioner for the promotion and protection of all human rights', 20 December. A/RES/48/141.

United Nations General Assembly (2012) Resolution 66/290, September, at https://documents-dds-ny.un.org.

United Nations General Assembly (2023) UN scale of assessments for the regular budget at https://www.un.org/en/ga/contributions/scale.shtml. Retrieved May 2023.

United Nations High Commissioner for Refugees (2022a) *Global Appeal 2022* (Geneva: UNHCR).

United Nations High Commissioner for Refugees (2022b) 'Statelessness around the world', at https://www.unhcr.org/ibelong/statelessness-around-the-world. Retrieved May 2023.

United Nations High Commissioner for Refugees (2022c) 'UNHCR warns of surging needs in Sudan amid skyrocketing prices and gaps in humanitarian funding', at https://www.unhcr.org/news.

United Nations High Commissioner for Refugees (2022d) Web site at https://www.unhcr.org. Retrieved May 2023.

United Nations High Commissioner for Refugees (2022e) Refugee data finder at https://www.unhcr.org/refugee-statistics.

United Nations Network on Migration (2023) Web site at https://migrationnetwork.un.org. Retrieved May 2023.

United Nations Population Division (2020) *Trends in International Migrant Stock: The 2020 Revision* (New York: UN Department of Economic and Social Affairs).

United Nations Population Division (2022) *World Population Prospects: 2022 Revision* (New York: United Nations Department of Economic and Social Affairs).

United States Energy Information Administration (2023) Data on oil production at https://www.eia.gov. Retrieved May 2023.

Van den Bossche, Peter (2021) *The Demise of the WTO Appellate Body: Lessons for Governance of International Adjudication?* WTI Working Paper No . 02/2021, World Trade Institute: University of Bern.

Van den Bossche, Peter, and Denise Prévost (2021) *Essentials of WTO Law*, 2nd edn (Cambridge: Cambridge University Press).

Van den Bossche, Peter, and Werner Zdouc (2022) *The Law and Policy of the World Trade Organization: Text, Cases, and Materials*, 5th edn (Cambridge: Cambridge University Press).

Van der Hoeven, Rolph, and Rob Vos (2022) 'Reforming the international financial and fiscal system for better Covid-19 and post-pandemic crisis responsiveness', in Elissaios Papurakis (ed.) *Covid-19 and International Development* (Cham, Switzerland: Springer).

Van Leeuwen, Judith, and Jason Monios (2022) 'Maritime commerce and transport: The imperfect match between climate change and the International Maritime Organization', in Paul G. Harris (ed.) *Routledge Handbook of Marine Governance and Global Environmental Change* (Abingdon: Routledge).

Velásquez, Germán (2018) quoted in Yves Beigbeder, *The World Health Organization: Achievements and Failures* (Abingdon: Routledge).

Verbeek, Nicolas (2022) 'The future of IMF and World Bank: New dynamics in times of COVID-19 crisis, 2020', in Madeleine O. Hosli, Taylor Garrett, Sonja Niedecken, and Nicolas Verbeek (eds) *The Future of Multilateralism: Global Cooperation and International Organizations* (Lanham, MD: Rowman & Littlefield).

Wade, Robert H. (2011) 'Emerging world order? From multipolarity to multilateralism in the G20, the World Bank, and the IMF', in *Politics & Society* 39:3, September, pp. 347–78.

Wagner, Markus (2022) 'World Trade Organization steps back from the brink of irrelevance … but …', at *Qrius* (https://qrius.com), 22 June.

Wakefield, Alison (2021) *Security and Crime: Converging Perspectives on a Complex World* (London: SAGE).

Waltz, Kenneth N. (1979) *Theory of International Politics* (Boston: McGraw-Hill).

Weiss, Thomas G. (2009) 'Preface', in John Mathiason, *Internet Governance: The New Frontier of Global Institutions* (Abingdon: Routledge).

Weiss, Thomas G. (2016) 'Rising powers, global governance, and the United Nations', in *Rising Powers Quarterly* 1:2, pp. 7–19.

Weitz, Richard (2018) *Assessing the Collective Security Treaty Organization* (Carlisle, PA: US Army War College Press).

Wessel, Ramses A. (2016) 'Executive boards and councils', in Jacob Katz Cogan, Ian Hurd, and Ian Johnstone (eds) *The Oxford Handbook of International Organizations* (Oxford: Oxford University Press).

Wesselink, Bert (2020) Directory of Development Organizations, at http://www.devdir.org. Retrieved May 2023.

Western, Shaina D., Sarah P. Lockhart, and Jeannette Money (2019) 'Does anyone care about migrant rights? An analysis of why countries enter the convention on the rights of migrant workers and their families', in *The International Journal of Human Rights* 23:8, pp. 1276–99.

Wickert, Christopher, and David Risi (2019) *Corporate Social Responsibility* (Cambridge: Cambridge University Press).

Willetts, Peter (2011) *Non-governmental Organization in World Politics: The Construction of Global Governance* (Abingdon: Routledge).

Willoughby, Robin, and Tim Gore (2018) *Ripe for Change: Ending Human Suffering in Supermarket Supply Chains* (Oxford: Oxfam International).

Wise, Timothy A. (2019) *Eating Tomorrow: Agribusiness, Family Farmers, and the Battle for the Future of Food* (New York: New Press).

Witter, Rebecca, Kimberly R. Marion Suiseeya, Rebecca L. Gruby, Sarah Hitchner, Edward M. Maclin, Maggie Bourque, and J. Peter Brosius (2015) 'Moments of influence in global environmental governance', in *Environmental Politics* 24:6, pp. 894–912.

Woellner, Robert A. (2020) 'Preface', in Robert A. Woellner, John Vorhees, and Christopher L. Bell, *International Environmental Risk Management*, 2nd edn (Abingdon: CRC Press).

Woodward, Richard (2009) *The Organization for Economic Cooperation and Development* (Abingdon: Routledge).

World Association of Non-Governmental Organizations (2023) Worldwide NGO directory at https://www.wango.org. Retrieved May 2023.

World Bank (2023) Outline of World Bank Group policy on universal health coverage at https://www.worldbank.org/en/topic/health/overview#1. Retrieved May 2023.

World Customs Organization (2023) Web site at https://www.wcoomd.org. Retrieved May 2023.

World Food Programme (2018) 'Humanitarian assistance continues to prevent a massive human catastrophe in Yemen but it is not enough'. WFP press release, 8 December.

World Food Programme (2023) 'Why WFP needs to be invited into a country before delivering food'. WFP news release, 12 January, at https://www.wfpusa.org.

World Health Organization (2019) *WHO Global Report on Trends in Prevalence of Tobacco Use, 2000–2025* (Geneva: WHO).

World Health Organization (2022) *World Health Statistics 2022* (Geneva: WHO).

World Health Organization (2023a) Coronavirus dashboard, at https://covid19.who.int. Retrieved May 2023.

World Health Organization (2023b) Web site at https://www.who.int. Retrieved May 2023.

World Intellectual Property Organization (2023) IP facts and figures, at https://www.wipo.int/en/ipfactsandfigures/patents.

World Resources Institute (2021) Climate watch, at https://www.climatewatchdata.org/ghg-emissions. Retrieved May 2023.

World Trade Organization (2020) 'Information on trade and trade policy measures', at https://data.wto.org. Retrieved January 2021.

World Trade Organization (2023a) Web site at https://www.wto.org. Retrieved May 2023.

World Trade Organization (2023b) Data on regional trade agreements at https://rtais.wto.org. Retrieved May 2023.

World Wide Fund for Nature (2023) Web site at https://www.worldwildlife.org. Retrieved May 2023.

Yanacopulos, Helen (2019) 'International NGOs in development studies', in Thomas Davies (ed) *Routledge Handbook of NGOs and International Relations* (Abingdon: Routledge).

Youde, Jeremy (2018) *Global Health Governance in International Society* (Oxford: Oxford University Press).

Zartman, I. William, Paul Meertz, and Mordechai Melamud (eds) (2014) *Banning the Bang or the Bomb? Negotiating the Nuclear Test Ban Regime* (Cambridge: Cambridge University Press).

Zinkina, Julia, David Christian, Leonid Grinin, Ilya Ilyin, Alexey Andreev, Ivan Aleshkovski, Sergey Shulgin, and Andrey Korotayev (2019) *A Big History of Globalization: The Emergence of a Global World System* (Cham, Switzerland: Springer).

INDEX

Boldface numbers indicate key references